The Body of the Queen

The Body of the Queen

Gender and Rule in the Courtly World, 1500–2000

Edited by

Regina Schulte

with the assistance of Pernille Arenfeldt,
Martin Kohlrausch and Xenia von Tippelskirch

Berghahn Books
New York • Oxford

First published in 2006 by

Berghahn Books

www.berghahnbooks.com

© 2006 Regina Schulte

Library of Congress Cataloging-in-Publication Data

The body of the queen : gender and rule in the courtly world, 1500-2000 /
edited by Regina Schulte ; with the assistance of Pernille Arenfeldt, Martin
Kohlrausch, and Xenia von Tippelskirch.
   p. cm.
Includes bibliographical references and index.
ISBN 1-84545-121-X (acid-free paper) -- ISBN 1-84545-159-7
(pbk : acid-free paper)
   1. Sex role--History. 2. Queens--History. 3. Courts and courtiers--
History. 4. Body, Human--Social aspects. I. Schulte, Regina, 1949-

HQ1075.B673 2005
305.48'09621--dc22

                                          2005057003

British Library Cataloguing in Publication Data

A catalogue record for this book is available from the British Library
Printed in the United States on acid-free paper

ISBN 1-84545-121-X hardback

Contents

List of Illustrations

Foreword

This volume is the result of a long-term research project that culminated in a four-day conference at the European University Institute in Florence in September 2001. The conference was preceded by two workshops in which a group of graduate students and scholars addressed the theme 'the Body of the Queen' and situated it within the context of historiographical traditions. From the beginning the group was interdisciplinary and international. Scholars with a background in literature, media studies and cultural studies as well as art historians and historians addressed the subject from their respective disciplines and focused on different historical periods. The contributions presented in this volume reflect the diversity and complexity of the discussions concerning the body of the queen and the double body of the king.

We would like to thank the Fritz-Thyssen-Stiftung for their financial contribution to the travel expenses of conference participants. The European University Institute is acknowledged for generously funding translations. Finally, we thank Almut Höfert and Sergio Amadei, both from the European University Institute, Marion Berghahn and Mark Stanton for helpful collaboration and advice.

List of Contributors

Dr Jill Bepler (Research Grants, Herzog August Bibliothek, Wolfenbüttel)

Professor Dr Claudia Breger (Dept. of Germanic Studies, Indiana University, Bloomington)

Professor Catherine Brice (Institut d'Etudes politiques de Paris)

Professor Susan Frye, Ph.D. (Dept. of English, University of Wyoming)

Dr Martin Kohlrausch (German Historical Institute, Warsaw)

Professor Louis Montrose, Ph.D. (Dept. of Literature, University of California, San Diego)

Professor Dr Regina Schulte (Chair of Modern and Contemporary History / Gender History, Ruhr-Universität, Bochum)

Dr Alexis Schwarzenbach (University of Zurich)

Professor Dr Katharina Sykora (Dept. of Art History and Media Studies, Hochschule für Bildendende Künste Braunschweig)

Professor Dr Juliane Vogel (Dept. of German Language and Literature, University of Vienna)

Professor Rachel J. Weil, Ph.D. (Dept. of History, Cornell University)

Professor Dr Bernd Weisbrod (Dept. of History, Georg-August University, Göttingen)

Professor Dr Horst Wenzel (Dept. of German Literature, Humboldt University, Berlin)

Professor Abby E. Zanger, Ph.D. (Dept. of History, Tufts University)

1

Introduction

Conceptual Approaches
to the Queen's Body

Regina Schulte

Does the queen have one body, or, like the king, two (Kantorowicz 1957)? How many 'bodies' can a queen possess or inhabit? In an enthusiastic review of Andrea Breth's Vienna production of Schiller's *Maria Stuart* in the *Frankfurter Allgemeine Zeitung*, the critic speaks of 'the queen's three bodies'.[1] The queen's body becomes a picture-puzzle made up of medieval theological discourses, politically verifiable facts and the projections that have always been trained upon the feminine. From the beginning, the body of the queen appears to have been incorporated into a political concept, that of the monarchy. We encounter a remarkable paradox here, though; it seems as if the political luminosity of this particular body was repeatedly reduced to its 'natural', its particularly gendered dimension, as if it were its femaleness that limited the ability of the queen's body to engage in politics. Its political strength seems to require the proximity of a male body – as the consort of the king, the mother of future sovereigns, the widow and preserver of the royal or dynastic legacy. The femaleness of the queen's body connotes a lack, but this very dimension opened up its capacity for politics in a specific historical context. For the king's body, too, had revealed a 'natural' side; it could be too young, or become ill, old and feeble-minded; it could be weak, or fall prey to its passions – its corporeality connoted it with deficiency, with femininity.

Was the king's body ideally always a male, or even an androgynous one, which united all genders within it, such as we can find in representations of Louis XIV?[2] Or was it necessary for the queen to be able to embody the male form, as in the case of Elizabeth I of England, who claimed to have the body of a woman but the heart and stomach of a king? The phrase is complex: she said 'of a king', not 'of a man'.[3]

Historians – including some feminists – have persisted in operating within this set of questions, with its dichotomous trap of male versus female and political versus natural. Ernst Kantorowicz exposes this very structure in his marvellous book on the king's two bodies, but only at the beginning of the work does he mention that it was the body of a queen – Elizabeth I – that revealed the full implications of the concept of the dual royal body.[4] The jurists of the Elizabethan court developed a concept that at once permitted the coronation of a valid sovereign, despite the succession of a woman, and placed limitations upon her. For political and legal reasons, it had become necessary in 1561 to equip the queen with two bodies, a natural one and a political one, with her body politic incorporated into her body natural.[5] Rachel Weil has pointed to the instability of the English monarchs' relationship to the female sex in the early modern period. 'Queens were not simply women, any more than kings were simply men. The notion that the monarch possessed two "bodies" mystically fused together in her person, her mortal body and the immortal body of the "king-who-never-dies", was available to insure that the ills to which all mortal flesh was subject (including femaleness) did not diminish the aura of divine authority attaching to the ruler's person.'[6] The symbolism and iconography that arose under Elizabeth acquired increasingly elaborate theoretical underpinnings, which were refined by the London Inns of Court.[7]

The legal construction developed by English jurists, which Shakespeare treats in Richard II[8] and which Elizabeth explicitly addressed,[9] was both brilliant and fateful. The next monarch but one could be beheaded quite legally, his physical body was subject to juxtaposition with a parliament that was capable both of preserving the king's body 'politic' and rejecting his body 'natural'. I long believed that the appearance of the unique Queen Elizabeth I was the consequence of a fantastic construction born of necessity, until I came to understand that this construction, which resulted from the secularisation of a previously theological concept, was fundamental to the inception of a new understanding of the monarchy, which, in its constitutional form, would later reach a high point under Victoria.

But different political worlds may exist side by side – for instance England and France with its Salic law – and the bodies of queens follow the structure of political versus natural more than just ideally. Perhaps we can even use the complexity and contradictions of female royal images and biographies to break through the dualistic thought structure prevalent in historical literature. In what follows I would like to pursue the cycle of various life-courses and show, using a few examples, that the political and natural bodies of the queen were inextricably intertwined. At the same time, I would like to emphasise and develop the function of the natural, corporeal image for the political context.

Initiations

Even as a young girl, Elizabeth I had woven her political ambitions and potential future as a queen into her handiwork and embroidery. A skill always regarded as female became a vehicle of political speech, and needle and thread produced writing, binding the recipient of affectionate gifts to a hand that would later take up the sceptre and the crown.[10] When Elizabeth entered London for her coronation in 1559, she had mastered the choreography of political discourse without being consumed by it. The young queen was greeted enthusiastically by Londoners as a figure of hope after dark political times:

> For all men hope in thee, that all virtues shall reyne,
> For all men hope that thou, none error wilt support,
> For all men hope that thou wilt truth restore agayne,
> And mend that is amisse, to all good mennes comfort.[11]

At this time, Elizabeth needed the support of the city, which devised a festive entrance ceremony in which it sought to commit the young queen to its interests on the day before her coronation. In *The Passage of Our Most Dread Sovereign Lady Queen Elizabeth*,[12] a text in which the city's elites captured the royal entry, the roles of the paternal city and the virtuous daughter, of Elizabeth as the city's wife and mother are played out, and the virgin queen is entangled in a tight network of economic reciprocities. Susan Frye has shown, however, that Elizabeth at no time relinquished her right of interpretation over these symbolic events, but rather developed a mastery of symbolic expression and self-representation that allowed her to shape her own role as queen while entering into a long and productive phase of collaboration with the city and its populace.[13] In a sense, she tailored her royal robes according to her own design. This ritual of entry and its sophisticated choreography became virtually symptomatic of the mastery with which Elizabeth developed from a maidenly, chaste and bride-like queen, whose hair in her coronation portrait still lies girlishly loose upon her shoulders[14] to an icon of a virgin whose husband was the kingdom – 'I am already bound unto an husband, which is the kingdom of England'.[15] Finally, in an elaborate semantic of love, she came to occupy the sacred place of the secularised Virgin Mary.[16] The metamorphoses of her body were accompanied by a maelstrom of political speculations about her willingness – and her ability – to marry, her political intentions, as well as by poetic and iconographic attempts at interpretation, attribution and transfiguration, with which an entire complex of political and cultural meanings was equipped, leading to the ultimate disappearance or mystification of her natural body. In her last, 'Rainbow' portrait (Figure 1.1), painted shortly before or after her death, Elizabeth looks younger than in any of the previous ones – her girlishly loose hair redder, her skin smoother, and her features softer – dressed in a gown composed almost solely of writing and symbols.[17]

It seems that, in her initiation into her status as sovereign and into absolute rule, Elizabeth succeeded in maintaining a high degree of self-determination by continually playing the two sides of the royal body against each other. In the seventeenth century, when the Spanish Habsburg princess Maria Teresa of Austria, bride of Louis XIV and future queen of France, was handed over in an elaborate ceremony at the Spanish-French border and made her nuptial entry, the circumstances were quite different. As Abby Zanger demonstrates in an impressive essay, the transfer rituals accomplished the transformation of the Habsburg infanta Maria Teresa into the Bourbon queen Marie Thérèse, transporting her from the symbolic system of one culture, the Spanish, into that of another, the French.[18] In essence it is a process of changing clothes; the body of the princess has already become that of a Bourbon before she ever steps onto French soil. Having shed both clothing and name, the princess stands literally and metaphorically naked, before being physically overcome in a genuine and symbolic act of fitting out with new garments. Never again will Austrian-Spanish thread or cloth touch the bride's body, which is now arrayed in the silks and laces of French fashion, made in Lyon and not in some foreign land. This ritual of adoption by the French court has also been claimed in the literature for Marie-Antoinette – for instance

NON SINE SOLE
IRIS.

Figure 1.1 Allegorical Portrait of Elizabeth I (The 'Rainbow' Portrait), artist unknown, c. 1600–03.

by Stefan Zweig – although it no longer took place in the same manner.[19] Perhaps this was also already a consequence of the softening of strict absolutist court ceremonial.

Nevertheless, a glance at this later Habsburg princess – Maria Antonia / Marie-Antoinette – provides important clues. She brought nothing with her: to the later torment of her imperial mother Maria Theresa she was not trained for her future role, not prepared for political action; she was, rather, a tabula rasa, young, cheerful and naïve. In her malleability she presented the ideal body of a bride who was to take shape in the splendour of the French court, and there only. One hundred and ten years before the entry of Marie-Antoinette, however, the iconography and the official account of 1660 in the pamphlet 'La pompe et Magnificence fait au marriage du Roi et de L'Enfante D'Espagne ….' show the role assigned to her predecessor Marie Thérèse in the ritual of royal entry that followed the dressing ceremony – she was above all an ornament, a jewel in the crown, 'a curio that could be placed into the royal collection',[20] and thus a function in the overwhelming absolute image of the French king. Beauty was an attribute of the king, and was indeed the king himself. The sight of the somewhat awkward, sweaty Spanish stranger only reflected his own refinement. At the same time, however, it was the perspiration of the newly married Marie Thérèse in her heavy French wedding gown, which was made of brocade and ermine despite the June heat, that led to a confusing and very concrete disturbance of the celebration. After the marriage ceremony the bride undressed and took to her bed, indifferent to all homage, thus withdrawing from the further festivities. Even with the strictest protocol, the body of the young queen was not completely controllable, and the transformation into a royal French body proved to be a process fraught with resistance and obstinacy.[21] Marie Thérèse remained in the king's shadow and with the birth of a dauphin her role in the Bourbon–Habsburg power play was over, and her body was banished from the king's presence. Thus it is perhaps not surprising that this queen is barely present in the iconography of the period.

Who produced the images, and who looked at them? Marie-Antoinette's enormous iconographic career had much to do with the change of audience;[22] she was the Other, the symbol and ugly face of decay, who could not and must not be symbolised within one's own, French, context. She, the foreigner, represented the corrupt body of the *ancien régime* king, as long as he had not yet been abandoned as a body politic in his own country.[23]

From the beginning, Marie-Antoinette's entry was laden with omens whose historiographic significance the seventeen-year-old could scarcely imagine: an unfortunate mural of the wedding of Jason and Medea on the island in the Rhine near Strasbourg when she was delivered to the French, and a fire that occurred during her entry into Paris that killed hundreds of people. Interpretations of omens, which already saw a bad end looming over the new bride, began to circulate, although now they came not from the court but from middle-class observers and writers, from the people.[24] Only when the royal bride adapted to the demands of incipient middle-class ideas about love and images of the sovereign would a safe entry be possible again: that is, when the bride could, as it were, rise from the yeast of the people, when her youth and innocence satisfied a new, strict, bourgeois moral canon, and when her beauty spoke of virtue and nature, not artifice. A new voice had been added now to royal historiography or hagiography, and the natural, chaste body of a queen close to the people should and must be its political dowry.

According to all the requirements of romantic notions of royalty – the Brothers Grimm had just rewritten their fairy tales – in the end it was Queen Louise of Prussia who lived up to the demands of the new era, outdone only by Elisabeth of Austria, popularly known as Sisi. Children of nature who came from the country, with a love story in which the prince recognised his future bride at first sight, fell in love with her and kissed her amidst the babbling of forest brooks, touched the hearts of first the Prussian and then the Austrian people. Henceforth, all queens would be moral and good. The others, the female monarchs of the past, were banished as envious, wicked stepmothers to the realm of witches, where cannibalistic, child- and man-eating monsters like Catherine the Great lived on as the good queens' evil twins.[25] Royal brides – Louise – kissed the children of the people and themselves wasted away in poetic verses. The citizens of the capital prepared celebrations for their royal entries, and were near neighbours to their well-known country estates. They drank water instead of wine and distributed bread to the common folk instead of mocking their starving subjects in the manner of Marie-Antoinette. They dressed plainly, affronting the extravagant court ladies with their simple appearance and behaviour, and communicated with the mother of the famous poet whose verses they scratched into the icy window of a poor cottager's dwelling.[26] And this body, which was glorified as 'natural', was their body politic, the programme in the visions of a queen in a constitutional monarchy.

Had a fundamental depoliticisation of the queen occurred? It appears that the middle class in particular placed its fantasies of redemption and hopes for a new beginning after the downfall of decayed royal dynasties and the demise of old, allegedly corrupt and immoral kings, in the virginal brides and queens of the early nineteenth century, as happened in Prussia, and in England with Victoria's ascent to the throne. This young queen promised innocence and purity, and her youth and femininity awakened popular recollections of earlier queens who had passed into legend – Elizabeth and Anne. Thus in romanticised pictorial and literary representations, the moment when Victoria received word that she would ascend the throne assumed a mythical quality. The accession was portrayed in an Annunciation scene, in which Victoria appeared as a secularised, modern Virgin Mary, a Madonna receiving the good news from a minister-angel kneeling before her.[27] The body of a young queen could provide material and a vehicle for messages of redemption, just as that of Marie-Antoinette had heralded disaster and later become a site of political and pornographic discourses on the corruption of the court, nobility and Church.

The Bodies of Queens

Before that, however, her mother Maria Theresa had depicted the ideal image of the queen of France for her daughter Marie-Antoinette and the image of the mother of the French dauphin, whose grandmother she, the Austrian empress, would be. In a correspondence lasting ten years she deluged Marie-Antoinette, like her other children, with instructions, orders and admonitions. She concerned herself with her daughter's appearance and proper conduct at the court of Versailles, attempting to turn her inexperienced and poorly prepared child into a queen of France on her own model.[28]

But what was the image that she had of herself as a monarch? As the first-born daughter of Charles VI, she had been forced, in the absence of a male heir, to succeed him upon his sudden death. At the age of twenty-three she found herself the almost wholly unprepared ruler of an immense and dangerous empire:

At that time I possessed the experience and knowledge necessary to rule such vast and far-flung lands all the less as my lord father had never seen fit to involve or instruct me in either domestic or foreign affairs. Thus I found myself all at once devoid of money, troops and counsel.[29]

That was how she described her situation eleven years after she ascended the throne, in a memorandum of 1750/51, when she was thirty-three years old and the mother of eleven children. In the meantime she had come to fill her role, was queen of Hungary and Bohemia and had refused to be crowned empress at Frankfurt at the side of her husband Francis Stephen of Lorraine, who had been elected emperor, 'since she esteemed this coronation less than the two masculine crowns [*couronnes masculines*] she wore herself, having once said that she preferred not to change her sex again at a coronation, and repeated to me today that this coronation was but a comedy in which she did not wish to participate.'[30]

Instead she turned her journey to Frankfurt into a 'private' triumphal procession through her lands. Along the way she played with the charm of her 'naturally beautiful' appearance, which in the eyes of the people seemed for a long moment to be freed from etiquette and the exigencies of royal disguise, and finally stole the show in Frankfurt from her officially imperial but still relatively powerless husband.

When His Imperial Majesty had nearly reached the Römer, accompanied by the constant joyful shouting with which the air fairly buzzed, Her Majesty the Empress-Queen, standing at the window and waving a white handkerchief, showed her heartfelt pleasure at the so successfully accomplished coronation of his Most Serene Highness her husband, and as soon as a small silence ensued, cried out a cheerful 'Vivat!' of her own.[31]

Which body of the empress-queen became visible here? Was it her private body, or the one that claimed the masculine crowns and political authority still more plainly at the moment when Maria Theresa used the offer of coronation as imperial consort merely as an occasion for a refusal and a folksy encounter with the people? Was she interested in a brilliant fusion, a dissolve, a constantly changing play with herself as queen, consort and, finally, the mother of many children and as many aspirants to royal roles? Maria Theresa was a master of the art of permanent transgression of the body politic and the body natural. A fine example is the famous scene of 7 September 1741 in which, dressed in mourning with a six-month-old infant (the long-awaited heir to the throne) in her arms and the crown of St Stephan on her head, she tearfully begged the representatives of the Hungarian nobility for their support (for the 'insurrection', that is, a levy *en masse*). Legend has it that the men, moved to tears themselves, 'threw themselves at their ruler's feet, drew their daggers and swore a sacred oath: "moriatur pro rege nostro Maria Theresia"'.[32]

Maria Theresa knew how to put her maternal body to good political use and to assert her political will by touching the emotions. The increasingly rigid disciplining of her everyday life and office, the perfection of her representations and the strictness of her canon of virtues were ultimately revealed when, after the death of her beloved husband, she put aside her jewels forever, wore nothing but mourning until the end of her life, and banished all gaiety from her surroundings. In this way she glorified and stylised her marriage as the 'most blessed' and as the flawless nucleus of her huge family and her empire, an example for all.[33]

At some point, however, the body natural of the weary old queen began to rebel. Letters were the central medium of her rule, her personal means of influencing and participating in the lives of her children. She wrote her letters largely in her own hand. Her last letter to Marie-Antoinette, written one month before her death, ends with the following words: 'I myself have been suffering for four weeks from rheumatism in my right arm, which is the reason that this letter is written less well than usual, and which causes me to close [now] with the assurance that you have all my love.'[34]

Queen Victoria was so successful because she could represent the bourgeois ideal of the royal couple who found their vocation in the family while at the same time apparently having no difficulty in wielding power and asserting their own (so-called natural) will. She was undoubtedly conservative and had no sympathy for female emancipation, and the affairs of the common people were more likely to touch her heart than to inspire her to political reforms. Why was she able to become such a strong force for stability in nineteenth-century England? At her coronation, the tears in her eyes were plainly visible,[35] and her emotionality brought her closer to the common people, and made her an ideal for middle-class Englishwomen.

She was perceived as the tireless, protective mother of the growing brood of children her voluminous body brought into the world. Rapturous poetry celebrated her: '"The blessings happy *peasants* have, be thine, O crowned queen". If Victoria does not quite become a peasant, she is likened to one. Democratised and domesticated – wedded *yet* crowned – Victoria upholds a romantic idea of the merrily married folk.'[36]

Victoria presented herself as the loving wife of her prince-consort, who competently relieved her of the duties of rule and became an essential part of her body politic, and whom she crowned a secret king.[37] It was to him, whom she adored, that she gazes devotedly upwards on countless paintings and photographs. She mourned his death to excess.

Queen Victoria refused to wear the crown without ever doubting that it belonged to her alone.[38] In her self-representations she did not compete with the beautiful queens of Europe, preferring the plainest, almost rustic, clothing. She looked like a woman of the people, and could be mistaken for one. Thus she could become a legend, as in one of the countless Highland tales about encounters with the queen, with a shepherd lad as hero:

> 'Gang out of the road, lady, and let the sheep gang by', he cried. Finding that his appeal produced no effect, he shouted yet louder, 'I say, gang back, will you, and let the sheep pass!' 'Do you know, boy, whom you are speaking to?' asked the Queen's attendant. 'I dinna know, and I dinna care', replied the exasperated lad; 'that's the sheep's road, and she has no business to stand there'. 'But it is the Queen', was the reply. 'Well', replied the astonished boy, 'why don't she put on clothes so that folks would know her?'[39]

The queen did not go about in disguise like the figure in a fairy tale in order to learn the secrets of the common folk. Instead, her clothing betrayed *her* secret to the people, who recognised her as one of their own, as Adrienne Munich notes in her excellent analysis of 'Queen Victoria's Secrets', the building blocks of her myth.[40] 'Intensively private in her domestic relations,' however, 'the Queen displayed her privacy for public consumption; she was alone and surrounded; autocratic and abject; charitable to the poor, egocentric and abrupt to others; immensely hardworking and immensely self-indulgent.'[41] The fact that she was regarded as a constant troublemaker who defied the ideas about queens held dear by the upper classes who actually ruled Britain, and who hoped that she would abdicate in favour of her son, does not appear to have bothered Victoria. Nor was she troubled by the family mutterings and newspaper gossip about her long-time Scottish manservant and lover Mr Brown, whom she mourned as publicly (much to the embarrassment of those in her immediate surroundings) as her late husband Prince Albert.[42]

It might appear that Victoria conquered a realm in which her political and natural bodies merged. Or that she was the right queen at the right time, with her naïvety, her delight in the theatrical, her sense of power and ultimately her immense wealth. Towards the end of her life she was the worst-dressed and the richest woman in the world. She managed at the same time to be racist and to love her Indian servants dearly; her close relationships with her dogs inspired animal protection laws that offended the hunt-loving aristocracy – she embodied all the paradoxes of a country that sought to be at once aristocratic *and* democratic, but nevertheless needed the protective, powerful and wilful body of a super-mother as well. Victoria was a fantasy and an invention of the nineteenth-century English middle classes, in whose minds the femaleness of the royal body served more to preserve than to dismantle the monarchy. Her magnificent eccentricity and wilfulness offered redemptive elements in dealing with a monarchy whose rigid fetters had given way, along with the severed heads of the *ancien régime*, to a semantic of flowing political discourses, within which the English monarchy could be stabilised. And in the discourses of the people these flows were connoted as feminine.

And yet, didn't Victoria's natural, self-willed body ultimately merge into an imperial fantasy? In closing, I would like to cite the ingenious beginning of Dorothy Thompson's biography of Victoria:

> By the time of her death her nine children, thirty-six grandchildren and thirty-seven great-grandchildren, with their spouses, constituted a flock of Battenbergs, Bernadottes, Bourbons, Bourbon-Parmas, Braganzas, Coburgs, Glücksburgs, Hapsburgs, Hessens, Hohenzollerns, Mecklenburg-Strelitzes, Romanovs, Savoys and Wittenbachs, enough to occupy most of the remaining thrones of Europe for the foreseeable future.[43]

There is, however, yet another, oft-repeated story about the elderly Victoria, according to which, by her own account, she felt utterly alone sitting amongst this multitude of kinfolk.[44] Was this, too, a self-polished jewel in the crown of an imperial queen and mother, or was it instead the contemplation of a woman in the full possession of her faculties, whose body sensed the nearness of death?

Translated by Pamela Selwyn

Notes

1. Gerhard Stadelmaier, 'Die drei Körper der Königin. Frauenbilderkrieg: Andrea Breths gloriose "Maria Stuart" kämpft in der Wiener Burg', *Frankfurter Allgemeine Zeitung*, 29 October 2001.

2. Cf. the picture of the young king as a dancer in Peter Burke, *The Fabrication of Louis XIV* (London and New Haven, 1992), 46.

3. Rachel Weil, *Political Passions: Gender, the Family and Political Argument in England 1680–1714* (Manchester and New York, 1999), 166; see also Marie Axton, *The Queen's Two Bodies: Drama and the Elizabethan Succession* (London, 1977).

4. Ernst H. Kantorowicz, *The King's Two Bodies: A Study in Medieval Theology* (Princeton, NJ, 1957).

5. Axton, *The Queen's Two Bodies*, 12; see also Susanne Scholz, *Body Narratives: Writing the Nation and Fashioning the Subject in Early Modern England* (London and New York, 2000).

6. Weil, *Political Passions*, 166. See also Fanny Cosandey, *La reine de France, Symbole et pouvoir XVᵉ–XVIIIᵉ siècle* (Paris, 2000), 361ff.

7. Kantorowicz, *King's Two Bodies*, Chapter 1; Axton, *The Queen's Two Bodies*, 12ff.; Roy Strong, *The Cult of Elizabeth: Elizabethan Portraiture and Pageantry* (London, 1977); Rudolf Braun and David Gugerli, *Macht des Tanzes – Tanz der Mächtigen. Hoffeste und Herrschaftszeremoniell 1550–1914* (Munich, 1993).

8. See the impressive interpretation of Shakespeare's *Richard II* in Kantorowicz, *King's Two Bodies*, Chapter 2.

9. 'And as I am but one body naturally considered, though by His permission a body politic to govern' is the earliest of Elizabeth's references to the doctrine of the king's two bodies, made on 20 November 1558 in her first speech before her coronation, to her secretary and lords. Elizabeth I, *Collected Works*, ed. Leah S. Marcus, Janel Mueller and Mary Beth Rose (Chicago and London, 2000), 52.

10. Susan Frye, 'Sewing Connections: Elizabeth Tudor, Mary Stuart, Elizabeth Talbot, and Seventeenth-Century Anonymous Needleworkers', in *Maids and Mistresses, Cousins and Queens: Women's Alliances in Early Modern England*, eds. Susan Frye and Karen Robertson (New York, 1999), 165–82, 167.

11. Quoted in Dorothy Thompson, *Queen Victoria: Gender and Power* (London, 1990), 27.

12. Richard Mulcaster, *The Passage of Our Most Dread Sovereign Lady Queen Elizabeth through the City of London to Westminster the Day Before her Coronation* (London, 1558[9]) (STC 7590). For excerpts from this account of the entry see Elizabeth I, *Collected Works*, 53–55.

13. Susan Frye, *Elizabeth I: The Competition for Representation* (New York and Oxford, 1993), 22ff.; see also Braun and Gugerli, *Macht des Tanzes*, 73.

14. Cf. the coronation portrait painted by an unknown artist around 1600 in Elizabeth I, *Collected Works*, 50.

15. Elizabeth I, *Collected Works*, Speech 3, Version 2, 1559. Her answer to the Commons' petition that she marry, 59; cf. Philippa Berry, *Of Chastity and Power. Elizabethan Literature and the Unmarried Queen* (London und New York, 1989), 66.

16. See John N. King, 'Queen Elizabeth I: Representations of the Virgin Queen', *Renaissance Quarterly* 43 (1990), 30–74.

17. On the 'Rainbow' portrait and the 'mask of youth', see Strong, *The Cult of Elizabeth*, 46–54, and *Gloriana: The Portraits of Elizabeth I* (New York, 1987), 146–61.

18. Abby Zanger, 'Fashioning the Body Politic: Imaging the Queen in the Marriage of Louis XIV', in Louise Olga Fradenburg, ed., *Women and Sovereignty* (Edinburgh, 1992), Yearbook of the Traditional Cosmology Society 7, 101–20. On the handing over of the bride on the banks of the River Bidassoa and on the marriage celebrations, see also Simon Schama, *Landscape and Memory* (New York, 1995), 334–35.

19. See Regina Schulte, 'Der Aufstieg der konstitutionellen Monarchie und das Gedächtnis der Königin', *Historische Anthropologie. Kultur – Gesellschaft – Alltag*, 6, 1 (1998), 76–103, here 76–77.

20. Abby Zanger, *Scenes from the Marriage of Louis XIV. Nuptial Fictions and the Making of Absolutist Power* (Stanford, Calif., 1997), 157.

21. Zanger, 'Body Politic', 111ff.

22. See Sarah Maza, *Private Lives and Public Affairs: The Causes Célèbres of Prerevolutionary France* (Berkeley, Los Angeles and London, 1993), esp. 167–211.

23. See Lynn Hunt, *The Family Romance of the French Revolution* (London, 1992), 89ff.

24. Schulte, 'Aufstieg', 76.

25. See Helmut Brackert, 'Hänsel und Gretel oder Möglichkeiten und Grenzen literaturwissenschaftlicher Märchen-Interpretationen', *Und wenn sie nicht gestorben sind ... Perspektiven auf das Märchen*, ed. H. Brackert (Frankfurt a.M., 1980), 9–38; Johann Gustav Droysen, *Vorlesungen über die Freiheitskriege*, 2 vols. (Kiel, 1846), 1, 374.

26. See Schulte, 'Aufstieg', 92ff.

27. Susan P. Casteras, 'The Wise Child and her "Offspring": Some Changing Faces of Queen Victoria', in *Remaking Queen Victoria*, eds. Margaret Homans and Adrienne Munich (Cambridge, 1997), 182–92, 197–98 f.; cf. Thompson, *Queen Victoria*, 24.

28. See *Marie-Antoinette. Correspondance secrète entre Marie-Thérèse et le Cte de Mercy Argenteau. Avec les lettres de Marie.Thérèse et de Marie-Antoinette*, ed. Alfred von Arneth and Matthieu Auguste Geoffrey, 3 vols. (Paris, 1874); Paul Christoph, ed., *Maria Theresia und Marie Antoinette. Ihr geheimer Briefwechsel* (Vienna, 1952).

29. Maria Theresa, *Briefe und Aktenstücke in Auswahl*, ed. Friedrich Walter, Freiherr-vom-Stein-Gedächtnis-Ausgabe, Ausgewählte Quellen zur Deutschen Geschichte der Neuzeit, ed. Rudolf Buchner, 12 (Darmstadt, 1968), 64.

30. Fred Hennings, *Und sitzet zur linken Hand. Franz Stephan von Lothringen* (Vienna, Berlin and Stuttgart, 1961), 265.
31. Hennings, *Und sitzet*, 280–81; see also Peter Berglar, *Maria Theresia* (Reinbek bei Hamburg, 1980), 48–49.
32. Edwin Dillmann, *Maria Theresia* (Munich, 2000), 36.
33. Cf. Gertrud Fussenegger, *Maria Theresia* (Munich, 1988), 263.
34. Christoph, *Geheimer Briefwechsel*, 343.
35. Cf. Adrienne Munich, *Queen Victoria's Secrets* (New York, 1996), 19.
36. Munich, *Queen Victoria's Secrets*, 21; the most important biographies of Queen Victoria are Lytton Strachey, *Queen Victoria* (1921; reprint Harmondsworth, 1971); Elizabeth Longford, *Victoria R. I.* (London, 1964); Stanley Weintraub, *Victoria: Biography of a Queen*, 2 vols. (London, 1987); and Dorothy Thompson, *Queen Victoria*; a good German selection of Victoria's voluminous correspondence with commentary is printed in Kurt Tetzeli von Rosador and Arndt Mersmann, eds., *Queen Victoria. Ein biographisches Lesebuch* (Munich, 2000).
37. Cf. Thompson, *Queen Victoria*, 36; Weintraub, *Victoria*, Vol. 1, 170–71.
38. Cf. Weintraub, *Victoria*, Vol. 1, 14, 138, and Dorothy Marshall, *The Life and Times of Victoria* (London, 1972).
39. Munich, *Queen Victoria's Secrets*, 59; on royal enthusiasm for the Scottish Highlands, see Hugh Trevor-Roper, 'The Invention of Tradition: The Highland Tradition of Scotland', in *The Invention of Tradition*, eds. Eric Hobsbawm and Terence Ranger (Cambridge, 1983).
40. Munich, *Queen Victoria's Secrets*.
41. Margaret Homans and Adrienne Munich, Introduction in *Remaking Queen Victoria*, eds. Margaret Homans and Adrienne Munich (Cambridge, 1997), 3.
42. On Victoria and John Brown, see among others, Thompson, *Queen Victoria*, 61ff.; Weintraub, Victoria, Vol. 1, 372ff.
43. Thompson, Queen Victoria, xiv.
44. *Queen Victoria in her Letters and Journals*, ed. Christopher Hibbert (London, 1984), 304.

Part I

Constructing the
Body Politic

2

How Two Ladies Steal a Crown

The Memoirs of Helene Kottannerin (1439–40) at the Court of Queen Elisabeth of Hungary (1409–42)

Horst Wenzel

Helene Kottannerin is the first woman author in the history of German language chronicle writing.[1] In her memoirs or *Denkwürdigkeiten* (probably dictated around 1450/52), she describes not only the open conflicts characterising the political scene around the Hungarian Queen Elisabeth after King Albrecht's death in 1439 but also writes of the behind-the-scenes negotiations and intrigues accompanying these political conflicts.[2] In this politically tense situation, Helene Kottannerin is not only chronicler, but also a protagonist whose account lets no doubt remain as to her own merits and services for God and the dynasty.

Helene Kottannerin was neither a nun nor a woman of high nobility, but came from a minor aristocratic family from the region of Ödenburg in western Hungary. She was married first to Peter Székeles, who later became mayor of Ödenburg (†1431), and then to the Viennese patrician Johann Kottanner (1432). She had children from both her first and second marriages, and thus definitely her own life apart from the queen. But as chambermaid and lady of the court she was also a person of great influence. She enjoyed the confidence of Queen Elisabeth, who was the daughter of Emperor Sigismund (1433–37) and since 1422 the wife of Albrecht V, Habsburg Duke of Austria. This marriage contributed decisively to Albrecht's being elected King of Hungary in 1437 and then King of the Germans as Albrecht II (1438–39). Johann and Helene Kottanner were in the service of the royal couple from 1436 on, Johann in the duke's service and Helene as chambermaid and attendant of Albrecht and Elisabeth's daughter, the young princess Elisabeth, born in 1436. With the royal court, they moved from Austria to Hungary in 1439 and in this year also Helene's account begins.

In her *Denkwürdigkeiten* Helene Kottannerin recounts the death of Albrecht II in 1439, and the competing actions of the Hungarian-Polish and Habsburg parties as each attempts to arrange a succession that would be advantageous for them. The Hungarian magnates want to marry their queen to Wladislaus of Poland (born in 1424, son of Wladislaus II). The pregnant Elisabeth, however, tries to delay the decision because she sees the possibility of securing the Habsburg position should a son be born. To forestall the opposing faction, Elisabeth takes possession of the Holy Crown of Hungary (Saint Stephan's Crown; see Figure 2.1), the most important of all the regalia necessary for the coronation of a new king.[3]

The birth of Ladislaus Posthumous (1439/40) validated her plans that also touched directly upon her own status and political future. The rapid coronation of the young Ladislaus Posthumous performed at the right place (Stuhlweißenburg) by the right person (the Archbishop of Gran) and with the holy crown was therefore a highly symbolic act and thus a great success for the Habsburgs.[4] But this success was short-lived. Helene's *Denkwürdigkeiten* end with the retreat of Elisabeth's household to western Hungary after the Hungarian magnates succeeded in crowning the Polish rival King Wladislaus with other royal regalia, namely the right sceptre and sword. The crown remains in Elisabeth's possession until 1440 when she hands it over to her son's new guardian Frederic IV. Only after the death of Wladislaus III in a battle against the Turks in 1444 can the Habsburgs finally reclaim the throne: Ladislaus Posthumous, posthumous son of Albrecht and Elisabeth, becomes Ladislaus V, King of Hungary (1452–57).

There are good reasons to assume that Helene Kottannerin began her memoirs shortly before this time in order to support Ladislaus's claims to the throne as well as to recall her own role in events.[5] Only a single manuscript has survived, today in the collection of the Austrian National Library (Hs. Nr. 2920).[6] The document can be understood variously as an historical record, an autobiographical account and a literary text. Space here does not permit a

Figure 2.1 St. Stephan's crown. Gold, jewels and enamel (after 1076).

comprehensive interpretation of the document, so I will limit my discussion to the following aspects:

1. First, how does Helene Kottannerin represent herself as protagonist in the events she describes in terms of her commitment to the court, in the first place to the queen and then to the young king? This relationship between service and independence not only hints at the complexities of her personality, but, importantly, it can help to reveal the self-construction or self-fashioning of the writing 'I'.

2. Related to her self-representation as a part of public courtly life, is Helene's description of her secret participation in the robbery of the crown, which she carries out on the orders and in the interest of the queen. This tension between public and non-public political manoeuvring characterises the queen's dual stratagem, but it also constitutes the realm in which Helene herself, as the queen's confidante, can act in ways the queen cannot.

3. Helene's *Denkwürdigkeiten* are not only an autobiographical document. The text offers an illuminating view into the principle of courtly, aristocratic representation. The coexistence of the two strategic levels within which the queen operates allows for an especially clear view of the ways in which courtly life is staged and the contrast between public self-representation and secret manoeuvring.

4. As chronicle writer Helene Kottannerin represents the Habsburg interpretation of historical-political events; she depicts these events from the Habsburg perspective and according to Habsburg interests. Her text does not strive to be objective but has a thoroughly propagandistic character, promoting one party in the conflict and disqualifying the claims of the other.

5. The text offers an early and especially clear example of the dialectic between ruler (queen) and servant (chambermaid), one that is not only of interest retroactively for medieval courtly literature but also anticipates that of the court under absolutism.

Self-representation

The question of the construction of the writing 'I' immediately raises the problem of the position of this text within the history of autobiographical writing. Particularly striking for such an early text is the strong emphasis the author places on her own person: 'And then his grace [Albrecht] sent a delegation to Vienna to fetch and bring to him in Pressburg his youngest daughter, Princess Elisabeth, with all her servants. And that happened. *And I, Helena Kottanerin, was there too ...*' '... and together they carried the Holy Crown and brought it into a pentagonal vault. *And I, Helene Kottanner, was there too ...*' (22) '... and they took the Holy Crown out of the box and examined it very carefully. *And I was there too*' (23).[7]

'I came along', 'I was present', and 'I, Helene Kottannerin, was also there' are the frequently repeated formulas that bring the author's self into play. The author's personal participation is emphasised again and again, but the narrated 'I' defines itself predominantly through participation in the events relevant to rule. The 'I' derives its meaning not from a look backwards, a retrospective view of its own history, but rather by looking at the political activities of the dukes and kings and through participating in their history. This might also explain why Helene Kottannerin limits her *Denkwürdigkeiten* to the years 1439–40. Her life before entering the queen's service and her life afterwards appear unimportant because they are not part of the dynastic story that is worth telling. Simultaneously with describing her participation she seems to emphasise her role as witness by repeatedly making reference to herself. Many of her statements confirm this, for example the report of the knighting ceremony of young Ladislaus, just eight weeks old: 'Then the lords dismounted from their horses and formed a wide circle of armoured men holding naked swords in their hands, and into the middle of that circle, *I, Helene Kottanner, had to carry the young king*' (42). 'Then *I, Helene Kottanner, took the king in my arms*, and the Lord of Freistadt, took the sword in his hand and made the king a knight'(43).[8]

It is the young king for whom Helene represents herself as being responsible. Queen Elisabeth has delegated important aspects of her role as mother to Helene, who appears as a substitute mother not only in private chambers but also in courtly ceremony: 'And the noble queen felt such awe for her son and was so meek, that I, humble woman, had priority over her grace that day and was to remain closest to the noble king, because I had held his grace in my arms during his holy anointment and coronation' (44).[9]

In this sense Helene defines herself by her participation in the queen's sphere, the queen who, as in Kantorowicz's theory of the king's two bodies, herself possesses in addition to her natural body a symbolic or representative body to which her entourage also belongs.[10] Helene Kottannerin adopts this perspective herself when she accepts the delegating queen's view as her own: 'Then the noble queen said to me: "What do you advise, dear Kottannerin? If I could divide you in three parts, I would gladly do it. I would like to keep you to myself, and I would also like to leave you with my son and I would also like to see you staying with my daughter."' (49)[11]

The royal body is able to multiply itself. Helene, in contrast, cannot be divided, but she considers it an honour and a justification of her public recognition that the queen wants her not only by her side but would also like to know that she is with her son and daughter. Personal identity here is not yet the product of various temporal and spatial experiences set within an autobiographical framework, but rather the accumulation of honour derived from proximity to the queen or the crown. According to the contemporary theory of the state, the final decision for Helene to remain with the young king means that she binds herself to the future of the kingdom, for as young as he might be, the king stands for the entire state.

On the other hand, it must be emphasised that the scattered glimpses Helene provides of very personal reactions clearly indicate that she does not only define herself through her proximity to the queen and the young king, but also has her own history and her own family. Interestingly, these passages are found in the portion of the text that describes the robbery of the royal crown. Her greatest service to the queen simultaneously demands the greatest risk in terms of her responsibility for her own children.

The Theft of Saint Stephan's Crown

The crown that the first Hungarian king, Saint Stephan, is supposed to have worn in his enthronement in the year 1000 remains the most important relic in Hungary to this day.[12] The people believed that only the legitimate ruler was entitled to this crown, which in its timeless dignity symbolised the continuity and the auratic dimension of rule that had to be continuously realised anew in different persons. In this way the crown also stands for the second body of the king (the body politic) that must be brought together with his natural, physical body (body physical): 'The perpetual, changeless crown symbolised the monarch's body politic.'[13]

Helene reports that the crown had been in the custody of Georg von Pálócz, Archbishop of Gran, together with the other regalia in his castle in Gran. After the death of the bishop, King Albrecht has the crown delivered to him at the castle of Plintenburg (Visegrad). Upon his death in 1439 disposition over the regalia passes to Elisabeth and the old custodian of the crown is replaced by a new keeper. As this is done the Hungarian nobles confirm that the crown is still in its place and seal the treasury once again.

In order to remove herself and her unborn child from under the power of the Hungarian nobles, the queen leaves the Plintenburg, taking her own crown and jewels with her, which Helene smuggles out hidden under her clothing. The crown of Saint Stephan remains sealed in the treasury, but the queen would like to obtain control of it as a guarantee for her own political future as well as that of her child. In the coronation of the hoped-for son, Elisabeth sees her only chance to retain power, knowing full well that the fact that her father was Emperor Sigismund will not protect her from a forced marriage to the young Polish ruler if she herself does not bring an heir into the world.

In consultation with her closest adviser, the Graf of Cilli, she asks Helene Kottannerin to undertake the difficult task of getting the holy crown out of the Plintenburg. In this delicate situation the queen herself cannot act and thus she places her hopes in her trusted chambermaid who, however, feels unequal to the task. Before describing the conspiratorial acquisition of the heavily guarded crown that forms the central event of her *Denkwürdigkeiten*, Helene characterises the conflict of loyalties between her obligation to the queen and to her own family: 'Then my gracious lady came to me and said that I should do it because there was no one she could trust who knew the place as well as I did. The queen's request frightened me, for it meant great danger for me and my little children. And I weighed the matter in my mind wondering what to do, and there was no one I could ask for advice except God alone. I said to myself that if I did not do it and something evil happened as a result, then I would have sinned against God and the world. And so I said to her that I was willing to undertake the difficult journey even at the risk of losing my life, but I asked that they give me a helper' (27).[14] This weighing of the danger that stands before her is one of the rare glimpses Helene provides into her private life. But in the end this conflict leads to the decision to avoid the greater 'wrong in the eyes of God and the world', and to carry out the task.

The secret central event is described in detail, and although Helene emphasises her own contribution, what dominates is the symbolic interpretation of the world according to publicly accepted structures. Helene describes the theft of the crown from the sealed treasury as a battle for righteousness and against its enemies, in other words as a conflict between good and evil. Already in the first sentence of her narration she claims to have God's assistance in what she does: 'But when the time had come when the Almighty God wished to perform His miraculous deeds, God sent us a man who was willing to abduct the Holy Crown. He was Hungarian ...' (28).[15]

God not only provides assistance, but he takes the leading role in the actions described as 'His miraculous deeds'. It is his will that the holy crown should end up in the hands of the Habsburgs, and thus a Hungarian noble turns up who with the help of his servant takes over the technicalities of the operation. Actually it is a well-prepared theft. Helene appears on the Plintenburg under the pretext of wanting to pick up the queen's ladies-in-waiting. The Hungarian carries two files in his slippers and new padlocks under his clothing. Helene has the queen's seal with her in order to reseal the room after the robbery (14:24ff.). During the night of 20 February 1440, when the young ladies and everybody are asleep (15:23–24), the thieves go to work. While the men file the padlocks Helene goes down on her knees to pray that it might all end well. Accordingly God also does his part and ensures that the guards notice nothing of the unavoidable hammering and filing: 'Then he removed from the lock the linen cloth which the castellan had wrapped around it and unlocked the door and went inside with his servant and they worked so hard on the other locks, that the sounds of their hammering and filing could be heard distinctly. But even if the guards and the castellan's men had been on the alert that night and actively watching the treasure entrusted to their care, then surely God Almighty would have stopped their ears to prevent them from hearing anything. But I alone heard everything very well and kept watch while invaded by many fears and worries, and I kneeled down in deep devotion and prayed to God and to Our Dear Lady, that they might assist me and my helpers' (29f.).[16]

Helene herself hears what sounds like armoured men at the door and takes them for ghosts. She reacts by praying and promising to undertake a barefoot pilgrimage to Zell, or to sleep without her feather bed every Saturday night and to recite a prayer of thanks to the Virgin Mary. While she prays the noises resume and she becomes convinced that the devil is trying to interrupt their good deed: 'But while I was praying like this, I seemed to hear loud noises and the din of armour at the door that led directly into the apartment of the ladies-in-waiting. This frightened me so much that my entire body began to shake with fear and I broke into a cold sweat and I thought that it must not be a ghost after all ... and said to myself that it surely was the Devil, who would have liked to foil our plan' (30f.).[17]

Good and evil, God and the Devil wrestle with each other and it is not clear who will get the upper hand. Seen in this way, Helene participates at least as actively in the events as the Hungarian helper who breaks the padlocks with the file and finally takes the crown out of its case. The man takes care of the mechanics while she defends against the devil's disruption by praying, making vows and calling on the Virgin Mary's protection. But they complete the action without attracting attention; the doors are locked with the new padlocks and sealed with the queen's seal. The crown is sewn into a red velvet pillow and taken from the Plintenburg to Kormon where the queen is residing, her pregnancy now far advanced.[18] The crown is transported on Helene's sledge, and she worries with good reason that as they cross the Danube the entire sledge might break through the ice. But they all arrive at their destination safely and Helene is received with relief and gratitude by the queen: 'who now knew well, that with the help of God I had been a good messenger' (33).[19] Barely an hour later the successor to the throne is born.

Helene's literary conception of herself is dominated by her involvement in a remarkable incident even though it is the queen and the nobles, the statesmen and otherworldly powers who appear to be the real protagonists determining the course of events. Nevertheless Helene feels herself to have been chosen, as 'special' in the sense of being a fitting instrument for the struggles of both mundane and divine powers. As she phrases it in the words of one of her confidantes: 'great things are entrusted to you' (32).[20] Her worries about the crown pursue her even into her dreams where communication with God customarily takes place. Traditionally nobles or clergy would have been predestined for such 'special missions'. In this text, however, the early modern era seems to manifest itself in that here it is a chambermaid – someone on the borderline between lesser nobility and middle class – who sets down in writing her experiences in the court of the Hungarian queen.

Public and Non-public Manoeuvring

The manoeuvring behind the scenes of the public representation of rule that Helene's *Denkwürdigkeiten* reveal gives an illuminating glimpse into the structures of rule. Private manoeuvring precedes or coincides with public manoeuvring. Whereas in the public realm Helene's position is far inferior to that of the court's noble representatives, she is a central figure in the realm of private action. The queen and other nobles around her ask Helene numerous times to engage in discreet or secret activities: 'Then the two counts I just mentioned came to me and talked to me *in secret*, and together we went to the door which gave access to the Holy Crown' (23); 'Her grace took me in her secret and said: "Dear, faithful Kottannerin, watch over my daughter and also over that room. Do not allow anyone to enter it except my daughter and yourself"' (24f.); 'Then, all of a sudden, her grace had to go to the countryside *in secret* and ordered me to go to the castle above to try and *secretly* bring her crown and jewellery down to the castle below. I did this and went to the queen's residence above and in utmost *secrecy* brought down from there my gracious lady's crown and all her jewelry on a sled, hiding everything under my clothes' (26).[21]

The phrasing *in ir gehaim* (to be taken into her confidence, secret activity, secret speech), *in gehaim, haimlich* (secret, discreetly, non-public, hidden, clandestine), together form a domain of significance that resists or opposes the public arena of meaning. Secret activity or activity in non-public spaces highlights the tension between public and hidden, a tension that seems constitutive of courtly activity and courtly representation.[22]

As long as rule has to be mediated through the person of a ruler it remains necessary to make that rule evident through signs and symbols. Rulers demonstrate their status through bearing, gesture, clothing, and through signs of rule, that is, through the symbolic extension of the ruler's body into the public space.[23] An entire spectrum of activities functioned in every encounter to underline that this relationship was intact; the honouring during the greeting, the banquet, the sociability during games or on the hunt, the bestowing of gifts upon departure. The language of signs and gesture was the language that dominated in the court and that filled the minds and horizons of the nobles in a way that written instructions could not yet compare to.[24]

Hans-Georg Gadamer expressed this in his characteristically succinct way by defining the 'being' of the ruler as a 'self display'

('Sich-Zeigen'), and thus simultaneously emphasising the ruler's subordination to his public status: 'whose being is so intrinsically enclosed in the "self-display" that he no longer belongs to himself'.[25] The artistry involved in this public self-display – which demands substantial effort to stage – was thematised by Machiavelli: 'Therefore is there no necessity for a Prince to bee endued with all these above written qualities, but it behooves well that he seeme to be so.'[26] The strenuous effort of this 'representation as if' already makes plain that there must be much more to courtly life than the public demonstration of status.

In contrast to the public sphere, in which the members of the nobility must constantly represent their social status, exists the non-public sphere, the backstage on which political arrangements, intrigues and confidential manoeuvring find their proper place. The representation of the theft of Saint Stephan's Crown is one example of this; another is supplied by Helene in an earlier passage where she describes the queen's reaction to the Hungarian nobles' unreasonable request that she marry the young Polish prince. While she publicly agrees to the demand, she privately arranges the conditions necessary to evade it: 'The Hungarian lords ... came to her grace and pressed the case of the King of Poland. Then someone advised her to feign her willingness to marry the Polish king, while pursuing in the meantime whatever would be best for her, and they would always be able to find a reason to get out of her promise ... Since the wise and noble queen understood this, she thought for a long time about possible ways to get the Holy Crown in her possession, away from the Hungarian lords. She thought namely that if she were to be delivered of a son, he should not be ousted from his realm, and that if she were to be delivered of a daughter, she might still be able to negotiate with the Hungarian magnates and obtain concessions from them' (26).[27]

Publicly the queen succumbs to the political pressure of the Hungarians but in secret she works to thwart the marriage plans, especially in view of the possible birth of a son and the resulting retaining of power. Another revealing example is the secret preparation for the hasty coronation of young Ladislaus: 'Shortly after that we received the news, which turned out to be accurate, that the King of Poland was on his way and planning to go to Ofen, as indeed happened, and so we quickly and secretly made preparations for the coronation ... Then the noble queen sent a messenger in utmost secrecy to the noble sovereign of Austria named Duke Albert and announced to him that she intended to have my gracious lord, King Laszla, crowned on the day of Pentecost' (40f.).[28] Even the Archbishop of Gran appears in Stuhlweißenburg on short notice at the queen's bidding, so that the public and formal coronation of the twelve-week-old successor in the end represents only a ratification of the power relationships that had already privately prevailed in the secret struggles for power.

Political Publicity

Helene Kottannerin sees herself as part of the royal *familia*, not only in her actions but also in her writing. Accordingly her description is anything but neutral or historically objective. She represents things from the viewpoint of the royal court and uses every opportunity to show time and again that God and the world too support the queen's will. This is particularly true of the queen's aspiration to unite the holy crown with the hoped-for son, for only the crown can make the heir into the successor.

When a fire breaks out in the queen's chambers it is quickly discovered and no one is injured. The chronicler sees this outcome of the incident as God's support for the crown and its future wearer, whom 'the evil one' ('der poes veint', 10:14) would gladly have harmed: 'And now take note of the miracle! The King who was to wear the Holy Crown was still safely enclosed in his mother's body and he and the crown, which the evil fiend would have liked to destroy with the fire, were hardly two cords removed from one another, but *God watched over us* and awakened the ladies in time' (24).[29]

During the transport of the crown there is another critical moment because the ice covering the Danube is already thin. But Helene and her fellow travellers cross the river safely. Once again Helene sees this as the protection of God, who is interested that the crown reach its destination and not sink to the bottom of the river: 'Then we reached the Danube, which was still covered with ice, but the ice had gotten thin in several places. When we were on the ice and had come as far as the middle of the Danube, the carriage of the ladies-in-waiting proved too heavy; the ice broke and the carriage toppled over, the ladies screamed, and there was much chaos and confusion. I was afraid and thought that we and the Holy Crown would all perish in the Danube together. *Yet God came to our rescue*' (24).[30]

For this reason, as Helene voices to the queen, it also seems to her like a miracle and a sign from God that in the hour of his birth the holy crown is already waiting for the young king. She logically thus draws a direct connection between Saint Stephan and the young king: 'But if it is true that the Holy Crown was sent to the Holy Saint Stephan by God and meant by God for him, it is also true that it was clearly God's will that the true heir, King Lászlá, and not the King of Poland, should receive the Holy Crown of Hungary' (35).[31] In carrying out the coronation in public ('according to the old tradition', [nach irer alten gewonhait (26:33)]) the old law will be satisfied.[32] This coronation in accordance with old tradition receives its higher meaning through its religious connotation, which Helene makes clear in her obvious reference to the form of the Trinity and the emphasis on the festival of the Pentecost. King Ladislaus, King Albrecht's son and Emperor Sigismund's grandson, has been crowned with the Holy Crown by the Archbishop of Gran on the holy day of Pentecost in Stuhlweißenburg (27, 14–17).[33]

The correctness of the succession is manifest in how much the body of the young king ('body natural') is predestined for the crown ('body politic'). Helene tells of the remarkable strength of the small child who proves capable of bearing the burden of the holy crown: 'as the Archbishop placed the Holy Crown on the child's head and held it there, he held up his head with the strength of a one-year old, and that is rarely seen in children of twelve weeks' (43f.).[34] According to tradition the legitimacy of the young king must be inscribed in his body. In this sense and with the same objective, Helene Kottannerin draws attention to the strength of the child's voice: 'But the noble young king had little joy of his coronation, for he cried so loud that it could be heard throughout the entire church and the common people marveled and said that it was not the voice of a child of twelve weeks but rather of a one-year-old, which he really was not' (44).[35]

The surprising strength of the young king is supposed to be seen as a sign of his royal predestination. The unusual birth of the child and the young king's conspicuous strength draw on ancient mythological heroes, but also on Christ himself: in this way the future ruler is already distinguished at birth, showing how important signs draw attention to his superior status. This tradition is apparently still so vital that it is transferred onto the young Ladislaus in order to present the legitimacy of his claim to rule and to make his legitimate claim to the crown recognisable and evident.

The clearest evidence of Helene's efforts to make the king's legitimacy unassailable can be seen in the way that she emphasises the presence of the complete regalia in young Ladislaus's coronation. Helen reports that the queen's cousin, Count Ulrich von Zilly, held the holy crown over the baby's head, while other prominent nobles carried the royal insignia – the orb, the sceptre and the legate staff: 'And Count Bartholomeus carried the apple, and the Duke of Lindbach named Thomas Szécsi, carried the sceptre. Another nobleman walked in front of the king with the legate staff, to show that no part of Hungary is a fief of the Holy Roman Empire. They also had by his side the sword with which his grace had been knighted' (44).[36]

But Helene's description here does not correspond with the historical facts, for the orb and sceptre were still on the Plintenburg and thus in the hands of the Hungarian party, a fact that had already been used by Ladislaus's opponents to argue against the legality of his coronation.[37] At the time of her dictation in 1450–52, Helene must have known that the royal regalia were incomplete, even if the queen had ordered surrogates to be made. But because tradition demanded that the authentic regalia were necessary for a legal coronation, Helene fabricates the 'truth' in writing.

Queen and Servant[38]

Despite widespread prejudice, already in the Middle Ages a considerable number of important women played leading roles in the political arena. But there are also genuine areas of feminine intimacy insulated from the male world and thus characterised by a particular feminine knowledge and responsibility. Helene's *Denkwürdigkeiten* are a revealing witness to this world, especially with regard to the queen's pregnancy and the birth of the heir to the throne: 'As I was talking to the noble queen like this, her grace told me that the women from Ofen had bathed her in a tub and that after the bath she had felt quite unwell. Hence I lifted up her gown to see her naked. Then I saw several signs that showed me clearly that the birth of the child was not far off' (33).[39] In this situation Helene assumes responsibility for the queen: 'Then I said: "Gracious lady, get up; it seems to me you will not go to Pressburg tomorrow." Then her grace got up from the bed and went and began to prepare herself for the heavy work.'[40] She sends for the women who are to be present at the birth and wakes the midwife: 'Margret, get up right away, her grace is going to have the child now' (34).[41]

It does not take longer than a half hour before 'the young king' sees the light of day, and Helene Kottannerin points out that this occurs just as the holy crown arrives from the Plintenburg: 'The child did not want to wait any longer; he wanted to rush to the Holy Crown before anyone else did, as if he had been told that the King of Poland was after his paternal heritage. And had he slept only one week more in the womb of his mother ... then the King of Poland would possibly have arrived in Weissenburg first' (35).[42]

The political dimension (body politic) seeps through Helene's depiction in her account of the practical care of the child (body natural); this is consistent with Plowden's point that the two bodies are not so clearly distinct from one another. The imperishable kingship takes material form in the natural body of the king, which thus also requires the best possible care. After the choice of a midwife Helene describes the selection of a wet nurse, herself the mother of a son and not a daughter: '... the other a wet-nurse to suckle the baby with her own breasts. And this wet-nurse had brought along her own child, a boy, for the wise say that the milk of a woman who has given birth to a son is better than the milk of a woman who has brought forth a daughter' (33).[43]

It seems remarkable that the *Denkwürdigkeiten* represent the conflicts, tensions and competitions in the inner chambers of the house and in the company of women as hardly less significant than those in the broader realm of the court. Indicative of this is Helene's account of how the women enviously observed who was allowed to be present at the birth and who not, because the question of presence (proximity to the king) is also a question of honour: 'And when the ladies from Ofen learned that my lady had been delivered of the child, they were happy, as they ought to have been, but they were also annoyed that they had not been present at the birth and they strongly suspected that this was my doing, even though it truly was not my fault, for there simply had not been enough time' (35).[44]

This commentary subtly hints at the personage whose prestige is most bound up with the birth of the king, that is, second only to the queen and before all others, the chambermaid Helene. Whereas the queen is the natural mother of the new-born child, Helene appears to be his second mother in more ways than one. First she procures the crown of Saint Stephan that guarantees the king the realisation of his kingdom, and then she stays with the queen during the birth of the baby. Later she takes on a recognisable role during the baptism, the knighting ceremony, and the coronation of the young prince; and, in a certain sense, she resumes this mother role many years later when she produces her memoirs that recall the many miraculous signs that distinguished the successor to the throne and are thus suited to support Ladislaus Posthumous on his final ascent to the throne. As the mother of the text she still acts out of responsibility for the queen, the young king, and the crown.[45]

Nevertheless Helene's perspective cannot be presumed to coincide completely with the viewpoint of the queen and the nobles surrounding her. The relation of lord to servant, of queen to chambermaid cannot be ignored, even though Helene cannot be classified as a mere servant in the modern sense of the word.[46] She is the 'servant' of the queen but also her confidante. We learn that the queen more than once asks Helene for advice: '"Well, what would you advise me now"' (46); '"What would you advise, dear mother Kottannerin"' (49).[47] We even learn that the 'servant' dares to criticise the queen when the queen seems convinced that Helene should secretly return the crown to its original place on the Plintenburg now that the changed political constellation seems opportune to do so. Helene decisively rejects this impossible request: 'When I heard this, I was so shaken by my wise lady's change of heart that I felt it in all my limbs, and I thought by myself that it must be an idea inspired from the devil. I could hardly control myself and answered angrily and spoke as follows: "Woman, stop that! I will not do it and will not risk my life like that and will not even help you with advice, ..." When the noble queen heard me answer her so rudely, out of anger, she kept silent and said neither yes or no and left me thus, without receiving an answer to her question, and also later she never talked to me about it again' (39).[48]

Confidentiality and private familiarity in the court are still far from indicating a suspension of class boundaries or a symmetric communication. Helene herself reports that she did not even have the opportunity to tell the queen the details of the spectacular theft of the crown.[49] The noble lords and ladies are dependent on their public appearance and on a highly stylised behaviour on the public stage, and for this reason they are to a large degree dependent on advisers and confidants, on their counsellors, secretaries or servants. As servant or chambermaid, the confidants of kings and queens are largely free of the obligations of public representation; they have a broader sphere of action to do what cannot be done without loss of reputation. When Helene (expecting a reward[50]) reminds Elisabeth of all the things she has done in her service, the queen articulates this distinction very clear-sightedly. She promises to raise the social rank of Helene's family if the political conflicts should go her way, and then continues: 'you have done for me and my children more than I would have been capable of in the position to do myself' (45).[51] *Noblesse oblige*, aristocratic status, must maintain its public representation, and thus it is absolutely necessary to hide from public view those dimensions of political manoeuvring that cannot be done in public, and to delegate these as far as possible to servants and confidants. In this way politically dependent servants (chambermaids, secretaries) become powerful and experienced bearers of secrets who at times could consolidate their position enough to invert the hierarchy of dominance and subordination. Drawing on Hegel, J. Peter Burgess has very aptly characterised this constellation: 'though the master relates to the servant as to a simple thing, the master cannot relate immediately ... to the world of objects. The master can only relate to objects of the world of things through the mediation of the servant ... The relation between master and servant is now asymmetrical: The servant is a mirror that reflects the master but the master is a mirror that reflects only his or her own image.'[52]

Summary

In the *Denkwürdigkeiten* of Helene Kottannerin the writing 'I' appears characterised by its participation in the affairs of the Hungarian court, in the public staging of rule, but also in the non-public hopes, intrigues, triumphs, and disappointments of Queen Elisabeth. In historical perspective it is not surprising that the chronicler appears primarily to be the mouthpiece of the court. She reveals herself as a representative of the Austrian-Habsburg party and as the confidante of Queen Elisabeth, whose son, born after the death of his father, Helene helps to ascend the Hungarian throne against the interests of the Hungarian magnates and the Polish royal house. Moreover, the political initiatives of Queen Elisabeth, whose retention of power and status depends on the succession, are just as impressive as the glimpse into the dual realms of public and non-public manoeuvring to win power. The queen's two bodies find their equivalent in the co-operation of two women, who significantly differ in their birth, status and their potential spheres of activity, but who together intervene with the greatest effectiveness in the political relations of their time.

Translated by Cynthia Hall

Notes

1. Karl Mollay, ed., *Die Denkwürdigkeiten der Helene Kottannerin*
   (1439–1440), Wiener Neudrucke 2 (Vienna, 1971), and 'Kottaner(in),
   Helene', in *Lexikon des Mittelalters* (Munich and Zurich, 1991), 5,
   1463; Ingo Reiffenstein, review of *Die Denkwürdigkeiten der Helene
   Kottannerin* (1439–1440), by Karl Molloy in *Sprachkunst. Beiträge zur
   Literaturwissenschaft*, ed. by the Austrian Academy of Sciences, III
   (1972), 164–166; Maya Bijvoet Williamson, ed., *The Memoirs of Helene
   Kottanner* (1439–1440), The Library of Medieval Women (Cambridge,
   1998) and 'The Austrian Chambermaid Helene Kotanner', in *Women
   Writers of the Renaissance and Reformation*, ed. Katharina M. Wilson
   (Athens, 1987), 326–49; Heide Dienst, 'Frauenalltag in erzählenden
   Quellen', in *Frau und spätmittelalterlicher Alltag* (Vienna, 1986),
   213–41; Winfried Stelzer, 'Kottanner, Helene', in *VFL* (Berlin/New York,
   1985), 5, 326–28. Christina Lutter, 'Lebensordnungen und
   Geschlechterbeziehungen am Beginn der Frühen Neuzeit,' in *Aufmöpfig
   und angepasst. Frauenleben in Österreich. Niederösterreichische
   Landesausstellung 1998, Schloß Kirchstein.* (Wien 1998), 51–60.
2. Mollay, *Denkwürdigkeiten*, 91; Bivjoet-Williamson, *Memoirs*, 6f.
3. See Bijvoet Williamson, *Memoirs*, 18f.
4. For in the Kingdom of Hungary they have three basic rules [to instate
   the king], and if one of them is not fulfilled, then they are afraid that he
   is king not in the whole sense of the word. The first claim is that a king
   of Hungary is to be crowned with the Holy St. Stephan's Crown, the
   second that the Archbishop of Gran shall crown the king. The third
   applies to the fact that the coronation must take place in
   Stuhlweissenburg. These three basic rules have been completely
   fulfilled with the noble King Ladislaus. 'Wann Si habent drew gesecz in
   dem Kungreich zu Vngeren. Vnd wo der ains abgeet, da mainen Sie, daz
   der nicht rechtlich Kung sey. Das ain gesetz ist daz,. vnd das haisst, daz
   ain Kung zu Vngern sol gekroent werden mit der heilig kron. Das ander
   , daz in sol kroenen der Ercz Bischoue zu Gran. Das dritt, daz die
   kronung sol beschehen zu Weissenburg. Die drey geseczt die sind
   volkomenlich gehalten worden zu dem edelen kung Lassla'
   (*Denkwürdigkeiten*, p. 27, lines 17–22).
5. Bijvoet Williamson, *Memoirs*, 6f.
6. Mollay, *Denkwürdigkeiten*, 91; for the manuscript tradition see 71.
7. The English-language passages from Helene's script are quoted from the
   English edition of Maya Bijvoet Williamson, though it has to be
   carefully compared with the German text, here: Bijvoet Williamson,
   Memoirs, 21. 'Vnd dar nach sandt sein gnad [Albrecht von Österreich]
   her wider auf Wienn vnd man prachte im sein Juengste tochter, frawn
   Elyzabethen mit irm hofgesind hin ab gen Presburg, das geschach. *Do
   was Ich, Helene Kottannerin auch da ...*' (9:8–11); '... vnd prachten sy
   die Heiligen kron vnd truegen die in ain Gwelb, das von fünf seiten
   auch gewesen was, *vnd Ich, Helena Kottanerin was auch dabe*i...'

(10:2); '... vnd nomen die Heiligen kron her aus vnd sahen die gar wol an. *Da was ich bei*' (10:40) [Italics by the author, H.W.].

8. 'Do stuenden die herren von den pherten ab vnd machten ainen weitten krais mit geharnaschten mannen und hetten plassen swert in den henden vnd enmitten in den krais, *do muest ich, elena Kottanerinn den Jungen Kung tragen* (26:13). *Da nam ich elena Kottannerin den Kung an meinen armb.* Vnd da nam der von der Freinstat das Swert in die Hant und slueg den Kung zu Ritter' (27:4).

9. 'Vnd die edel KungInn die erat Ieren Sun als hoch Vnd was als diemuetig, daz ich armme fraw deselbigen tags muest vor iren gnaden gen zu aller nagst bey dem edelen kunig. Darumb daz ich sein gnad zu der heiligen salbung und kronung an meinem arm het gehalden' (28:19–23).

10. According to Axton the theory of the king's two bodies gets specified in the contention for the succession to the throne in Elizabethan England: 'it was found necessary by 1561 to endow the Queen with two bodies: a *body natural* and a *body politic*.' (p. 12). She later quotes Plowden, seemingly the most influential of the contemporary legal experts: 'For the King has in him two Bodies, viz. a Body natural, and a Body politic. His Body natural (if it be considered in itself) is a Body mortal, subject to all Infirmities that come by Nature or Accident, to the Imbecillity of Infancy or old Age, and to the like Defects that happen to the natural Bodies of other People. But his politic is a Body that cannot be seen or handled, consisting of the Policy and Government and constituted for the Direction of the People, and the Management of the publick-weal ...' Marie Axton: *The Queen's Two Bodies. Drama and Elizabethan Succession.* (London, 1977), 17.

11. 'Do sprach dy edel kungin zu mier: "wie rat ir liebe Kottannerinn, mocht ich ew in drey tail getailen, das tet ich gern. Ich behielt euch selber gern und liesz euch gern bei meinem Sun, vnd hiet euch gern bei meiner tochter"' (32:29–32).

12. Alfried Wieczorek and Hans-Martin Hinz, eds., *Europas Mitte um 1000. Beiträge zur Geschichte, Kunst und Archäologie.* Exhibition Catalog (Stuttgart, 2000), 534f. See also László Veszprémy, 'König Stephan der Heilige', in Wieczorek and Hinz, *Europas Mitte*, 2, 875–79.

13. Marie Axton, quoting Plowden, in *The Queen's Two Bodies* (London, 1977), 25.

14. 'Do kam mein gnedige fraw an mich, daz ich das tueen solt, wann die gelegenhait nymant also wol wesset als ich, dem Si dar zu vertrawn mocht, vnd das erkam ich hart, wann es was mir vnd meinenn klainen kinden ain swer wagnuss, vnd gedacht hin vnd her, was ich dar Inn tueen solt vnd west auch nyemantz Rats ze fragen. Dann got allain vnd gedacht, ob ich das nicht tet, gieng Dann icht vebel dar aus, so wer die schuld mein gegen got und gegen der welt, Vnd willigat mich der sweren rais in wagnuss meins lebens, vnd begerat ains gehilfens' (13:36–14:3).

15. 'Do nue die recht zeit kam, an der got der almechtig seine wunderwercch wuerchen wolt, da schickchat uns got einen man, Der

sich willigat her aus gwynnenn die Heiligen kron, vnd der was ain Vnger' (14:20–22).

16. Do nam er das tuech mit dem petschad ab dern slos, daz der purkgraue dar het gelegt, vnd sperrat auf vnd gien hin. In mit seinem diener vnd arbaitat vast an den andern slossen, daz das slahen vnd feillen vueberlaut was,/ vnd waren die wachter vnd des purkgrafen volck diselbig nacht gar muenter von der sarig wegen, die sy dar auf heten, dennoch het got der almoechtig Ir aller oren verschopt, daz sein ir kainer nicht horat. Dann ich horat es alles wol, vnd ich was die weil in der huet mit grossen angsten vnd sorgen, vnd ich knyeat nider mit grasser andacht vnd pat hincz got vnd hincz vnser lieben fraun, daz Si mir vnd meinen helferen bei gestuenden' (15:39–16:8).

17. 'Vnd da ich nach an meinem gepet was, da deucht mich aber wie ain rosz geprecht vnd ain gerumppel mit Harnasch an der tuer wer, da der recht eingankch was in das frawn Zymer. Do erschrakcht ich als hart, daz ich vor angsten alle zitern vnd swiczen ward, vnd gedacht, es wer nicht ain gespenst … vnd gedacht mir wol, daz es der tewfel wër vnd die sach gern vnderstanden hiet' (16:25–35).

18. 'When the Holy Crown was completely free, we again closed the doors everywhere, replaced the locks that they had removed, pressed my lady's seals on them once more, and locked the outer door again, and tied the piece of cloth with the seal on it as we had found it and as the castellan had put it here. And I threw the files in the privy in the room of the ladies, where you will find them, if you break it open, as proof that I am speaking the truth. We carried the Holy Crown through the chapel of Saint Elizabeth, to which I, Helene Kottanner, still owe a chasuble and an altar cloth to be paid of by my gracious lord, King Ladislaus. Then my helper took a red velvet pillow, opened it, removed part of the feathers, put the Holy Crown into the pillow, and sewed it back up' (31). [Da nue die heylig kron gancz [schuldig] ledig was, da tet wier die tuer wider zue vberal vnd sluegen ander slos wider an der slosz stat, die man ab het gesprochen vnd trukchten meiner gnedigen frawn Sigel wider auf, vnd die ausser tuer sperrat wir wider zu vnd legaten das tüehel wider mit dem petschaft hin wider an, als wier es heten funden vnd als der purkgraf hin an het gelegt, vnd ich warf die feil in das secret, das in dem frawnczymer ist, do wirt man die feil Inn vinden, wann man es aufpricht, zu ainem warczaihen. Vnd die Heiligen kran die trueg man durch die kapellen aus, dar Inn rast sand Elspet, da belaib ich, Helena Quottannerin ain mesgbant vnd ain Altertuech hin schuldig, das sol mein gnediger [frawn be] herr Kung Lasla beczalen. Do nam mein helfer ainen Ratsamedeinen polster, vnd trennat den auf vnd nam der vederen ainen tail her aws, vnd tet die heilig kran in den polster vnd neyat in wider zu (17:1–13)].

19. '… die wesssat nue wol, daz ich ain gueter pot gewesen was mit der hilf gotes' (18:31–18:36). See also 23:25–24:14.

20. 'euch sind gross sach enpholchen' (18:10f).

21. 'Do kamen die vorgenanten Zwen grafen zu mier und namen mich *in ir gehaim* vnd giengen mitenander zu der tuer, da man zu der Heiligen

kron in gieng'; (10:33–34) '... Do nam mich ier gnad *in ier gehaim* vnd sprach: "liebe vnd getrewe Quottannerin, lasst euch mein tochter enpholhen sein,vnd auch die kamer, da laszt niyemt in gen Dann mein tochter vnd ir."' (11:34–36) 'Nu het ir gnad muet her auf in das lannd *in gehaim* vnd pat mich, ich solt auf das haws vnd solt versuechen, ob ier kran vnd ander ier klainat mocht hinab zu ier bringen in den hof *in gehaim*. Vnd das tet ich vnd kam auf das haws vnd in meinem gewant pracht ich dar von *in grosser gehaim* meiner gnedigen frawn Kran al all Ir klainat auf ainem Sliten' (13:12–17) (my italics, H.W.).

22. Horst Wenzel, 'Repräsentation und schöner Schein am Hof und in der höfischen Literatur', in *Höfische Repräsentation. Das Zeremoniell und die Zeichen*, eds. Hedda Ragotzky and Horst Wenzel (Tübingen, 1990), 171–209; 'Einführung: Aufführung und Repräsentation', in *'Aufführung' und 'Schrift' in Mittelalter und Früher Neuzeit*, ed. Jan-Dirk Müller (Stuttgart and Weimar, 1996), 141–48; 'Öffentlichkeit und Heimlichkeit in Gottfrieds "Tristan"', *ZfdPh* 107 (1988), 335–61; 'Das höfische Geheimnis: Herrschaft, Liebe, Texte', in *Schleier und Schwelle. Geheimnis und Öffentlichkeit. Archäologie der literarischen Kommunikation*, eds. Aleida Assman and Jan Assmann (Munich, 1997), V:1, 53–69; 'Öffentliches und nichtöffentliches Herrschaftshandeln im "Erec" Hartmanns von Aue', in *Das Öffentliche und Private in der Vormoderne*, eds. Gert Melville and Peter von Moos (Cologne, Weimar and Vienna, 1998), 213–38; 'Öffentliches und nichtöffentliches Herrschaftshandeln', in *Formen und Funktionen öffentlicher Kommunikation im Mittelalter*, ed. Konstanzer Arbeitskreis für mittelalterliche Geschichte. Vorträge und Forschungen (Stuttgart, 2001), 247–60; Horst Wenzel and Christina Lechtermann, 'Repräsentation und Kinästhetik. Teilhabe am Text oder die Verlebendigung der Worte', *Paragrana. Internationale Zeitschrift für Historische Anthropologie* 10, (2001), 191–214.

23. Gert Althoff, *Spielregeln der Politik im Mittelalter. Kommunikation in Frieden und Fehde* (Darmstadt, 1997).

24. See for example C. Müller and H. Haferland, 'Gefesselte Hände. Zur Semiose performativer Gesten', *Mitteilungen des Deutschen Germanistenverbandes* 44, (1997), 29–53.

25. 'Wessen Sein so wesenhaft das Sich-Zeigen einschließt, der gehört sich selbst nicht mehr', Hans-Georg Gadamer, *Hermeneutik I*, in *Wahrheit und Methode. Werke 1* (Tübingen, 1986), 147.

26. 'A uno principe, adunque, non è necessario avere in fatto tutte le soprascritte qualità ma è bene necessario parere di averle'. Niccolò Machiavelli, *Il Principe. Der Fürst*, ed. Philipp Rippel (Stuttgart, 1986), 138. Here: Niccolò Machiavelli, *Nicholas Machiavel's Prince* (London 1640; reprint Amsterdam/New York 1968), 139.

27. 'Die Vngrischen herren ... drungen Si aber an von des von Polan wegen. Do ward Ír geraten, Si solt sich willigen den von Polan zenemen, vnd solt die weil trachten, was ir das peste were, man wurd dannoch wol ainen sin vinden, daz Si da von kem, ... Da das dy weis vnd die edel

KungInn verstuend, do ward Si gedenkchen vnd trachten nach der Heiligen kron, wie Si die in ir gewalt moecht bringen von den vngrischen herren. Das tet Si auf die maynung, ob das wer, daz Si ainen Sun geperet, daz der von dem Reich nicht wuerd verdrungen, trueg Si aber ain tochter, so mocht Si dennoch dester pas ainer taiding bekomen von den vngrischen herren' (12:20–36).

28. 'Nicht lang darnach do kom ain gewisse potschaft, der Kung von Polan der zug da her vnd hiet willen gen Ofen, als es dann geschach, vnd *muesten vns haimlich vnd eylund zu richten* zu der krönung ... Da sandt die edel KungInn *in grosser gehaym* zu dem edelen fursten von Osterrich, genant Herczog Albrecht, vnd tet im zu wissen, Daz Si an dem heiligen Phingstag [15. Mai 1440] wolt lassen krönen meinen gnedigen herren Kung Lassla (24:17–25:7).

29. 'Vnd merckt das wunder: Es was der Kung noch verslossen in mueter leib, der die heilig kron auf solt tragen,vnd die warn kawm zwo klafter von einander, die hiet der poes veint gern gelaidigt mit der pruenst. Aber got was huetter, der het sy zu rechter zeit aufgewecht...' (11:12–15)

30. 'Do kam wir an die Tuenaw, die was dennoch gestoessen mit eis. Aber es was an ettlicher stat nue duenn warden. Do wir nue auf da eys komen, vnd wol enmitten auf der Tuenaw, da prast der wagen mit Junkchfrawen ein, vund viel vmb vnd was ein geschray von den Junckfrauen vnd macht ains das ander nicht gesehen. Do erkam ich hart, vnd gedacht, wier muesten mitsambt der heyligen kran in der Tuenaw beleiben. Aber got was unser helfer, daz kain mensch vnder das eys nicht kam.' (18:18–24)

31. 'Vnd als das war ist, daz die heilige kron gen vngeren dem heiligen sand Steffan von got gesandt vnd gemaint ist, Als war ist das, daz es got hat scheinperleichen wellen, daz der recht erb Kung Lassla die heiligen Kran zu Vngeren solt auf tragen, vnd nicht der von Polan' (20:22–26).

32. Then my gracious lady sent for the eldest townsmen, just in old fashion, and she had them see the Holy Crown and arranged everything in such a way that it was in accordance with customs and as it had been handed down from ancestry. And there were some townspeople who remembered that Emperor Sigismund had been crowned on these premises too, and that they had been witnesses. 'Da sandt meiner frawn gnad zu den eltisten burgeren, die dann dar zue gehorten, vnd liess sye die Heiligen kron sehen, vnd hies es zu richten, als es dar zue gehort vnd von alter her komen ist. Vnd warn ettlich burger da, die des gedachten, daz man Kaiser Sigmund auch gekronet het , vnd die da bei gewesen waren' (26:17–21).

33. 'Kung Lassla, Kung Albrechts Sun vnd Kaiser Sigmunds Enykel, Der ist an dem heiligen Phingstag [15.Mai 1540] mit der heiligen Kron von dem ErczBischoue von Gran zu Weissenburg gekroent worden' (27:14–17).

34. 'da im der Ercz Bischoue dy heilig kron auf sein haupt saczt vnd im die hielt, daz er das haubt als kreftikleichen auf hielt, es wer ainem kind genueg gewesen ains jars alt, vnd das wirt selten gesehen von kinden, die zwelf wochen alt sind' (27:24–27).

35. 'Der edel Jung Kung der het ain klaine frewd zu seiner kroenung. Wann er waynat mit lautter stym, daz man es horat als weit die kirchen was, daz sein das gemain volkch wunder nam, vnd sprachen, es wer nicht ain stym als ain kind bey zwelf wochen, es wer ainme kind geueg, das bey ainem Jar wer, des er doch nicht was' (27:37–28:1). See also Mollay's afterword, p. 81.

36. 'Vnd graf Bärtelme der trueg den Apphel, Vnd ain Herczog von Lynndbach, genant der Seczýtamesch, der trueg das Zeppter. Man trueg auch vor dem edelen Kung ainen legaten stab, Darumb daz kain von Vngeren ze lehen hat von dem Heiligen Roemischen Reich. Man trueg im mit das swert, da man sein gnad mit zu Ritter het geslagen' (28:14–18).

37. Mollay, *Denkwürdigkeiten*, 82.

38. Bijvoet-Williamson, *Memoirs*, 65.

39. 'Da ich mit der edeln KungInn also redat, do ward mir ier gnad sagen, wie sie dy fraun von Ofen gepetten hieten in ainer wannen, vnd wie ir nach dem pad gar swer wer worden. Do hueb ich die huel auf vnd wolt Si plasse sehen. Do sach ettliche warczaichen, Dar an ich wol erkant, daz es von dem kind gepern nicht verr was.' (19:14–18).

40. 'Do sprach ich: "gnedig fraw stet auf, mich bedünkcht wol, ier wert morgen nicht gen Prespurgk faren." Do stuend íer gnad auf vnd gieng vnd begund anzeheben zu der sweren arbeit,' (19:21–24).

41. '"Margret, stet pald auf, meiner frawn gnad, die get zu dem kind."' (19:21–29).

42. 'Der Kung wolt nicht lenger peiten, er wolt eylen zu der heiligen kran, ee daz ain annder këm, Wann wer het im das gesagt, daz der von Polan stellat nach seinem veterlichen erb, vnd hiet er nuer ein wochen nach in seiner mueter leib geslaffen, ... So wer der von Polan villeicht ee gen Weyysenburg komen' (20:16–22).

43. 'das ander was die am, die das kind neren solt mit den prusten, vnd diselb am het íer kind auch mit bracht, das was auch ain Sun. Wann es mainen die weisen, es sei die milch pesser von der frauen, die ainen Sun bringt denn von ainer tochter.' (19:6–8).

44. 'Vnd do die frawn von Ofen des Inne wuerden, daz meiner frawn gnad des kindes genesen was, des waren sie fro, als es wol pilleich was. Aber darumb, daz Sy da bey nicht waren gewesen, da waren sy gar vnmuetig vmb, vnd ich ward gar hoch vnd vast darInn verdacht vnd es was doch an mein schuld, wann die zeit die was zu kuercz' (20:12–18).

45. There is strong evidence that she produced her memoirs to support king Ladislaus before he ascended the throne in 1452. The text has actually been understood in this sense, as a political document. The names of Helene and her Hungarian helpers were not mentioned in the first edition of the manuscript, probably to protect their owners. Mollay, *Denkwürdigkeiten*, 72, 91.

46. 'The "servants by remuneration" are free people who place themselves in the service of a master: among them, some serve in exchange for board and clothing only; others receive a salary in addition; still others

work "for remuneration only", seeing to all their needs by themselves. There are, finally, those who serve not "for money or out of compulsion, but for mere and sincere pleasure, feeling great affection towards their master's virtue". The ones in this position "are called servants, but they are not truly so, they are, rather, courtiers". 'From Raffaela Sarti, 'Telling Zita's Tale. Holy Servants' Stories and Servants' History', in *Narratives of the Servant*, eds. Regina Schulte and Pothiti Hantzaroula, Working Papers of the European University Institute, HEC 1 (2001), 1–30, here 1.

47. '"nue wie welt ir nue raten"' (30:3); '"wie rat ir liebe Kottannerin"' (32:29–30).

48. 'Do ich das hort, do erkam ich also hart, das ich in allen meinen glidern enphand, daz sich der muet der weisen frawn also verkert het, vnd gedacht mir wol, daz es ain einplasen von dem tewfel wer. Vnd ich moch nicht lenger peitten, vnd gab ir ain antburt aus zoren, vnd sprach also: "Fraw, do lasst von, des tuen ich nicht vnd wag mein leben in solcher mass nicht mer vnd rat auch dar zue nicht, es ist allbeg in der stauden pesser denn in dem stockch. Widergeben kombt ir albeg wol, der yczund ewer fruendt ist, der moecht villeicht darnach ewr veindt werden." Da das die edel KungInn horat, daz ich ier aus zoren also groebleich het geantburt, do swaig Si stil, vnd sprach weder Ja noch nain vnd gieng also von mier vngeanttbuertt, vnd redat auch furbas aus den sachen nicht mer mit mier' (24:1–11).

49. 'But of the wondrous and truly miraculous assistance of God which had manifested itself there, her grace knows nothing, and she died before she had the opportunity to learn of it. It was never possible for me to be alone with her long enough to tell her the entire story from beginning to end, for we were not together much longer' (33). [Aber dy wunder vnd die zaichenlich hilf gotes, die sich da vergangen hat, der wessat ier gnade nicht, vnd ist auch also gestorben, daz Si sein ny Inn ist worden. Es kund sich nye gefuegen, daz ich also lang allain bey ier gewesen wer, daz ich ir das von dem anfang vncz an das end hiet mogen gesagen. (18:2–36)].

50. According to a document of 1452 Helene Kottannerin was rewarded for her services with a gift from the royal possessions. Later she and her family were given the Kisfald property on the Schütt island, part of the royal possessions belonging to the Preßburger Burg. See Mollay, *Denkwürdigkeiten*, 71.

51. Das habt ir wol verdient Vnd habt das an mir vnd an meinen kinden getan, dazz ich selber nicht hiet getuen moegen noch kunnen.' (28:30–36).

52. J. Peter Burgess, 'In the Service of Narrative. Master and Servant in the Philosophy of Hegel', in Schulte and Hantzaroula, *Narratives*, 31–45; here 41.

3

Elizabeth When a Princess

Early Self-representations in a Portrait and a Letter

Susan Frye

Elizabeth I was not always the towering monolithic figure that the 'Ditchley' portrait presents, with her head in the heavens and her feet planted firmly on the map of England (see Figure 4.8). She was not always the elder stateswoman whose bodily image asserted her dominance, not always presiding over the golden age of English literature and the beginnings of the English exploration – and exploitation – of the New World. However, picturing Elizabeth Tudor as a young woman can be a difficult historical project, in part because one of the principal obstacles to imagining the young Elizabeth is Elizabeth herself. As she grew older, Elizabeth systematically worked with key contemporaries to erase or rewrite the perils of her youth. In visual terms, this erasure resulted in a variety of portraits taken in her sixties that do not show her chronological age, like the 'Rainbow' Portrait at Hatfield Hall. Such representations fooled no one into thinking Elizabeth had suddenly become young. Instead, they asserted Elizabeth's continuing political vitality.[1] This image of the queen's youthful political vitality proved so important to many of her peers, and to those who looked back on her reign with nostalgia in the seventeenth century, that such representations of political youth continue to obscure Elizabeth's physical youth.

This article attempts to look beyond our dominant sense of the Elizabeth of the 1580s and 1590s in order to rejuvenate Elizabeth in a way quite different from the youthful portraits painted in the closing years of her reign. Specifically, I will be looking at examples of her self-representation during her early and mid-teens, especially a portrait that I argue she commissioned, *Elizabeth When a Princess*, and a letter written about the same time that suggests the portrait was painted for her brother, King Edward VI. Recovering the young Elizabeth provides the opportunity to understand more about where she came from, the uncertainties that surrounded her, and the consequent sense of her vulnerability that she retained even at the height of her power. This is not a story about Elizabeth as victim, but of her responses to the political moments in which she found her physical and intellectual self, responses that help us to understand her development as a writer of speeches as well as of poetry, as the author not of her own destiny, as earlier historians might have it, but as the author of the negotiation of her always-changing political position. Her ability to manoeuvre within a very small space proved invaluable when she ascended the throne.

I am not going to claim, however, that we can recover Elizabeth as a psychologically consistent individual. This act of feminist historicist analysis derives from this historical moment, as does my interest in questions about why people construct Elizabeth through the lens of her later years. Specifically I want to ask two questions that I think of as revisionist. First, how might looking at Elizabeth's life as the product of attitudes towards gender refocus her youthful vulnerability for us? And second, if we gain a more immediate and less teleological sense of Elizabeth's youth, what can we learn about her responses to the often murderous court politics of the mid-sixteenth century?

My answer is that the one recoverable area of Elizabeth's early life that demonstrates her ability as a developing political entity is her gift giving, in which materials passed from her hand to the hands of those in power over her. Through gifts of needlework-covered manuscripts at the ages of eleven and twelve, and the gift of her portrait when she was fourteen, Elizabeth demonstrated her ability to combine self-representational strategies in the attempt not only to survive but also to get to court. To be physically at court was to be where the conversation was and the writers were and where decisions about royal marriages and even the succession were weighed. And even if she were not at court, Elizabeth's gifts served to *remind* the people in power that she was out there – resourceful, fully cognizant of her society's modes of self-expression and self-display.

Before I examine the politics of the young Elizabeth's gift giving, let me provide a compressed chronology of her childhood and early youth, the context in which she sought favour. The Princess Elizabeth was born to her father, Henry VIII, and her mother, Anne Boleyn, on 7 September 1533. From the moment of her birth, gender was all. Had she been a boy, her mother would have lived and she would have been the indisputable heir to the throne of England. At the age of three months, Elizabeth was settled away from her parents in her own elaborate establishment at Hatfield. At the age of one, marriage negotiations began for her hand.[2] In 1536, two months before her third birthday, her father beheaded her mother for treasonous adultery with five men, one of them Anne Boleyn's own brother. Two months later, the Second Act of Succession allowed the King in Parliament to declare both his daughters to be bastards. Elizabeth was three years old, and Mary, his daughter by his first wife Catherine of Aragon, was twenty years old. Although Elizabeth and Mary were restored to the succession in 1544, they were never legally legitimate again. When she was declared illegitimate in 1536, Elizabeth was no longer titled 'The Princess Elizabeth' but 'The Lady Elizabeth'. In 1537, when Elizabeth was four, the King's new wife, Jane Seymour, gave birth to Edward, and died a week later. Henry, after a brief marriage to Anne of Cleves, from whom he was quickly divorced, then married Katherine Howard, whom Elizabeth knew and who was beheaded for adultery when Elizabeth was eight.

When Elizabeth was ten, Henry VIII initiated a period of relative peace in the family when he married the kind and brilliant Protestant humanist, Katherine Parr. When she was fourteen, Henry VIII died and her brother ascended the throne as Edward VI. Four months later, Katherine Parr, with whom Elizabeth was then living outside of London at Chelsea and at Hatfield, hastily married her former suitor Thomas Seymour, the Lord Admiral and brother to the man who served as Edward's regent – the Lord Protector, Duke of Somerset. Later that same year, Katherine Parr died in childbirth. A few months later, when she was fifteen, Elizabeth was investigated and interrogated about a supposed sexual relationship with the same Thomas Seymour, who was beheaded for treasonously attempting to marry her. Edward VI died when he was sixteen and Elizabeth was twenty. On his deathbed, Edward passed over his beloved sister Elizabeth to name their cousin, Lady Jane Grey, Queen of England.

Thus in 1555, Elizabeth's half-sister Mary marched on London to defend her claim to the throne, attracted widespread support, and imprisoned Jane Grey and her ambitious family. The following year, at the age of twenty-one, Mary accused Elizabeth of having plotted to marry Edward Courtenay, the last surviving Plantagenet, in order to seize the throne as part of Wyatt's rebellion against Queen Mary.[3] She was thrown into the Tower within days of the beheading of Jane Grey, Jane's husband and Jane's ambitious father-in-law on Tower Green. The Spanish actively called for Elizabeth's execution, but due to a lack of evidence this proved impossible to accomplish, for which Mary apologised to the Spanish. A few months later the Lady Elizabeth left the Tower for house arrest at Woodstock. At the age of twenty-three, after two years of imprisonment, Elizabeth was released and invited to Mary's court because of the belief, which proved unfounded, that the queen was about to produce an heir. When Elizabeth was twenty-five, her sister died, and she ascended the throne on 17 November 1558.

Given the eight beheadings that dot this chronology, the two women who died in childbirth and the third who died trying to have a child, we might well ask how Elizabeth survived to ascend the throne. She was physically vigorous, and that was obviously a help, but she also negotiated these crises in familial politics with courage and care by asserting both physical and intellectual strength.

How did Elizabeth negotiate her position as a highly connected bastard? She wrote letters, she made visits, she assiduously practised the prevailing religion of the moment, she sought counsel, and, perhaps most interesting of all if we want to look at a number of strategies operating at once, she gave gifts. Gift giving at the Renaissance court was a highly symbolic act that has recently drawn commentary from anthropologists and historians.[4] The gift one gave a personage at court was a painstakingly considered form of self-representation. The gift connected giver and recipient by making a statement about their shared relation to larger groups and networks, while the point of the gift was to create a bond through what the gift said about the power of the recipient and the submission of the giver. The ideal court gift expressed the giver's self-perceived place within the 'reciprocal expectations'[5] of the court, and thus made a clear statement about the discrimination, merit and position of the giver within the court hierarchy.

If the responsibility for repaying the debt incurred by a gift lay with its recipient, the responsibility for a thoughtful and imaginative gift lay with its giver.

So what did Elizabeth give when she was of the court but nowhere near its centre? Her first recorded gift at the age of six was

a cambric shirt she had sewn herself for her brother Edward –
whether it was her choice to sew this gift or not, the shirt formed a
suitable self-representation as dutiful sister to her father's heir,
being properly trained in the appropriate roles of the feminine.[6]
After another gift of needlework to Edward, the next gifts we know
are those she gave as an eleven- and twelve-year-old girl, when she
sought to demonstrate her accomplishments as an educated young
woman to her father, Henry VIII, and to her educated stepmother,
Katherine Parr, by presenting them with matched sets of
needlework-covered calligraphic manuscripts as her New Year's
gifts of 1544 and 1545.[7] For all their display of her abilities in
needlework and in writing two different italic hands, these gifts also
demonstrated her intellectual and religious relationships to the
court.

Her three surviving manuscript volumes in fact contain
ambitious translations: in 1544 she translated part of Calvin's
Institutes for her stepmother, and for her father she translated
Katherine Parr's prayers in English into Italian, Latin and French. In
1545, again for Parr, she translated Marguerite de Navarre's *Glass of
the Sinfull Soul*, a Protestant text that John Bales published on the
Continent in 1548[8] – Elizabeth's first publication.

To her father, Henry VIII, Elizabeth's gifts demonstrated her
proper upbringing as the daughter of one of the best-educated
humanist princes in Europe, and thus her suitability for her position
as third in line to his throne. The year 1544, after all, was the year
in which she and Mary were restored to the succession. Elizabeth's
seeking of her father's approval and attention seems not to have
been wholly successful, however. Her father's complete approval
depended on the one factor over which she had no control – her
female sex, and was thus reserved for her brother Edward.
Nevertheless, she continued to pursue a connection that was far
more important personally and politically to her than it ever was to
him.

To her stepmother, Katherine Parr, Elizabeth's gifts demonstrated
her commitment to an already existing alliance that offered her
more intellectual and emotional nurturance than her dynastic ties
to her father. In the absence of her father's interest, Elizabeth
reached out to Parr through the association of the discourses of
Protestant humanism and emblematically ciphered needlework.
Translating Marguerite de Navarre for Katherine Parr meant
asserting their bond through religion, female kinship and

authorship. In her 'Epistle Dedicatory' the young Elizabeth connects herself physically to Parr's body, writing that the work came from Parr's 'humble daughter', who 'knowing the affectionate will and fervent zeal which your highness hath toward all godly learning as also my duty toward you ... hath moved so small a portion as God hath lent me to prove what I could do'.[9] In other words, this is a gift that 'proves' what the twelve-year-old Elizabeth can do.

Elizabeth's gift brings together the memories and activities of six different women: Elizabeth, Marguerite de Navarre, Katherine Parr, Anne Boleyn, and even Lady Margaret Beaufort, who was Henry VII's mother and Elizabeth's great-grandmother. In his recent edition of *The Glass of the Sinful Soul*, Marc Shell points out that Marguerite de Navarre very likely had presented Elizabeth's mother, Anne Boleyn, with a copy of this Protestant work when they renewed their association in 1534–35.[10] Moreover, Elizabeth's choice of the title, 'The Glass of the Sinful Soul', echoes the choice that her great-grandmother made when *she* translated a work from the French titled 'The Mirror of Gold for the Sinful Soul'.[11]

The several strategies that Elizabeth developed through these gifts benefited her later in her political career. In presenting such elaborate gifts from her own head and hand, yet carefully situated in approved intellectual and domestic competence, Elizabeth's self-representation as a proper young woman and her judgement of what would attract the attention of her parental audience proved equally flawless. At the same time, however, the gifts served notice that she was capable of combining strategies for self-representation that moved beyond accepted gender roles into the world of the decision makers, whose minds were likewise trained in humanist and religious discourse.[12]

The second form of gift that Elizabeth gave was her portrait. We know of one early portrait that was almost surely a gift to her brother, the painting now displayed in the Queen's Withdrawing Chamber at Windsor Castle as *Elizabeth When a Princess* (see Figure 3.1). There also exists a letter from the Lady Elizabeth to her brother King Edward, which accompanied a portrait – perhaps this portrait, perhaps another – that she sent him.[13] Like the needlework-covered translations that she gave her father and stepmother, the gift of her portrait sought to affirm and strengthen a bond between herself and her brother with the implied hope that she would not only retain his favour but be invited physically to the court, where she might at least have a chance to influence decisions concerning

Figure 3.1 Elizabeth when a Princess (c. 1546).

her allowance, her education, her housing and her future husband.

The portrait appears in the inventory taken on Edward VI's accession in 1547 as 'A table with the picture of the ladye Elizabeth her grace with a booke in her hande her gowne like crymsen clothe of golde with workes', so that we know it was painted by September of 1547.[14] The letter is dated only '15 May Hatfield'. Although we can't say for sure whether the letter and the portrait arrived at Edward's door at the same time, the two are worth discussing together because they allow a comparison of Elizabeth's visual and textual strategies for representing herself.[15] In preparing this article, I read all the extant letters to and from the children of Henry VIII that we as yet recognise. In this rather scant correspondence, Edward's letters to his father, Richard Coxe his tutor and later almoner, Katherine Parr, and his sister Mary are very much in evidence. Only two of his letters to Elizabeth survive, however, and the letter under discussion is the only letter of Elizabeth's to survive to her brother. The easy tone of his letters to her suggest that one possible reason that their correspondence did not survive is that their letters were intimate enough to require destruction. Considering the relation between the portrait and the letter not only makes visible aspects of each that have not been commented on, but also highlights Elizabeth's early use of the political interplay between the visual and the textual.

The fact that she felt it necessary to accompany her portrait with a letter, that sending a portrait alone was not enough, signals a strong desire to preface the portrait in a way at once careful and bold. In fact, Elizabeth's letter disturbs the usual economy of the female dynastic portrait, painted by a man, paid for by a man, and which then becomes the object of the male gaze. Both her portrait and her letter work to create images of Elizabeth's dignity and intelligence that intrude into the world of the court by acknowledging the young king's relative power while working hard to condition his response as the immediate audience of her visual and textual images.

If – as I believe – this is a portrait of Elizabeth in the apparel that she wore for her brother's coronation, then this particular portrait would have served as an eloquent reminder of his sister's claim to his continuing regard.

Why is it likely that Elizabeth is wearing her coronation finery in this portrait? Henry VIII's children, though well lodged, fed and tutored, were not constantly receiving new clothing. Privy Council and other domestic records, though far from complete, record block grants for the children's households, but also sometimes record individual expenditures for their clothing, furs, coffers, stables, attendance and tutelage. In one case clothing records take the form of warrants drawn on the king's wardrobe and grouped around Christmas and the New Year. In another, an inventory closely records yardage of cloth given to members of the royal family.[16] Gifts of clothing are therefore unusual enough to be remarked on in the records.

When Edward received a special gift of jewellery and clothing from his father in the summer of 1546, he wrote gratefully acknowledging Henry VIII's 'great and costly' gifts, especially 'these fine gifts of jewelry', the 'neckchains' and 'necklaces' and 'garments … to adorn and furnish me with all the accomplishment fitted to a prince'.[17] These gifts arrived about the same time that Edward's portrait was painted at Hunsdon in summer, 1546, as we know from the scenes of Hunsdon in its background, and were probably sent for inclusion in the dynastic portrait of the Prince of Wales that seems to be by the same unknown hand as that of *Elizabeth When a Princess*.

Elizabeth received a great deal of new clothing in April 1547, when the Privy Council footed an enormous bill for the Lady Elizabeth that must represent attire for her father's funeral and brother's coronation the month before and may also include payment of some back bills. The pertinent Act of the Privy Council reads in part, 'To my Lady Elizabeths taylour 25 pounds 10 shillings 7 pence; for a bill of her embroiderers, 41 pounds 5 shillings; for a bille of her robes, 73 pounds 12 shillings and 4 pence'.[18] These large numbers are repeated in the warrant for the money in a different notation. Considering that her brother's coronation cost a modest 442 pounds 10 shillings 0 pence,[19] Elizabeth's total expenditure of more than £170 may well mark not only a new reign but also provide an appropriate occasion to inscribe this new beginning in a technically meticulous painting like this one. The minute details of jewels, embroidery and rich cloths are so carefully rendered that they become a major focus of the portrait. The care that the painter took in rendering the many embroidered details recalls the huge embroidery and robes bill, as does the woven stuffs making up her dress of which, writes Janet Arnold, the red cloth 'may have been cut velvet, but it is more likely that the material … [is] silk. … The undersleeves and matching forepart are in a very rich material with a white satin ground and raised looped pile of gold thread'.[20] This particular material is identical in type to the rich cloth hanging above Edward's head in the companion portrait of him.

Elizabeth's portrait was an ideal gift in that it asks that we read and consider the young Elizabeth. She had an immediate need to place herself at court when absent, to strengthen her connection with her brother, and to plead for the chance to represent herself in person. In representing Elizabeth as established in her *richesse*, the portrait provides crucial evidence of Elizabeth's developing ability to use to advantage any form of representation that might bring her closer to the decision makers of the realm. And even though she may not have had complete control of her pose or paid the artist herself, it is at least equally possible that she determined her pose and even commissioned the portrait. Her half-sister Mary, for example, commissioned a portrait of herself in 1544, no doubt in order to mark her return to her father's favour when he restored her to the succession.[21]

The gift of the portrait works like her needlework-covered translations to figure and establish her familial and intellectual connection with the monarch. After Edward's birth, brother and sister spent indeterminate periods of time together, usually at Ashridge and Hatfield. They were educated, sometimes together, by leading Protestant humanists – first, Richard Coxe, and then John Cheke, as well as Roger Ascham and William Grindal. Edward himself recounted in his journal how he and Elizabeth had been brought together to hear the news of their father's death at Enfield.[22]

Nowhere were familial relations more political, however, than at the Renaissance court. Despite Elizabeth's and Edward's affection for one another, the king was a minor whose first regent, Edward Seymour, the Lord Protector, largely controlled access to the king. If Elizabeth's letter was written in May of 1547, then it was also written during the renewed courtship between Thomas Seymour and Katherine Parr, a courtship marked by two surviving letters from Seymour, one of which asks for Parr's portrait. The result was a marriage as early as mid-May and certainly by June 1547 which, coming a scant four months after Henry VIII's death, ensured his brother the Lord Protector's anger. The young king himself wrote in his journal that 'the Lord Protector was much offended' (Edward VI, p. 6). Elizabeth, who had been staying with the queen since her father's death, in May of 1547 was already grouped with Parr and Seymour in events that would place her outside the King's presence for some time because the Lord Protector controlled access to Edward. If the letter accompanied some portrait in May of 1547, in part then they comprised Elizabeth's attempt to intrude into the court dynamics working to exclude her.

Only after Parr's death in childbirth later that year, the investigation of Thomas Seymour's supposed lovemaking to Elizabeth, and his, and then his brother the Lord Protector's executions, did Northumberland come to power and Elizabeth come to court. The favour of the king was necessarily temporary, however. Had Elizabeth been present as she wished when her brother was dying, Northumberland might not have so easily prevailed on him to name Jane Grey as his heir. In any case, these are the shifting climates of political favour into which Elizabeth's portrait and letter worked to impose her presence.

In the portrait, Elizabeth's implicit dynastic claims take on a religious dimension appropriate for the Protestantism fashionable at the court of Edward VI. Elizabeth stands between two books – the folio in the background on a lectern in part suggesting the Old Testament, and the smaller quarto held with her left hand in part suggesting the New Testament. Books as testaments and books held by female subjects in portraits are fairly common elements in portraits of this period. In placing an emphasis on reading, the books invite their audience to read the portrait. At the same time, the books imply rather than seek to enforce Elizabeth's religiosity – the pages in the large book are left thoughtfully blank; the small book may be Latin or English or Greek. What is clear is that the artist represents his sitter as someone with whom one must reckon. The direct, firm and intelligent gaze of this fourteen-year-old replicates the authoritative gaze of Holbein's Henry VIII. In this portrait, its intelligence is confirmed by the small book in her hand, which we know that she is reading, first, because her index finger is inside the book, as if holding her place; and second, a small bookmark protrudes from it. The gesture of her holding a book that she is reading sets up the association between her book and her intellect that validates her intelligence by linking it to her implied piety. Like the gaze directed at the onlooker, the gesture communicates a working intellect. Yet the gesture ends tucked neatly within the authorisation of religion and scholarship with Elizabeth's finger in her book. It is also worth noticing that the smaller book both covers and reminds the onlooker of Elizabeth's female sexuality.

In the corresponding portrait of Edward, *his* left hand touches the edge of his doublet touching his codpiece, with the gesture to his own masculinity making a dynastic statement similar to several portraits of Henry VIII featuring his codpiece. Elizabeth's holding the book parted by her left index finger over the position of her own sexuality – the book placed at the bottom of the triangle formed by her girdle and at the top of the triangle formed by her foreskirt – makes the corresponding statement that her sexuality is both important and covered in a gesture no less significant than her brother's.

In her letter accompanying her gift of her portrait, the Elizabeth in prose, like the Elizabeth in paint, asks us to read her image with a care for what is going on inside of her mind, and to use her physical presence in the picture and in her 'hand' as the means to come to know that mind. At the same time the letter, like the portrait, is a presentation piece. As Lynne Magnusson has pointed out, letters before the nineteenth century were not usually private expressions.[23] The letter is carefully written in her increasingly accomplished italic hand, with sixteen ornamental capitals. The most frequently ornamented words are 'Majesty' and, as if to emphasise her self-assertion, the pronoun 'I'. Aside from its visual polish and appeal (except for the extra word 'of' in the first line, which is carefully crossed out), Elizabeth has artfully constructed the letter to shape the response of her brother as audience of his sister and her portrait.

The main difference between the portrait's representation of Elizabeth and her letter's self-representation is that while the portrait makes both overt and covert dynastic claims for the Lady Elizabeth, the letter is far more reticent. This is to be expected, because in the portrait she is ostensibly being represented by the artist, so that she is free to dress up in all her finery, to look directly at her audience, to hold the book in a gesture that simultaneously evokes her ability to have children in the line of succession and asserts her chaste scholarship. The textual Elizabeth also dresses up appropriately. But in order to present her *self* presenting her portrait, she clothes that self in the shifts and disguises of the rhetoric that she and her brother had been schooled in by the best humanist minds in England. Theirs was a rhetoric whose nuances she could be sure that her brother would recognise.

When she became queen, Elizabeth often began her letters directly, even bluntly, while remaining adept at circumlocutions when she wished to be circumspect. The directness arises from the moments when Elizabeth felt in control and so are associated with her monarchy. To Sir John Perrot, Lord Deputy of Ireland, she wrote on 14 April 1586, 'Let us have no more such rash unadvised journeys without good ground, as your last fond journey into the North'.[24] From Hatfield, probably in 1547, the Lady Elizabeth began her letter to her brother the king with a long sentence telling him how much his request for her portrait has added to her emotional riches. It is a sentence remarkable for the delicacy with which she intrudes into her brother's consciousness.

> Like as the rich man that daily gathereth riches to riches, and to one bag of money layeth a great sort till it come to infinite, so methinks your Majesty, not being suffied with many benefits and gentleness showed to me afore this time, doth now increase them in asking and desiring where you may bid and command, requiring a thing not worthy the desiring for itself, but made worthy for your Highness's request.

Elizabeth's next sentence to Edward begins more plainly but soon moves again into the circumlocutions of humility: 'My picture, I mean, in which if the inward good mind toward your Grace might as well be declared as the outward face and countenance shall be seen, I would not have tarried the commandment but prevent it, nor have been the last to grant but the first to offer it'. I unravel this sentence to mean: I am sending you my picture as you requested. If you could see my inner mind as easily as you see my outward face in this portrait, you would believe me when I tell you that I would not have kept you waiting to receive it, but would have anticipated your request and offered this portrait to you before you could ask for it.[25] This reading of the sentence suggests that the portrait predated Edward's request to have it sent to him, possibly because he knew she had commissioned it.

She insists further that as audience of the picture and letter, he should not simply look at the surface of the painting – at her external self – but consider the interior self that it represents. As she says next, 'For the face, I grant, I might well blush to offer, but the mind I shall never be ashamed to present.' It is a clear sentence about the relation between the visual representation of the corruptible body and the incorruptible mind. Elizabeth may 'blush' to offer her face, but interestingly enough, she is definitely not modest about presenting her intellect, any more than she was when at the ages of eleven and twelve she presented her father and stepmother with their New Year's gifts. Those gifts, like the presentation of the combined painting and letter to her brother, suggest in both the visual and textual registers a demure femininity together with a boldness and strength of mind. As she writes in the letter's next sentence, 'though the grace of the picture the colours may fade by time, may give by weather, may be spotted by chance; yet the other [that is, her mind] nor time with her swift wings shall overtake, nor the misty clouds with their lowerings may darken, nor chance with her slippery foot may overthrow'. Again, in this contrast between body and mind, the mind becomes one with the incorruptible soul. This last sentence is, stylistically, the high point of the letter. If it sounds familiar, it is because it derives from the same constellation of rhetoric and images of mutability from which so much of Renaissance literature draws its power.

Elizabeth's management of rhetoric and imagery brilliantly seconds her portrait's invitation to couple the sight of her body with the awareness of an intelligence validated by its religious context. Then she moves one step further, saying that this 'inward mind' actively wishes that she might be with him in person. Her plea to attend him and the frank admission that being close to him would do her 'great good' ends in a moment of classical allusion from their shared education: 'and again because I see as yet not the time agreeing thereunto, I shall learn to follow this saying of Horace, "Feras non culpes quod vitari non potest".' This Latin phrase is actually an artful paraphrase of the last two lines of Horace's Ode I:24, the 'Lament for Quintilius' addressed to Virgil about Quintilius's death.[26] The ode concludes, 'It is hard, but whatever cannot be corrected becomes bearable through patience'. Elizabeth's paraphrase translates as 'May *you* not blame what cannot be avoided', so that she changes the subject to 'you'. In other words, *Edward* need not blame what cannot be avoided – namely, the fact that they are being kept apart. The ways that Elizabeth changes rather than quotes Horace may well assume that Edward would recognise this famous line from the odes of the first book that they may have studied together. In this way, she could send him a necessarily subtle but pointed allusion to their shared inability to change the political world in which they found themselves – a ciphered message, which like the portrait's assembled references, makes political claims in the personal register. From this paraphrase she turns tactfully in her final sentence to leave him in control.

Through the letter's careful construction, the Lady Elizabeth produces a verbal portrait of herself consistent with the visual portrait whose surfaces likewise draw us from purely public representation to the consideration of her capabilities. The letter's attempt to structure the response to her gifts is the most dramatic early instance of Elizabeth's awareness of both the limitations and potential of her portraiture.

Without the strategies that Elizabeth brought into play to display herself – without *Elizabeth When a Princess* – the many later portraits of Elizabeth might never have been painted. Thus Elizabeth's gifts to the figures controlling her access to power reveal her ability to screen as well as declare her femininity and her piety in ways that allowed her to use her female body and hand to declare her intellect and her resolve. These gifts encapsulate her learning, her rhetorical expertise, her fusion of caution with boldness, and her awareness of the importance of coupling the visual and the textual. The gifts that the young Elizabeth presented within the enclosed but always shifting politics of the Tudor court prefigured the strategies used to present her as queen to the whole of England.

Notes

1. I am grateful to a number of people for their comments on this article. I presented early versions of this work at the Tate Gallery of Art in London in conjunction with the Dynasties Exhibit, where Karen Hearn provided many useful comments; at Vassar College, where Karen Robertson and Jim Brain made valuable suggestions; and a later version under the auspices of the European Institute in Florence, where I also received valuable suggestions. For a longer discussion of the relation between Elizabeth's youthful portraiture and her attempts to maintain political vitality, see Susan Frye, *Elizabeth I: The Competition for Representation* (New York, 1993), 98–104.

2. Elizabeth was born in 1533; in 1534, Eustace Chapys, the Spanish Ambassador, wrote to Charles V's secretary about her first known marriage negotiations, noting that Henry, 'having been told that there was a rumour of a future marriage between the Infanta [Mary Tudor] and the dauphin [of France], sent for the secretary of the French embassy at this court to propose that of his own bastard daughter to the duke of Angoulême'. Chapys to Francisco de los Cabos, 13 October 1534. Pasqual de Gayangos, (ed.), *Calendar of State Papers Spanish. Henry VIII* (London, 1886); reprint (Nendeln, Liechtenstein, 1969), Vol. 5; part 1, 1534–1535, 279.

3. See Frye, *Elizabeth I*, 72–77 for a lengthier account of this imprisonment. See also *Calendar of State Papers Domestic, Mary,*

1547–50, eds. Robert Lemon and Mary Anne Everett Green (London, 1856–72), especially item numbers 2:20, 3:31, 34; 8:52, 54; *Calendar of State Papers Spanish*, vols. 12 and 13, esp. 4, 5, 7, 8, 12, 17, 18, 19, 24 February; 1, 9, 14, 27 March; 3,17,22 April; 22–25 May; 4 June 1554; 21 April, 6 May 1555; *Calendar of State Papers Venice*, 1556–57, ed. Rawdon Brown et al. (London, 1864–1947), Vol. 6, 1056–59, 1076. J.R. Dasent (ed.), *Acts of the Privy Council of England*, 1554–56 (London: HMSO, 1890–1907), 5:28, 29, 38, 79, 83, 109–10, 119; Henry Machyn, *The Diary of Henry Machyn, Citizen and Merchant-Taylor of London from A.D. 1550 to A.D. 1563* (London, 1850), 51–60; J.G. Nichols ed., *The Chronicle of Queen Jane and of Two Years of Queen Mary Written by a Resident of the Tower of London* (London, 1850), 34–76.

4. On the social and political implications of gift giving, see the germinal anthropological work, Marcel Mauss, *The Gift*, trans. W.D. Halls (1950; reprint New York, 1990); see also David Cheal, *The Gift Economy* (London, 1988).

5. The phrase is David Cheal's, who points out that 'Interpersonal dependence is everywhere the result of socially constructed ties between human agents', so that 'the contents of those ties are defined by the participants' reciprocal expectations. It is these reciprocal expectations between persons that make social interaction possible, both in market exchange and gift exchange' Cheal, *Gift Economy*, 11.

6. According to the New Year's lists of gifts to Prince Edward from 1538 to 1539, 'The Lady Elizabeth' provided Edward with 'A shyrte of comeryke of her owne woorkynge'. In 1539–40, 'A braser of nedleworke of her owne makyng' is also recorded from 'The Ladye Elizabeth'. J.G. Nichols, ed., *Literary Remains of King Edward the Sixth* (London, 1857), Vol. 1, cclxii, cclxv.

7. Margaret Swain first pointed out that the three extant manuscripts point to a missing fourth manuscript, with each pair containing a manuscript for Henry VIII and one for Katherine Parr ('KP' on the cover of the Bodleian manuscript). See Swain, 'A New Year's Gift from Princess Elizabeth', *The Connoisseur* (August 1979), 258–66. For a discussion of the politics of Elizabeth's youthful needlework in the context of the needlework of Mary Queen of Scots and Elizabeth Talbot, Countess of Shrewsbury ('Bess of Hardwick'), see Susan Frye, 'Sewing Connections: Elizabeth Tudor, Mary Stuart, Elizabeth Talbot, and the Seventeenth-Century Anonymous Needleworkers', in Susan Frye and Karen Robertson, eds. *Maids and Mistresses, Cousins and Queens: Women's Alliances in Early Modern England* (New York, 1999), 165–82.

8. Elizabeth's three extant calligraphic manuscripts are 'The Glass of the Sinful Soul', Bodleian Library, Oxford, Cherry 36, included in Marc Shell, *Elizabeth's Glass* (Lincoln, 1993), 111–44. Her manuscript was first published by John Bale as *A Godly Medytacyon of the Christen Sowle* (Marburg: Dirik van der Straten, 1548). Elizabeth's English translation of John Calvin's *Institution Chrétienne*, is MS, Scottish Record Office; and her translations into Latin, French and Italian, of

Katherine Parr's *Prayers, or Meditations*, title 'Precationes sev meditationes' are British Library, MS Royal 7.D.X.MS.

9. Bodleian Library, Oxford, Cherry 36, fol. 2r–2v.

10. Shell, *Elizabeth's Glass*, 3.

11. J.E. Neale, *Queen Elizabeth I: A Biography* (1934; reprint 1957), 10.

12. Since I began work on this article, David Starkey has published *Elizabeth: The Struggle for the Throne* (2000; reprint New York, 2001), which arrives at very different conclusions about Elizabeth's relationship with her father. Starkey, instead of considering Elizabeth's New Year's books as gifts submitted in matching pairs to Katherine Parr and her father, Henry VIII, finds that the extant gift to her father is 'prodigious' and that presented to her stepmother as merely 'impressive'. As a result, Starkey finds that what mattered to Elizabeth was her relations with her father. But as art historian Griselda Pollock notes in *Vision and Difference: Femininity, Feminism and the Histories of Art* (London, 1988), 'High Culture systematically denies knowledge of women as producers of culture and meanings' (17), and I have tried to provide the context for Elizabeth's work as including her knowledge of women who created culture and meaning. Elizabeth produced her volumes in part because they connected her to the learned and devout women in her family, and it is possible to consider Elizabeth's connections to her mother, stepmother and grandmother without neglecting her sense of her dynastic connection to her father.

13. The letter is British Library, Cotton MSS Vespasian, F iii.

14. The 1547 inventory taken of Henry VIII's goods following his death is British Library, Harleian MS 1419; the quotation is listed under the 'Stuffe and Implumentes at Westminster', fol. 131^v. This inventory of thousands of items that detail the royal material culture of England at mid-sixteenth century is now available as *The Inventory of King Henry VIII: The Transcript* (Vol. 1), ed. David Starkey (London, 1998), where the painting of Elizabeth is item number 10719.

15. Janet Arnold has argued that *Elizabeth When a Princess* and the letter dated 15 May Hatfield belong together in Arnold, 'The "Pictur" of Elizabeth I when Princess', *Burlington Magazine*, Vol. 123 (1981), 303–4. I argue that although we can never know for certain that they do belong together, they are useful to discuss together. Given how few works of art survive from this period and how curiously little of the correspondence between Elizabeth and Edward is extant, it would be quite amazing if the portrait and letter actually do belong together. Moreover, we cannot know how many portraits of Elizabeth may have come into existence in spite of Henry VIII's insistence on the control of his children's portraits. Mention is made in diplomatic correspondence of a hastily completed portrait sent to France as part of marriage negotiations early in Edward's reign (*Calendar of State Papers Spanish*, Vol. 10, 215), so that it is difficult to say how many portraits of Elizabeth there were.

16. See for example *Acts of the Privy Council of England, 1547–1550*, ed. John Roche Dasent (London, 1890), Vol. 2, 74, 196.

17. Prince Edward to Henry VIII, 4 August 1546, from Hundsdon, translated from the Latin of BL MS Harleian 5087, in James Halliwell ed., *Letters of the Kings of England* (London, 1846), Vol. 2, 15.

18. *Acts of the Privy Council* (1547–50), Vol. 2, 86.

19. W.K. Jordan, *Edward VI: The Young King: The Protectorship of the Duke of Somerset* (London, 1968), 66.

20. Arnold, 'The "Pictur" of Elizabeth I', 303.

21. Karen Hearn, *Dynasties: Painting in Tudor and Jacobean England* (Peterborough, 1995), 47.

22. Edward VI kept a diary in the third person in which he recorded that 'After [the king's] death incontinent came Edward, Early of Hertford, and Sir Anthony Browne, Master of the Horse, to convey this prince to Enfield, where the Early of Hartford declared to him and his younger sister Elizabeth the death of their father'. Edward VI, *The Chronicle and Political Papers of King Edward VI*, ed. W.K. Jordan (Ithaca, 1966), 3–4.

23. See Lynne Magnusson, 'Reading Courtly and Administrative Letters', chapter 4, in *Shakespeare and Social Dialogue: Dramatic Language and Elizabethan Letters* (Cambridge, 1999), 91–113.

24. Elizabeth I, *The Letters of Elizabeth I*, ed. G.B. Harrison (London, 1968), 175.

25. Here I disagree with G.B. Harrison's rather curious note about what 'prevent' means in this context. Whereas he interprets 'prevent' to mean 'forestall', I follow the OED's second meaning of 'anticipate'. Elizabeth I, *Letters*, ed. Harrison, 15.

26. My thanks to my colleague, Carolyn Anderson, who helped me track down the origin of Elizabeth's play on Horace; I quote her translation of the final line of Ode 1:24: 'durum: sed levius fit patientia' (http://www.perseus.tufts.edu/cgibin/ptext?lookup=Hor.+Carm.+1.24.1).

4

Elizabeth through the Looking Glass

Picturing the Queen's Two Bodies

Louis Montrose

In sixteenth-century Europe, the monarchical state was given iconic form in the royal portrait. The proliferation of images of Habsburg, Valois and Tudor princes provides compelling visual evidence for the consolidation of monarchical authority, and for the highly personalised nature of the political process, during the early modern period. This personification of the state in iconic and verbal representations of the royal body was shaped by the contingent particulars of a prince's gender, age and physiognomy – as well as by the abilities and motives of those who represented them, either visually or textually. My concern is with the iconic and rhetorical strategies entailed by the representation of royal authority in the person of Queen Elizabeth I – a woman who was not merely a royal consort, nor even a regent, but an unmarried prince regnant; and with the problems and opportunities that these unusual circumstances presented to the project of royal representation. Here I can only begin to suggest the dimensions of this issue, through a brief consideration of the Queen's image in relation to those of her father, Henry VIII, and her half-sister, Mary I, and at different points in her own reign and lifecycle, putting particular emphasis on the final years.

The perception and promotion of the royal image were components of a dynamic process that, in both its motives and its impact, was just as likely to be contestatory or hortatory as it was to be celebratory. Elizabethan royal images were employed in a wide range of cultural work, which included enhancing and subverting the charisma of the queen; legitimating and resisting the authority of her regime; pursuing foreign policy through strategic royal courtships; seeking to influence royal sympathies in matters religious, civic and military; and pursuing personal advancement through courtly flattery. Various competing and opposed interests were at work in the production and apprehension of visual representations of the monarch, and in the textual representation of royal icons and spectacles. Here I include not only texts which describe visual representations of the Queen, but also those which record the visual spectacle of the Queen's self-presentation: For when she was in state, enrobed, bejewelled, bewigged and painted, Elizabeth herself was a living icon – or, as opponents of her regime would have had it, a vain and blasphemous idol.

A number of recent writers on Queen Elizabeth have claimed that when she received visitors in the Privy Chamber at Whitehall Palace, she liked to stage herself before the imposing image of her father that dominated Holbein's great wall painting of the Tudor dynasty.[1] I am unaware of any Elizabethan source for this claim; nevertheless, it is both attractive and plausible, and it holds significant implications for a study of the queen's own royal image. Holbein's monumental wall painting for the Privy Chamber at Whitehall dates from some three decades after the accession of Henry VIII, and it eschews the imagery of martial and amorous chivalry that was associated with the young king; nevertheless, it projects more powerfully than any other Henrician icon the gender-specific resonance of the royal body. In this work – of which only part of the original cartoon survives – the painter vividly portrays the power of the reigning monarch as manifest in the size, strength and carriage of his body.[2] Extant seventeenth-century copies of the painting, made before its loss in the 1698 fire which destroyed Whitehall, indicate that in the final version, Holbein gave Henry VIII a fully frontal pose (see Figure 4.1). Of the four royal figures represented, only the king regnant looks directly at the viewer. There is an emphatic contrast between his thrusting pose and the self-contained demeanour of his deceased father, Henry VII, the founder of the Tudor dynasty, who stands behind him. Neither of the royal consorts – Elizabeth of York and Jane Seymour – engages the viewer's gaze; each demurely clasps her hands together, a chaste and obedient female instrument of the Tudor dynastic imperative.

The graphic contrast between the figures of Henry VIII and Henry VII parallels the Latin inscription on the central tablet, in which the regal accomplishments of the son, who had routed the Pope and restored an English *imperium*, surpass those of the father, who had healed internecine strife by uniting the dynastic houses of Lancaster and York.[3]

Karel van Mander, writing at the beginning of the seventeenth century, remarked of Holbein's likeness of Henry VIII that 'the King as he stood there, majestic in his splendour, was so lifelike that the spectator felt abashed, annihilated in his presence'.[4] How much more awesome, then, must have been the effect when the King himself was actually present and in state in the Privy Chamber. In a memoir composed upon the death of Queen Elizabeth, Sir John Clapham remarked of her father that 'the greatness of his personage seem[ed] to carry a kind of proportion with the greatness of his state.

Figure 4.1 Henry VII, Elizabeth of York, Henry VIII, and Jane Seymour, by Remigius van Leemput, 1667.

And surely among other outward gifts of nature, the stature and lineaments of body are not least to be respected, specially in such princes as appear themselves in person at solemn interviews and public assemblies, as this king ofttimes did'.[5] In the real presence of the king – who was, as the Henrician Bishop Gardiner put it, 'the image of God upon earth' – Holbein's icon was made flesh, the royal supremacy over both Church and State was incarnated.[6]

The theme of Holbein's painting was the succession and filial emulation of the Tudor dynasty; however, since none of Henry VIII's progeny were actually represented in Holbein's painting, the spectacle of the living Queen Elizabeth standing or seated before the images of her father and grandfather could have conveniently presented a powerful visual assertion of her legitimate succession to the body politic of Tudor kingship. This celebrated work continued to adorn the wall of the Privy Chamber at Whitehall throughout Elizabeth's reign; and it was there that she frequently entertained ambassadors and others whom she sought to impress with her regal authority and to honour with her special favour. However, if she did indeed pose herself before this portrait of her progenitors, Elizabeth would also have foregrounded her anomalous condition: a queen regnant and (as Francis Bacon later put it) 'a lady solitary and unmarried'. Elizabeth did explicitly employ rhetorical strategies of identification with her father – as, for example, in her address to a joint delegation of lords and commons during the notably outspoken parliament of 1566. In the course of her angry response to pressuring that she marry and secure the succession, she asserted that, 'thowghe I be a woman yet I have as good a coreage awnswerable to mye place as evere my fathere hade'.[7] As is suggested in this very example by the Queen's initial conditional clause – 'Thowghe I be a woman' – such strategies of identification were double edged. They always risked emphasising precisely the condition that Elizabeth wished to neutralise: namely, the radical difference between the Queen and her father, a difference that was culturally grounded in the assumed innate inferiority of Elizabeth's gender, in her naturally deficient female body, and in all of the attitudes, practices and policies that flowed from that perceived difference.

The unprecedented historical circumstance of two successive queens regnant (Mary and Elizabeth Tudor) impelled the English political nation to speculate – and to act – more boldly than they might otherwise have done about issues of authority, liberty, counsel and commonwealth. At the same time that loyal

Protestants defended Elizabeth's rule as providentially sanctioned, they did so only in terms of a mixed monarchy, in which the royal prerogative was limited by a masculine political nation, as embodied in the Privy Council and Parliament. Within this paradigm, if the ruler's divinely appointed office was to preserve the commonwealth, it was a sacred duty of the political nation to ensure that she met her responsibilities. The humanist concept of counsel assumed unprecedented importance during the reigns of Henry VIII's three children – successively, a male in minority and two females. Sir Thomas Smith considered it imperative that child or woman rulers 'never lacke the counsell of such grave and discreete men as be able to supplie all other defectes'.[8] A Secretary of State and Privy Counsellor to Queen Elizabeth, Smith clearly thought of himself as one of those men.

Although none of Henry VIII's children are represented in the Whitehall wall painting, it nevertheless appears to project its dynastic theme beyond past and present. The year in which it was painted, 1537, also saw the birth of Prince Edward; this blessed event promised to secure, at last, the continuity of the Tudors in the male line.[9] Thus, the prominence and ample proportions of the king's codpiece would seem to be especially appropriate to the dynastic theme of this particular painting.[10] Henrician iconography frequently embodied royal power and prerogative in the king's phallic self-assertion. Elizabethan iconography, after the first decade of the reign, began to embody royal power and prerogative in the queen's virginal self-sufficiency. This was the case even as Elizabeth continued to pursue various marriage negotiations through the beginning of the 1580s; during the final two decades, after all prospects of marriage had ceased, such iconography became both ubiquitous and extravagant. Elizabeth's iconic strategies may be usefully compared not only to those of her father but also to those of her Catholic half-sister and immediate predecessor, Queen Mary.

The unprecedented accession of a woman to the English throne impelled Mary's parliamentarians to pass 'An Acte declaringe that the Regall power of thys realme is in the Quenes Majestie as fully and absolutely as ever it was in anye of her mooste noble progenytors kynges of this Realme'. And the prospective marriage of Queen Mary to Philip of Spain impelled them to enact a statute declaring

that youre majestye as our onely Quene, shal and may, solye and as a sole quene use, have, and enjoye the Crowne and Soveraynte, of, and over your

Realmes, Dominions, and Subjectes ... in suche sole and onelye estate, and in as large and ample maner and fourme ... after the solemnisation of the sayde maryage, and at all tymes durynge the same ... as your grace hath had, used, exercised and enjoyed ... before the solemnization of the sayde mariage.[11]

The motivation for such legislation was not enthusiasm for the principle of female rule but rather an urgently felt need to assert the precedence of the legitimate inheritrix of the English crown over her foreign consort, despite the inferiority of her gender.[12] That Mary's status as queen would be fundamentally unaffected by her marriage to Philip had already been stipulated in the well-publicised marriage treaties; and, as Susan Doran has suggested, Queen Mary herself may have been more careful of her authority vis-à-vis her husband than frequently she has been given credit for.[13] Nevertheless, in the unprecedented circumstances of a queen regnant's marriage to a foreign prince, the English political nation had a vested interest in ensuring that an implicit contradiction between the dominant domestic paradigm of husbandly authority and the anomalous political circumstance of female rule would not lead to an erosion of English sovereignty, thereby endangering the security and privileges of the queen's natural subjects. That such concerns had some foundation is suggested by the proclamation of the new regnal style, which gave precedence to Philip; and also by the most widely disseminated official icons of the reign: the coins, charters and seals which represented Philip and Mary as joint sovereigns, with a single crown suspended between them.[14]

The most striking of Mary's official portraits as Queen was painted in 1554, by Antonis Mor, a Netherlander in service to the Habsburg family (Figure 4.2).[15] Mor's work conveys a strong illusion of volume and depth, and a pronounced use of chiaroscuro; the Queen appears close to the viewer, her pose is naturalistic and animated, and her strongly lit face reveals signs of aging and irregularities of complexion. Mor was not in the employ of the Queen or the English court. His patrons were the Emperor Charles V, who had arranged the marriage of Queen Mary to his son, Philip of Spain, in order to further his dynastic interests, and who had originally commissioned the portrait; and Philip himself, who was newly married to Mary and at the English court when the portrait was painted, and who adopted Mor as his own court painter in the year the portrait was made. We can assume that Mor's powerful

Figure 4.2 Queen Mary I, by Antonis Mor, 1554.

patrons must have approved of the apparent naturalism with which he represented the royal bride. A decade later, during Queen Elizabeth's own Habsburg courtship manoeuvres, she told the envoy of the Emperor Maximilian of her determination that 'she would take no man whom she had not seen ... She knew very well how the King of Spain had cursed the painters and envoys when he first beheld Queen Mary, and she would not give the Archduke Charles cause to curse'.[16] Joanna Woodall has suggested that Mor's likeness is a response to, or a compensation for, such flattering portraits.[17] Mary wears a large and splendid pendant jewel that was a Habsburg wedding gift; and the pious Queen grasps a red rose, an emblem not only of the Tudor dynasty but also of her sacred namesake – and, perhaps, evocative of her supposed pregnancy, which was rumoured within weeks of the marriage. If Mary's pregnancy had been genuine, and had succeeded in producing an heir, the likely political consequence would have been England's absorption within the European hegemony of the Habsburg dynasty and the entrenchment of its recent official return to the Catholic church: there would have been no Elizabethan age. Thus, while Mor represents Mary in state, a queen regnant seated upon her throne, other aspects of the painting's style and composition, as well as the circumstances and agents of its commission, suggest that both Mary and her throne were being valued as potential Habsburg possessions and as instruments of Habsburg statecraft. Indeed, Karen Hearn has suggested that 'the broader iconography of the portrait ... characterises the Queen as a Habsburg consort, rather than an English sovereign'.[18] Significantly, in a small full-length double portrait of Philip and Mary dating from 1557, it is Mor's 1554 portrait that provides the model for representing the Queen. The Mor portrait of Queen Mary circumscribes her within the interests and agendas of the Emperor Charles V and Prince Philip; the control of the English Queen's image by her new Spanish husband was a synecdoche for the Habsburg dynasty's intended control of her body and her state.[19]

For those whose visual image of Queen Elizabeth has been formed by the striking allegorical portraits of her later years, the extant portraits from the first decade of her reign are notable only for their relatively understated treatment of their regal subject; absent are the elaborate iconography of monarchy and the overt personal symbolism that are characteristic of such later royal portraits. In a representative example, she appears as a virtuous and beautiful lady – and, perhaps, as a potential royal bride and mother: the emphasis is upon her body natural rather than upon her body politic.[20] Personal symbolism makes a discreet entrance into Elizabethan royal portraiture in the two finely drawn and brilliantly coloured oil portraits attributed to the young Nicholas Hilliard and painted in the early 1570s. In each of these pictures, the Queen wears a large jewel suspended from a necklace: one, the image of a life-rendering pelican, tearing its breast in order to succour its young with its blood; the other, the image of the singular and self-renewing phoenix upon its burning pyre.[21] Each jewel gives symbolic form to a royal trope that would be elaborated in word and image throughout the rest of the reign: the Pelican, that of the Queen as a nurse and mother to her people, willing to sacrifice herself for their welfare; the Phoenix, of the Queen as a unique and self-sufficient being, whose constancy was given verbal form in her motto, *semper eadem*.

The paired icons of the Pelican and the Phoenix provide a matrix for much of the work of the Elizabethan political imaginary. Together, the Pelican and the Phoenix may be understood as symbolic responses – or mythical solutions – to the persistent Elizabethan political quandaries of royal marriage and succession. And, like the problems, the solutions were inflected by considerations of gender. The Pelican is associated with the Queen's displacement of her maternity from her offspring to her subjects – a trope that was initiated by Elizabeth herself in a speech to her second parliament in 1563, in response to their urging that she marry and produce an heir: 'I assure yow all that though after my death yow may have many stepdames, yet shall yow never have any a more naturall mother then I meane to be unto you all.'[22] There is evidence that maternal tropes had already been turned against Elizabeth's hapless predecessor. According to David Loades, Mary's reign had witnessed the circulation of 'crude woodcuts ... which portrayed [Mary as] a many-breasted queen suckling bishops, priests and Spaniards'.[23] If Elizabeth was aware of such anti-Marian polemics, she was making emphatically clear in her 1563 parliamentary speech that her maternal care and sacrifice would be on behalf of her 'natural' subjects, and not on behalf of Jesuits and Spaniards. The Phoenix, on the other hand, was associated with the quasi-mystical powers inhering in the Queen's virginity. The prominence of this image and its associated motto in the later years of the reign suggests that the perceived succession crisis was being given imaginary resolution in a fantasy of the Queen's perpetual self-renewal.[24]

In her royal image, as in every other aspect of her rule, Mary's female example proffered to Elizabeth a uniquely relevant precedent, whether the response was emulation or calculated antithesis. The bejewelled *imprese* worn as pendants by Elizabeth in the Pelican and Phoenix portraits make the strongest possible iconographic contrast with the Habsburg wedding present worn by Mary in Mor's portrait. Equally strong – and of equally strong political resonance – is the stylistic contrast between Mor's work and those attributed to Hilliard. The Elizabethan portraits are in the highly decorative nativist English style, and display an affinity with the jewel-like art of the limner or watercolour miniaturist; stylistically, the Marian portrait is a continental renaissance painting in the tradition of Titian. This emphatic contrast of cultural styles subtly underlines the contrast between the 'mere English' Elizabeth and her half-Spanish half-sister and the latter's Habsburg consort. Through both its style and its iconography, Mor's fine portrait subtly affirms precisely those likely consequences of a dynastic marriage that Elizabeth worked so assiduously to avoid – at the same time that she sought to extract maximum diplomatic advantage from her erstwhile availability.

The fact that the monarch was an unmarried woman had ensured from the inception of the reign that issues of gender and sexuality would be foregrounded. The Queen and her subjects habitually articulated their political relationships in conjugal-amatory and maternal-filial metaphors; and such a transfer of domestic gender paradigms to the public domain eased the negotiation of anomalous female rule. However, the cult of royal virginity that made the Queen the inviolable object of universal desire emerged in the later 1570s, at least in part as an assertion of opposition to the Queen's marriage negotiations with the French and Catholic Duc d'Alençon and the perceived threat that this alliance represented to the future of the Protestant English commonwealth. In its exorbitant final phase, the quasi-idolatrous cult of the virgin queen more clearly came to serve the strategic interests of the monarch and her increasingly authoritarian and isolated regime. During the last decade and a half of the reign – in what political historians are now calling 'the second reign of Elizabeth I' – potentially destabilising religious and political initiatives and widespread socioeconomic discontent catalysed the regime's efforts to secure popular support. The queen was promoted as an exception to disabling gender norms, in whose inviolate sexuality and self-sacrificing maternal care was a quasi-sacramental source of the nation's welfare.[25]

This ideological programme is given compelling iconic form in the so-called 'Ditchley' portrait of Queen Elizabeth, painted in the early 1590s by Marcus Gheeraerts the Younger. This impressive painting, the largest known portrait of Queen Elizabeth, represents her standing, like some great goddess or transfigured Virgin Mary, with her feet upon the globe and her head amidst the heavens. She is exquisitely clothed in a gown of maidenly white silk with silver thread, richly embroidered and bejewelled; the matching hanging sleeves extend to the ground, creating an appearance of angel's wings. The cosmic background divides into sunlight and storm; according to the now-fragmentary sonnet inscribed on the canvas, these signify, respectively, the heavenly glory and divine power of which the Queen is the earthly mirror. The sonnet form of the inscription, and its still partially legible images and tropes, link it to the Petrarchan-Neoplatonic royal panegyrics that were the currency of court poetry and pageantry in the 1590s. The sonnet's opening sentence – which reads simply, 'The prince of light' – clearly refers to Queen Elizabeth herself. With its cosmological and apocalyptic resonances, this functions as an appropriate title of address to the mortal deity who, as God's anointed substitute, embodies the sun which shines upon England.[26] Such royal solar symbolism reaches its apogee in the so-called 'Rainbow' portrait (Figure 1.1). Produced at the very end of the reign, the 'Rainbow' portrait fashions a visual apotheosis of the aged Queen.[27] The motto inscribed above the rainbow grasped by the Queen – 'NON SINE SOLE IRIS', or, 'no rainbow without the sun' – identifies Elizabeth as the sun. The uncovered bosom and unbound hair of the portrait's subject signify her status as a maiden; at the same time, the youthful beauty of her face, her long, flowing tresses, and the richly embroidered flowers on her bodice all suggest that she is being represented not only as a virgin but also as a bride.[28] I suggest that the marriage being figured is neither to Christ nor to any of the Queen's many disappointed suitors but rather to 'all my husbandes, my good people', as she herself put it in a comment reported by one of her courtiers and her godson, Sir John Harington.[29]

In the 'Ditchley' portrait, the Queen stands upon a cartographic image of Britain, deriving from Christopher Saxton's collection of printed maps. The painting divides England into counties, each separately coloured, and marks principal towns and rivers. Much of the monarch's island nation is enclosed by the hem of her gown and hanging sleeves, a compositional feature perhaps recalling the iconography of the *Madonna della misericordia*, widely disseminated during the fourteenth and fifteenth centuries, which represented Mary as Our Lady of Mercy, spreading her cloak over the mortal suppliants gathered at her feet.[30] The 'Ditchley' portrait's images visually literalise Elizabeth's own description of herself in 1601, in what was to be her final parliamentary address, as 'a taper of trewe virgin waxe to wast my self and spend my life that I might give light and comfort to those that lived under me'. Similarly, upon the death of the Queen, Thomas Dekker played upon this Elizabethan appropriation of Marian imagery, describing his late queen as one who had 'brought up even under her wing a nation that was almost begotten and born under her, that never shouted any other *ave* but for her name, never saw the face of any prince but herself'.[31] The Ditchley icon's representation of the Queen as standing upon her land and sheltering it under her skirts suggests a mystical identification of the inviolate female body of the monarch *with* the unbreached body of her land. At the same time, it affirms her distinctive role as the maternal protectress of her people. She is both 'A Virgin Mother and a Maiden Queene' – both the Pelican and the Phoenix.[32]

This painting also asserts in spectacular fashion another aspect of Elizabeth's personal symbolism that derives from her body politic – namely, her princely rule; it affirms her power over her land and over its inhabitants. The cartographic image imposes territoriality upon place, transforming the *land* into a *state*; and by the division of the state into the counties that constituted its core administrative units, its inhabitants are more precisely and securely marked as the monarch's political and juridical subjects. Roy Strong comments that, 'in the "Ditchley" portrait Queen, crown, and island become one. Elizabeth is England, woman and kingdom are interchangeable'. This seems to me to be only partially true, for it elides the theme of sovereign power and rule that is emphasised both in the icon and in its accompanying verses. In melding the nurturant mother with the absolute ruler, the representational resources of the 'Ditchley' portrait are concentrated upon Elizabeth's *possession* of England.[33] In terms of its sheer scale – both its physical size and its imaginative scope, its realisation of the divine source of royal power in the superhuman proportions of the royal body – the 'Ditchley' portrait strikes me as one of the clearest Elizabethan equivalents of Holbein's icon of Henrician kingship. As in Holbein's portrait of King Henry VIII – although by means radically different from the phallic symbolisation of kingly *virtù* – the 'Ditchley' portrait of Queen

Elizabeth seems designed to elicit from its beholders feelings of awe and devotion, love and fear, and an unquestioning assent to their own subjection.

However, one of Gheeraert's stylistic choices introduces a dissonance into this icon of quasi-divine sovereignty: namely, his use of chiaroscuro to model Elizabeth's facial features, which creates a relatively naturalistic image of the sovereign at three-score years of age. Indeed, the verisimilitude in the handling of Elizabeth's physiognomy contrasts sharply with the highly decorative patterning of her clothed body and the exorbitant conceit governing the whole work. A comparison with the 'Rainbow' portrait emphasises the stylistic incongruity of the 'Ditchley' portrait. Like the oil paintings of Gheeraerts, the portrait miniatures and drawings of his brother-in-law Isaac Oliver reveal a pursuit of the norms of high Renaissance painting, including linear perspective, chiaroscuro, and plasticity of forms.[34] At about the same time that Gheeraerts painted the 'Ditchley' portrait, Oliver limned a strikingly naturalistic miniature of the Queen. The apparent verisimilitude of this unfinished portrait was an experiment that was not repeated: This seems to have been Oliver's first and only commission from the Queen.[35]

To undertake to represent the monarch was to engage in a potentially dangerous manipulation of symbolic power; and the Elizabethan regime was concerned to regulate the production and dissemination of the royal image. As early as 1563, a proclamation was drafted in an attempt to curtail the grievous and offensive 'errors and deformities' in widely available representations of the Queen, in 'painting, graving, and printing'. The intent was to regulate the production and distribution of the royal image according to a single model posed for, and approved by, the Queen; this was alleged to be necessary because 'hitherto none hath sufficiently expressed the natural representation of her majesty's person, favour, or grace'.[36] However, this proposal seems not to have been enacted. And in 1596, the regime was once again ordering the collection and destruction of such unofficial likenesses as might be objectionable to their royal subject.[37] More than thirty years on, the official tone was stronger and more urgent than it was in 1563. Those without sufficient skill to present a true likeness of the Queen were now characterised as abusive, and their work was said to be unseemly; the proposed remedy now included the confiscation and destruction of extant offensive works and the subjection of future production to a process of review by a court official. Furthermore, the emphasis in 1596 was not upon what in 1563 was characterised as 'the natural representation of her majesty's person, favor, or grace' but rather upon defining the skilful artisan as one who, in representing 'her Majesty's person and vysage', fully conveyed 'that beutyfull and magnanimous Majesty wherwith God hathe blessed her'. In other words, between 1563 and 1596 there was a subtle shift in the regulatory language from a verisimilar representation of the young queen's body natural – the 'natural representation' of her 'person, favour, or grace' – to an idealised representation of the aged queen's body politic – 'that beutyfull and magnanimous Majesty wherwith God hathe blessed her'. I suggest that the shifts in emphasis and tone between the regulations drafted near the beginning and near the end of the reign are due at least in part to the growing disjunction between the political ideal of the Queen's beauty – which was abstract and timeless – and an artistic project of 'natural representation' that more sharply observed the realm of the senses and might thus subvert the royal charisma.

During the last decade of the reign, it was not Isaac Oliver but Nicholas Hilliard who embodied the ideals encoded in the 1596 regulation; he could best imitate the Queen's 'beutyfull and magnanimous Majesty', and it was to his studio that royal patronage flowed. The officially sanctioned pattern for 'her Majesty's person and vysage' that Roy Strong has called 'the mask of youth' dominated production of the royal image from the early 1590s. This pattern is most strikingly represented in the face of the 'Rainbow' portrait but it is primarily associated with the portrait miniatures of Hilliard and his studio. Characteristic is a miniature limned by Hilliard c. 1600, set in a jewelled locket, with a star-burst design on the case.[38] Like the contemporaneous 'Rainbow' portrait – but without recourse to any arcane symbolism – this intimate picture evokes Elizabeth's mystical virginity by representing her as a young and radiant maiden, her bosom uncovered, and her unbound hair flowing onto her shoulders. Not only in their youthful and idealised rendering of the Queen but also more generally in their linear, decorative and brilliantly coloured style, Hilliard's miniatures exemplify an aesthetic at variance with that evident in the work of his younger contemporary, Isaac Oliver.

As it happens, the only textual evidence we have for the Queen's artistic opinions and preferences is recorded by Nicholas Hilliard and concerns Elizabeth's resolute aversion to the application of chiaroscuro. In his *Treatise concerning the Arte of Limning*, which was apparently composed around 1600, Hilliard recounts a conversation that he had with the Queen on the occasion of painting her portrait: noting the 'great difference of shadowing in the works, and diversity of Drawers of sundry nations', the Queen opined 'that best to showe ones selfe, nedeth no shadow of place but rather the oppen light'; accordingly, she chose to pose for her portrait 'in the open ally of a goodly garden, where no tree was neere, nor anye shadowe at all'.[39] Hilliard concludes that 'beauty and good favor is like cleare truth, which is not shamed with the light, nor neede to bee obscured'. This flattering comment can be juxtaposed to an almost contemporaneous remark in Sir John Clapham's memoir of the reign. Discussing his late queen's predilection for flattery, Clapham urges the importance of recording monarchs' vices as well as their virtues, concluding that 'by flattery in describing their actions, like a painted face without a shadow to give it life, the credit of such things as are truly reported would be much doubted and diminished'.[40] It is evident from the pattern of royal patronage and the regulatory attempts of the Elizabethan government that, as she grew older, chiaroscuro became too revealing of the work of time and mutability for a Queen whose personal motto declared her to be singular and constant.

A number of Elizabethan subjects astutely observed the politics of the Queen's self-display, although – like Clapham – they tended to commit their observations to writing only after her death. John Hayward, a writer of politic histories who was imprisoned for sedition near the end of Elizabeth's reign, subsequently wrote a shrewd account of her early years as Queen. In his account of Elizabeth's passage through London on the day before her coronation in 1559, Hayward notes her care regarding the royal furnishing of both herself and her train. He commends her for 'knowing right well that in pompous ceremonies a secret of government doth much consist, for that the people are naturally both taken and held with exteriour shewes … The rich attire, the ornaments, the beauty of Ladyes, did add particular graces to the solemnity, and held the eyes and hearts of men dazeled betweene contentment and admiratione'.[41] 'Dazeled betweene contentment and admiratione' captures nicely the complex experience of solace and awe that could hold 'the eyes and hearts of men' in willing subjection to the charismatic power of the prince – an effect here produced by a combination of costume, ceremony and feminine beauty.

Writing in the months following the Queen's death, John Clapham provides a useful counter-perspective to Hayward's account of her early years. Clapham discusses the altered circumstances in which the Queen deployed this 'secret of government' at the end of her reign: 'In her latter time, when she showed herself in public, she was always magnificent in apparel, supposing haply thereby, that the eyes of her people, being dazzled with the glittering aspect of those accidental ornaments would not so easily discern the marks of age and decay of natural beauty' (86). This strategy seems to have worked well upon Thomas Platter, a Swiss traveller who saw the Queen in 1599. In his diary, he carefully recorded a detailed description of her gown, headpiece, jewellery and gloves, concluding with the observation that 'she was most gorgeously apparelled, and although she was already seventy four [sic], was very youthful still in appearance, seeming no more than twenty years of age'. However, three years later, when the Duke of Stettin-Pomerania and his entourage saw the Queen, his diarist observed more sharply: 'To judge from portraits showing her Majesty in her thirtieth year, there cannot have lived many finer women at the time; even in her old age she did not look ugly, *when seen from a distance.'*[42] The royal pageantry and iconography of late Elizabethan culture display an exorbitance in verbal, visual, and sartorial rhetoric that seems intended to produce a symbolic compensation for the Queen's natural decline. Such 'exteriour shewes' may have continued to be relatively effective in dazzling a majority of 'the people'; however, in the eyes of at least some beholders, it seems that such hyperbolic strategies worked to the contrary effect, magnifying rather than mystifying the discrepancy between the Queen's natural and politic bodies, and thus subverting her *arcana imperii* or 'secrets of government', as Hayward calls them.

As the most immediately conspicuous and versatile manifestation of royal magnificence, costume was at the centre of attention in royal portraiture and courtly ceremony. In their dispatches and diaries, foreign visitors to the English court almost invariably described in detail the Queen's features, carriage and wardrobe; and in their reports to the Queen, English ambassadors frequently described the appearance, demeanour and dress of foreign queens and court ladies. When the Venetian Secretary Scaramelli reported to the Doge and Senate upon his first official audience with the Queen, which took place just a few weeks before her death, he began with the following description:

The Queen was clad in taffety of silver and white, trimmed with gold; her dress was somewhat open in front and showed her throat encircled with pearls and rubies down to her breast. Her skirts were much fuller and began lower than is the fashion in France. Her hair was of a light colour never made by nature, and she wore great pearls like pears round the forehead; she had a coif arched round her head and an Imperial crown, and displayed a vast quantity of gems and pearls upon her person.[43]

It is the colour, fabric and style of the Queen's dress, and the size, shape and abundance of her jewels that make the most immediate visual impact upon the Venetian Secretary. The spectacle of the Queen in state was clearly contrived to dazzle the ambassador – to create an aura of imperious magnificence, one that put both the Queen and her Kingdom on an equal footing with *la Serenissima*. It is clear from Elizabeth's reported remarks that the occasion was a very important one for the aged Queen, and one very long in coming:

Her countenance, which had hitherto been placid and almost smiling, assumed a graver aspect, and she said, 'I cannot help feeling that the Republic of Venice, during the forty-four years of my reign, has never made herself heard by me except to ask for something; nor for the rest, prosperous or adverse as my affairs may have been, never has she given a sign of holding me or my kingdom in that esteem which other princes and other potentates have not refused. Nor am I aware that my sex has brought me this demerit, for my sex cannot diminish my prestige nor offend those who treat me as other Princes are treated, to whom the Signory of Venice sends its Ambassadors'. (533)

Elizabeth's blunt comment to Scaramelli reflected a forty-four year struggle: one of the challenges faced by the Elizabethan regime had always been to ensure that the Queen's sex did not diminish her prestige. The Venetian despatch is a valedictory reminder that, in the Elizabethan case, personal vanity and *arcana imperii* were of a piece.

In February 1603, shortly before the Queen's death, John Manningham recorded in his diary the following anecdote: 'Sir Christopher Hatton and another knight made challenge whoe should present the truest picture of hir Majestie to the Q[ueene]. One caused a flattering picture to be drawne; the other presented a glas, wherein the Q[ueene] saw hir selfe, the truest picture that might be.' Although the story is likely to have been apocryphal, it is nevertheless of historical interest as a record of late Elizabethan attitudes and perceptions. The scenario is one of typical courtly rivalry for the attentions and approval of the prince; but because this prince is a woman, the scenario is also atypical in being predicated upon gendered assumptions regarding *vanitas*, assumptions that the singular Elizabeth confounds. The politic courtier praises the Queen's moral virtue, flattering her with the implication that she disdains flattery.[44] In his almost contemporaneous memoir, written in the months immediate following the Queen's death, Clapham writes that:

> It is credibly reported that, not long before her death, [the Queen] had a great apprehension of her own age and declination by seeing her face, then lean and full of wrinkles, truly represented to her in a glass; which she a good while very earnestly beheld, perceiving thereby how often she had been abused by flatterers whom she held in too great estimation, that had informed her to the contrary.[45]

Like some of his contemporaries, Clapham might have chosen to focus, misogynistically, upon the personal vanities of the female monarch; instead, he reflects upon the collective ethical and political dilemmas of court society and monarchical government: endemic corruption and sycophancy, and the constant danger that the subject's duty to proffer wise counsel will be perverted by narrow and ruthless self-interest.

Other anecdotal evidence consists largely of court gossip that is of considerably less moral probity than Clapham's observations, and is characterised by a pervasive and casual misogyny. Soon after John Manningham recorded his anecdote, the Queen was dead; and Henry Chettle wrote in *England's Mourning Garment* that 'She never could abide to gaze in a mirror or looking glasse ... When I was yong, almost thirtie yeeres agoe, courting it now and than: I have seene the Ladies make great shift to hide away their looking glasses if her Majestie had past by their lodgings'. After 1603, textual records of such gossip multiplied – although most, unlike Chettle's, focused on the Queen's declining years. In his recorded tabletalk, playwright and poet Ben Jonson made a couple of particularly wicked remarks about the late Queen's chastity and beauty: of the former, 'that she had a Membrana on her which made her uncapable of man, though for her delight she tryed many' – in effect, that she was rampantly unchaste, and only remained a virgin despite herself; and of the latter, that 'Queen Elizabeth never saw her self after she became old in a true Glass. they painted her & sometymes would vermilion her nose'.[46]

Here Jonson pithily confounds Manningham's simple opposition between the 'flattering picture' painted to represent the Queen and the true picture revealed by her reflection in the glass: for Jonson, the putatively 'false' glass merely gives a truthful reflection of the 'flattering picture' that has been painted in cosmetics directly upon the old Queen's face; his iconoclastic quip renders the royal image not merely a false idol but a ridiculous one. Even Protestant divines shared this discourse: in his memoir of the Jacobean court, Bishop Godfrey Goodman recalled that in the later years of Elizabeth's reign, 'there was ... a report that the ladies had gotten false looking-glasses, that the queen might not see her own wrinkles'.[47]

Such anecdotes as these are of more than anecdotal interest: as manifestations of a collective Elizabethan political imaginary, they are indicative of the problems surrounding the production of the royal image, the potential dangers of representing the queen to herself, and the hollowness of the royal 'cult', especially in the later years of the reign. They are also, of course, part of a venerable misogynistic discourse about female vanity, envy and spite, a discourse in which old women were assigned an especially ignominious role. And this discourse was but the underside of that which venerated youthful female beauty, grace and charm. In the Elizabethan case, at issue was the predicament of a ruler who – perhaps out of personal inclination, and undoubtedly out of political necessity – had exploited the charismatic potential of certain culturally constituted feminine ideals, ideals with which the accidents of nature and the ravages of time were becoming increasingly incompatible. As we have seen, when Isaac Oliver limned his unfinished miniature of the aging monarch in the early 1590s, he provided her with a looking glass in which she might see her wrinkles. He received no further patronage from the Queen, who preferred the flattering pictures offered by Hilliard. During the final decade of the reign, as if in compensation for Oliver's image, Hilliard produced numerous variations upon an idealised, youthful and beautiful royal visage. We are frequently asked to comprehend such images in Neoplatonic terms, as idealisations of the Queen's virtue and authority, as metaphorical portraits of her chaste mind, her beautiful soul. Yet there is considerable evidence that, at least for those within the orbit of the court, for whom the Queen was a relatively familiar presence, the whole enterprise of later Elizabethan royal panegyric was pervaded by a distinctly cynical air. In effect, the gossip that represented the Queen as a vain, foolish and wrinkled old woman – an object of pathos, or derision–divested her of the body politic of kingship by confining her within a body natural that was culturally defined by the deficiencies of her gender, age and marital status. The lengthening tenure of Elizabeth's rule may well have served to enhance her political experience and acumen, but it also eroded the efficacy of those very symbolic forms through which her regime sought to secure the devotion of her subjects.

Notes

1. For example, Leah Marcus writes that 'as a young woman, Elizabeth had liked to place herself directly in front of the giant Holbein portrait of Henry VIII at Whitehall, challenging those present to measure her own bearing and authority' against those of her father. Leah Marcus, *Puzzling Shakespeare* (Berkeley, 1988), 55. She cites the biography by Paul Johnson, *Elizabeth I* (London, 1974), 79. A very similar assertion is made in Christopher Haigh, *Elizabeth I* (London, 1988), 21. None of these writers cites any Elizabethan source.

2. A detailed analysis and contextualisation of the painting, extensively illustrated, is to be found in Roy Strong, *Holbein and Henry VIII* (1967), reprinted with a new preface in Strong, *The Tudor and Stuart Monarchy: Pageantry, Painting, Iconography*, Vol. 1. Tudor (Woodbridge, England, 1995), 1–54; see esp. 31–49. I am indebted to Strong's discussion, and have also benefited from Christopher Lloyd and Simon Thurley, *Henry VIII: Images of a Tudor King* (London, 1990), esp. 28–29. The present discussion revises and considerably expands one that I initially presented as part of a comparison of Holbein's image of Henry with the *Armada* portrait of Elizabeth, in 'The Elizabethan Subject and the Spenserian Text', in *Literary Theory/Renaissance Texts*, eds. Patricia Parker and David Quint (Baltimore, 1986), 303–40.

3. The inscription, which was reproduced in the Restoration copy by Remigius van Leemput, was transcribed from the now-lost original by the Moravian Baron Waldstein when he visited London in 1600. See *The Diary of Baron Waldstein, A Traveller in Elizabethan England*, trans. G.W. Groos (London, 1981), 57. Groos provides the following translation (56):

If you find pleasure in seeing fair pictures of heroes
Look at these! None greater was ever portrayed.
Fierce is the struggle and hot the disputing; the question:
Does father, does son – or do both – the pre-eminence win?
One ever withstood his foes and his country's destruction,
Finally giving his people the blessing of peace;
But, born to do things greater, the son drove out of his councils
His ministers worthless, and ever supported the just.

And in truth, to this steadfastness Papal arrogance yielded
When the sceptre of power was wielded by Henry the Eighth,
Under whose reign the true faith was restored to the nation
And the doctrines of God began to be reverenced with awe.

4. Quoted in Strong, *Holbein and Henry VIII*, 35; and in Lloyd and
Thurley, *Henry VIII*, 29. Strong, *Holbein and Henry VIII*, n. 20, points
out that it is not absolutely certain that van Mander is referring to the
Whitehall wall painting, and that he probably gained his knowledge of
Holbein's portraits of Henry VIII at second hand from his master, Lucas
de Heere, who was active in England during the second decade of
Elizabeth's reign.

5. John Clapham, *Elizabeth of England: Certain Observations Concerning
the Life and Reign of Queen Elizabeth*, eds. Evelyn Plummer Read and
Conyers Read (Philadelphia, 1951), 49.

6. Stephen Gardiner, *De Vera Obedientia* (1535), quoted in Lloyd and
Thurley, *Henry VIII*, 32.

7. The Queen's address to a delegation from both houses of parliament,
delivered on 5 November 1566; printed in *Proceedings in the
Parliaments of Elizabeth I*, ed. T.E. Hartley, 3 vols. (London, 1981–95), I,
145–49; quotation from 148. Also see her comments to the parliament
of 1593, two versions of which are printed in *Proceedings in the
Parliaments of Elizabeth I*, III, 28 and III, 173.

8. *De Republica Anglorum: A Discourse on the Commonwealth of
England*, ed. L. Alston (1906; reprint Shannon, 1972), 30. Among
historians of political thought addressing these issues, A.N. McLaren is
exceptional in her appreciation of the dynamics between gender and
political culture. She writes that, 'In Elizabeth's reign the mixed
monarchy posited a political configuration in which the virtue of the
male political nation could be seen as constraining, with God's
oversight and in the interest of England's imperial identity, the
tyrannical proclivities of a female ruler'. *Political Culture in the Reign
of Elizabeth I* (Cambridge, 1999), 236.

9. See Strong, *Holbein and Henry VIII*, 46–49. Jane Seymour, represented as
Henry's consort in Holbein's painting, died twelve days following the
birth of her son, on 24 October 1537. In terms of our calendar, the year
1537 would have run from 25 March 1537 to 24 March 1538. There is no
certain evidence regarding the chronological relationship between the
completion of the painting and either the birth of Prince Edward or the
death of Queen Jane. In a variant Restoration copy of Holbein's Whitehall
wall painting, also by Remigius van Leemput and probably commissioned
by the late Queen's relatives, the Seymour coat of arms appears upon the
central altar in place of the inscription; in front of the altar, in the centre
foreground of the painting, stands the young Edward VI, in a pose that
imitates his father's. See Strong, *Holbein and Henry VIII*, 31, and plate 25
(n.b., the captions for plates 25 and 26 have been reversed).

10. The royal codpiece is conspicuous in Holbein's 1540 *Henry VIII and the Barber-Surgeons* (see Strong, *Tudor and Stuart Monarchy*, plates 55–56; Lloyd and Thurley, *Henry VIII: Images of a Tudor King*, plate 53; but, interestingly, not in the three-quarter-length portrait of the king in old age, existing in several versions, that is attributed to both Hornebolte and Holbein; see Roy Strong, *Tudor and Jacobean Portraits*, 2 vols. (London, 1969), 2, plates 313–14.

11. Quoted in J.M. Richards, 'Mary Tudor as "Sole Quene"? Gendering the Tudor Monarchy', *Historical Journal* 40 (1997), 895–924, 903–4 and 908–9 respectively.

12. As one Marian writer put it, in a text not printed until Elizabeth's accession, 'As for wysdome and pollicie, seing it consisteth in folowing the counsayl of many godly, learned, & long experienced heades, it were better to have a woman, who consideringe her owne weakenes and inabilitye, should be ruled thereby, than a man which presuming upon his owne fond brayne, wil heare no advise save his owne'. *The Mirror for Magistrates*, ed. Lily B. Campbell (1938; reprint New York, 1960), 420.

13. The proclamation was issued on 14 January 1554, and is printed in *Tudor Royal Proclamations*, eds. Paul L. Hughes and James F. Larkin, 3 vols. (New Haven, 1969), 2.21–26. The terms of the articles seem to have been widely known: Bodin discusses them in the course of his disquisition on gynaecocracy in *The Six Bookes of a Commonweale* (1576; 1606 English translation), 749–50. On Mary not allowing 'power and authority to slip from her hands into those of her husband', see Susan Doran, *Monarch and Matrimony: the Courtships of Elizabeth I* (London, 1996), 8–9, and the works cited therein.

14. For the Proclamation of the regnal style of Philip and Mary (25 July 1554), see *Tudor Royal Proclamations*, eds. Hughes and Larkin, 2.45–6. For the iconic record in official documents, see Erna Auerbach, *Tudor Artists* (London, 1954), 96–101 and plates 28–33; and Richards, 'Mary Tudor as "Sole Quene"?', 915–19.

15. Three autograph versions of Mor's portrait are extant. My discussion of it is indebted to Joanna Woodall, 'An Exemplary Consort: Antonis Mor's Portrait of Mary Tudor', *Art History* 14 (1991), 192–224. Woodall contextualises Mor's portrait of Mary, and his clientage to both the Emperor Charles V and his son Philip, in terms of Habsburg diplomatic strategies and artistic tastes.

16. Adam Zwetkovich to the Emperor Maximilian, London, 4 June 1565; translated and printed in Victor von Klarwill, *Queen Elizabeth and Some Foreigners* (New York, 1928), 218.

17. See Woodall, 'An Exemplary Consort', 214–16.

18. See Karen Hearn, *Dynasties: Painting in Tudor and Jacobean England 1530–1630* (New York, 1996), 54–55; she continues that, 'in contrast to the contemporary full-length image by Hans Eworth ... which works within English pictorial conventions, the type of seated format and aspects of the costume link [Mor's painting] with a visual "genealogy" of Habsburg brides'.

19. Philip's favourite, Ruy Gómez de Silva, writing from England shortly after the King's arrival there, concluded a letter to the Emperor's Spanish Secretary as follows: 'To speak frankly with you, it will take a great God to drink this cup ... . I have made every preparation for doing my share; and the best of it is that the King fully realises that the marriage was concluded for no fleshly consideration, but in order to remedy the disorders of this Kingdom and preserve the Low Countries' (Ruy Gómez de Silva to Francisco de Eraso, from Winchester, 29 July 1554; trans. and printed in *Calendar of Letters, Despatches and State Papers Relating to the Negotiations Between England and Spain*, Vol. 13, July 1554–November 1558, ed. Royall Tyler (London, 1954), 6.

    On Philip's attitude towards his English marriage and his role in governing Marian England, see D.M. Loades, *The Reign of Mary Tudor* (London, 1979), 109–47, 211–51; and David Loades, 'Philip II and the Government of England', in *Law and Government under the Tudors*, eds. C. Cross, D. Loades and J.J. Scarisbrick (Cambridge, 1988), 177–94. In the latter study, Loades summarises that 'the whole pattern of Philip's involvement with England, and particularly after the failure of his dynastic hopes, indicates that he saw it primarily as a base and a source of supply for his perpetual struggle against France' ('Philip II and the government of England', 191).

20. By an unknown artist, and painted c. 1565–70, this portrait is catalogued as P.17 in Roy Strong, *Portraits of Queen Elizabeth I* (Oxford, 1963); it is reproduced with several other roughly contemporaneous examples in Roy Strong, *Gloriana: The Portraits of Queen Elizabeth I* (London, 1987), 58–61.

21. The paintings are catalogued as P.23 and P.24, respectively, in Strong, *Portraits of Queen Elizabeth I*; and discussed in Strong, *Gloriana*, 79–83. To my knowledge, both the dating and the attribution to Hilliard are unchallenged.

22. The Queen's answer to the Commons' petition, 28 January 1563; printed in *Proceedings in the Parliaments of Queen Elizabeth I*, ed. Hartley, 1.95.

23. David Loades, *Mary Tudor: A Life* (Oxford, 1989), 335. Loades cites no sources.

24. At the Queen's death, that fantasy was easily converted back into the doctrine of the king's immortal body politic, and made serviceable for Jacobean panegyric:

    See how our *Phoenix* mounts above the skies,
    And from the neast another *Phoenix* flyes,
    How happily before the change did bring
    A Mayden-*Queene*; and now a manly *King*.

    (I. L., *An Elegie upon the death of the high and renowned Princesse, our late Soveraigne ELIZABETH* [1603], reprinted in *Fugitive Tracts*, ed. W.C. Hazlitt, 2 vols. (privately printed, 1875), Vol. 2 [unpaginated].)

25. On 'the second reign of Elizabeth I', see the studies collected in *The Reign of Elizabeth I: Court and Culture in the Last Decade*, ed. John Guy (Cambridge, 1995) and especially the editor's Introduction, 'The 1590s: The Second Reign of Elizabeth I?', 1–19; also see McLaren, *Political Culture in the Reign of Elizabeth I*, 8–9, 159–60, 238–39.

   On the royal iconography of chastity and the Queen's association with the goddess Diana, see Philippa Berry, *Chastity and Power: Elizabethan Literature and the Unmarried Queen* (London, 1989); John N. King, 'Queen Elizabeth I: Representation of The Virgin Queen', *Renaissance Quarterly* 43 (1990), 30–74; Susan Doran, 'Juno versus Diana: The Treatment of Elizabeth I's Marriage in Plays and Entertainments, 1561–81', *Historical Journal* 38 (1995), 257–74; Helen Hackett, *Virgin Mother, Maiden Queen: Elizabeth I and the Cult of the Virgin Mary* (New York, 1995). Influential earlier studies include Elkin Calhoun Wilson, *England's Eliza* (1939; reprint London, 1966), 167–229; Frances Yates, *Astraea: The Imperial Theme in the Sixteenth Century* (London, 1975), 29–120; Roy Strong, *The Cult of Elizabeth: Elizabethan Portraiture and Pageantry* (London, 1977); and Strong, *Gloriana*.

26. For reproductions of details and analogues, a transcription and partial reconstruction of the sonnet inscribed on the canvas, and a commentary different from but complementary to my own, see Strong, *Gloriana*, 134–41. The painting takes its modern title from the placement of Elizabeth's feet in Oxfordshire, in the vicinity of Ditchley, which was the estate of Sir Henry Lee. Lee was a central figure in the development of Elizabethan tournaments and chivalric symbolism, and was the Queen's champion until his retirement from the tilt in 1590. He was also a major patron of Marcus Gheeraerts the Younger. The Queen visited Lee at Ditchley in 1592, and Strong surmises that the portrait was executed at about this time and in connection with this occasion; eighteenth-century visitors to Ditchley recorded seeing the painting there.

27. I have analysed this painting in detail in 'Idols of the Queen: Policy, Gender, and the Picturing of Elizabeth I', *Representations* 68 (Fall 1999), 108–61; see 139–48. Although the painting is undated and unsigned, there is general agreement that it must have been painted c. 1600–1603; there is no consensus as to the painter, although John de Critz, Marcus Gheeraerts the Younger and Isaac Oliver have all been suggested. See Strong, *Gloriana*, 156–61, for a detailed and important discussion of style and iconography, with illustrations of possible iconographic sources; also see Strong, *The Cult of Elizabeth*, 52–54. The painting is catalogued and its attributions and recorded history are discussed in E. Auerbach and C.K. Adams, *Paintings and Sculpture at Hatfield House* (London, 1971), 59–61. Strong reads the painting in relationship to John Davies's *Hymnes to Astraea* (1599), a cycle of lyrics in praise of the Queen, and suggests that Davies was responsible for the painting's programme. Davies also wrote related texts for royal entertainments sponsored by Sir Robert Cecil in 1602. The painting appears in the earliest Cecil family inventories, and is presumed to have been

commissioned by Sir Robert Cecil, Lord Burghley's second son and inheritor of his position as the Queen's Principal Secretary and closest adviser. The painting's connection to Cecil and to entertainments devised by Davies is elaborated in Mary C. Erler, 'Sir John Davies and the Rainbow Portrait of Queen Elizabeth', *Modern Philology* 84 (1987), 359–71. Erler establishes a relationship between the painting and two entertainments in 1602, at each of which the Queen was presented with the gift of a rich mantle; on this basis, she proposes that the painting probably dates from the last year of the Queen's life, although she does not rule out the possibility that it is posthumous.

Significant earlier discussions of the picture's iconography include Frances Yates, 'Allegorical Portraits of Queen Elizabeth I at Hatfield House' (1952), reprint in Yates, *Astraea*, 216–18; and René Graziani, 'The "Rainbow" Portrait of Queen Elizabeth I and its Religious Symbolism', *Journal of the Warburg and Courtauld Institutes* 35, 1972, 247–59. For a recent study of the painting as 'a political allegory, one whose religious dimensions underpin an iconographic representation of sovereign self-investiture', see Daniel Fischlin, 'Political Allegory, Absolutist Ideology, and the "Rainbow Portrait" of Queen Elizabeth I', *Renaissance Quarterly* 50, 1997, 175–206; quotation from 177.

28. The continental traveller, Paul Hentzner, observed of Elizabeth in 1598 that 'her bosom was uncovered, as all the English ladies have it, till they marry', see *Paul Hentzner's Travel in England during the Reign of Queen Elizabeth*, trans. Horace, Earl of Oxford (London, 1797), 34.

29. See 'My *Notes* and *Remembraunces*', in Sir John Harington, *Nugae Antiquae*, ed. H. Harington, 3 vols. (1779; reprint Hildesheim, 1968), 2, 223.

30. On the popularity of this cult in pre-Reformation England, see Eamon Duffy, *The Stripping of the Altars: Traditional Religion in England 1400–1580* (New Haven, 1992), 264.

31. *The Wonderful Year* (1603), in Thomas Dekker, *Selected Prose Writings*, ed. E.D. Pendry (Cambridge, Mass., 1968), 33.

32. The phrase 'A Virgin Mother and a Maiden Queene' occurs in the anonymous elegy, 'Singultientes Lusus', printed in *Sorrowes Joy; or, A Lamentation for our late deceased Soveraigne Elizabeth, with a triumph for the prosperous Succession of our gratious King James* (1603), reprint in John Nichols, *The Progresses, Processions, and Magnificent Festivities of King James the First*, 4 vols. (1828), 1, 15.

33. For the quotation from Roy Strong, see *Gloriana*, 136.

34. Thus, if the attribution of the 'Rainbow' portrait to either Gheeraerts or Oliver is correct, we must conclude that the painter was instructed to abandon his own style in order to conform to the alien style of Hilliard, and to the clear preferences of the Queen.

35. There is an illustrated, descriptive catalogue of miniatures and drawings by Oliver in Roy Strong, *Artists of the Tudor Court* (London, 1983), 97–116; and a profusely illustrated catalogue of portraits signed by or attributed to Gheeraerts the Younger in Roy Strong, *The English Icon*

(London, 1969), 269–304. On Oliver and the Queen, see Strong, *Artists of the Tudor Court*, 124–26, and *Gloriana*, 142–45. For a detailed description of Oliver's miniature of the Queen, see Jill Finsten, *Isaac Oliver: Art at the Courts of Elizabeth I and James I*, 2 vols. (New York, 1981), 2, 27–30. Both Strong and Finsten suggest that the unfinished state of the miniature may indicate that it was intended for use as a pattern, and both surmise that it may also have remained unfinished due to the dissatisfaction of the Queen. In any event, only one finished miniature is known that is derived from it, and even there the features have been softened; the same is true of the popular 1592 engraving by Crispin de Passe, which also apparently derives from Oliver's image. The several paintings of the Queen that derive her image from the 'Ditchley' portrait by Gheeraerts also soften her facial features. For reproductions of these paintings, see Strong, *Gloriana*, plates 142, 143, 152.

36. The draft for the proclamation is printed in *Tudor Royal Proclamations*, 2, 240–41; quotation from 240.

37. The *Acts of the Privy Council* record the following minute from 1596: 'A warrant for her Majesty's Serjeant Painter and to all publicke officers to yelde him their assistance touching the abuse committed by divers unskillfull artizans in unseemly and improperly paintinge, gravinge and printing of her Majesty's person and vysage, to her Majesty's great offence and disgrace of that beutyfull and magnanimous Majesty wherwith God hathe blessed her, requiring them to cause all suche to be defaced and none to be allowed but suche as her Majesty's Serjant Paynter shall first have sight of.' (*Acts of the Privy Council of England*, ed. J.R. Dasent, 32 vols. (London, 1890–1907), 26, 69).

38. On the 'mask of youth', see the following studies by Roy Strong: *Portraits of Queen Elizabeth I*, 94–97; *The Cult of Elizabeth*, 46–54; *Artists of the Tudor Court*, 126–32; *Gloriana*, 146–51. The Hilliard miniature in the jewelled locket is catalogued as M.21 in Strong, *Portraits of Queen Elizabeth I*; and is fully described in Strong, *Artists of the Tudor Court*, 128. Although primarily associated with miniatures, the 'mask of youth' is evident in such large-scale oil paintings as the 'Procession' picture and the 'Hardwick' portrait, both dating from around the turn of the century, as well as in the 'Rainbow' portrait. These paintings are catalogued as P.101, P.95 and P.100, respectively, in Strong, *Portraits of Queen Elizabeth I*.

39. Nicholas Hilliard, *A Treatise concerning the Arte of Limning*, eds. R.K.R. Thornton and T.G.S. Cain (Manchester, 1981), 86. For the sake of clarity, I have slightly modified the punctuation in this transcription. The treatise is apparently unfinished, and appears to have been drafted c. 1600.

40. John Clapham, *Certain Observations Concerning the Life and Reign of Queen Elizabeth*, 97.

41. Quotation from John Hayward, *Annals of the First Four Years of the Reign of Queen Elizabeth*, ed. John Bruce (1840; reprint New York, 1968), 15.

42. See *Thomas Platter's Travels in England 1599*, trans. Clare Williams, London, 1937, 192; and 'Diary of the Journey of Philip Julius, Duke of Stettin-Pomerania, Through England in the Year 1602', ed. Gottfriend von Bülow, *Transactions of the Royal Historical Society* (new series) 6 (1892), 1–67, quotation from 53 (emphasis added).

43. Giovanni Carlo Scaramelli, Venetian Secretary in England, to the Doge and Senate, London, 19 February 1603; translated and printed in *Calendar of state papers and manuscripts relating to English affairs, existing in the archives and collections of Venice, and in other libraries of Northern Italy*, eds. Rawden Brown et al., 9 vols. (London, 1864–98), 9, 531.

44. See *The Diary of John Manningham of the Middle Temple, 1602–1603*, ed. R.P. Sorlien (Hanover, New Hampshire, 1976), 188.

45. John Clapham, *Certain Observations Concerning the Life and Reign of Queen Elizabeth*, 96.

46. See: Henry Chettle, *Englandes Mourning Garment*, E2, quoted in Ben Jonson, ed. C.H. Herford, P. Simpson, and E. Simpson, 11 vols. (Oxford, 1925–51), 1.166; and 'Ben Jonson's Conversations with William Drummond of Hawthornden', in Jonson, *Ben Jonson*, ed. Herford and Simpson, 1.141–42.

47. Godfrey Goodman, *The Court of James I*, ed. J.S. Brewer, 2 vols. (London, 1839), 1.164.

5

Royal Flesh, Gender and the Construction of Monarchy

Rachel Weil

The title of this volume invites three questions. First, *why queens*? In other words, what can we say about the queen's body that is not also true of the king's body, and what insights are to be gained by focusing on queens rather than kings? Second, *which queens*? What were the differences between the bodies of queens regnant and queens consort, queens in absolutist monarchies and queens in constitutional ones, queens who give birth and those who don't? Finally, *which bodies*? How does Kantorowicz's famous account of the difference between the body natural and the body politic apply to the case of queens?

In her groundbreaking 1997 book, *Scenes from the Marriage of Louis XIV*, Abby Zanger poses some intriguing answers to the first and third of these questions. She argues that the mortal and fleshly body of monarchy, identified with the body of the queen, can contribute to the construction rather than the deconstruction (or destruction) of royal power. She thus questions what has been a central assumption in the pioneering feminist work of Lynn Hunt and Sarah Maza on the body of Marie Antoinette. Both Hunt and Maza describe the Queen's body as a point of attack upon the institution of monarchy, a site of corruption and an opportunity for denigration. Their assumption, then, is that flesh is somehow antithetical to monarchy; that royal power somehow relies upon covering up the fact that royal persons are mortal. The same assumption seems also to be present in models of French absolutism which emphasise the superhuman powers with which the monarch was invested by virtue of his identification with a perpetual, immortal body. Again, Zanger points out, royal mortal bodies play no positive role in this account. She seeks to restore the balance by investigating the body of the queen consort, the Spanish infanta Maria Teresa who was married to Louis XIV in 1660. The queen's body in this case is by definition mortal and fleshly; to transcend mortal flesh would after all defeat the purpose of a royal wedding, which is sexual reproduction. In the marriage, then, the fleshly body must somehow be acknowledged, made visible, and united with the body of the king; such a process, Zanger suggests, may risk compromising the king's immortality, but ultimately, because the king's body successfully assimilates that which contradicts it, it enhances royal power at a symbolic level.[1]

I mention Zanger's book here for two reasons. First, as a historian of political culture in late Stuart England, Zanger's project of asking what royal mortal flesh, as opposed to the immortal royal dignity, can do *for* the power of monarchs or the legitimation of monarchy as an institution is very fruitful for me. Royal flesh was much discussed in the late seventeenth and early eighteenth centuries. My own work has explored the meaning of that discussion in, for example, the political pornography of Charles II's reign, which provided graphic images of the king's sexual doings, or in the 'bedchamber narratives' which purported to give insider accounts of the health, inclinations and emotions of Queen Anne. In both cases I have emphasised, first, the fictionality of these accounts – that is, the fact that they are about the 'real' body does not make them less mythic – and second, the usefulness of the fictions to those who produced them. Insofar as they allowed others to manipulate royal images to their own ends, they made monarchy more rather than less secure as an institution.

But although I find Zanger's questions to be close to my own, her work also underscores for me the importance of context: queens' bodies do not mean the same thing everywhere, because royal power does not operate or legitimate itself in the same way everywhere. Zanger's arguments and insights cannot be directly applied to the English case, for reasons that lie in the differences between the English and French polities in the early modern period.

First, and most obviously, England had no equivalent of the French Salic law; whereas French queens by definition were queens consort (or queen mothers), unable to rule in their own right because of the Salic law barring women from the throne, England had queens who ruled in their own right , and who, coincidentally, were not mothers. These included Mary I (r. 1553–58) Elizabeth I (r. 1558–1603), Mary II

(r. 1689–95) Queen Anne (r. 1702–14). The queens regnant were clearly distinguished from the queens consort (the six wives of Henry VIII, Anne of Denmark, Henrietta Maria, Catherine of Braganza, Mary of Modena), although one of them, Mary II, who was part of a monarch known as *William-and-Mary*, was oddly in the position of being monarch and consort at once. Because queens sometimes ruled in their own right, the gendering of the two bodies was less clear in the English than in the French case, and female flesh was even more tightly mixed up with monarchy than it is in Zanger's account of the royal marriage. In the case of the French royal marriage, as Zanger describes it, there was a rough dichotomy between king/male/immortal body and consort/female/mortal body. This is not to say the dichotomy was stable, and Zanger explores its instability with great subtlety. Nonetheless, female was coded mortal or fleshly in the French royal marriage ceremony, and this equation of woman and flesh was buttressed by centuries of cultural tradition in the West.[2] Zanger's description of the body of the queen consort in France thus underscores the peculiar situation of a queen regnant (as opposed to a married king regnant) in England: the female and mortal flesh to which she was indissolubly united was her own, not that of a spouse.

A second difference between the French and English cases is that of political organisation and culture. Without wishing to repeat early modern clichés about English liberty, it is fair to say that English monarchs never achieved the centralised, 'absolutist' power of Louis XIV.[3] By reign of two latter early modern queens, Mary II and Anne, the English polity was self-consciously non-absolutist, defining itself against the 'tyranny' of the French system. Historians of England have emphasised the manifold ways in which the very fiction of the king's two bodies has served to *limit* rather than enhance the power of actual living monarchs. Marie Axton, for example, has shown how the Roman Catholic jurist Plowden, in the reign of Elizabeth I, used the fiction that 'the king never dies' to make a case for the succession of the Catholic Mary Stuart to the throne. Mary's claims were blocked by the will of Henry VIII, which had stipulated that Stuarts be barred from the throne of England. But, Plowden argued ingeniously, Henry VIII's will was not valid, because Henry VIII had never died. In this case, the fiction of monarchical immortality was used to frustrate the desires of the dead monarch, Henry VIII, and the living one, Elizabeth I (who of course also did not want to recognise Mary Stuart's claims).[4] For

Ernst Kantorowicz, the existence of an immortal body was ultimately the basis for constitutionalism: it was in the name of the immortal king, after all, that parliament declared war on the person of Charles Stuart:

> Without those clarifying, if sometimes confusing distinctions between the King's sempiternity and the king's temporariness, between his immaterial and immortal body politic and his material and mortal body natural, it would have been next to impossible for Parliament to resort to a similar fiction and summon, in the name and by the authority of Charles I, King body politic, the armies which were to fight the same Charles I, king body natural.[5]

For Kantorowicz, fictions about the immortal body of the monarch were not necessarily created by monarchs, but by other people seeking to justify something. That is why his book pays such loving attention to the distinct manifestations of the 'body politic' – that is, to the differences between the *Crown* (or collective powers of the government), the *Dignity* (the *corporation sole*, consisting of a line of kings over time), the *corpus mysticum* (or that to which the king is married as Christ is married to the Church), and the population of the state imagined as a body of which the king is the head. For Kantorowicz, the 'body politic' of the king was not a coherent, unified concept: rather, there were so many versions of the body politic because there were so many uses to which the notion of the king's two bodies was put.

The observation that the monarch's possession of a body politic might in some cases act as a check or limit on his or her power makes Zanger's question once again extremely pertinent. How would the monarch's possession of a 'body natural' actually enhance or construct royal power?

I take it as given here that the body natural is as much of a fantasy as the body politic. And it is a vehicle of political argument, but mobilised in a different way. Stories of the body natural take for granted the weakness, vulnerability, mortality, uncontrollability and passions of their subject, but they do not give any access to the actual literal body of the monarch.

As I have argued in previous work, stories about the body natural of the monarch became an important dimension of political discourse. In Charles II's reign, for example, tales of the King's sexual adventures provided a complex language for talking about the paradoxically simultaneous threats of royal tyranny and royal impotence. Charles's overactive penis was equated with his overmighty sceptre: that is, he was a tyrant. And at the same time, Charles's sexuality was presented as exhausting him, draining his fluids, and exposing him to infection or poisoning at the hands of Roman Catholic French whores, agents of the King of France who sought to dominate English king and English nation alike. While such stories contained implicit criticisms of Charles II's behaviour, they were not attacks on monarchy; rather, they contributed to a resacralisation rather than a desacralisation of the monarch's body precisely through their intense concern with it and expression of a desire to protect it, and thus held the criticisms made firmly within the framework of ideological royalism.[6] Rendering visible (or alluding to) the mortality of a monarch, as Zanger says, need not tear down monarchy as an institution.

Two further observations should be made about the political pornography of Charles II's reign. First, it is very hard to pull the two bodies of the king apart analytically. Charles's mortality and vulnerability were emphasised, but they were not confined to his private self; it was precisely in his vulnerability that he was identified with the equally vulnerable nation. Second, although the specific implications of Charles's maleness were never explicitly discussed in writings of the period, assumptions about masculine sexuality informed the discourse and structured its poetics. The notion that male sexual ejaculation is at once an expression of power and a diminution of power (because the loss of vital fluids weakens the body) made possible the portrayal of Charles as simultaneously too powerful and too weak. Charles's maleness also explains something that, strikingly, no one to this day seems to think needs explanation: that the authors of virtually all political pornography of the type I am describing were men. It would be hard to imagine a way for a woman to write about Charles's body. Rules about what women could say about male sexuality were operative though unacknowledged in Restoration political pornography.

Both of these observations apply to early modern English queenship. The first – that the two bodies are hard to separate – is perhaps counterintuitive. It is something of a commonplace that queens were able to rule because their immortal bodies compensated for the disability (femaleness) attached to their mortal ones. Thus, Elizabeth was 'King Elizabeth', and had 'the heart and stomach of a king'. However, as Carole Levin among others has perceptively noted, Elizabeth was never a purely masculine figure, but somehow both 'king and queen' at once, sometimes using her sex as an ideological and diplomatic tool.[7] Mary II's femaleness was also central to representations of her, most of which stressed her status as a wife.[8] It would be unrealistic to imagine that a queen's subjects failed to notice that their ruler was female. The mortal body of the queen (or king) was not trumped, pulverised or rendered entirely irrelevant by its union with the eternal body of the sovereign. Its particular qualities were visible, and symbolically powerful. It could be detached from and reattached to the monarch's political persona in complex ways, in accordance with political needs.

The second point – that gender was present though unacknowledged in discussions of royal flesh – is also equally true of English queens regnant. Their biological sex, though usually not openly discussed, was mobilised to make certain kinds of stories plausible. My example here is Queen Anne. Women as well as men wrote about Anne, in marked contrast to Charles II's case. Moreover, although very few claims about Anne centred overtly on gender (no one said, 'Anne is female, therefore X') images of Anne, positive and negative, rang the changes on the quality of 'tenderness'.

To understand the importance and meaning of Anne's 'tenderness', a brief digression is necessary on the political context in which tenderness was useful. Anne's reign was characterised by a 'pathological fear' of bedchamber favourites. Edward Gregg's definitive biography of Queen Anne provides a convincing explanation of why ministers, politicians and propagandists were so eager to regard the Queen as a political cipher. Anne, Gregg notes, was particularly determined to keep herself free from domination by either the Whig or the Tory party, or by her own ministers. To this end, she habitually encouraged politicians who were not part of her ministry, or who belonged to the party out of power, to visit her in private. Insofar as Anne's secret dealings with these politicians took place in her bedchamber, and insofar as the meetings were facilitated by female servants who controlled access, there was some truth to the idea that bedchamber women were powerful. But it was the Queen, and not the female favourites, who called the shots.[9]

Thus, expressions of anxiety about the influence of a female favourite usually came from those currently in office who expressed frustration at their lack of more complete and secure control. Anne's Whig friend, the Duchess of Marlborough, for example, was attacked at precisely the moment when Anne disappointed Tory expectations that she would definitively suppress occasional conformity. The roles were reversed in 1707 and 1708, when Anne's reluctance to appoint Whigs to the cabinet, and her appointment of Tory bishops, caused her Whig ministers to wonder at her resistance. They concluded that she was subject to the 'secret influence' of her new favourite, Abigail Masham. Ministers and party politicians developed fantasies of the power of bedchamber favourites because such fantasies allowed them to ignore the basic structural contradiction of their situation. It was essential for any politician hoping to gain the trust of the Queen to proclaim his independence of party loyalty. But all of the Queen's ministers (Marlborough and Godolphin on the Whig side, Harley and Bolingbroke on the Tory side) were compelled to ally themselves with, respectively, Whigs and Tories. By exaggerating the influence of bedchamber women, the ministers resolved the contradiction between maintaining their own identities as virtuous and disinterested royal servants and engaging in precisely the kind of partisan politicking that they had promised to help the Queen to stamp out. The belief in the influence of favourites also allowed them to avoid the truth that they did not want to admit: that Anne was herself trying to be independent of them.[10]

The problem facing Anne's ministers was how to explain Anne's decisions as the result of pressure, without seeming to wish to simply exert pressure themselves. The notion that Anne was 'tender' helped them to do so. Bedchamber narratives emphasised Anne's 'tenderness'. Indeed, she was downright squishy. To be tender meant, first of all, to be permeable, open to pressures and influences of the external environment, lacking inner density. In that sense, 'tenderness' drew on an age-old Aristotelian view of the female constitution as soft, cold and wet rather than hard, hot and dry. In his analysis of the causes of Anne's death, the Queen's Whig physician, David Hamilton, explained that Anne died because the 'gouty humour' located in her knee and foot was 'translated' to her brain. This 'translation' was made possible by the 'preparatory sinking of her spirits and weakness of her nerves' that had, apparently, been brought about by political events. At the beginning of the reign, Anne's health had been good, because a 'succession of pleasures' (such as her victories against Louis XIV) had 'undoubtedly refreshed her mind, and strengthened her spirits'. But in the last seven years of the reign (1707 onwards) 'there happened a succession of disquiets, which by grieving her mind, made her less able to resist outward impressions and importunities, a compliance with which has loaded the latter part of her life, with reflections, and her memory with reproaches; and by impairing her health and weakening her nerves, rendered them less able to resist this last translation of the gout, which was the cause of her sudden death'.[11] The disquiets were both personal and political: the rise of the Tory Robert Harley, the fall of the Whig ministers Marlborough and Godolphin, and Anne's loss of her subjects' love through the shameful Peace of Utrecht and her Tory ministers' flirtation with the Pretender. Anne's physical, personal and political troubles were, for Hamilton, closely related and mutually reinforcing: her ill health led her to abdicate responsibility to evil advisers, which in turn led her to make bad political decisions, thereby damaging her health.

Thus, for David Hamilton, Anne' s tenderness was an excuse to exert pressure. He was in a position to do so. Hamilton was a court insider, and one of the only Whigs who had access to the Queen after the fall of the Whig ministry. But having condemned, as her doctor, those who made the Queen uneasy by pressuring her, he had to explain that his form of pressure was designed to make her 'easy'. He did so by painting the Queen as someone who was *so* susceptible to pressure that she needed to have counter pressure applied in order to make her do what she had really wanted to do all along. When Anne criticised Godolphin in Hamilton's presence, Hamilton took it as evidence that the Queen had been under pressure from the Tories. It was, he wrote,

> a plain demonstration, of the success of outward endeavor to impress the Queen against him [i.e. Godolphin] and that though there had been a great disquieting struggle between her own inclinations, and the force of outward pressure, yet she was a yielding. For to my own personal knowledge, her natural calmness, was such, that a continued teasing, as she termed it herself, would make her yield, unless she stood in the middle between the teasings of two different sorts, and then her affection and personal respect would cast the balance between the two advisors, as is the common temper of a good natural disposition.[12]

Hamilton's elaborate narrative about the Queen's health and emotions reconciled a number of contradictions. He could distinguish between those who 'made the Queen easy' and those who 'teased and pressured her', while justifying the pressure he himself exerted. He could devote himself to the welfare of the Queen's private body, appearing to cordon it off from the hurly-burly of party struggle, while carrying out party agendas in the Queen's bedchamber.

The Queen's almost literally physical 'tenderness' was also, when inflected by her femaleness, a quality that allowed (Whig) politicians to achieve a delicate and otherwise improbable combination of praise and criticism of the Queen, a feat which in turn enabled them to present Anne's death as a welcome relief without seeming to have wanted it in the first place. Mourning the best of queens while cheering her demise was no easy task, but writers were able to exploit the fact of Anne's sex to create narratives that obscured the contradictory nature of their claims. The key to their strategy was the fact that 'tenderness', when embodied in a woman, was a multivalent, morally ambiguous quality. When it took the form of compassion, tenderness was generally praiseworthy. It was thus used by opponents of the war of the Spanish succession, for example, to explain Anne's decision to sign the peace of Utrecht in 1713.[13] But 'tenderness' could also be understood in a more negative way, as 'easiness', a desire to please people. 'Easiness', of course, might have a positive connotation: it was related to civility and politeness, and was for theorists of politeness in the early eighteenth century the quality that made women a civilising influence. But moralists frequently saw a danger: too much easiness threatened a women's virtue and reputation. Thus Halifax, in his *Advice to a Daughter* (1688) , warned that 'civility' and 'easiness' could destroy reputation:

> Therefore nothing is with more care to be avoided, than such a kind of civility as may be mistaken for invitation; and it will not be enough for you to keep yourself free from any criminal engagements; for if you do that which either raiseth hopes or createth discourse, there is a spot thrown upon your good name.[14]

The simultaneously positive and negative connotations of easiness were a perfect vehicle for those who wished to explain Anne's behaviour as the result of outside pressures without appearing to insult the Queen. Joseph Smith described the Queen as having 'tenderness to a fault' in relation to both her people and ministers.

> So far from invading the public rights of the community ... she seemed rather inclined to give up her own. [She was] so far from avenging the injuries, indignities, and insults thrown upon her, that she rejoiced in the

happiness and prosperity of all about her, even of those whose party prejudice, pride and ambition ... made them forget they were either servants, or subjects.[15]

The diary of David Hamilton showed a similar confusion about what to praise and what to blame. In the entry for 29 December 1711, Hamilton said that he had advised the Queen to discipline her ministers and commented on the personality trait which inhibited her from doing so. Anne was

a pattern of patience, and her bearing so much turned her into a subject to be afraid, instead of a queen to cause terror in others. This I can demonstrate by letting the whole world know, that she even denied her own inclinations, that she might not provoke those about her, and so by the provocations be made uneasy in her own mind.[16]

In a defence of Anne's character written after her death, Hamilton described her as possessed of 'civility and good breeding', having 'a mind pious towards God, willing to please all its fellow creatures', and desiring 'to make all her subjects easy, instead of reproaching them, as they have done her. I have stood in amaze myself, to hear her make excuses for others'.[17]

Although the first passage was an analysis of the causes of Anne's political problems, while the second was meant as praise of her character, they said essentially the same thing. Anne's patience, her solicitude for others, was the quality that allowed the ministers to destroy her reputation; but it also vindicated her from whatever charge it was that was levelled at her in reputation-destroying fashion.

The link between tenderness, easiness, dangers to female reputation also provided a way of expressing relief at Anne's death without blaming her for the loss of reputation that had brought it about. To say that Anne's reputation had been damaged was not to say she was guilty of anything except the loss of reputation. It was widely recognised that reputation was about public appearance and perception: a good reputation was not the same thing as true virtue and innocence. Yet, it was also recognised that the distinction was for all practical purposes moot. Women were responsible for reputations as well actual behaviour. The penalty for losing one's reputation, even if innocent of actual wrongdoing (as Samuel Richardson's *Clarissa* was to show) was death.

Post-mortem narratives about Queen Anne eerily echo the cautionary tales presented in contemporary advice literature, and carry the same moral ambiguity. Anne was said to have lost her reputation and suffered dishonour. For her damaged reputation, moreover, Anne was simultaneously blameworthy and innocent. The Whig Charles Povey exploited the connection between lost reputation and death to convey a double message about the nature of the Queen's guilt: although he affirmed her innocence, the innocence was only established by her death, which in turn was presented as an expiation of her sins. As Anne awoke to the 'ill prospect of affairs', Povey tells us, she was

> taken with very violent fits that seized on her spirits and nerves; so that she could not live three months longer, to see herself betrayed and her kingdoms involved in civil war, and foreign troops ... coming over to engage in the grand combat.

> To prevent this, her Majesty's sacred life fell as a victim. For she is now stripped into a naked spirit, and set on shore in the invisible world where that divine ray, I mean her soul, dwells in bright regions of light and glory, and is not to answer for the late, base treaty of peace ... though signed by her own hand.

> As the change is happy to the queen by being released from sighs, sorrows and tears; so I am sure the advantage is great to Europe.[18]

Thanks to the elusive nature of guilt when discussed within the framework of reputation, no one could be blamed for being glad Anne was dead, yet Anne could be mourned and exonerated.

So far I have discussed the way that other people made use of stories about the Queen's body. But it must also be added that Queen Anne herself was capable of putting her own mortal body – her desires, frailties, and emotions – into the public eye to achieve her own political goals. In 1710, she successfully won her battle to determine the personnel of her own bedchamber, marshalling parliament to prevent a Whig move to remove the Tory favourite Abigail Masham from her bedchamber by asserting that she could 'love whom she pleased'. Ironically, by proclaiming and drawing attention to her mortal body, Anne was waging political war. She not only found a way to keep a Tory in her bedchamber, and thus maintain access to Tory politicians to counterbalance pressures from her Whig ministry; she also publicly embarrassed the Duke and Duchess of Marlborough, who had led the attack on Masham. The demand that Masham be removed was made to look like an intolerable intrusion into the Queen's private life, and that the Marlboroughs sought it was presented as a first step in their scheme to usurp all royal authority. As the Tory *Letter to the Examiner* described it, they had attempted to 'take that privilege from her [Anne], which the meanest of her subjects enjoy, and slavery was to pursue her even to her bedchamber'.[19] The more Anne made reference to her mortal body, the more powerful in this case her political position became.

I have argued in this paper that royal flesh, the mortal body of the monarch, was useful to monarchy as an institution; sometimes it was used by the monarch, sometimes by writers using particular images of the monarch to buttress particular political arguments or legitimate themselves as political actors. I do not believe that this statement is necessarily more true of female than of male royal flesh. Nonetheless, I have also argued that the monarch's gender mattered to the way in which this process occurred. It may be possible that the relation between the monarch's two (or three or four) bodies was differently configured in the case of queens than of kings, simply because it was traditionally harder to remove women from their own flesh. And it is certainly true that female flesh had different connotations and capacities from male flesh – it is hard to imagine writers handling a king's tenderness or a queen's sexual prowess in the same way as they handled Anne's and Charles II's physical qualities. But the monarch's mortal body, I have also insisted, was a product of politics as much as biology, and it was to be found as much in the minds, needs and ambitions of those who imagine it as it was in the monarch's physical flesh.

Notes

1. Abby E. Zanger, *Scenes from the Marriage of Louis XIV: Nuptial Fictions and the Making of Absolutist Power* (Stanford, 1997); Lynn Hunt, 'The Many Bodies of Marie Antoinette' and Sarah Maza, 'The Diamond Necklace Affair Revisited', in *Eroticism and the Body Politic*, ed. Lynn Hunt (Baltimore, 1991).
2. A classic scholarly account is Ian Maclean, *The Renaissance Notion of Woman* (Cambridge, 1980).

3. This is not to deny that our picture of French absolutism has been importantly modified by William Beik, who shows the extent to which royal authority depended upon local co-operation. See his *Absolutism and Society in Seventeenth-century France* (Cambridge, 1985). Nonetheless, the English monarchy can be said to have been relatively 'weaker' than the French, insofar as it lacked a standing army and insofar as representative institutions (parliament) continued to operate on a national scale.

4. Marie Axton, *The Queen's Two Bodies: Drama and the Elizabethan Succession* (London, 1977).

5. Ernst Kantorowicz, *The King's Two Bodies: a Study in Medieval Political Theology* ([1957] Princeton, 1981), 20–21.

6. Rachel Weil, 'Sometimes a Sceptre is Only a Sceptre: Pornography and Politics in Restoration England', in *The Invention of Pornography*, ed. Lynn Hunt (New York, 1993).

7. Carole Levin, *The Heart and Stomach of a King: Elizabeth I and the Politics of Sex and Power* (Philadelphia, 1994).

8. See Rachel Weil, *Political Passions: Gender, the Family and Political Argument in England 1680–1714* (Manchester, 1999), chapter 4.

9. Edward Gregg, *Queen Anne* (London, 1984), especially 181, 197–98, 403–4. See also Philip Roberts, *The Diary of Sir David Hamilton 1703–14* (Oxford, 1975), introduction; Robert Bucholz *The Augustan Court: Queen Anne and the Decline of Court Culture* (Stanford, 1993), 156–88.

10. These arguments are developed at length in Weil, *Political Passions*, chapters 7 and 8.

11. Roberts, *Diary of Sir David Hamilton*, 3–4.

12. Ibid., 7.

13. *Memoirs of the Conduct of her Late Majesty and her Last Ministry, Relating to the Separate Peace with France. By the Right Hononrable* [sic] *the Countess of* ——- (London, 1715).

14. George Savile, Marquess of Halifax, *Advice to a Daughter* [1689], printed in Walter Raleigh ed., *The Complete Works of George Savile, First Marquess of Halifax* (Oxford, 1912), 28.

15. Joseph Smith, *The Duty of the Living to the Memory of the Dead* (London, 1714), 6–7.

16. Roberts, *Diary of Sir David Hamilton*, 35.

17. Ibid., 68.

18. Charles Povey, *An Inquiry into the Miscarriages of the Last Four Years Reign* (London, 1714), 7–8.

19. *Letter to the Examiner* (London, 1710), 13.

Part II

Transgressing the Body Natural

6

What the King Saw in the Belly of the Beast or How the Lion Got in the Queen

Allegories of Royal Procreation in the 1622 Royal Entry into Lyon

Abby E. Zanger

In October 1622, Anne of Austria, Queen of France, and the Queen Mother, Marie de Medicis, travelled to the city of Lyon to join the King, Louis XIII, who had just completed a seven-month military campaign against the Huguenots in southern France. These campaigns culminated in the retaking of Montpellier and a treaty with the Protestant nobility.[1] As was usual when a monarch visited a city, Lyon staged an elaborate entry for the king.[2] The event of 11 December was organised around the theme 'Le Soleil au Signe du Lyon', a not so subtle conceit justified by the name of the city, Lyon, and the fact that Louis's July conquests had occurred under the astrological sign of the lion. Running through this conceit was another leitmotif, one that seems particularly interesting in the context of this volume of essays on queens' bodies: the reiteration at various points throughout the entry iconography that Lyon had been the site of Louis XIII's conception. This essay focuses on the curious constellation of images concerning conception that emerge in the entry literature. Indeed, metaphors of conception provide a particularly interesting optic from which to consider the representation of the queen's body, both because conception was seen as playing a central role in preserving the dynasty and because of the way contemporary notions of procreation positioned the woman as liminal insofar as conception was seen as an activity animated by virile, male matter that took place inside a female receptacle.[3] In what follows I shall be arguing that representations of the queen's body will serve very much as receptacle in the entry literature, where representations of the queen provide a pretext for a larger political struggle occurring between king and city in the entry ritual. I shall also suggest that it is only in understanding how the queen's body is deployed in this literature that one can fully understand the symbolic and political meaning of the entry reporting.[4]

Indeed it is the reporting of the entry that concerns me primarily in this discussion, and not the historical event as it may have actually occurred, were such a reality even possible to relate. It is thus necessary to begin with a brief overview of the sources used here, namely two illustrated folio accounts of the entry, both published in Lyon within two years of the event. One, referred to largely in the second half of this discussion, was published in 1623, under the title *RECEPTION DE TRES-CHRESTIEN,TRES-IUSTE, ET TRES-VICTORIEUX MONARQUE LOUIS XIII. Roy de France & de Navarre, premier Compte & Chanoine de l'Eglise de Lyon et De tres-chrestienne, Tres auguste, & Tres-vertueuse Royne ANNE D'AUSTRICHE: Par Messieurs les Doyen, Chanoines, & Comtes de Lyon, en leur Cloistre & Eglise, le XI. Decembre, M. DCXXII* (Lyon: Jaques Roussin, 1623). This sixty-seven-page text focuses primarily on the last entry monument and on the reception in the church at the end of the entry, including the presentation of gifts. It also includes a description of the fireworks and dramatic presentations staged in the evening and days after the entry. The other source, referred to primarily in the first part of this discussion, was published a bit later, in 1624, in multiple editions, under variations of the title *L'ENTREE DU ROY ET DE LA ROYNE dans sa ville de Lyon: ou LE SOLEIL AU SIGNE DU LYON. D'OU SONT TIREES QUELQUES PARALLELES AVEC LE tres-Chrestien, tres Juste, & tres-Victorieux Monarque LOUYS XIII, Roy de France & de Navarre. Ensemble un sommaire recit de tout ce qui s'est passé de remarquable en ladite Entree de sa Majesté,& de la plus Illustre Princesse de la Terre, Anne d'Austriche, Royne de France & de Navarre, dans sa Ville de Lyon le 11. decembre 1622* (Lyon, Chez Jean Jullieron, 1624). At 187 pages, it is considerably longer than *La Reception*. It contains a brief introduction, the texts of speeches given by city dignitaries on the morning of the entry, and descriptions of all twelve entry monuments; it does not describe the final ceremonies, gifts, fireworks, or other later dramatic presentations. Note that this text presents itself in opposition to *La Reception*, declaring it is the true and correct version of the events in its preface. Despite these differences, the conceit of the 'Sun in the Sign of the Lion' and the recurrent mention of conception are central organising themes in both volumes. These themes are, furthermore, unique to the Lyon entry. They do not appear in descriptions of entries Louis XIII made into other cities, such as Arles, Avignon and even Paris during this period, although there are passing wishes for a long-awaited dauphin expressed in some of those texts.[5]

We turn now to the entry proper. Its organising principle is presented in the first pages of the folio produced in 1624 under the title *ENTREE DU ROY ET DE LA ROYNE dans sa ville de Lyon: ou LE SOLEIL AU SIGNE DU LYON*. The conceit runs as follows: the Sun, 'King of Planets' is visiting the cities of his kingdom, the signs of the Zodiac, and has arrived at the Lion/'Signe du Lyon' (4). The Sun (i.e. the King) shares a special affinity with this sign/city and each of the twelve entry monuments offers another dimension of Louis' leonine and solar qualities, the beauty and purity of his spirit, his strength and courage, his wisdom, clemency, piety, and so forth, such that the affinities between the solar King (of France) and that of beasts seamlessly merge into a lionisation of Louis, his wife, *and* the city into which they were welcomed.

That is the basic frame of the entry allegory, which embellishes the relations between city and king as each monument embroiders aspects of his solar and leonine metaphors. Of particular interest for this discussion is a strand of this conceit that likens the relation between Sun and Lion to a marriage (between king and city). Marriage being a contractual relation in early modern Europe, it is not surprising that it would serve as an organising metaphor for a royal entry, a ritual deeply embedded in the adjudication of political relations between sovereigns and the cities into which they were welcomed.[6] In the Lyon entry description, however, the coupling of the King/Sun and Lion/City is expressed specifically in terms of fertility:

The Sun is recognised by the Ancients as the husband of the earth, all the more so because she derives her fertility from him. And if ever this Father of light pours his sweet influence into the breast of Nature, it is particularly when he is lodged in the sign of the Lion/Lyon, when we see ears of wheat ripen little by little, grapes and other fruits change their dead and dull complexion into a lively colour and sweet ripeness ...

Le Soleil est recognu des Anciens pour mary de la Terre, d'autant qu'elle emprunte de luy sa fecondité. Et si jamais ce Pere de lumiere verse ses douces influences dans le sein de la Nature, c'est lors particulierement qu'il est logé au Signe du Lyon, que nous voyons les espics de bled se dorer peu à peu, & les raisins, & autres fruicts, changer leur teint mort & terny en une vive coleur, & douce maturité ... (5–6)[7]

Here, following contemporary notions of procreation, the Sun/King provides the heat that animates the Earth/Lion. This figuration of the encounter between king and city threads throughout the entry monuments, in allusions increasingly sexual, as opposed to focusing on the contractual nature of marriage.

One good example of this tendency is the description of a figure in a painting on the first entry monument. The figure in question is a woman on a lion, described in the following manner:

This princess is the earth, The Sun is her husband, particularly when he is in the sign of the Lyon, which by the [fecond] heat that he communicates to his dear consort makes her happily birth the flowers, fruits, and crops, which fleck the fields, are heavy in the trees, & guild the country-side.

Cete Princesse est la terre, le Soleil est son espoux, particulierement lors qu'il est au Signe du Lyon, que par la feconde chaleur qu'il communique à sa chere espouse, il luy fait heureusement enfanter les fleurs, les fruicts, & les moissons, qui esmaillent les preries, chargent les arbres, & dorent les campagnes. (32)

Note here that the pairing of Louis and Lyon is again characterised as rich and fertile. Like the first example, this is also a pastoral image, recalling the similes of fertility after war of Virgil's *Eclogues*.[8] It again recalls Aristotelian principles of generation in which it is the male who provides the heat that energises the reproductive process, animating foetal matter in the cold and dry female.[9]

A similar scenario is presented in the fourth monument of the entry. There the pastoral motif is transformed to a bestial one when the leonine city is depicted as literally heated up in Louis's presence, as he is in hers:

Lions, say the naturalists, never make such a parade of their forces, never display themselves in any season as so passionate and wild, & and as having so much knowledge of the excellence of their nature as when the Sun is in the sign that bears their name: & this great and powerful City never makes such a vigorous parade of its forces & doesn't believe it can arrive at a greater height of glory as when she considers herself in the midst of the most tender affections of her king, from which, alone, like the Lyon in the Sun, she takes her force, life, & the brilliant lustre of his/her glory.

... les Lyons, dient les Naturalistes, ne font jamais tant de parade de leurs forces, & ne se monstrent en aucune saison si furieux, & avoir tant de cognoissance de l'excellence de leur nature, que lors que le Soleil est au Signe qui porte leur nom: & cete grande & puissante Ville ne fait jamais plus puissamment parade des ses forces, & ne croit pouvoir arriver en l'apogee d'une plus grande gloire, que lors qu'elle se considere logee au milieu des plus tendres affections de son Roy, duquel seul, comme le Lyon du Soleil, elle prend sa force, sa vie, & le lustre brillant de sa gloire. (58)

In a striking invocation of a natural history of lions that the entry literature adapts from Aristotle via Pliny, the description proposes an explicitly sexual pairing between king and city, one that is focused less on the king's divine, then on his mortal, one might say, bestial urges. Note, however, that the pairing is homo-social. The city wife is a lion, not a lioness, thus capable of generating fertile heat according to Aristotelian notions of the humours. But the lion draws heat from the sun in whose 'tender affections he is lodged', suggesting his fertility is always derivative, feminised, if not female, in the presence of the king.

It is against this repetition of Lyon, or the lion as the perfect milieu or fallow field in which the king/sun might wish to roll around, that the entry reminds the reader that the very king it is welcoming into its city, 'nostre Soleil François', was conceived there, 'avoit esté conceu dans son Lyon' (14). This allusion glorifies the city, while it also seems to underscore a vexing political dilemma by recalling just how quickly Henri IV and Marie de Medici (present at the entry) conceived Louis XIII – more or less on their wedding eve in Lyon in December 1600. Unlike the fantasmatic coupling of the Sun in the sign of the Lion, or that of Henri and Marie, Anne and Louis's seven-year marriage was barren. Indeed Anne had suffered a miscarriage just before departing for Lyon. Nonetheless, or perhaps because of this bareness, the entry descriptions are full of wishes for a Dauphin.[10] This connection between the conception of the future king and Lyon was readily available in 1622. Rubens' Medicis cycle canvas, The *Marriage Consummated in Lyon*, offers one contemporary acknowledgment of this connection with its depiction of Marie and Henri as Jove and Juno hovering over a chariot pulled by two lions. On the lions are two cherubs, representing their future children and in the background is a cityscape of Lyon.[11] Another can be found in a pamphlet published either just before or at the same time as the entry, *L'Horoscope du Roy, Par lequel la Ville de Lyon pretend qu'ayant beu [sic] l'honneur de la Conception de sa Majesté, qu'elle est sa vraye Patrie & non le lieu de sa Naissance* (Lyon: Jean Jullieron, 1624) written by François Goujon, a Lyonnais lawyer and the municipal magistrate (*premier échevin*) who was involved in planning and executing the entry ceremonies.[12] More will be said about this text in the ensuing discussion.

We now turn, however, to what is probably the most intriguing treatment of conception found in the entry literature. It is found in the earlier folio produced for the entry, *LA RECEPTION DE TRES-CHRESTIEN,TRES-IUSTE, ET TRES-VICTORIEUX MONARQUE LOUIS XIII* (Lyon: Jaques Roussin, 1623). As noted above, this text largely discusses the end of the entry, describing the final monument and focusing most fully on the reception in the church following the procession, including the presentation of gifts. It also includes a description of the fireworks and dramatic presentations staged in the evening and in the days after the entry.[13] It is the description of the gifts and their exchange to which I draw your attention now, a description beginning on page 25 of the folio, titled separately as the 'BRIEFVE DESCRIPTION DES PRESENS faicts à leurs Maiestez par la Ville de Lyon, à cause de ladite Entree, comme encore du feu d'artifice, & batteau de la Royne'. It describes two approximately 10–inch-high solid-gold lions seated on square pedestals adorned by '*escussions*' or *blazons*, given to the king and queen. Unlike the monuments, which one must largely imagine via erudite descriptions and often incomplete woodcuts, detailed engravings are provided of the gifts (Figures 6.1 and 6.2). These items expand considerably on the curious coupling between Louis and Lyon that is alluded to in the entry itself.

While the entry ceremony stresses a broad range of the king's leonine attributes, the gift to the king (Figure 6.1) focuses on Louis's martial strengths in displaying what is described as 'the portrait of

Figure 6.1 Gift for the King Louis XIII (c. 1622).

Figure 6.2 Gift for the Queen Anne of Austria (c. 1622).

his Majesty, dressed as Jupiter, and the lighting bolt in his hand, with which he destroyed the Giants who had the presumption to want to scale the mountains and ascend to the inaccessible Heights of his authority./le portraict de sa Majesté, vestu en Jupiter, & le foudre en main, duquel il abbattoit les Geans, voulans par des montagnes de presomption mal entassees, escheller le Ciel inaccessible de son authorité' (*BRIEFVE DESCRIPTION*, 27). The story of Jupiter vanquishing the giants is a common baroque topos, as is the association of Jupiter with the king. Here, of course, the giants are also associated with the Protestant menace, a fact made clear in the text, which describes the king represented as Jupiter:

> where Your Majesty is represented as Jupiter, who with his thunderbolt puts down the arrogant rebellion of the Giants, who vainly raise their hopes and dare to make an attempt against the government of the world. Sire, we do not count on the gifts of your Majesty because everything belongs to him, but we consecrate this present to his valour and we admire even more this eminent virtue in his Majesty with which, beyond the martial titles of a great captain and of a conqueror of cities, he has acquired that of founder of public tranquillity and of Father of his people, by the peace he has given to his kingdom & we very humbly beseech your Majesty to make these clement effects felt by this city, granting us, by his goodness the demands contained in the notebook that necessity compels us to present, & our wishes will never be more ardent than in praying to God for his posterity and health.

> où V.M. est representee en Jupiter, lequel avec le foudre abbat l'orgueil & la rebellion des Geans, qui ensloient vainement leurs esperances, & osoient entreprendre sur le gouvernement du monde. SIRE, nous ne faisons pas estat de faire des dons à V.M. puis que tout est à elle, mais nous consacrons ce present à sa valeur, & admirons encore plus cete eminente vertu en V.M. avec laquelle outre les tiltres guerriers de foudre, & de preneur de villes, elle s'est acquise ceux de fondateur du repos public, & de Pere de son peuple, par la paix qu'elle a donné à son royaume, & supplions tres-humblement V.M. en faire ressentir les douces influences à cete Ville, nous accordant par sa bonté les demandes contenues au cahier, que la necessité nous contraint de presenter, & nos voeux ne seront jamais plus ardens qu'à prier Dieu pour sa prosperité & santé. (26)

The focal point of the image is not Zeus, however, but the giants. The banner declaring what has happened – 'His nigra ad Tartara

mittit / He sends these men to the Underworld' – seems to barely
hold back the mountains, which push inexorably upward, while one
giant on the far right even seems to be climbing towards Zeus.[14]
With the Protestants expelled from Montpellier and the signing of a
new treaty, one might expect a clearer image of triumph over the
forces of evil. This blason actually seems modelled on a 1620
woodcut depicting triumph over the Protestant menace (Figure 6.3).
The image on the lion, however, suggests threat, not victory.
Something is threatening to crawl up and strike Jupiter, but what?

The queen's statue provides insight into this danger and it is
interesting that the account devotes considerably more attention to
the queen's gift. It is described as follows: 'On the shield of the present
[offered to the queen] was a sleeping Queen, at the bottom of whose
stomach a crowned arm emerging from the clouds attached a medal
with the figure of a Lyon on it./Dans l'escusson du present faict à la
Royne, l'on voyoit une Royne dormante, aux bas de l'estomac de
laquelle, un bras couronné sortant des nuees attachoit une medaille,
portant la figure d'un Lyon' (27). Note the image turns from the
martial to the marital in showing not *the* queen, but *a* queen, not in
active combat, but passive, asleep. While she slumbers, an arm
reaches down and places a medallion on her stomach. The image of a
lion is inscribed on it. The printed account records the speech the
Presvost des Marchands makes to the queen in handing over the gift:

> Madam, Among the trophies of peace, born of the victorious arms of the
> King, the people have no longings nor wishes more ardent than to see their
> tranquillity affirmed by the blessings of a royal issue. We foretell in this
> present, that the City of Lyon is offering to Your Majesty, that which the
> whole world wishes for passionately. The Father of Alexander dreamed
> that he lay a golden medal on the Queen his wife, on which was engraved
> a figure of a Lion, which was interpreted and followed by the birth of a son
> who was in his time a Lion in courage, and the greatest Prince in the
> World; may our wishes obtain for you from the Heavens a long sweet
> marriage, and may a generous posterity carry to future centuries the
> tranquillity we taste under your Empire.

> MADAME, Parmy les triomphes de la paix, nez des victoirieuses armes du
> Roy, les peuples n'ont des voeux, ny des souhaits plus ardens, que de veoir
> leur repos affermy par les benedictions d'une lignee Royalle, nous
> presageons en ce present d'honneur, que la Ville de Lyon fait à V. M. ce que
> tout le monde souhaitte passionnément. Le pere du Grand Alexandre

Figure 6.3 Embleme de la Revolte des Huguenots contre le Roi (1620).

songea qu'il mettoit une medaille d'or à la Royne sa femme, où estoit gravee la figure d'un Lyon, ce qui fut interpreté, & suivy de la naissance d'un fils, qui a este en son temps un Lyon en courage, & le plus grand Prince de la Terre; puissent nos voeux obtenir du Ciel une longue duree aux Myrthes de son mariage, & qu'une genereuse posterité transporte aux siecles suivans les douceurs que nous goustons sous son Empire. (BRIEFVE DESCRIPTION, 28)

The story seems a straightforward wish for an heir and the Latin text surrounding the image – 'Haec Omina Reges Claros Signant / These omens signify illustrious kings' – seems to reinforce that idea. But perhaps there is more to the retelling of the opening of Plutarch's 'Life of Alexander'. In that narrative, the queen is cast under suspicion, as is the parentage of Alexander, when the king has a dream that he seals up the queen's womb. On the seal is engraved the figure of a lion. The king's counsellors offer the interpretation that he should watch closely over his wife. One oracle, however, gives the dream a more positive twist: the queen must be pregnant 'since men do not seal up what is empty'. Nonetheless, the story continues by recounting Philip's ongoing suspicions of his wife, especially when he spies a snake visiting her.[15] In Plutarch, Philip ultimately loses an eye for his indiscreet voyeurism. Nonetheless, when Alexander later goes off to war, his mother Olympias confides in him the secret of his divine conception, even while, Plutarch notes, she later repudiates this story. The entry folio sanitises the story, however, omitting not only the king's suspicions, but also the part where the queen dreams her womb is struck by a thunderbolt and then by fire everywhere.[16]

So what do we have in the entry's allusion to the dream of the lion? A tale of cuckoldry and castration neatly sanitised? A tale of divine parentage highlighting what is otherwise left unspoken? If this is the case, what is said or not said by the gift? The answer to this question may perhaps be found in reading between the two *blasons*. On the first sits the King/Jupiter. Out of the second emerges the crowned arm, no longer throwing a bolt of lighting, but certainly virile in inserting the lion/embryo into the sleeping queen.[17] With the depiction of this act of impregnation we certainly return to the unspoken question of the parentage of the offspring. We also might ponder the nature of the offspring. For while what is inserted into the queen is the arm of the man/king, what is inserted by the arm is the medal/embryo/lion. This is a process of dizzying *mise-en-abîme*. For not only does the image contain a medallion of a lion within a lion, but the interior medallion is being placed in the belly (or is that the breast) of the woman, herself in the belly of the beast. What we seem to have here are concentric circles of merging significance from beast to belly to b(r)east to belly yet again. That Anne might become pregnant in Lyon (if not in and of the lion) simply multiplies the repetition, or one might say repetition compulsion of the image, since it insists on what we have seen in the first folio, namely that Lyon is the place where dauphins are conceived in an eternally repeated cycle of civil qua bestial intervention. Such activities do not necessarily produce a dauphin, however. It seems they may spawn a lion. We might say here that the folio description of the gift has actually shifted Lyon from position of virago wife to that of sire and offspring.[18]

That this usurpation by Lyon of the position of sire and heir is, if not a *coup de foudre*, at least a blow of sorts, seems likely. For the sexual act that seems to impregnate the queen by sliding from one statue to the other, an act undertaken by Louis *qua* Zeus, incarnates Jupiter's uncontrollably avid sexuality – or rather, the avid desire of the city of Lyon whose lion serves not only as the womb for these acts, but, upon closer inspection, is actually in the process of devouring the entire scene. For if one looks at both statues, one notes that the *blasons* are laid out not just on the belly of the beast, but also in it. And if one examines the frame of the scene, one realises that it is not just the edge of the *blason*, but rather a mouth: at the very top of the shield are the upper lips of the lion, matched below with his lower lips, now apparently a gaping mouth. In slipping from wife to offspring, the lion seems to devour the royal family, usurping all the positions in a baroque *mise-en-scène* of incorporation that seems to underscore the very craft and power of the city to devise its own conceit (the perfect fantasy of auto-generation!).

What might we conclude about this series of allegories shifting around Lyon, Louis, Anne, and the as yet inconceivable dauphin, allegories that seem to alter and bend expected genealogies if not in favour of the royal couple, surely in favour of the city? First and foremost, we should recognise that this allegorical bite or act of, if not carnal incorporation, perhaps civic digestion, merges and repeats the sociopolitical gesture of the entry ritual. For if the entry is staged to celebrate and lionise the king, it is offered as a present, however coerced, to the royal couple. Both gift exchange, as Marcel Mauss has described the phenomenon, and the entry, as it has been treated by historians, are rituals that displace civic enmity, subsuming it in organised symbolic gestures.[19] What better symbol to utilise in such an instance than the lion, described in Pliny's *Natural History* (a much cited text in the entry folio) as 'the only big cat who shows mercy to its supplicants', that is, which is both ferocious and clement, which both bites and caresses.[20] The city leaders seem to have understood this affinity between lion, gift and entry. When handing the lions to the king and queen, they reminded them the gifts would not give them real riches, only symbolic ones: '[words of the *Prevost des Marchands*] such presents are not offered to enrich Kings, but to immortalise their glory and witness for posterity by these marks of obedience and affection, the sentiment and inclination that the people have for their Majesties ... / tels presens ne se faisoient pas pour enrichir les Roys, mais pour immortaliser leur gloire, & tesmoigner à la posterité par ces marques d'obeyssance & d'affection, le sentiment & inclination que les peuples avoient pour leurs Majestez ...' (26). Honour bestowed, according to Mauss, creates a relation of obligation on the part of the recipient. Give the gift that keeps on biting. I underscore biting here, since, as historian Bernard Guénée has shown, at its origin in the thirteenth century the entry largely involved providing foodstuffs to the king and his retinue. Little by little, that process was displaced as endpoint of an increasingly complex allegorical programme, which nonetheless continued to conclude with banqueting and gift exchange. The latter retained traces of its origin since gifts offered evolved from food to items associated with eating, i.e. gold and silver dishes, platters, utensils ... precious objects ... lions. Small wonder then that the final meal of the 1622 Lyon entry would involve swallowing the king and queen, instead of the opposite. That gesture suggests the city's clergy, if not its ruling council, recognised entries had evolved beyond their purpose in the sixteenth century, when, as Guénée has argued, in a political climate on the cusp between Feudalism and Absolutism, the entry provided bourgeois city leaders a rare opportunity to engage in dialogue with the monarch.[21] The work of historian Lawrence Bryant complements Guénée's thesis in proposing that the entry into Paris in the Renaissance served to mask and adjudicate tensions between the city and the monarch in a period marked by a shift between two different models of rule, one juridical, the other dynastic.[22] When the dynastic model gained precedence over the juridical one, the entry would die out as a form of political ritual, no longer necessary since the struggle between city and monarch was firmly tilted in favour of the latter. In 1622, however, the tension was not yet resolved.

We can now situate the genealogical conceits around the queen's insemination in terms of the power play(s) going on in a ceremony adjudicating city-state relations. Each role in which Lyon posited herself in the entry can be understood in terms of contemporary notions of monarchical prerogative being worked out in many spheres in this period. The work of Sarah Hanley on how marital metaphors expressed contemporary notions of monarchy is particularly useful for teasing out the significance of these positions.[23] According to Hanley, the 'marriage maxim' first emerged as a description of monarchy in the sixteenth century in works of French jurists who insisted on the contractual nature of the relation between king and kingdom. By referring to the relation as 'like a marriage', the jurists actually held the king's power in check, since any 'dowry' brought to the so-called marriage would be inalienable. In this sense Lyon's purpose would be well served in presenting herself in the position of wife vis-à-vis the entering monarch. If she could not become the woman on top, at least as the woman entered she could remind the king of his legal obligations to her fisc, the dowry she brought to the king.

The marriage maxim provided jurists with a way to describe kingship in terms of legal codes. But theorists of the monarchy also had recourse to models of natural law to explain problems of succession when they utilised a vocabulary related to Aristotelian notions of generative theory in which the male passes active seed into a passive female receptacle. This 'seminal theory of kingship', as Hanley and others have termed it, was utilised to argue for exclusively male succession – remember that in Aristotelian theory the female was a product of defective male generative matter. Male-right, or should we say City-right, could be used by the city to both flatter the king and itself, something that emerges in the entry programme's insistence on the 'honour Heaven bestowed on Lyon by the conception of his Majesty. / l'honneur que le Ciel luy a fait de la conception de sa Majesté'. Avid readers of Aristotle via Pliny, as mentioned above, the entry composers would have such notions of natural law at hand. These ideas about generation allowed the city to posit itself as matter the king-foetus sucked in his most impressionable foetal state as, for example, when noting:

> the honour that Heaven offered [the city] by the conception of his Majesty gives her the glorious title of his true mother country, for having sucked in [humer] the Lyonnais air during the first two months of life,

giving [us] the courage to say that it is Lyon's sole prerogative to 'carry' Dauphins.

l'honneur que le Ciel luy a fait de la conception de sa Majesté, qui luy donne le tiltre glorieux de sa vraye patrie, pour avoir humé l'air Lyonnois environ les deux premiers moys de sa vie, luy donnant le courage de dire, qu'il n'appartient qu'à Lyon de porter des Dauphins. (123)

Of course the valuing of the amniotic milieu might also challenge seminal theory. For it seems to give considerable power to the womb, even if that womb is usurped by the male lion in the simile. This position is nuanced in the text mentioned earlier, Goujon's *Horoscope of the King*, which offers a detailed, one might say painstaking, argument for the importance of conception over birth (26). Goujon's argument is at once natural and juridical. On the one hand, he argues for the import of the amniotic milieu in forming the king:

It seems to me that I hear [Nature] say, that presumption and reason is correct to attribute the honour of one's native land to the place where we are conceived, rather than to the place which received us emerging from the mother's belly, because man suffers nothing in the maternal bosom equal to the calamities that proceed from birth, which introduces man into a valley of miseries, a world of obstacles, & an ocean of tears.

Il me semble que je luy [La Nature] entends dire, que la presomption & raison est plus grande d'attribuer l'honneur de la patrie au lieu où nous sommes conceus, qu'à celuy là qui nous recoit sortant du ventre de la mere, puisque l'homme ne patit rien dedans le gyron maternel, à l'esgal des calamitez qui procedent de la naissance, laquelle introduict l'homme en une valee de miseres, un monde de traverses, & un Ocean de larmes. (*Horoscope*, 5–6)

Here Goujon underscores Lyon as the peaceful site of the king's conception, opposing it to the pain of the Parisian birth. But he also argues that the site of conception merits juridical rights over that of birth, rights established by the 'seul droit d'ainesse', (8) the laws of primogeniture. Note of course that here again Lyon has fudged on its position in the French royal genealogy, identifying itself as womb and heir. Both roles, of course, have distinct rights in royal genealogy, contractual rights as wife or inheritance rights as child.[24]

It now seems likely that in welcoming the king and queen, Lyon proposed a multi-valent allegory that played out a complex struggle with royal power over city-state relations. Indeed, when Louis XIII met with the municipal magistrates (*échevins*), and Provost or Judge (*prévôt*) of the city at the end of the entry to receive their gifts, he was also given a *cahier* or written petition of griefs and requests.[25] The *cahier* reviewed the city's dire fiscal situation and reclaimed lost rights, most particularly its status as free of the crown, a status it claimed was illegally usurped by Henri IV in 1595.[26] The petition complained as well of the continued erosion of economic benefits once linked to those rights, that is, freedom from certain taxes and the right to be sole port of entry for certain foreign goods and thus recipient of the revenues of import duty. These prerogatives were perhaps even more critical to the city and its economy after it had been required to invest huge sums to produce twelve entry monuments or stations. Add to this cost that of weeks of lodging the queen and queen mother and their court, and later the king and his retinue, the expense of crafting the golden statues for the king and queen, of providing meals, and presumably of composing, illustrating and publishing the entry descriptions later offered to the king and queen and one begins to perceive that the 1622 encounter between king and city was not so much concerned with the fertility of the royal couple as it was with the fecundity (or lack thereof) of city (and monarch's) treasury, that is, with contractual relations between two corporate bodies.

In the face of such immense monetary investment and perhaps strains, it is not surprising that the ceremony would have recourse to an allegory that could turn in many directions, juridical, natural, economic, etc., containing, but also perhaps allowing aggression to simmer below the surface.[27] The dizzying allegorical effect of the golden lions and of the entry allegory more generally can now be understood in terms of the multiple tactics various constituencies in Lyon were using to struggle with the emerging absolute power of the king. It is crucial to use the word tactic here – suggesting the activity of the subaltern according to de Certeau – because, in the final analysis, the city could be said to have lost the struggle with the king. For after the entry, instead of giving the Lyonnais tax relief, the king availed himself of whatever materials (tapestries, paintings, etc.) he wished, giving them to members of his retinue even when it would have been normal for the entry's underwriters to have expected their return.[28] So in some sense the king refused the civil gestures of the gift-exchange ritual and acted like the absolutist king he was in the process of becoming. According to Mauss, choosing not to return the gift is the most dangerous position in the gift-exchange ritual because it recognises and exposes the antagonism of the interaction. If successful, however, it is the stance of the sovereign, the habitus of a person (or beast) so powerful he/it does not need to engage in acts of civic mollification.[29] And that was indeed the course taken by the king. He did not reciprocate.[30] Where did that response leave the city? Spurned woman, barren wife, empty womb, sidelined mother, younger son and dispossessed heir? Take your pick from the various genealogical positions traditionally assumed by or tangentially related to the queen of France in the early modern period.

It is perhaps useful to add an afterthought to the material presented in this discussion. It concerns the position of the queen, for perhaps at times it seemed she slipped somewhat from view in this analysis of the entry folios, eclipsed not by the king, but by the lion, who swallowed her, penetrated her, and birthed itself out of her figural body. Indeed, perhaps the queen's body is less represented in the 1622 Lyon entry descriptions than it is pressed into the service not of state building, as was the case of Louis XIV's queen in his marriage (and of Anne of Austria, in hers), but of city building, however futile that act might have been.[31] This treatment of the queen's body occurs in an allegory that, in invading and ingesting the queen, plays with the boundaries of its own genealogical and geopolitical conceits. I have described this phenomenon as a kind of dizzying *mise-en-abîme* and as an allegorical bite. Ultimately what may interest us most about this process is how allegory is such a malleable and shifting process, as shifting and shifty as conception, construed as both active and passive in early modern natural philosophy. Indeed much of what I outlined in this discussion is a series of shifts or displacements, that is, allegorical moves. From *allos*, meaning other, and *agorein*, to speak publicly, as well as *agora*, assembly, meaning to speak in public assembly of what is other, allegory is a form of displacement. As such, it is quite different from the aesthetic most often associated with baroque political force, the Italian perspectival mechanism exemplified by Velasquez's painting *Las Meninas* or the classical stage. Mechanisms of perspective pin the viewer in one place, clearly establishing hierarchies and viewpoints. Allegory, by displacement, moves the viewer and blurs relations. Like the entry monument, it invites the spectator to circle, peer up, down and around, perhaps even enter, the object.[32] This phenomenon of moving, seeing many things at once, the displacement and substitution of allegorical metonymy and metaphor seems incarnated by the figure of the lion *and* that of the queen in the entry descriptions. It is almost as if the queen, in being equated with the lion, becomes another monument or gift, decorated, entered, and/or shifted around, to mention just a few of her figured body's positions. It is her symbolic malleability, finally, that makes her so amenable to this kind of allegorical processing and such a rich body for interpretation by the Lyonnais in their ultimately futile supplication to the rising monolithic power of the emerging absolutist king.

Notes

1. On these campaigns and Louis's travels, see Ruth Kleinman, *Anne of Austria, Queen of France* (Columbus, 1985). See also the issue of the journal *Dix-septième siècle*, no. 212 (July–September 2001), which focuses on royal entries. Most particularly, see essays by Marie-Claude Canova-Green, Marie-France Wagner and Daniel Vaillancourt.
2. Note that much of the entry would have been dictated by the monarch, or his agents. On this point see, Daniel Nordman, *Un tour de France royal. Le voyage de Charles IX (1564–1566)* (Paris, 1984).
3. For my ideas about the focus on procreation by state apparatuses, see my book, *Scenes from the Marriage of Louis XIV: Nuptial Fictions and the Making of Absolutist Power* (Stanford, 1997), and my essay, 'Making Sweat: Sex and the Gender of National Reproduction in the Marriage of Louis XIII', *Yale French Studies* 86 (1994), 187–205. For contemporary notions of procreation and conception, see Jacques Gélis, *L'Arbre et le Fruit: la naissance dans l'occident moderne* (Paris, 1984), Thomas Laqueur, *Making Sex: Body and Gender from the Greeks to Freud* (Cambridge, 1990), and Evelyne Berriot-Salvadore, 'Le Discours de la Médecine et de la Science' in *L'Histoire des femmes*, Vol. 3, eds. Georges Duby and Michelle Perrot (Paris, 1991). I refer to this status as liminal because liminality, as characterised by Victor Turner, is the unknowable and chaotic that nonetheless, and because of its status as outside and excluded, structures and defines that from which it is excluded. On liminality, see Turner's 'Betwixt and Between: The Liminal Period in *Rites de Passage*', in *The Forest of Symbols* (Ithaca, NY, 1967).
4. This essay is part of a larger project I am engaged in on the nature of political allegory in seventeenth-century France. I first became interested in political allegory when writing my book on the marriage of Louis XIV to the Spanish infanta María Teresa of Austria, *Scenes from the Marriage of Louis XIV*. What I called nuptial fictions in that

study were fictions that manipulated the portrayal of the queen in order
to buttress and promote representations of the king. In particular, I
noted the role played by the queen in showing that the king was virile,
virility being a strong symbolic position of governance in France where,
as the work of Ernst Kantorowicz has shown, the separation between
the king's two bodies was never as important as it had been for fictions
of kingship in England. For the case of Louis XIII, whose virility was
often cast in doubt, such a symbolic apparatus of virility was crucial.
This essay looks back to issues of impotence in the political body, that
is, to representations of Louis XIII and Anne of Austria, which concern
their lack of an heir. It is a complement to my earlier essay, 'Making
Sweat: Sex and the Gender of National Reproduction in the Marriage of
Louis XIII', which discussed the representation of Anne of Austria
during the marriage mass celebrated in Bordeaux in 1615. In that essay I
argued that the queen's representation was pressed into the service of
state building, paradoxically, by portraying the queen as virile, as
almost like the king, precisely because her virility advertised the
dynasty's ability to reproduce itself. Another title for this new essay
might be 'Sex and the City', since this discussion overviews how the
entry literature presses the queen's representation into the service not
of state building, but of city building.

5. Other entry pamphlets for this period are available in the Lb^{36} rubric of
the *Catalogue de L'Histoire de France* at the French National Library.
Essays in *Dix-septième siècle*, no. 212, mentioned above, are useful in
contrasting the various entries of this campaign.
6. On the entry as matrimonial rite, see Jean Boutier, Alain Dewerpe, and
Daniel Nordman, *Un tour de France royal*, 296. On the French entry
more generally, see Bernard Guénée, *Les entrées royales françaises de
1328 à 1515* (Paris, 1968) and Lawrence Bryant, *The King and the City
in the Parisian Royal Entry Ceremony*, (Geneva, 1986).
7. This, and all translations, are my own.
8. I am thinking here of lines from the fourth *Eclogue*: 'Soft spikes of grain
will gradually gild the fields, / And reddening grapes will hang in
clusters on wild brier ...' See Virgil, *The Eclogues*, trans. by Guy Lee,
Harmondsworth (England, 1984), 57.
9. Again, see Gélis, Laqueur, Berriot-Salvadore, and my own essay 'Making
Sweat' for details on these processes as understood in this period.
10. As for example the following verse from the final entry monument:
'Royne nostre sage Iunon, / De qui le celeste renom / Remplit l'un &
lautre hemisphere, / Ce Ciel qui vous fait à la foys, / Et soeur, &
espouse de Roy, / Promet que vous en serez mere.' (*Entree*, 126) A rough
translation of these lines runs as follows: Queen, our sage Juno /
celestial renown / Fills one and the other hemisphere, / This Heaven
which makes you at once, / Sister and Wife of the King, / Promises that
you will become a mother (of kings).
11. The plan for this painting was probably conceived by this date, if not
the painting itself. The finished image's symbolism is well explicated by

Ronald Forsyth Millen and Robert Erich Wolf in *Heroic Deeds and Mystic Figures: A New Reading of Rubens' Life of Maria de Medici* (Princeton, 1989), 73–81.

12. Note that the *Horoscope* was published in the same year and by the same publisher as *L'ENTREE DU ROY ET DE LA ROYNE*.

13. At sixty-seven pages, this volume is considerably shorter than the other folio, perhaps because it focuses only on the culmination of the entry, the ceremonies in the cathedral at the end of the procession. The folio's writers, the Church dignitaries, were responsible for these ceremonies. That there may have been tension between the Church and city leaders, at least with regard to their various ceremonial contributions, is suggested by the fact that the folio published by the city fathers presents itself as attempting to rectify errors in the volume published by the Church dignitaries. Nonetheless both are describing the same general events and thus both have conception as one of their organising leitmotifs.

14. The other Latin motto in the text reads: 'Vanum Sine Numine Nomen, A Name is vain without a will'.

15. The queen, Olympias, is also identified with Orphic snake ceremonies and Bacchic revelries in Plutarch's text.

16. For Plutarch's treatment of Alexander's conception, see Plutarch, *The Age of Alexander*, trans. by Ian Scott-Kilvert (New York, 1973), 252–54. This material was available to the entry organisers in *Les Vies des Hommes Illustres Grecs et Romains*, trans. Amyot (Paris: Guillaume Auvray, 1600), Vol. 2, 135–39.

17. This crown and arm can also link the image to the Assumption of the Virgin, which often includes the Virgin ascending into the clouds, with the presence of a descending cloud. Of course here the illusion is merged with the Annunciation, although none of that event's iconic illusions are present in this vignette. Perhaps the message is that Anne will be the new Eve and her offspring will save the world.

18. The image of Lyon as child is reinforced one page later in the description of the fireworks that followed the ceremony of gift giving. One 'machine', as fireworks were called, included 'un Lyon portant trois fleurs de Lys', each lily standing for the king, the queen and the city of Lyon, the perfect trinitarian family (29)

19. Marcel Mauss, *The Gift*, trans. Ian Cunnison (New York, 1967) and Bryant, *The King and the City*.

20. Pliny, *Histoire Naturelle*, Livre VIII, ed., A. Ernout (Paris, 1952), 40. I have translated the quote into English.

21. Bernard Guénée, p. 24

22. Lawrence Bryant.

23. See Hanley's 'The Monarchic State in Early Modern France: Marital Regime Government and Male Right', in *Politics, Ideology and the Law in Early Modern Europe*, ed. Adrianna Bakos (Rochester, 1994). The following information is drawn both from this essay and from personal conversations with Sarah Hanley.

24. When the city returns itself to the role of child, however, it returns from natural to juridical concepts. For in presenting itself inside the queen or as the third lily, it invokes the laws of primogeniture.

25. Sebastien Charlety, 'Le Voyage de Louis XIII à Lyon, en 1622: Etude sur les relations de Lyon et du pouvoir central au début du XVIIe siècle (1595–1622)', part 2, *Revue d'histoire moderne et contemporaine*, no. 2 (Jan.–Feb. 1910), 497. The document is mentioned in the account of the gift-exchange ceremony, which refers to the 'notebook, that necessity constrains us to present' (*Reception*, 26).

26. Sebastien Charlety, 'Le Voyage de Louis XIII à Lyon ...' part 1, *Revue d'histoire moderne et contemporaine*, II (1900–01), 349. On the history of Lyon see also Charlety, *Histoire de Lyon depuis les origines jusqu'à nos jours* (Lyon, 1972) and Arthur Kleinclausz, *Histoire de Lyon* (Lyon, 1948).

27. This is also an attribute of the central figure of the conceit, the lion. Clement, he carries within the threat of explosion. Indeed references to biblical and classical sources on the lion that run throughout the folio account of the entry underscore in particular the uniquely dual character of the lion as both fierce and just.

28. Charlety, II, 499.

29. See Mauss, *The Gift*, 41. See also, Natalie Zemon Davis, *The Gift in Sixteenth-Century France* (Madison, 2000), 90–95 where the author discusses the entry as gift exchange. As Davis points out, in Henri II's 1548 entry into Lyon, the king did not reconfirm the city's privileges as he did in the private meetings months earlier: 'Thus the king enhanced the sovereign quality of his act by preferring to make it a response to subjects come to him in obedient homage rather than a response to subjects receiving him with gifts and with didactic hospitality which might seem to oblige him' (94).

30. Charlety, II, 499.

31. At least that is the argument I make about Anne and María Teresa in *Nuptial Fictions* and 'Making Sweat'.

32. I am indebted to Gordon Teskey's discussion of allegory in his book, *Allegory and Violence* (Ithaca, 1996), for the way he conceives of allegory as a participatory process that invites the viewer to collaborate.

7

Posterity and the Body of the Princess in German Court Funeral Books

Jill Bepler

In contrast to the examples of England and Sweden, the laws of
succession in early modern Germany generally precluded female
rule. Female government was usually restricted to the role of
regent in a husband's absence, or after his death during a son's
minority.[1] The sheer number of territories which formed the Holy
Roman Empire in the early modern period (estimated at around 420[2])
shows that a comprehensive gender-studies-based investigation of
the court culture of the Empire and the role of the princess within it
is sorely needed.[3] In this context the following will examine some
aspects of a genre which was expressly aimed at creating an image of
the princess for posterity. Nowhere, of course, was the body of a
princess more literally a subject of observation and reflection than at
her funeral. Her corpse was frequently put on public display for
several days, and even in small residence towns it could have been
viewed by thousands of people.[4] The coffin was carried through the
streets in ceremonial procession and was placed before the altar
during the service. The mourning decorations often included
portraits of the deceased. Her body was represented both visually and
verbally in commemorative publications: a variety of texts stemming
from the occasion constantly refer back to the body of the princess;
engravings of portraits 'to the life' were accompanied by those of her
lying-in-state.

Printed funeral sermons for members of the upper nobility
formed part of the currency of self-representation of the courts of
the German Empire from the mid-sixteenth to the mid-eighteenth

centuries. With the advent of printing and the circulation of engravings and woodcuts, a far larger audience could be reached than those who had actually attended the deathbed or the funeral, or those travellers who visited the epitaphs and monuments erected in memory of the deceased. One of the topoi of the printed funeral sermon was that a paper monument could be expected to preserve the memory of the deceased more dependably and even more durably than any architectural structure.[5] From the 1620s onwards there was a burgeoning production of funeral books at the Protestant courts of the Empire, which ran parallel to the development of the lavishly illustrated festival book.[6] Funeral books were printed in large quantities for distribution both at home and abroad[7] and their production was carefully orchestrated and overseen by the members of the ruling dynasties themselves. At first quite modest, they became increasingly complex publications aimed at recreating the elaborate ceremonies and decorations accompanying the funerals themselves. They not only documented the event, but provided a highly stylised version of it, and of the deceased, for posterity.[8] The splendour of such books was often in direct contrast to the actual political significance of the dynasty involved and in some cases the publications were direct reflections of dynastic rivalry and conflict.[9]

The standard format of the funeral sermon preached for all classes of society[10] dictated the core around which, in the context of a court publication, ceremonial, pictorial, literary and musical elements could be grouped. In the course of the sixteenth century it became usual for the sermon to contain a detailed curriculum vitae of the deceased, which, in the case of funeral sermons for the princes of the Empire, adopted some of the elements of the chronicle literature of earlier generations. This genre can be seen as one of the first in which depictions of women's lives were accorded equal space with those of their male counterparts.[11] Funeral books for female members of ruling houses provide us with an insight into the way in which gender roles were inscribed for posterity and at the same time established as paradigms.[12] In some cases, where reality fell short of the role model, some funeral books show how conflicting tensions could be overcome by discreet omissions or by the skilful reworking of the life they presented.

The genre of the funeral book itself is, of course, shaped by its primarily religious and devotional function. Its political aspects became increasingly important as its potential for dynastic self-representation, often in rivalry with other houses, was recognised. These texts also reached a broader public, however, for whom the political undertones of inner dynastic communication were of secondary importance. Contemporary evidence suggests that funeral books were both read and collected in order to satisfy a thirst for biographical literature as well as for devotional purposes in the *ars moriendi* tradition. An obsession with the lives of royalty and its success as a marketable commodity is not an invention of our own day and age. Long before the advent of the newspaper and the yellow press, even the most devout reader could to some extent satisfy a longing for this kind of reading. The distinction between edification and entertainment was blurred, which explains the longevity of the popularity of the genre. Looking back in 1727, Christian Gerber, a compiler of exemplary biographies gleaned from funeral sermons, described the interest in biographies of the famous which had led to his own lifelong fascination with the genre of the funeral sermon: 'In truth I can say that from my youth I have been so inclined, and thus in my childhood loved to read stories of the lives of the holy people in the Bible, especially of the Kings, whose actions and fates are described quite fully in the Book of Kings and Chronicles ... after that I also started to enjoy reading the biographies or Curricula Vitae of famous people which are printed in funeral sermons and to note the good and the best from them. I still think that the best part of funeral sermons are the curricula vitae, even if they are not based on the truth.'[13]

The enormous number of printed funeral sermons in circulation in early modern Germany had thus generated a wealth of biographical literature *avant la lettre*. The fact that these biographies were written with a specific purpose and were not necessarily true in all respects makes them none the less valuable, as Gerber clearly states. The following will look at the way in which such texts contributed to the construction of an image of the princess for posterity.

The Natural Body of the Princess in the Funeral Book

In his book on death and ritual in post-Reformation England, Nigel Llewellyn distinguishes between the natural body and the social body.[14] The social body is the construct developed in the liminal phase between life and death, the picture which remains for posterity. Llewellyn emphasises that our own concept of life and death as binary opposites differs greatly from that of earlier periods. He suggests that we should imagine another phase in the process leading from the one to the other, which he terms 'dying'. This can be a preparatory period of indeterminate duration in which the social body emerges, to be sustained in future memory by artefacts or texts. The creation of the social body is a process of conscious construction in which the deceased herself or himself may well have been actively engaged, whether in the detailed instructions for the display of his or her body, the way in which the funeral or burial should be conducted, or in the commissioning or personal preparation of such artefacts as coffins, shrouds, coffin inscriptions and decorations, epitaphs or texts to be preached or read out at the funeral. It is often the case that the definitive version of the curriculum vitae was written personally by the deceased well in advance.

The introduction of the natural body into the German funeral book was in itself a slow process. Martin Luther rejected the idea that the funeral should be used as an occasion to celebrate the deceased and his or her individual life and saw it instead as an opportunity for moving his funeral congregations to repentance by confronting them with the imminence of their own deaths.[15] Thus at first the deceased was the occasion but not the subject of the funeral sermon. Gradually, however, preachers began to focus on the exemplary role of the deceased as a model of 'holy living and holy dying' and he or she thus moved to the centre of funeral rites. The curricula vitae in funeral sermons for all levels of society which were read out to the congregation also began to pay particular attention to the final illness and the death of the deceased. These lengthy descriptions often contain graphic details of symptoms of illnesses and the various stages of physical decline.[16] No apparent difference is made between the varying levels of society, and the bodily functions and malfunctions of the princess are just as frankly described as those of the burgher's wife. The way in which the deceased bears up in illness and pain, the patience which he or she demonstrates, is interpreted as the final test of his or her Christianity and courage in the face of adversity. This holy dying is, of course, best exemplified in the death of a Christian ruler. The consort plays a particular role as a model of piety for her subjects. She is apostrophised in early funeral sermons as a 'pillar of prayer', supporting the realm and guaranteeing the righteousness of the political successes of her husband in the division of labour which characterises both Protestant[17] and Catholic[18] princely 'working couples'[19] of the early modern period. It is this topos of the pillar of prayer which leads to the pathetic fallacy in which the body of the princess and the body politic are linked, as in the introduction to the sermon for Louise Henrietta of Orange, wife of Friedrich Wilhelm Elector of Brandenburg, in Berlin in 1667: 'For just as upon eclipses of the sun and moon there are upheavals in the elements and in the blood and the state of mind of men: so experience has shown that upon the deaths of God-fearing princes and princesses burdensome changes usually follow.'[20]

The natural body of the princess was as conspicuously absent from early funeral books as it was in those printed for her more humble subjects. When the Electress Anna of Saxony[21] died in 1586 numerous publications commemorated the event.[22] None, however, contained references to her physical appearance, whether in life or in death, and no portraits or illustrations accompanied them. The funeral rites for the Electress constructed her social memory out of exclusively Christian moral attributes: her piety, charity, and her missionary zeal for the Lutheran church. The Lutheran concept of the superiority of the housewife over all other possible forms of social role for the female also dominated the portrait of the princess.[23] The Electress Anna is shown to have been the supreme 'housewife'. Her motherly concern for the court and her husband's well-being, her modesty in manners and dress and the shunning of vanity provides the ultimate female role model for her subjects. While her husband wrestled with the enemy in the field, the Electress supervised the morals of the court and ensured his victories by the power of her prayer.[24] Nearly twenty years later the same image of the princess/housewife still prevails and, for example, informs the description of Hedwig of Brandenburg, widow of Duke Julius of Brunswick-Wolfenbüttel, who died in 1602: 'Thus her royal Highness (even in her final weakness), like all her daughters and her ladies of the chamber, never sat idle but always had work in her hands, in particular, like Tabitha, sewing garments for the poor. Thus, when the time was right, her royal Highness and her ladies prepared apothecary's wares to dispense to the poor and for this purpose gathered violets and roses, carnations and redcurrants, and peeled quinces ... [25]

A commemorative broadsheet printed by Elias Holwein on the death of Hedwig[26] portrays her in a simple widow's dress (Figure

7.1). This mode of depiction, focusing on moral attributes, remained at the core of the funeral biography of the German princess right through into the early eighteenth century, but her physical body and its functions were gradually brought into play and several themes are introduced which run parallel to the moral construction

Figure 7.1 Commemorative leaflet for Hedwig of Brunswick-Wolfenbüttel, 1602.

throughout. The equation of majesty with beauty and beauty with majesty gains in importance. Physical attributes are seen as an expression of magnanimity, but there is also the rejection of outward physical beauty in favour of the beauty of the soul, and these are themes which are present in differing degree in the texts and their accompanying illustrations. It seems that at first physical details were merely used to enhance the exemplary moral characteristics of the princess and only later did the balance shift away from this subordination towards the idea that beauty itself was the ultimate expression of majesty, giving the princess the star-cult status which she has retained until today.

The Natural Body as the Ultimate Test of Faith – Pregnancy and Illness

The physical body of the princess comes into focus first in funeral biography in its function in the indeterminate liminal phase of 'dying', for the endurance of all weakness and illnesses could be interpreted as a test of Christian virtue, as trial runs for a final deathbed encounter. Just as the binary terms of life and death do not adequately encompass the concepts underlying early modern death ritual, so do our ideas of a 'good death' vary.[27] In the early modern period sudden death was considered not a blessing but a sign of Divine wrath. 'Dying' constituted a lengthy process of exercise and preparation, both mental and physical, which occurred not only individually and in private but also included social components. Thus funeral biographies pay great attention to illness and in particular to the physical trials of the deathbed and thus reveal 'a dissociation of private and public social spheres'.[28] The necessary description of stoic endurance of excruciating pain or debilitation as witness to an exemplary Christian death means that the natural body of the princess enters the public domain in a drastic way that even our prurient age would find surprising.

The biography of Sophie Jagiellon, widow of Duke Heinrich of Brunswick-Wolfenbüttel, recalls that three days before she died in 1575 she expressed a wish to take communion, 'so long as she was not too much overtaken by weakness and the continual vomiting did not prevent her.'[29] The biography of Elisabeth Charlotte of the Palatinate, widow of Elector Georg Wilhelm of Brandenburg, published in 1660 describes her physical decline from dropsy in graphic detail: her lungs were full of water, her lips had turned black

and her body was quite brown from lying on her sickbed.[30] The
whole life of Louise Henriette, first wife of Brandenburg's Great
Elector, is described at her death in 1667 as a chain in which one
illness or accident was linked to another and she is compared to
someone lying in a fever, suffering from one day to the next. Her
body had been severely weakened by a series of miscarriages. All of
these physical tribulations are interpreted as preparations for her
final illness at the age of thirty-nine.[31] Similarly weakened by
pregnancies and miscarriages, Sibylla Ursula Duchess of Holstein-
Glücksburg died at the age of forty-two having given birth to a
stillborn daughter in 1672 (Figure 7.2). All three children she had
carried to term before that died straight after birth. Her biography
describes graphically how in the last ten weeks of her final
pregnancy she developed a quartain fever.[32] This kept her bedridden
with leg sores and meant that she could only take nourishment in
liquid form. The onset of labour and the birth of her daughter were
fatal to both. These descriptions are randomly selected and could be
added to endlessly. They form part of what has been termed the
'aesthetics of loathing', rooted in Luther's graphic description of the
total corruption of the flesh as a welcome prerequisite of the
resurrection in his four sermons on the resurrection and the
Apocalypse based on Corinthians 15.[33] Similarly the sufferings of
Job provided the biblical imagery for the description of bodily

Figure 7.2 Sibylla Ursula von Holstein-Glücksburg lying in state.

affliction and physical suffering. In the funeral biographies the social body of the princess is constructed in the *memento mori* tradition, as a reminder of the vanity of all things human and the corruptibility of the flesh. Her exalted status is seen in the Dance of Death tradition as irrelevant to the salvation of her soul. There is, of course, also only a thin line here to the figure of *Frau Welt*, the Janus figure of beauty and putrefaction. However, with her piety and her willingness to meet death, rejecting the body in favour of the soul, the princess of the funeral book serves to teach the art of holy dying in the *ars moriendi* tradition as an example to all levels of society.[34]

The pregnancies and illnesses of the majority of princesses in early modern Germany provided these standard patterns of exemplary Christian endurance in which faith overcomes physical suffering. Two examples of funeral books, personally commissioned and planned by grieving husbands in the mid-seventeenth century, give us insights into the production of such commemorative texts. Ludwig VI of Hessen-Darmstadt and Friedrich I of Saxony-Gotha were close friends[35] and, as members of the first German academy, the *Fruchtbringende Gesellschaft*, both had literary interests and wrote poetry. When the wife of Ludwig VI died in childbirth with her tenth child in 1665 he was inconsolable.[36] His mourning found its expression in an outpouring of poetry.[37] Some of these poems were included in the funeral book he had published for her, which draws a harmonious portrait of a beloved princess who had fulfilled all the duties associated with her station and whose death was a confident affirmation of her piety. One key element in this standard pattern of holy dying always stressed in funeral biographies is the conscious intellect, able to affirm belief in the face of affliction right up to the moment of death. When this exemplary constancy in the face of pain and death is not manifested, for example when not only the physical but also the mental faculties of the dying person disintegrate at the same time, a problem of interpretation arises.[38] The example of the death of Magdalena Sibylla of Saxony-Weissenfels, wife of Duke Friedrich I of Saxony-Gotha, offers a rare example of how such a situation was dealt with. As in the case of Ludwig VI of Hessen-Darmstadt, both the funeral book commissioned for the occasion[39] and autobiographical texts by the husband are extant.

The recently published private diaries of Duke Friedrich of Sachsen-Gotha, kept between 1667 and 1686,[40] provide an opportunity to examine how such a case could be interpreted for posterity in the funeral book. Friedrich's diaries make the reader very aware of the fact that in the miniscule territories which made up the Empire, attending christenings and funerals constituted a major part of everyone's social life. In 1669, at the age of twenty-three, Friedrich married Magdalena Sibylla of Saxony-Weissenfels. It was a marriage of love, opposed by his father. Magdalena Sibylla's first pregnancy and safe delivery a year later are a matter of great concern and forward planning on Friedrich's part, as we see from the diary. By the time her last child arrives, eleven years later, he is less closely involved. However, the diaries do reveal a great affection both for his wife and his children and he always rushes to their sickbeds, even from a great distance, whenever summoned. The deaths of two children affect him greatly, as he records in his diary. It also reveals him at pains to attend the sickbeds of dying relatives where he often stays awake all night, whether at the side of his mother-in-law, father, mother, sister-in-law or his own children.

After the birth of their seventh child in 1677, Friedrich's diary notes the first major dispute with his wife. In the ensuing period several more follow, leading up to her final illness after the birth of their eighth child at the end of 1680. The first indication in the diary that her illness was not merely physical comes in an entry about discussions on what he calls his wife's 'condition': 'In the afternoon I spoke to the court preacher for three hours about my wife's condition, in the evening it was very bad again.'[41] On the next day he noted that things had worsened: 'My wife was in a very bad way and started to talk madly'.[42] Fearing that a mania would set in, he spent the next morning with her in her room and later sat with her until three in the morning. However, this was the point at which the Duchess showed clear signs of being mentally disturbed: 'Then the real raving started, which was a great misery. God has sent me great crosses this year but none so great as this that I should have such a desperate situation with my wife. God be with her and help me out of this great misery and let things go with the patient according to His holy will. He knows that it is all for the good of her soul.'[43] In a clear moment the Duchess movingly took leave of her children, but then relapsed into 'dementia'. On 3 January 1681 Friedrich noted: 'On this day the mania was all too strong, for she raged terribly, and ran around in the nude. Because of this I was in an awful condition and was unable to conduct any business.'[44] The next day saw a violent culmination of the Duchess's malady:

I did not get up until 10 o'clock because of attending her yesterday. My wife was still in a very bad way all night. Near to the morning, and at about 2 o'clock, she was somewhat quieter, NB I ate with her at lunch time, but she came out with strange stories. But at 2 o'clock the raving started again, and everything had to be cleared from the chamber and the cabinet and coloured hangings had to be brought back into the chamber[45], which lasted until 5 o'clock, after that she was somewhat quiet again and the court preacher was summoned to her. At 8 o'clock in the evening the fury began again with such intensity that force had to be used, but I nearly caught the best of it, for she got hold of me and gave me three heavy blows to the body so that I almost stopped breathing. Because of this I also had to vomit somewhat.[46]

Three days later the Duchess died.

Like Ludwig VI of Hessen-Darmstadt, Friedrich commissioned a funeral book in his wife's memory (*Ehrengedächtnüs*, 1681) naming himself as its author on the title page: 'Erected with a faithful and loving heart by the deeply grieving husband she has left behind' and also contributing his own mourning poems. Friedrich's diary reveals that he spent a whole afternoon personally vetting the funeral biography which was to be read out at the service and later included in the printed volume.[47] This funeral biography takes pains not to gloss over his wife's difficult death and even her mental illness completely, but to interpret them in such a way as to strengthen the impression of her Christian endurance rather than weaken it. Early bouts of melancholy are seen as proof that although blessed with a fine bodily constitution, the Duchess had rejected her own body in favour of a spiritual union with Christ and a longing for death: 'Her God, rich in love, who endowed her Royal Highness with such indescribable gifts of the spirit, had also given her a healthy and magnificent physical constitution, however because at the same time her heavenly spirit was far more strongly attached to her beloved Jesus than to her unsullied royal body, her commerce was more with heaven than with earthly things: and thus some years ago she began to harbour thoughts of death and as time went on she let this be seen more and more clearly.'[48] Physical problems had exacerbated the melancholy and in her final pregnancy the Duchess developed a tertian fever, resulting in 'various pernicious affects, such as particular shortness of breath, illness of the pancreas and liver, as well as blockage of the mesentery and the small arteries, which all remained with her, so gradually causing Melancholicam hypochondriacam.'[49] The fits to which the Duchess was subject are described, not however as violent explosions of aggression, but as a gradual drain on her physical and mental resources. Although the symptoms of her final illness left her with neither direct control over her mind nor her body, the funeral biography claims that her uncontrollable verbal outpourings (described by Friedrich in his diary as 'ravings' or 'strange stories') were expressions of religious fervour. In keeping with the Duke's own alchemical interests, her illness and death are compared to a purification process: 'Her Royal Highness was like the finest gold which is preserved in the furnace by the heat of the fire, giving off one glorious spark of faith after the other and proving immutable.'[50]

Her 'passions' are likened to the testament of faith of the three men in the fiery pit of the Old Testament (Daniel, 3). In all the cases of depictions of the body of the princess in funeral books discussed so far, the main emphasis was placed on the natural body as an encumbrance, as a trial of endurance which the princess shared with all lesser mortals.

The Natural Body Versus the Royal Body – the Aesthetics of Majesty

The ultimate celebration of the body of the princess at the transition from Baroque to Early Enlightenment is contained in the funeral work for the first Queen of Prussia, Sophie Charlotte of Brandenburg-Prussia, who died in 1705 and was buried with great pomp and ceremony. [51] During her final illness Sophie Charlotte herself predicted: 'how many useless ceremonies people will perform for this body.'[52] The funeral publication provided an opportunity for a bombastic representation of dynastic power, in which Prussia's newly-founded monarchy and Germany's only queen is celebrated. The production of the publication took nearly two decades, lasting into the year 1723.[53] As Gerhild Komander stresses, the Prussian crown, as yet still an unusual attribute, is present in all the texts and allegorical illustrations in the volume.[54] All the components of earlier exemplary depictions of princesses of the Empire are contained in the publication for Sophie Charlotte, although their weighting has shifted. The Queen is not presented as a model of holy dying to which all can aspire but as the unattainable embodiment of majesty. The funeral biography celebrates the Queen's beauty as a natural expression of her inner majesty. Like her earlier counterparts, she is also said to have placed little value on her exalted position and excelled in all the regal virtues of modesty, magnanimity, and charity to her subjects. There is, however, little praise of the Queen as an exemplary Christian.[55] This aspect is in fact almost completely replaced by her worldly rank. The place accorded to her Christianity in a summary of the quintessential aspects of her life is revealing: 'In short, her life consisted almost solely in the performance of the duties of her Christianity, the exercise of nameless virtues, in fruitful conversation, in the frequent reading of good books, correspondence with her nearest relatives and friends, in the undertaking of so many journeys, and in other similar actions befitting so great a Queen.'[56]

The dictates of the genre mean that Sophie Charlotte's religiosity is of course a regular theme, but the imagery associated with it is consistently congruent with her status. Death is here in no way the great leveller. The afterlife is imagined to be yet another even more magnificent court at which Sophie Charlotte will naturally assume the highest rank, and where her majesty will outshine all else: 'And thus she will shine better, more beautifully and more majestically there than we ever saw her here. Yes, already she is adorning the court of the King of Kings in a never-ending succession of gala days amidst many thousand angels ...'[57] This theme is taken up in one of the engravings for the funeral publication in which allegorical figures accompany the Queen not towards heaven, but to her reception into the pantheon of the Gods (Figure 7.3). The funeral book describes the debilitation of Sophie Charlotte's natural body in her final illness in the same drastic detail as in earlier cases: 'When she almost forced herself to cough in order to free herself as much as possible from the phlegm which had gathered and to be able to breathe, some clear blood emerged instead of phlegm, and almost at the same time all of her strength deserted her. All of which, especially the suffocation and the blockage of her throat, despite the fact that she developed a continual warm sweat, persisted in such a way that the blessed Queen herself also thought that it might possibly be in great part due to rising vapours ...'[58]

The Queen's reaction to her distressing symptoms is interpreted, however, not as an exemplary Christian attitude towards death in the *ars moriendi* tradition, but as a heroic, almost military, stance: 'As all who stood about can testify, she did not show the least faintheartedness: but from that time forward she courageously confronted her death.'[59] The final words of the Queen as reported are

Figure 7.3 Sophie Charlotte of Brandenburg-Prussia, Allegory of glory, 1705/1723.

thus not a statement of faith, but a statesmanlike final command to her gentleman of the chamber: 'Greet the King from me and say adieu to him and my son and thank the King for all his love. I wish the King all happiness and I recommend all my servants to the king and my son for their recompense. ... I would have more to say to you Head Chamberlain but I cannot go on and am too weak.'[60]

In the funeral publication for this first German Queen in the early modern period the supreme quality of both her natural and her social body is that of its beauty. The funeral oration by the court poet Benjamin Neukirch celebrates Sophie Charlotte both as a heroine and as the figure in which all female beauty has found its ultimate culmination. Neukirch's own dedicatory preface to the King elucidates the way in which the funeral publication sets out to construct the image of the Queen for posterity: 'When they wanted to form the Greek Venus, they composed her from the inventions of different artists. Perhaps a picture will emerge here from the contributions of so many poets and orators which will, if not completely then at least in part, resemble our incomparable Queen and demonstrate for posterity the reason why she was so highly loved by your Majesty, so deeply admired by all, and lastly why she was buried in a manner so much more magnificent than any other Queen.'[61]

The natural body of the Queen becomes the subject of adulation, an expression of consummate majesty, and it is therefore Nature herself who most deeply mourns her passing: 'Finally Nature herself mourns and shudders at the violent force of Death, because he destroyed in an hour a work she had taken a thousand years to perfect.'[62] The social body of the princess is no longer constructed as a generally acceptable accumulation of exemplary Christian virtues, but as an unattainable embodiment of majesty, whether in life or death. She was thus also able to provide the focus for a developing cult of patriotism – at the end of his oration Neukirch addresses the 'Prussian subjects' and assures them 'there are no more beautiful memorial pillars than those erected in the breasts of the people (*Bürger*).'[63]

The Dysfunctional Body – Infertility and Infidelity

Despite the number of funeral sermons for princesses of the Empire, there were those the genre did not encompass. The political and dynastic significance of a dead princess varied in accordance with her own relevance for her own or her husband's dynasty, and this was above all dependent on her capacity as a child-bearer.[64] Unmarried princesses beyond marriageable age were rarely commemorated in funeral volumes, unless they achieved significance as abbesses or canonesses. Another group excluded from 'dynastic memory' in this way were those who had been deserted or divorced by their husbands, often through no fault of their own. An example of this is Christina Margaretha of Mecklenburg-Schwerin, who lived at the court of her married sister in Wolfenbüttel from 1652 until her death in 1666. No printed funeral volume commemorated her death, but her sister, Sophie Elisabeth of Brunswick-Lüneburg, had the story of her desertion inscribed on her tomb in the family vault.[65] Others were consigned to anonymity by virtue of their own indiscretion, such as Sophie Dorothea of Braunschweig-Lüneburg, wife of the Hanover Elector Georg Wilhelm, the future George I of England. She is better known as the Princess of Ahlden, the place of her decade-long incarceration after her infamous affair with Count Königsmarck was discovered and she was banished from court. The bulk of funeral sermons for princesses of the Empire are thus for consorts, widows or children, commissioned by their husbands, sons or parents as part of their own dynastic *memoria*. As was stressed earlier, the funeral sermon for the consort who fulfilled the dynastic and exemplary expectations directed towards her by bearing sufficient children to guarantee the continuance of the dynasty and provide a model of piety is often couched in the same terms as that for the good housewife. The difference is only one of degree, in that the princess is seen not just as a mother, but as a mother to the nation, 'Landesmutter'. A prime example of this role of conformity is given in the funeral volume for Magdalena Sibylla of Saxony, widow of the Elector Johann Georg I, who, when she died in 1659, was apostrophised in terms of her piety and, above all, her fecundity. She is shown to have been responsible for an unrivalled expansion of the family tree, guaranteeing the future of the Wettin dynasty by bearing ten children, and living to see fifty-five grandchildren, twenty-eight great grandchildren, a progeny of ninety-three in all, fifty males and forty-three females.[66]

In contrast to those princesses who could be commemorated as guarantors of dynastic stability there are consorts whose funeral books address, directly or indirectly, their manifest failure in this respect. In these cases, the body of the princess becomes a focus of attention because there is a conflict with its public role. The funeral volume published on the death of Erdmuth Sophie of Saxony, Markgräfin of Brandenburg-Bayreuth, in 1670 provides a case study.

Erdmuth Sophie was twenty-six when she died. There are several points in her funeral book which reveal tensions within the portrayal of the private and public body of the princess. The commemorative volume contains an important sub-text, for the authors were forced to battle against the 'common knowledge' picture of the Markgräfin's life in an effort to establish their own version and harmonise reality and ideal.

The court at Bayreuth was, like many smaller courts in Germany, a centre of literary activity with good connections to the literary circles of nearby Nürnberg, foremost among them the poet Sigmund von Birken, who could be employed on an ad hoc basis for the composition of texts for court occasions.[67] As the name of the line implies, Brandenburg-Bayreuth was also dependent on the central Brandenburg dynasty, of which it had formed a part since the extinction of the Franconian line.[68] Intermarriage with Brandenburg princesses had cemented these political ties throughout the early modern Period. When Christian Ernst of Brandenburg-Bayreuth married Erdmuth Sophie of Saxony in 1662, he was in fact marrying his first cousin. As the treasured only daughter of the Elector and Electress of Saxony she was given a good education at the court of Dresden, one of the most cultivated in Germany. Erdmuth Sophie's intellectual and literary ambitions were not restricted to the field of devotional literature in which so many of her contemporaries indulged. Her main interest was in history and politics and in 1666 she anonymously published a work entitled *A Treatise on the Ages of the World/on the Estates of the Roman Empire and the Consitution of the same* (*Handlung von der Welt Alter/des Röm. Reichs Ständten und derselben Beschaffenheit*), whose popularity is shown by the several editions it enjoyed over the next decades. Her physical beauty was obviously well known and she had a robust constitution which allowed her to engage in riding and hunting. She died in 1670 after a chill taken when riding in foggy and wet weather developed into what seems to have been a consumptive fever. Her marriage had remained childless.

There are several points which called for special treatment by the authors of Erdmuth Sophie's funeral biography. The most important was her infertility, which had obvious dynastic repercussions. The fertility of princes was hardly ever called into question and childlessness was seen as a failure of the princess, unless her husband was manifestly impotent. The celebration of fecundity cited from the funeral volume for Magdalena Sibylle of Saxony is, however, the general foil against which childlessness must be read, also provided by the funeral volume for Erdmuth Sophie's own mother-in-law Maria Elisabeth, who died of smallpox soon after giving birth to her sixth child in 1664, her children being cited as proof of her good marriage. We can gauge the importance of the question by looking at sources which describe a period of infertility and not a permanent state. The psychological strain of childlessness is revealed in the funeral volume for Louise Henrietta of Orange, first wife of the Great Elector of Brandenburg, who died in 1667. Two years after her marriage in 1646 she gave birth to a son, who died within the year. Several miscarriages followed, and it was not until eight years later, in 1655, that she finally gave birth to another son, who was followed by other children. In this situation, where childlessness is seen as a hiatus, the biographer gives a clear picture of what this could mean for a princess. He describes 'the long loneliness which this caused, especially because of the careless tongues which added to it by insinuating that it was her fault that the Brandenburg tree was being uprooted and would perish ...'[69] In another text for Louise Henrietta by Friedrich Spanheim, printed in the same funeral volume, the topic is taken up again. The purpose of princely marriages, it is stressed, is to guarantee the continuance of the dynasty.[70] Spanheim asserts that in biblical terms Louise Henrietta 'was not a Michal but a Lea or Rachel, not a crippled but a plentiful and fertile vineyard'.[71]

It is against this background that the many references to Erdmuth Sophie of Brandenburg-Bayreuth's lack of children in her funeral volume must be read. The volume begins with three prefatory poems. The first interprets the title-page engraving and it is followed by two elegies by Sigmund von Birken. Birken laments Erdmuth Sophie's childlessness:

> Hätt Sie mögen doch zuvor eine Fürsten Mutter werden
> Diese liebe LandesMutter! und so bliebe doch von Ihr
> ob Sie uns der Himmel nahm/ etwas wehrtes noch auf Erden;
> also sähe man noch tröstlich/ in den Ihren/ Ihre Zier.[72]

> (If only she could have first become the mother of a prince, this dear mother of the nation! Then, despite heaven taking her from us, something of value would still remain here on earth and we would be comforted by seeing her qualities in her children.)

The theme is taken up again at the end of the volume in the poems with which the section of consolation poetry begins. The first three are written in the name of the widower's stepbrothers, children of his father's second wife, Marie Elisabeth, whose death in 1664 of smallpox was mentioned above. Erdmuth Sophie is apostrophised by all three with reference to her lack of children as a surrogate mother to the orphaned princes. The poem for the eldest, Erdmann Philipp, claims

Ob Sie in den MUTTER-Orden
Gleich nicht aufgenommen worden
Lebt Sie doch nicht Kinder-loß:
Mutter können wir drey Weysen
Vor und nach dem Tod Sie heissen.[73]

(Even though she was not accepted into the order of mothers (*Mutter-Orden*) she did not live childless: we three orphans can call her mother before and after death.)

In her curriculum vitae Erdmuth Sophie's unexpected barrenness is also directly addressed: 'People lived in the good hope and persuasion that because these high born princely persons had come together in the bloom of their youth, in their 18th year, with good physical constitutions and health, also with good physical appearance and love and friendship, that by God's grace the fruits of marriage which the princess herself desired would soon follow, in accordance with Psalm 113, "he maketh the barren woman to keep house and to be a joyful mother", that she would be made the happy mother of a child and that she herself, the often-mentioned Electoral grandparents, especially however this land and principality, would be made happy thereby.'[74] In all these texts Erdmuth Sophie's childlessness is juxtaposed, if not linked, with her intellectual and literary ambitions. The lines just quoted from the poem by her eldest stepson continue:

Ja aus deß Gehirnes-Schoß
Ist so manches Kind gestiegen
daß Sie nicht kan Fruchtloß liegen.[75]

(Yes, various children emerged from the womb of her brain, so that she cannot lie [in her grave] without fruit.)

The funeral biography also posits a direct link between barrenness and women's intellectual activities:

> And because as we have already mentioned her Highness was not blessed by God with the desired marital blessings [i.e. children], for her recreation and her diversion she turned her thoughts to other things and to building. Especially, when she was at home and had completed her devotions, her Highness delighted in political texts and historical descriptions, reading them diligently and commanding her ladies to follow her example, and to remain in her chambers and pay attention. And because, by daily practice, she attained a particular understanding and knowledge in this area, she composed a tract out of all sorts of useful material and had it printed here in the year 1666 under the title A Treatise on the Ages of the World, on the Estates of the Roman Empire and the Constitution of the same etc., without any mention of her name, however, and she communicated it only to those who enjoyed her special trust and confidence. And this book has also been reprinted in other places since.[76]

The intellectual activities of the princess, when not restricted to the writing of devotional texts in accordance with her role as a 'pillar of prayer', were often explained as masculine aspects of her mind.[77] In his prefatory poem for the funeral volume Sigmund von Birken writes, 'Masculine was the great mind in the delicate frame of her body'. The idea of her androgynous mind is taken up in a consolatory poem by Johann Christoph von Pühel:

> Ach ach! es ist erblast/ die Königin der Frauen/
> Ein Spiegel aller Zucht/ in dem man konte schauen
> Als in einem Band verknüpfft der höchsten Tugend-Schaar/
> So theils nicht wohl weiblich/ und theils kaum männlich war.[78]

> (Oh! Oh! the queen of women is become pale, a mirror of all virtues, in which the highest assembly of virtues were reflected as if they were bound in a cord, and they were partly not properly female and partly hardly masculine.)

Another masculine attribute associated with Erdmuth Sophie by her biographers was her love of hunting and riding, all traits which by their very diffuse contextualisation with her childlessness gain in significance. Erdmuth Sophie's natural body and her physical beauty, demonstrated in the portrait accompanying the volume, is also a recurring theme in the funeral book. It occurs in the context of her literary talents and thus underlines the feminine aspects which her mind negates.

> Hat Ihr edler Zeitvertreib unsre Sprach nit adeln können
> mit den bästen Poesyen / mit den wohlberedtsten Kiel?
> Auch so muste Venus selbst Ihr den Schönheit Vorzug gönnen:
> weil der allerschönsten Tugend ein gleich schönes Haus gefiel.[79]

(Did not her noble pastime ennoble our language with the best verses, with the most eloquent quill? Even Venus herself had to allow her precedence in beauty, because the most beautiful of virtues enjoyed an equally beautiful dwelling.)

The poem written in the name of her youngest stepson, aged five, laments the loss of her beauty:

> Soll Ich nicht umbschräncket seyn
> von Euch mehr/ Ihr Marmor-Arme?
> Ach! Ach! Daß es GOTT erbarme/
> blast der Hände Helffenbein!
> soll der schönste Busen mich
> nicht mehr an sein Herze drücken[80]

(Shall I no longer be embraced by you, arms of marble? Oh! Oh! The ivory of her hands pales so that even God takes pity. Shall the most beautiful bosom no longer press me to its heart?)

In the context of her illness, Erdmuth Sophie's outward beauty becomes part of the motif of vanity and the deceptiveness of outward appearances. Her misleading outer shell masks an advanced state of inner physical corruption, which is described in drastic detail:

As far as her bodily constitution is concerned, everyone could see with their own eyes that her Highness had at all times had a beautiful figure and face, a straight and well-proportioned body and that she had a cheerful disposition, and according to outward appearances she could have been thought to be of the best and most healthy nature that could be found.

Especially because food and drink agreed with her Highness very well, and she not only slept well, but she could take part in and endure all sorts of exertions. The conclusion proved far different, however, and showed that she had always been subject to attacks of thin and acrid fluxes, or, as the doctors call it, by destillationibus tenuibus, salsis & acris.[81]

The inner corruption caused by these unnoticed fluxes is described in dramatic detail as the state of her health declines and she is shown to have 'a strange weakness of the stomach and a notable inability to digest', caused by the malevolent disposition of her pancreas and liver, with accumulations of 'fluxes of Tartaric matter and gall', which prove fatal.

Because it became apparent that there was also an inflammation of the inner organs and a febris scorbutica, together with a continual salivation which lasted until her blessed end, with fermentatione atrabilaris & tartarei or continuous eruption of the Tartaric fluxes which beset her Highness with such heartfelt fear that it was often feared that she would suffocate as a result of the fact that the viscera secundae concoctionis, the liver and pancreas, as has already been briefly mentioned, were so weakened they could not generate healthy and pure blood any more, whereas the malignant vapours rushed to the heart via the normal air and blood arteries and so assaulted, dissipated, and destroyed its spirit and its vital energy that from day to day the weakness and debility gained the upper hand and her already debilitated strength was completely consumed.[82]

In over seven folio pages the physical degeneration of the young Markgräfin is depicted until she finally dies surrounded by members of her family and court and with the hand of the court preacher blessing her. The aspects of the funeral volume highlighted above should not create the impression that any aspersions were cast directly or indirectly on Erdmuth Sophie's piety. As already mentioned, it was asserted that she only turned her attention to her daily reading of historical and political texts after she had completed her devotions. Her final illness and her steadfast faith, even on her deathbed, is in accordance with her exemplary function within the constraints of the genre. It is what is said over and above these standard elements that attracts attention.

This is particularly the case with the image which the funeral volume projects of the happy, companionate marriage led by

Erdmuth Sophie and her young husband Christian Ernst, to whom the work is dedicated and by whom we must assume it was commissioned. In the context of her barrenness the curriculum vitae notes that this situation did not make the Markgräfin despair, but that she comforted herself with her husband's pious personal motto, which taught that the God-fearing can make the best of everything. The text then proceeds with a depiction of her great conjugal love: 'The blessed princess loved her husband and master with all her heart and so passionately that she could hardly be parted from him, or when he was away on a journey she could not go to bed until she had certain and positive news of his condition and his expected return. Her highness kept mostly to her rooms, held her prayers in the morning and evening with seemly devotion and gave thanks to God that in His paternal goodness He had kept him and her other relatives safe from harm.'[83] When the Markgräfin fell ill, Christian Ernst, who was paying a visit to the Berlin court, hastened to her bedside, which, according to the biographers, he hardly left until she died. Her mother, Magdalena Sibylle, had also been summoned from Dresden and remained with her until her death. Both the Electress and the Elector, Johann Georg II, attended the funeral in person and thus both parents were in the congregation to hear their daughter's funeral biography read out in public. Like many of those in court circles who perhaps only read the version of Erdmuth Sophie's vita propagated by her widower, they were well aware that this version did not accord with reality, especially as far as the relations between the married couple themselves were concerned.

The only lengthy study of Erdmuth Sophie to date was published in 1975 in a journal for Franconian regional history by Joachim Kröll.[84] The archival material unearthed by Kröll in Bamberg and Merseburg shows that all those involved in the production of the funeral volume – Christian Ernst, his court preacher Kaspar von Lilien, and his Chancellor von Stein – had been involved in intensive plans for a legal separation of the marriage. In 1668, two years before the Markgräfin's death, Christian Ernst had travelled to Berlin to discuss the matter with the Great Elector, the head of the Brandenburg dynasty, under whose protection he had placed himself. The Elector pledged his assistance in the divorce and advised Christian Ernst how best to proceed in the light of difficulties which might arise with the Markgräfin's family in Dresden. The young Markgraf believed that he had evidence of

Erdmuth Sophie's adultery with his equerry Achatz Friedrich von der Schulenburg, and indeed that he claimed to have learned that she had already had illicit affairs in Dresden even before her marriage. The extensive correspondence concerning the marriage dispute contains letters and statements from the Markgräfin herself, from the Electors of Brandenburg and Saxony, from von der Schulenburg, and from members of the Bayreuth privy council. In a letter to his wife's father, the Elector of Saxony, Christian Ernst not only claimed to have letters in his possession proving that two years after their marriage the Markgräfin had already had an affair with one of his former equerries, von Oeppe, but also that Erdmuth Sophie had denied him his conjugal rights several times and that she had taunted him in public with unseemly words. All of this, he asserted, was well known to her parents. In order to avoid further public scandal, the Markgraf agreed to a reconciliation with his unfaithful wife, not before demanding, however, that Saxon officials should remonstrate with her and persuade her to alter her behaviour towards him, if only for the sake of appearances. Against the backdrop of this semi-public knowledge, the description of the Markgräfin's deathbed repentance and her confession in the funeral volume take on a special significance: 'And afterwards, although she was very weak and had lost all her strength, she made her quite lengthy confession with great piety and devotion, also shedding many tears, and she received Holy absolution with a glad heart and spirit.'[85]

Christian Gerber was cited at the beginning of this essay as a reader of court funeral books. He claimed that the best part were the biographies, even if they did not always represent the truth. Contemporary readers were fully aware of the conventions of the genre and the tensions which they caused. The importance attached to such monuments in paper can be shown by a final example, in which an attempt was made to use the genre for the purposes of social rehabilitation. The Elector Palatine, Karl Ludwig, brother to Sophie of Hanover and father of Liselotte von der Pfalz, caused a European scandal when he rejected his wife Charlotte of Hessen-Kassel and went through a bigamous marriage ceremony with one of her ladies-in-waiting, Louise von Degenfeld.[86] Charlotte held out in Heidelberg for quite some time, but eventually she returned to her family in Kassel and was one of those abandoned princesses for whom there was no commemorative funeral volume. Karl Ludwig and the Raugräfin, as she became known, lived in Schwetzingen, but

Louise von Degenfeld remained a social outcast. Her death in 1677 posed enormous problems of protocol, for there was no proper place for the body of a bigamous wife. In order to overcome the problem of 'where', Karl Ludwig had her body buried at night in a vault in the foundations for a church in Friedrichsburg which had yet to be built. No sermons appear to have been preached on this occasion.

Taking the offensive, however, Karl Ludwig also had a funeral volume published in her honour entitled *Leyd- und Ehren Grabmahl* (Funeral monument of suffering and honour). The problems confronting the compilers of this work are shown by the components missing from this volume which usually form the standard core of such works. The folio format and the general appearance of the volume may seem consistent with the ceremonial status of a consort. It consists of a main text with the curriculum vitae, a consolatory letter addressed to the daughters of the Raugräfin, a collection of 20 epicedia, and a report of the ceremonies which took place at the vault a short time after the burial. The central text around which all other texts in a funeral book are usually grouped, the funeral sermon by a court preacher, is completely missing here. The text of the *Leyd- und Ehren Grabmahl* begins with what would probably be best defined as an *Abdankung* (oration), the secular speech given after the burial outside the church by a lay person. It is into this speech that the curriculum vitae was incorporated. This text is anonymous, as are all the other prose texts in the volume. Recurring reference is made to the concept of 'impartial judgement', to which a person may only truly be subjected once they are dead. Much attention is paid to the Raugräfin's physical beauty. She is apostrophised as incomparable and her beauty as superior to that of any Venus of antiquity. Both her lack of princely lineage and her marital status, referred to as the fact that the Elector had been moved 'to take her to him in the form of a marriage and to enter into conjugal relations with her'[87], are quickly passed over. The reader is referred several times to acts and documents which will soon be published in her vindication. Only in one point can her life claim to have conformed to the ideal pattern of the consort and this is broadly vented: her enormous fecundity. Much is made of the fact that her thirteen children were a sign of God's blessing on her union, and her death shortly before coming to term with her fourteenth child is seen as a heroic act.

The ceremonial report of the nightly burial ceremony itself draws attention to the fact that there were no ambassadors from other courts present. The only religious elements in the funeral in the volume are found in the description of the foundation-laying ceremony for the church in Friedrichsburg. There was a speech on the occasion by the Heidelberg professor of theology, Johann Ludwig Fabricius. He refers to the mourning clothes worn by the Elector Palatine and the court, but fails to mention the Raugräfin personally or her death. His speech is called a 'sermon' in the funeral volume, which it is not. An aura of religious service is thus created in the text and indirectly linked to the Raugräfin, where it was impossible in reality.

The difficulties and convolutions expressed in this volume and its attempts to assimilate an outcast into the mould of the ideal consort represent an extreme in dynastic publishing strategy. It demonstrates, however, that contemporaries clearly attached great importance to funeral books and their biographies as a means of generating a portrait of the deceased for posterity, 'even if they are not based on the truth'.[88]

Notes

1. Heide Wunder, 'Er ist die Sonn', sie ist der Mond': Frauen in der Frühen Neuzeit (Munich, 1992), 205ff.; Heide Wunder, 'Herrschaft und öffentliches Handeln von Frauen in der Gesellschaft der Frühen Neuzeit', in Frauen in der Geschichte des Rechts. Von der Frühen Neuzeit bis zur Gegenwart, ed. Ute Gerhard (Munich, 1997), 27–54; Heide Wunder, Helga Zöttlein and Barbara Hoffmann, 'Religiosität und politisches Handeln von Frauen vom ausgehenden 16. bis zum Beginn des 18. Jahrhunderts', Zeitsprünge. Forschungen zur Frühen Neuzeit 1/1 (1997), 75–98.
2. Gerhard Köbler, Historisches Lexikon der deutschen Länder. Die deutschen Territorien vom Mittelalter bis zur Gegenwart, 5th edn (Munich,1995), XIV.
3. The catalogue of the exhibition Sophie Charlotte und ihr Schloss. Ein Musenhof in Brandenburg-Preußen (Munich/ London/ New York, 1999), 65, sums up the present situation in the words: 'No comprehensive study on the topic of the consort of the ruler in the Baroque period is known to us'.
4. In his diary Friedrich I of Saxony-Gotha noted that in three days over 3,600 people in the small town of Gotha had viewed his sister's body on its lit de parade: '18.6.1682 Mourning clothes were donned and I had sermons preached in the morning and afternoon in my chambers. In the afternoon I viewed the body. On this day I signed 63 letters, on this day more than 80 people viewed the body. 19.6.1682 In the morning I wrote

to my sister in Darmstadt, to little Christine in Eutin, to Princess Sophie Agnes, and to Herr Ludolf by my own hand, also dispatched 36 letters of notification, on this day 2402 people have been up here to view the body. *20.6.1682* ... On this day 1136 people have been up here who viewed the body.' Roswitha Jacobsen ed., *Friedrich von Sachsen-Gotha und Altenburg: Die Tagebücher 1667–1686, Zweiter Band Tagebücher 1678–1686* (Weimar, 2000), 213f.

5. Joseph Leighton, Poems of Mortality in the German Baroque, *German Life and Letters*, 36 (1982/83), 241–57.
6. Jill Bepler, 'German Funeral Books and the Festival Description. A Parallel Development', in *The German Book 1450–1750*, eds. John Flood and William Kelly (London, 1995), 145–60.
7. Jill Bepler, Birgit Kümmel and Helga Meise, 'Weibliche Selbstdarstellung im 17. Jahrhundert. Das Funeralwerk der Landgräfin Sophia Eleonora von Hessen-Darmstadt', in *Geschlechterperspektiven. Forschungen zur Frühen Neuzeit*, eds. Heide Wunder and Gisela Engel (Königstein i. Taunus, 1998), 441–68, here 442.
8. Jill Bepler, 'Ansichten eines Staatsbegräbnisses. Funeralwerke und Diarien als Quelle zeremonieller Praxis', in *Zeremoniell als höfische Ästhetik in Spätmittelalter und Früher Neuzeit*, eds. Jörg Jochen Berns and Thomas Rahn (Tübingen, 1995), 183–97.
9. Jill Bepler, 'Das Trauerzeremoniell an den Höfen Hessens und Thüringens in der ersten Hälfte des 17. Jahrhunderts', in *Frühneuzeitliche Hofkultur in Hessen und Thüringen*, eds. Jörg Jochen Berns and Detlef Ignasiak (Jena, 1993), 249–65.
10. Rudolf Lenz, *'De mortuis nil nisi bene'? Leichenpredigten als multidisziplinäre Quelle unter besonderer Berücksichtigung der Historischen Familienforschung, der Bildungsgeschichte und der Literaturgeschichte* (Sigmaringen, 1990).
11. Jill Bepler, 'Women in German Funeral Sermons: Models of Virtue or Slice of Life?', *German Life and Letters* 44 (1991), 392–403.
12. Jill Bepler, '"Im dritten Gradu ungleicher Linie Seitwarts verwandt". Frauen und dynastisches Bewußtsein in den Funeralwerken der Frühen Neuzeit', in *Dynastie und Herrschaftssicherung in der Frühen Neuzeit. Geschlecht und Geschlechter*, ed. Heide Wunder (Berlin 2002) (Beiheft 28 Zeitschrift für Historische Forschung), 135–60.
13. Christian Gerber, *Historia derer Wiedergebohrnen in Sachsen, Dritter Theil; Oder Exempel hoher und vornehmer Personen weiblichen Geschlechts , mit denen sich im Leben und Tode viel Merckwürdiges zugetragen; Als eine Continuation von M. Bruno Quinos, weil. Pred. in Zittau, Disce Mori, Oder Sterbe-Kunst; sowohl aus gewissen Urkunden, als eigener Erfahrung gesammlet* (Dresden, 1727), 351.
14. Nigel Llewellyn, *The Art of Death. Visual Culture in the English Death Ritual c. 1500–c. 1800*, London, 1991. In her comprehensive study, Beatrix Bastl, *Tugend, Liebe, Ehre. Die adelige Frau in der Frühen Neuzeit* (Vienna/Cologne/Weimar), 2000, which encompasses all phases

of women's lives, Bastl goes beyond this binary model and examines numerous 'border situations' in which the woman's body assumes symbolic significance. Her fascinating study is based on archival sources and artefacts. My concern here is exclusively with printed sources and their reflection of the media presentation of the woman's body after her death.

15. Irmgard Wilhelm-Schaffer, *Gottes Beamter und Spielmann des Teufels. Der Tod im Spätmittelalter und Früher Neuzeit* (Cologne/Weimar/Vienna), 1999, 196f.

16. Rudolf Schlögl, 'Öffentliche Gottesverehrung und privater Glaube in der Frühen Neuzeit. Beobachtungen zur Bedeutung von Kirchenzucht und Frömmigkeit für die Abgrenzung privater Sozialräume', in *Das Öffentliche und Private in der Vormoderne*, eds. Gert Melville and Peter von Moos (Cologne/Weimar/Vienna), 1998, 196f.

17. Jill Bepler, 'Die Fürstin als Betsäule – Anleitung und Praxis der Erbauung am Hof', *Morgen-Glantz* 12 (2002), 249–64.

18. Charles W. Ingrao and Andrew L. Thomas, 'Piety and Patronage: The Empress-Consort of the High Baroque', *German History*, 20/1 (2000), 20–43.

19. Wunder, *'Er ist die Sonn'*, 57f.

20. Bartholomaeus Stosch, *Die Selige Hofnung*, in: *Sieben Leichenpredigten ...* (Cölln an der Spree, 1668), 4.

21. Katrin Keller, 'Kurfürstin Anna von Sachsen (1532–1585). Von Möglichkeiten und Grenzen einer "Landesmutter"', in *Das Frauenzimmer. Die Frau bei Hofe in Spätmittelalter und früher Neuzeit*, eds. Jan Hirschbiegel and Werner Paravicini, (Stuttgart, 2000), 263–85.

22. *Sechs und vierzig Leichpredigten* (Leipzig, 1588); Jill Bepler, 'im dritten gradu', 139–41.

23. Claudia Opitz, 'Hausmutter und Landesfürstin', in *Der Mensch des Barock*, ed. Rosario Villari (Frankfurt am Main, 1999), 344–70.

24. *Sechs und vierzig*, 38.

25. Basilius Satler, *Ein Predigt gethan bey der Begrebnis ...*, (Wolfenbüttel, 1602), fol. Jiii^v.

26. John Roger Paas, *The German Political Broadsheet 1600–1700*, Vol. 1: *1600–1615* (Wiesbaden, 1985), 133.

27. Wilhem-Schaffer, *Gottes Beamter*, 104f.

28. Schlögl, *Öffentliche Gottesverehrung*, 195.

29. Jan Pirozynski, *Die Herzogin Sophie von Braunschweig-Wolfenbüttel aus dem Hause der Jagellonen (1522–1575) und ihre Bibliothek* (Wiesbaden, 1992), 245.

30. Bartholomäus Stosch, *Wahres Christenthumb Der Weiland Durchleuchtigsten Fürstinn* (Berlin, 1660), 88f.

31. Bartholomäus Stosch, *Sieben Leichenpredigten Nebst unterschiedlichen Anderen Traur-Schrifften* (Berlin, 1668), 107f.

32. *Fürstl. Schleßwig-Holstein-Glücksburgische Gedächtniß-Seule* (Hamburg, 1672), 59.

33. Johann Anselm Steiger, *Schule des Sterbens. Die 'Kirchhofgedanken' des Andreas Gryphius (1616–1664) als poetologische Theologie im Vollzug* (Heidelberg, 2000), 50.
34. On the question of the topoi of the death scenes in funeral sermons and their exemplary function see Wilhelm-Schaffer, *Gottes Beamter*, 190f.
35. Roswitha Jacobsen, 'Fürstenfreundschaft. Landgraf Ludwig VI. von Hessen-Darmstadt und Friedrich I. von Sachsen-Gotha und Altenburg in ihren Selbstzeugnissen', in *Ars et amicitia. Festschrift für Martin Bircher zum 60. Geburtstag*, eds. Ferdinand van Ingen and Christian Juranek (Amsterdam, 1998), 475–502.
36. Helga Meise, *Das archivierte Ich. Schreibkalender und höfische Repräsentation in Hessen-Darmstadt 1624–1790* (Darmstadt, 2002), 236.
37. Ibid., 283f.
38. On the treatment of signs of mental illness in German royal families of the sixteenth century see the case studies in: H.C. Erik Midelfort, *Mad Princes of Renaissance Germany* (Charlottesville/London, 1994).
39. *Ehren Gedächtnüs Der Weiland Durchleuchtigsten Fürstin und Frauen Magdalenen Sibyllen ... Aus treu-liebendem Hertzen auffgerichtet Von Dero hinterbliebenen höchstbekümmerten Herrn Gemahl* (Gotha, 1681).
40. Roswitha Jacobsen, *Friedrich I. von Sachsen-Gotha und Altenburg: Die Tagebücher 1667–1686, Erster Band Tagebücher 1667–1677* (Weimar, 1998).
41. Ibid., 147.
42. Ibid.
43. Ibid., 147.
44. Ibid., 148.
45. The rooms of the ducal family were all hung with black mourning drapes due to the death of Friedrich's mother two weeks previously.
46. Ibid.
47. The Duchess died on 7 January 1681 at midnight, the Duke remained at the side of the body until at 2 a.m. it had been 'properly prepared'; the next day he wrote letters of notification to the family. On 9 January the body was dressed for burial and put in the first coffin, on the 11th the Duke viewed the body 'which was still very fine', on the next day he inspected the burial vault, on the 14th he checked through 'matter for the curriculum vitae' and searched her papers in vain for notes she might have made on a Bible verse for the sermon, on the 16th the first sermon was preached on the text he had selected himself and the body was placed in the second coffin, which he did not have closed until 20 January. On the 21st the coffin was taken to the vault for burial and the next day the funeral ceremonies took place at part of which the curriculum vitae was read aloud. Jacobsen, *Friedrich I*, 149–51.
48. *Ehren Gedächtnüs*, 1681, fol. Gii[v].
49. Ibid., Giii[v].
50. Ibid., Giiii.

51. Uwe Steiner, 'Triumphale Trauer. Die Trauerfeierlichkeiten aus Anlaß des Todes der ersten preußischen Königin in Berlin im Jahre 1705', *Forschungen zur brandenburgischen und preußischen Geschichte*, n.s., 11 (2001), 23–52.

52. Christine van den Heuvel, 'Sophie von der Pfalz (1630–1714) und ihre Tochter Sophie Charlotte (1668–1705)', in *Deutsche Frauen der Frühen Neuzeit. Dichterinnen – Malerinnen – Mäzeninnen*, eds. Heide Wunder and Kerstin Merkel (Darmstadt, 2000), 77–92, here 89.

53. *Sophie Charlotte*, 227.

54. Gerhild Komander, 'Tod und Trauer am brandenburg-preußischen Hof', in: *Sophie Charlotte und ihr Schloss. Ein Musenhof in Brandenburg-Preußen* (Munich/London, 1999), 174.

55. Ibid., 175.

56. *Christ-Königliches Trauer- und Ehren-Gedächtnüs* (Berlin 1705), fol. J1^{v}.

57. Ibid., 37.

58. Ibid., fol. L2^{v}.

59. Ibid., fol. M2^{v}.

60. Ibid., fol. N2.

61. Maria Fürstenwald (ed.), *Trauerreden des Barock* (Wiesbaden, 1973), 364.

62. Ibid., 378.

63. Ibid., 379.

64. Bastl, *Tugend, Liebe, Ehre*, 431f.

65. The inscription records the Duchess's second marriage in 1650 'to the most illustrious Prince Christian Duke of Mecklenburg with whom she lived until the year 1652 when she was forced by his bad behaviour to resolve to move to the residence of her brother-in-law in Wolfenbüttel, the illustrious Prince, and (because she was shamefully deserted by her husband) she remained there until the year 1666 ...' Mechthild Wiswe, *Die Särge im jüngeren herzöglichen Grabgewölbe der Hauptkirche Beatae Mariae Virginis*, in: *Die Hauptkirche Beatae Mariae Virginis in Wolfenbüttel*, ed. Hans-Herbert Möller (Hannover, 1987), 199.

66. Jakob Weller, *Chur-Sächsischer Macht: und Ehren-Schild/ Das ist: Drey Christliche Leich-Predigten/von Der Unüberwindlichen Sachsen-Burg* (Dresden 1659), 236. See: Bepler, *Im dritten Gradu*, S. 146.

67. Joachim Kröll, 'Bayreuther Barock und frühe Aufklärung 1. Teil: Markgräfin Erdmuth Sophie (1644–1670) und ihre Bedeutung für Bayreuth', *Archiv für Geschichte von Oberfranken* 55 (1975), 55–174.

68. Köbler, *Historisches Lexikon*, 46.

69. Stosch, *Die selige Hofnung*, 39.

70. Ibid., 22.

71. Ibid. Michal was one of David's wives, whose barrenness was generally considered to have been a divine punishment for her vanity.

72. Kaspar von Lilien, *Höchst-betraurlicher Kronen-Fall ...* (Bayreuth, 1670), unpag.

73. Ibid., 265.

74. Ibid., 35.
75. Ibid., 265.
76. Ibid., 39.
77. In 1735 David Fassmann wrote a fictive debate between Markgräfin Erdmuth Sophie and Sophie Charlotte Queen of Prussia, in the 'Empire of the Dead', on the question of the appropriate education of princesses. Their biographies are taken directly from their funeral sermons. David Fassmann, *Gespräche in dem Reiche derer Todten, Zweyhundert und erste Entrevüe der ersten Königin von Preussen, Sophie Charlotte, Und der ... Marggräfin von Bayreuth, Erdmuth Sophia ...* (Leipzig, 1735), 672–754.
78. Von Lilien, *Höchst betrauerlicher ...*, unpag.
79. Ibid.
80. Ibid., 267.
81. Ibid., 39.
82. Ibid., 40.
83. Ibid., 37.
84. Kröll, Bayreuther Barock.
85. Ibid., 42.
86. Johann Jakob Moser, *Familien-Staats-Recht Derer Teutschen Reichsstände Zweyter Theil* (Frankfurt/Leipzig, 1775), 402f.
87. *Leyd- und Ehren-Grabmahl Der Weyland Hochgebohrnen Frauen ...* (Heidelberg, 1677), 6.
88. Gerber, *Historia*, 351.

8

'Madame, Ma Chère Fille' – 'Dearest Child'

Letters from Imperial Mothers to Royal Daughters

Regina Schulte

Empress Maria Theresa of Austria and Queen Victoria appear to have had a good deal in common. Both ascended the throne in the absence of a male successor, and both married men whom they loved and who supported them as the rulers of vast empires. Their large broods of children and immense girth are additional similarities, as is the shape of the long widowhood that followed the deaths of their husbands. Yet the two women differed fundamentally in the way they saw themselves and in their functions as queens and mothers, and their disparate life patterns were rooted in the epochal differences between their monarchies. In the following analysis of the letters of these two female rulers to their daughters, who were also destined to become queens, I would like to work out what the differences were between what they could feel and express about themselves and their daughters in the contexts of their times. I will take up two forms inherent in the letters themselves, as metaphors or as analytical probes: the portrait as a rigid normative outer skin of representation and the epistolary novel as a narrative structure of middle-class individuality. In their female variant, they point all the more clearly to the traces of transformation that had become inscribed on the bodies of queens over a century, from the aristocratic culture of the *ancien regime* to the middle-class foundation of constitutional monarchy.

Maria Theresa to Marie-Antoinette

'I await Liotard's picture with great impatience, but in all your finery, and neither in morning garb nor in gentleman's attire. For I love to see you in the position that is your due. I kiss you,'[1] wrote Maria Theresa in 1770 to her daughter Marie-Antoinette. In what follows, I do not intend to introduce a painting of Marie-Antoinette by Jean-Etienne Liotard, Elisabeth-Louise Vigée-Lebrun or other famous painters, but rather to uncover that particular 'portrait' of the imperial daughter Marie-Antoinette for which Maria Theresa had yearned for so long.

> I would like to have your figure in court dress [she wrote in 1777] even if the face is not such a good likeness. In order not to inconvenience you too greatly, it will suffice to have the figure and the attitude with which I am not familiar, and which pleases everyone so much. Since I lost my daughter so young, when she was a child, the desire to know how she has developed will excuse my importunate request, which comes from a heart full of maternal affection.[2]

Maria Theresa was, however, precisely *not* asking for the individual and 'like' portrait of her distant daughter, whom she had lost as a child, and whom she would never see or touch again. What she longed to see was the result of the transformation of the childish body natural of the Austrian princess into the body political of the French dauphine. She awaited the painting that represented the queen of France, who was the person she wanted to see.[3] It is as if Maria Theresa had already had a version of this picture in mind before she even married off her daughter, as if she were simply waiting for confirmation. I will try to locate this projected portrait in the letters she wrote to Marie-Antoinette over a period of ten years. I would like to reveal that image which Maria Theresa herself devised of her daughter as queen of France, her own interior portrait, which the official portrait painters long failed to provide to her satisfaction.

On 21 April 1770, Empress Maria Theresa's dearest wish in regard to the politics of marrying off her children was fulfilled.[4] Her youngest daughter, the fourteen-and-a-half-year-old Maria Antonia, left Vienna to wed the dauphin of France and live as his wife at Versailles. The marriage of the young princess, the last of a series of daughters of Maria Theresa's destined for the thrones of Europe, to the grandson of Louis XV, the sixteen-year-old Louis, Duc de Berry, had long been planned in the framework of an expansive foreign policy co-engineered by Count Wenzel von Kaunitz, and was intended to be understood as a pledge in the alliance between the houses of Habsburg and Bourbon, which had existed since 1756. The Habsburg–Bourbon friendship was to be further cemented through a family alliance. The main players in this political matrimonial spectacle had never met, but since love matches such as that between Maria Theresa and Francis Stephen of Lorraine owed far more to good luck than to intention, etiquette and ceremonial would determine the couple's first steps. With the day of this marriage begins Maria Theresa's documented attempt to transform her inexperienced and poorly prepared daughter into the queen of France. As in the earlier instances of her daughters Maria Amalia and Marie Caroline, she provided her with the instruction, also dated 21 April, to 'read every month [her] prescriptions for conduct'.[5] These instructions applied to her married state and position as a princess, and were imbedded in the catalogue of Habsburg virtues and a bundle of religious duties and practices. From now on, however, Marie-Antoinette would also be accompanied for ten years and several months by the tireless advice and reproaches, religious admonitions and suggestions for reading, rules of conduct and corrections that came from the distant but controlling eye of her mother (who loved her 'more than anything').

> At the beginning of each month I will send a courier from here to Paris. You could prepare your letters before his arrival, so that you might send them back with him immediately … You can also write to me by post, but only trivial matters that anyone might know about. I do not think that you should write your family, except for special occasions and the emperor, with whom you will reach an agreement regarding this point.[6]

She asked Marie-Antoinette to destroy her letters, which would allow her to write more freely, and promised to do the same with her daughter's correspondence. In this way she created a secret alliance, without, however, letting Marie-Antoinette know that she maintained an extensive secret correspondence at the same time with her local confidant in Versailles, Count Mercy-Argenteau, in which she shared and discussed all those secrets, passing on Marie-Antoinette's secret letters, and that he had already provided her with much of the information she gleaned from her daughter under the pressure of secrecy.[7]

In her letters, Maria Theresa began by assigning her daughter a place in the 'family' in distant Versailles, under 'good' King Louis XV, an 'affectionate father ... who will also be your friend, if you deserve it', whom she should love and obey, whose thoughts she should ascertain, whom she should follow, and whose orders and instructions she should await.[8] She then outlined the duties of a wife: she should obey her husband in all things and have no other ambition than to please him and do his will. 'The only true happiness in this world is a happy marriage: I can testify to that. Everything depends upon the woman, if she is compliant, kind and amusing.'[9] The framework and main characters of the future family portrait were set out, and it was now up to the daughter to discover the motivations underlying her mother's concern that the content be filled, and form and trappings conform to her standards.

A Mother's Love

My dear daughter, here are four points that I recommend to you with all the love of which you know I am capable: Do not say that I scold, that I preach. Say rather: Mama loves me very much and is constantly concerned about me and my well-being. You must believe her and comfort her by following her advice. You will feel easy in this, and in future every shadow that has so vexed you will be banished from my confidence.[10]

Maria Theresa repeatedly emphasised her fond love for her daughter, ever the devoted mother who spent 'precious moments with [her] tenderly beloved daughter',[11] whose 'fond kisses' end many letters, and who would make her 'dear daughter' happy 'if it cost me my life'.[12]

This imperial-maternal love traversed national borders. Maria Theresa sent a gift in which the daughter's delicate bloom appears transformed into a diamond-studded carnation in a vase embellished with pictures of the imperial palace at Vienna:

I was so glad that you were pleased with my flower [wrote Maria Theresa] and I hope that it fits well in the vase. It arrived just at the right moment to be of service to you at the reception of the diplomatic corps. It is my dearest wish that all of Europe know how much I love you, and that my happiness rests in that of my children.[13]

All of Europe would know, but most particularly the 'evil neighbour',[14] the much detested Frederick II of Prussia, before whom Maria Theresa paraded not just a beloved daughter, but also the successful alliance between Austria and France. This special maternal gift for a special occasion presented not just a nostalgic memento of Viennese valuables, but also positioned both daughter and imperial-royal portrait of love and family on the European stage.

The Place of the Dauphine/Queen

Maria Theresa asked her daughter to provide the most precise descriptions of her daily routine in Versailles – from her morning devotions to accounts broken down by the hour and minute of her meals, meetings of the royal family and the court, evening entertainments and finally going to bed. Maria Theresa followed the daily movements, conduct and appearance of her daughter through the eyes of the confidant she had sent to Versailles, Count Florimond de Mercy-Argenteau and his spies, and through the father-confessor Abbé de Vermond.[15] With their reports and Marie-Antoinette's monthly letters in hand, she began to intervene incessantly in Marie-Antoinette's life in Versailles. She waited impatiently for every scrap of news, in order to answer immediately with corrective advice. Every letter begins 'My dear Madame daughter!'

She worried about the correct style of behaviour for her daughter in courtly Versailles. The appropriate degree of proximity and distance became a decisive means of properly occupying the place of dauphine and queen within the family, at court and in public: 'Avoid familiarity, for that would impress no one, because it is common; kindness is what creates closeness and reassures everyone ... Do not tolerate gossip; make people be quiet instead, or at least avoid or withdraw from them.'[16] The omniscient Maria Theresa informed her daughter that her excessive familiarity had already provoked gossip, so that she could no longer be distinguished from the other princes and princesses. She advised her nevertheless not to play up her God-given dignity before others. 'One must remain in one's place and know how to play one's role; this puts oneself and everyone else at ease. Be obliging and attentive to all, but avoid familiarity.'[17]

Maria Theresa invoked her own role as 'friend' and 'affectionate mother' and her experience to protect Marie-Antoinette from the traps of the court and of her own dependence and carelessness. She should not let herself go in regard to her conduct or her figure, and should resist the advice of the family at the French court (most likely Louis XV's sisters), since it was her prerogative 'to set the tone in Versailles'.[18] Maria Theresa tirelessly warned against excessive intimacy, against gossip and intrigues, admonishing her daughter of the necessity to reassert her select position frequently, since it was imperilled from all sides, and a fifteen-year-old could all too easily fall prey to the dangers of court life. Equipped with a good figure and many assets, which from Maria Theresa's perspective could readily win hearts, inattention and carelessness could nevertheless have dire effects, destroying the balance of the artfully arranged and carefully practised game of encounter and gifts. Maria Theresa tirelessly drummed into her daughter that her place was not among equals – girlfriends, the court youth, or family members – and that her grace, her smile, her kindness and gentleness belonged not to her but to the state. Their wrong application or careless use would only serve the interests of court cabals.

> Nevertheless I cannot hide my sorrow, because I am told from all sides that you have greatly neglected your civilities and courtesies, as you do not have something pleasant and appropriate to say to everyone and do not treat anyone with particular respect.[19] I hear that you have been letting yourself go greatly in this respect ... Worse than anything else, however, is the claim that you have given court society cause for ridicule, by laughing right in people's faces: to do so would be to commit an enormous error, and one could quite rightly doubt the goodness of your heart; in order to please five or six young ladies or gentlemen you would lose all the rest. This error, my dear daughter, cannot be taken lightly in a princess; the consequence would be that all the courtiers, who normally comprise the idle and least commendable people in the state, come to wait upon you, while decent people keep their distance because they do not wish to expose themselves to ridicule ...[20]

Instead of neglect, thoughtless or random favouritism and wasted laughter, what the princess required was a differentiated pattern of attentions. This included the practice of bestowing particular respect (*Auszeichnen*), which Maria Theresa referred to tirelessly:

> It is important, however, to show people particular respect, and you must not neglect to do so.[21] ... I recommend above all that you bestow respect upon foreigners and address them directly, likewise persons of middling age and station who wait upon you. You cannot imagine the impression a look, a greeting or a word from you makes upon such people: it will

become known throughout the kingdom. These good folk are accustomed to being dealt with only when young people or courtiers wish to make fun of them.[22]

In the game of distance and attention, the dauphine/queen marked her place in the context of the court and court society. Her behaviour towards the common people, in contrast, should be characterised by charity and kindness. Maria Theresa used Marie-Antoinette's gift of one thousand écus to the Hotel-Dieu after a disastrous fire as an opportunity for another lesson.

My dear little one, we must set this example, and that is an essential and very sensitive point of our position: the more often you are able to exercise charity and demonstrate generosity without incommoding yourself, the better it will be; and what would be regarded as boastfulness and extravagance in another is suitable and necessary for us. We possess no other means than charity and kindness; this is particularly true of a dauphine or the wife of a monarch.'[23]

'Generosity' (Güte) is a key term in Maria Theresa's instructions for her daughter's behaviour towards her subjects, in order to win their 'love', which constituted the strength and the happiness of the royal station. Neither Marie-Antoinette's beauty, which was in truth not so overwhelming, nor her talents or knowledge – 'You doubtless know that none of this exists',[24] according to a not untypical harsh remark of her mother's – were the important thing. What truly counted were good-heartedness, openness and attentiveness.

The Facets of Beauty

In this way, the empress worked on the body of her daughter to create the figure of the queen within the configuration of the court, trying to visualise her, to envision her movements, and was pleased that her daughter was making progress as a dancer. She sought to reconcile Marie-Antoinette's outward appearance with her own notions of proper royal bearing.

The courier finds that you have grown taller and gained weight. Had you not reassured me with the whalebone corset you wear, this circumstance would have caused me concern because I feared that you were getting stout, and already have the waist of a woman without being one. I beg you not to let yourself go or neglect yourself. That would be ill-suited to your age and even more so to your station.[25]

Gowns, corsets, waists, bodices, teeth and hair – no detail was too petty for Maria Theresa to offer her daughter advice about it. After the death of Louis XV in 1774, Maria Theresa asked again for a portrait of her daughter the queen, this time in a note to Count Mercy-Argenteau.[26] In 1775 the tone of Maria Theresa's letters to her daughter became harsh; Marie-Antoinette's coiffure especially assumed importance:

> I cannot avoid mentioning a point that many of the papers repeat often enough: I am speaking of the wig you wear. It is said to be thirty-six inches high from the roots of your hair and decorated with so many feathers and ribbons that the height is increased still further ... A pretty young queen with so many assets has no need of such foolishness; on the contrary, simplicity of coiffure allows one's appearance to shine forth all the more brightly and better befits a queen's rank.[27]

Marie-Antoinette's predilection for expensive jewellery, with the attending press scandals, aroused Maria Theresa's ire once again: 'A ruler demeans herself when she decks herself out, all the more so ... when she spends so profligately. I am all too familiar with this penchant for reckless extravagance; I cannot remain silent because I love you for the sake of your happiness, and not for the sake of flattery.'[28]

A passion for finery, reckless spending, playing cards all night, long horseback rides, chasing from one pleasure to the next, masquerades, opera balls, which had the worst reputation, a neglect of the duties of representation in favour of shutting herself away in the Trianon with a circle of favourites – these were the realms in which Maria Theresa risked losing control over her daughter, where she did not believe her written protestations of moderation and restraint, as she informed her confidant Mercy, and where for a moment she saw a grim fate looming over her daughter. 'My daughter, my dear daughter, the first queen, when will you finally be yourself? The thought is intolerable to me,'[29] she lamented. Maria Theresa became a Cassandra. She read, listened and watched for signals of the future catastrophe on the body of the queen-daughter, interpreting the signs of disorder, of the transgression of, injury to and disregard for the boundaries drawn around the ideal body of the queen, the demarcations of the physical and cultural body. Excess and disregard for the body's appropriate social and political space threatened the political core of Maria Theresa's dream, the Austrian-French alliance, 'the only alliance that is natural and practical for our countries, and which is sealed by such tender ties and similar manner of thought, because it is so necessary for the religion, happiness and well-being of thousands of persons,'[30] and for 'the good fortune of both our states and our families.'[31] Maria Theresa believed, however, that her daughter's way of life was threatening her grand design:

> Your fortunes could change utterly, and you could be cast into the greatest misfortune by your own fault. That is the consequence of this terrible obsession with pleasure, which leaves you no time for other occupations. What books are you reading? And you dare to speak up constantly in the most important business of state and the choice of ministers? ... I hope I shall not live to see this misfortune.[32]

Maria Theresa's clairvoyance in regard to Marie-Antoinette's future is chilling, but it may illustrate the extent of the old empress's experience in court and political matters. Perhaps her instinctive feel for politics nevertheless failed to tell her that the degree of her intervention in her daughter's life and the politics of the French court would lead to the catastrophically growing enmity towards the *Autrichienne* assuming even more fateful proportions.

The Body of the Royal Childbearer

From the very beginning, it was all the more important for Maria Theresa to keep a strict eye on the true and secret focus of her passionate interest. Her rigid monthly correspondence kept to a rhythm inherent to her daughter's own body. It had to be kept under observation, its signs deciphered, its regularities and disruptions precisely noted and interpreted. For seven endless years nothing in her daughter's monthly cycles pointed to pregnancy, and Marie-Antoinette was repeatedly compelled to report the return of her 'indisposition'. Maria Theresa begged her daughter to seek the constant proximity of her husband, to share her bed with him instead of sacrificing her nights to the compulsive gaming that was also ruining her reputation.[33]

All letters from Paris report that you sleep apart from the king and enjoy his confidence only to a limited degree ... and if he no longer comes to your bed for the sake of an heir, then one will have to dispense with one ... Your sole duty must consist in being with him as often as possible during the day, keeping him company, being his best friend and confidante ... so that he may never find more comforts and security elsewhere than in your society.[34]

The cohabitation of husband and wife, the royal couple, was the ultimate precondition for the conception of the passionately desired heir to the throne of France, who would be Maria Theresa's grandson. Many factors had to be taken into consideration, however. On the one hand, the body of the queen must not become exhausted by riding, lack of sleep or dancing all night. It was the precious vessel of maternal imperial visions, and 'Your health ... does not belong to you alone; you must preserve it for our sake and that of the state.'[35] The king had brothers, and their wives might bear sons – this good fortune, since envy is deleterious to dignity – was an occasion for directing one's attention all the more firmly and urgently to one's own 'good fortune', the good fortune of the state, and of peoples. 'The slightest event is meaningful to me, since I love you so tenderly and am concerned for your well-being.'[36] 'The mere thought that a courier might bring me news of a pregnancy makes me lose my head with happiness and impatience'.[37]

When Marie-Antoinette was finally able to announce her pregnancy, the empress was beside herself with joy. 'You send me great and unexpected news! May God be praised! And may you, my beloved Antoinette, be strengthened in your splendid position by giving France an heir'.[38]

A flood of good advice now washed over the pregnant Marie-Antoinette. Her mother noted the child's first stirrings, discussed the issue of breastfeeding, the choice of *accoucheur* and of the right wet-nurse, and offered suggestions on caring for the future dauphin:

Particularly in the first year, everything depends upon the care that children receive: I am speaking of sensible and natural treatment, not swaddling them too tightly, not keeping them overly warm and not overfeeding them with gruel and food; and above all, a good and healthy wet-nurse is necessary ... [39]

The mother drew here on her own rich experience from sixteen births. She refers to her daughter affectionately as 'my little woman'. 'I kiss you tenderly, my dear little Mama, and your child.'[40] In this letter, Maria Theresa pours out her heart, all of her bitterness at the war policy of Frederick II of Prussia, her 'cruel enemy'. She speaks to her daughter as to an equal, an adult. Perhaps for a moment, as a future royal mother, Marie-Antoinette had arrived at the same level as Maria Theresa – perhaps she, too, had embarked on an endless series of pregnancies.

Marie-Antoinette gave birth to her child – having learned her mother's lessons about proper conduct in the courtly sphere. The birth of a royal infant, perhaps a dauphin, was a public event according to French custom, and occurred in the presence of the entire court and many guests from the provinces who had gathered for the occasion. Marie-Antoinette almost died from the birth, from her attempts to retain her composure before an audience, from suppressing her cries. Mercy, who still felt the pain, reported to Maria Theresa:

> The violence she did herself in order not to complain called forth a slight nervous convulsion ... Only now do I feel the full force of the pain that this caused me ... The convulsion that plagued the queen had several causes: firstly, the restlessness of the presence of too many people; secondly, the efforts the queen made not to complain; thirdly, she was shaken when the child did not cry and she believed it to be dead; fourthly, when the child did cry, this evoked a mighty contrast between pain and joy. The king and almost all of the people followed the child, which was taken to an adjacent room, and the king did not witness the misfortune, which was remedied in four minutes by the accoucheur's presence of mind ... The queen does not yet know the sex of her royal infant.[41]

The child was a girl, baptised as Princess Maria Theresa Charlotte.

Once again, in April 1779, the empress raised her voice, now insistently and impatiently: 'What you report to me of your dear daughter causes me great joy. Yet I must confess that I am insatiable; she needs a companion, and he should not be long in coming. ...'[42] In nearly every letter Maria Theresa now repeated her urgent call for a dauphin. In 1780, only a few months before her death, with the increasing sense that time was growing short, she wrote in an at once flattering and threatening tone:

No occupation is dearer to me than that with my children. Those are the only happy moments in my wearisome life. The lovely queen of France contributes not a little to this, but we need a dauphin. I was discreet until now, but with time I will become importunate. It would be a sin not to bring more children of this dynasty into the world ... I kiss you tenderly.[43]

The dauphin was not born until a year after Maria Theresa's death.

Maria Theresa had waited eight years 'with such yearning' for 'this dear and longed-for portrait'.[44] In the portrait of Marie-Antoinette that finally reached her in 1779, however, her daughter's form had assumed the contours of a mother. It showed a queen whose body might already carry the future dauphin within it. For a moment, even the grim shadows that Maria Theresa saw looming over her daughter's fate appeared to have been banished. 'Your large portrait brings me great joy. Ligne has found a likeness in it; but for me it suffices that it portrays your figure, with which I am very satisfied.'[45]

The Body of the Empress

I wondered whether Maria Theresa had written the well over a hundred letters to her daughter with her own hand. Twice I found myself confronted with passages that provided an answer, and which suddenly and poignantly revealed moments of the most unguarded and intense closeness.[46] These passages were intended to make her daughter see and feel the body of the elderly, overworked and exhausted empress and mother at the same time, as if the one had merged with the other.

> Since my style and my handwriting are no longer the best, and since my arms and eyes often fail to serve me, I will be compelled in future to make use of another's hand. You will excuse the ink spots and corrections in this letter; I had to rewrite it three times, and the wind blew it to the floor twice. You know how draughty my apartments are.[47]

Which of Maria Theresa's voices speaks here, which maternal body accompanies her beloved daughter, who ultimately followed scarcely any of her instructions, and whose letters of reply contain cover-ups, and often bald-faced lies? Was there ever any true communication between the two women? It seems unlikely. Maria Theresa seems to have realised this, increasingly predicting a catastrophe which she hoped she would not live to see. Perhaps, though, Maria Theresa's letters to her queen/daughter were also texts about herself, Maria Theresa. After a series of problematic – and in some cases disastrous – attempts to marry off her children throughout Europe, the letters might be considered as addressing her own struggle against the collapse of her notions of the ideal royal parent-couple, which, as her life and letters reveal, contained elements of bourgeois enlightened ideas that were still paradoxes in the waning *ancien regime* of courts, and which were permitted to exist at most in the fantasies of a people waiting on the horizon.

Victoria to Vicky

In what follows I would like to compare the correspondence of Maria Theresa and her daughter Marie-Antoinette with that of another mother–daughter pair, Queen Victoria and her eldest daughter Vicky, crown princess and later queen of Prussia, focusing on the letters they exchanged between 1858 and 1901. As in the case of Marie-Antoinette, the correspondence began with the marriage of the seventeen-year-old Vicky, 'the object of our hopes and desires',[48] to Crown Prince Frederick William of Prussia in 1858, a love-match that also corresponded to the political and dynastic interests of Victoria and her husband Albert. In the hope that her daughter would soon be the queen of a progressive, enlightened and united Germany,[49] the marriage had been carefully planned years in advance, so that this loving couple would finally reflect in a double sense the English royal parents.

Empress Maria Theresa had married the boy who had grown up with her at the court in Vienna for several years, and whom she loved, the 'only object of my love, who has known my heart in this world and was the aim and goal of all my actions and of all my love' – a legitimate love[50] she did not permit to her daughters, only one of whom married for love. 'Happiness' was otherwise understood within the categories of the courtly catalogue of virtues. Queen Victoria, in contrast, apparently considered it important for her daughter to make a love-match, and celebrated the romance of the engaged couple in private and public letters beginning in 1855.

> I must write down at once what has happened – what I feel and how grateful I am to God for one of the happiest days of my life! When we got off our ponies this afternoon Fritz gave me a look which implied that his

little proposal to Vicky ... had succeeded ... that while riding with her ...
They were interrupted in fact 3 times ... At last towards the end of the ride,
he repeated again his observation about Prussia; she answered she would
be happy to stay there for a year. He added he hoped always always – on
which she became very red ... We kissed and pressed our poor child in our
arms and then Albert told her how the Prince ... looking up joyously and
happily in my face – she was kneeling. Had she always loved him? 'Oh
always!' ... Fritz was there, and ... she threw herself into his arms, and
kissed him with a warmth which was responded to by Fritz again and again
and I would not for the world have missed so touching and beautiful a sight
... It is his first love![51]

That same evening Queen Victoria recorded this betrothal scene in
great detail with dramatic flourishes, composing a little melodrama
with a happy end, a genre scene that we find reflected in some of the
pictures that Victoria and Albert had painted around this time.
Reading this passage, I was reminded of the text and the scene that
Victoria recorded in her diary on the evening of her own
engagement, 15 October 1839,[52] and others that she would write in
later years in letters to Vicky, for she still had many more children
to marry off. From the outset, the initiation to marriage through a
love scene, a first glance, a sudden recognition, was a significant
element of the legend that Mother Victoria wove around her own
person as well. In this tale of marriage the daughter thus stepped
onto a new stage not just in her own life but also in that of her
mother, since the betrothal text was also the beginning of a new, if
secondary, romance that Victoria would embroider into her own life.
'I must write it down at once.'

As in the case of Maria Theresa, I would like to examine the
mother's letters in particular as part of a royal correspondence, that
of a reigning queen in a constitutional monarchy, whose political
interventions and perceptions were strongly influenced at the time
of Vicky's marriage by the liberal views of her husband. He laid the
groundwork for and structured her everyday political tasks to a
significant extent, for example by reading documents in order to
present them with commentary for her signature, and by explaining
complex political processes in clear and simple summaries, and was
a man at whose side the work of a monarch appeared to be jolly and
quite manageable.[53] At this time Victoria's life was also absorbed by
her duties in the inner circle of her large family. She regarded and

presented herself above all as a wife and as the mother of her (at that point) nine children, the youngest of whom was just one year old. Victoria herself was thirty-nine.

Victoria's first letter was written after her daughter, having been married with great pomp in the Chapel Royal of St James's Palace in London, left Buckingham Palace on 2 February 1858 for the journey to Germany. It already assumes the tone that would mark her letters to her daughter for the next forty years: emotional, chatty and associative.

> My first occupation on this sad, sad day – is to write you. An hour is already past since you left ... I struggle purposely against my feelings not to be too much overcome by them, as it is our duty to do, but I feel very sick when I think all, all is past ... and nothing here but a sad, sad blank! Yet it is cruel, very cruel – very trying for parents to give up their beloved children, and see them go away from the happy peaceful home – where you used all to be around us.[54]

She portrays herself as overcome with the pain of separation, a feeling that would pervade her letters in the days and weeks to come. She invokes the image of loving parents among their children, and the descent of the cosiness and tranquillity of home into black depression ('a sad, sad blank') when children grow up and go off into the world. Victoria invokes archaic images of middle-class familial bliss and endless rivers of tears. In so doing, she establishes a connection to her distant daughter from the outset, for when she writes, floods of words and sentences cross the Channel. 'Every thing I do makes me think of you, makes me long to tell you all about it.'[55]

From her first letters on, Victoria established an intimate mother–daughter relationship, in which her desire to express herself and her feelings freely appears to be the motive force behind her writing.

> [T]he delightful intercourse between us – so soothing and satisfactory to our hearts and so very much to my heart which requires sympathy, and the possibility of pouring out its feelings quite openly to one who will feel for and understand me! And this I have found in you, my dearest child.[56]

Her epistolary embraces are, however, meant not only for her child. Rather, Victoria is seeking a companion, an intimate friend, a peer with whom she 'shall agree in many things much more than we used to do. Indeed ever since you married ... There is no longer anything between us which I cannot touch with you – and a married daughter, be she ever so young, is at once, on a par with her mother.'[57] There should be no secrets that Victoria could not share with her daughter. Only with her marriage and the future selected for her could Vicky occupy this place in Victoria's emotional landscape, and only after her daughter had left could she discover her love for her, for in a letter of 1855 to Princess Augusta of Prussia she had still written that she found

> no especial pleasure or compensation in the company of elder children. ... And only very exceptionally do I find the rather intimate intercourse with them either agreeable or easy. You will not understand this, but it is caused by various factors. Firstly I only feel properly à mon aise and quite happy when Albert is with me; secondly I am used to carrying on my many affairs quite alone, accustomed to the society of adult (and never with younger) people – lastly, I still cannot get used to the fact that Vicky is almost grown up. To me she still seems the same child, who had to be kept in order and therefore must not become too intimate.[58]

Previously, she had scarcely noticed Vicky, who was rather an annoyance, a creature to be kept at arm's length and educated. If, however, we look at the mass of many-paged letters that made their way to Berlin beginning in 1858, it appears as if a floodgate had opened up for Victoria, or as if she had discovered a vessel into which she could pour herself without inhibition: 'I see my letter is getting long but I always feel I have so much to say to you that I have to write volumes – were I not to check myself.'[59] Vicky's at first surprised, then affectionate and respectful yet self-assured and articulate manner of responding to her mother, and even cautiously contradicting her when she spoke as the queen, lends both correspondences a unique authenticity. It was precisely the mirror of the homesick but sober Vicky that appeared to provide the framework for Victoria's pleasure in writing.

> Indeed it is as you suppose my greatest delight to write to you which I do whenever I have a spare moment and you are so easy to please, dear Mama, you allow me to write short or long ones just as I like. I never had a correspondence that I enjoyed so much because it is so natural and like thinking aloud ... It seems to me as if we never understood each other so well and never enjoyed exchanging every passing feeling and thought so

much and with so little restraint; it is indeed a blessed feeling ... It overcomes distance, it lessens the pain of separation, it is always with us.'[60]

The correspondence also provided the daughter with a new, unique opportunity, and this form of communication with her mother helped to lessen her loneliness in Berlin.

Victoria's and Vicky's declarations stand at the beginning of a gigantic body of letters, and formed the basis of an exchange whose variety and thematic richness touched on all aspects of their lives and can only be analysed in fragments here. I would like to stick to the trail of the queen's body here. It is clear from the beginning that it does not fit into the mould of Theresian rules of conduct and upbringing. I also will apply it only partially to Victoria's ideas or fantasies about her daughter as a future queen, instead reading her letters to her daughter as statements about her own female, maternal, royal and imperial body. The figure of the daughter is, in a sense (as was ultimately the case for Maria Theresa as well), the framework in which Queen Victoria herself appeared. I shall remain in the realm of the mother, as it were, before reversing the mirror that these letters hold up, and asking in what way the daughter's letters to her mother also manifest the image of the royal daughter.

The Orders of Writing

Prince Albert had expressed worries about the exuberant writing mania of mother and daughter, believing it needed to be given a more orderly form, for Victoria apparently liked to dominate even when she loved. She had revealed this during the negotiations of the formalities of her marriage with Albert, and even in this exciting new romance with her daughter she imposed a schedule. It did not matter that it was occasionally ironically undermined by Vicky, as by the father whom she supposedly resembled. The very chaos of the rules guaranteed that they would be obeyed. 'My intention for the future would be to write regularly to you on Mondays (by post) Wednesdays (by messenger) and Saturdays (by post) – I mean to send them off on those days. An additional letter would be besides of course.'[61] The secret of the letters lay in the existence of the messenger, that is, in the circumstance that the Wednesday letters were sent secretly, and could not be opened by the Post Office, that the secrets contained within should not be discovered and even the most scandalous and intimate revelations should be protected. The same may have applied to the 'additional letters besides of course' that were sent on Tuesdays, Thursdays and Sundays, and perhaps even twice daily. And Victoria, whose own handwriting was practically illegible, also had her own ways of reminding her daughter to watch her spelling and bring chronological order into her news and sentiments. One could number the letters, and make sure that their format fit into the proper containers.

> Your letter received today of the 30th ought to be numbered 84 instead of 78!! So that the next would be 85 – or – if you have written since – the one you write after this, should be 86. If you remembered them down in your remembrancer as I do, and looked before you wrote, you would not make mistakes.[62] ... Now I must end, else I could go on for hours.[63]

Royal Curiosity or the Entry into a New World

Victoria had not yet seen much of Europe, and apart from her concern for the well-being of her beloved child, Vicky's marriage also represented a window on the world, on another important royal court. It offered a glimpse of figures she could only guess at from the accounts of her German husband. But first Victoria entered this foreign land through her daughter, and, apart from her worry that the heat in Prussian palaces might endanger her child's health, she was above all curious – 'excuse Mamas curiosity'. 'Don't trouble yourself with descriptions of great things, ... but give me your feelings and your impressions about people and things, and little interior details'.[64] Victoria wanted to know about her daughter's emotions, her pain, happiness and the feelings aroused in her by the people she encountered daily, in the royal family. She wanted to know everything about the king and queen – 'How I do long to hear all about the King and Queen and family'[65] – at the court in Berlin, in the immediate surroundings of her ladies-in-waiting and servants – a desire which moved Vicky over the years to provide a wealth of complex descriptions and portraits of persons, through which Berlin's court landscape appears as in a distorting mirror, the curtain pulled back to reveal the stage of daily encounters, official occasions, petty intrigue and gossip. Victoria loved this just as Maria Theresa had.

Victoria also gave her daughter suggestions about how to behave, but rather reticently, trusting the upbringing she had received at home, and it does not seem that she was seeking to control her, as had been the case with Maria Theresa. Instead, Vicky served as her eyes and as a medium of her insatiable curiosity. One might even regard her as Victoria's spy, being her mother's private eye behind the political scenes of Berlin. In the secret pact she made with her, the imperial family and the court society of Berlin and Europe, but also of England, is scrutinised from within, commented upon and subjected to scathing remarks. Beautiful, tedious, mediocre and ugly but always interesting figures attract all manner of comment, from recognition, admiration and condescending notice to pity. Nevertheless, Victoria's first wish was to 'see' her daughter in her mind's eye – and she often asked for the details of her clothing:

> [W]hat dress and bonnet did you wear on landing? And what bonnet the 2 next days? ... I see by the papers you wore a green dress at the Cologne concert. Was that the one with black lace? ... I really hope you are not getting fat again? Do avoid eating soft, pappy things or drinking much ...[66]

Victoria loved photographs, and now they were the right medium. She wanted to see snapshots of her daughter on her bridal journey, on the street, at balls and receptions in Berlin, to be proud of her appearance, and imagined herself as part of the admiring crowd. Clearly, however, she also wanted to be acknowledged for her own contribution to Princess Vicky's successful performances, secret and yet visible to all. 'There is another thing which I tell nobody, but which you will remember my telling you to be sure to do – and which has produced the greatest effect: viz: your trying to kiss the King's hand. Don't you remember me telling you to be sure to do this?'[67]

The entry into Berlin had been accomplished and the official programme completed, but Victoria longed to follow her daughter into her new home, asking for the most precise descriptions, down to the arrangement, number and temperature of the rooms. Moreover, she awaited and repeatedly insisted on news of the daily round, details of the young couple's everyday life, comparing it with her own. She wanted to know everything, precisely, punctually and immediately:

> ... and you must tell me exactly how your hours are – what you do – when you dress and undress and breakfast, etc., for you know all what we do to a minute but unfortunately we know nothing and that makes the separation so much more trying ... You must not be impatient at Mamas curiosity but you must remember how hard it is for me not to know what you are doing.[68]

Victoria explained her curiosity in terms of her impatience, or was this impatience rooted in the unbearability of the removal of her beloved daughter's daily presence? But hadn't she once been more of an annoyance than anything else?

Marriage – the Ideal Couple

On Vicky's wedding day, Victoria composed a sort of manifesto for her daughter, a serious and solemn letter on the subject of matrimony and her views of the relationship between husband and wife and woman's role in marriage:

> It is a very solemn act, the most important and solemn in every one's life, but much more in a woman's than in a man's. I have ever looked on the blessed day which united me to your beloved and perfect Papa – as the cause not only of my own happiness (a happiness few if any enjoy) but as the one which brought happiness and blessings on this country! You have also the blessing of a dear, kind, excellent husband who loves you tenderly devotedly. Let it be your study and your object to make his life and his home a peaceful one and to be of use to him and be a comfort to him in every possible way.[69]

Victoria's ideal of matrimony was deeply middle-class. She celebrated the wife as a creature who affectionately and devotedly served her husband and cared for and protected her home. Happiness reigned where the family romance was realised in intimacy, dedication and submission,

> ... in devoting oneself to another who is worthy of one's affection;[70] ... You feel and appreciate the inestimable blessing of a perfectly united marriage – where there is perfect confidence – love and affection. It is the greatest blessing which mortals are allowed to enjoy and surely a foretaste of future life![71]

Hadn't Maria Theresa written something similar to her daughter? Nevertheless, Victoria's marital heaven was not wholly trouble-free, for repeatedly, as if Victoria had suddenly shaken herself in the midst of her hymn of praise for matrimonial harmony, in the very same sentence another voice breaks through for a moment, a tiny crack appears in the public portrait, and she warns her daughter. She complains of the self-absorption and egotism of men, and instead of celebrating the joy of submission, she suddenly expresses solidarity with the downtrodden of her sex, and laments woman's miserable lot. Such emotional moments could even remind her of the dismal fate of women of the lower classes. She had, after all, read Dickens, and certainly did not mean the wives of rebellious workers.

> The woman's devotion is always one of submission which makes our poor sex so very unenviable. This you will feel hereafter – I know; though it cannot be otherwise as God has willed it so ...[72] The poor woman is bodily and morally the husband's slave. That always sticks in my throat. When I think of a merry, happy, free young girl – and look at the ailing, aching state a young wife generally is doomed to – which you can't deny is the penalty of marriage.[73]

All the same, Victoria was the queen and absolutely determined to present herself with her consort Prince Albert as the very incarnation of married bliss: 'You know, my dearest, that I never admit any other wife can be as happy as I am – so I can admit no comparison for I maintain Papa is unlike anyone who lives or ever lived and will live.'[74] The incomparable union of her royal parents set standards for their daughter's marital happiness. It might appear at times that a disturbing trace of envy dictated Victoria's letters to the newlywed. Vicky did not have a chance because she, Victoria, was the greatest and he, Albert, was perfect. And he could be the greatest because he was 'worthy of her affection', because she, Victoria, had chosen him. The glorification of her marital happiness was expressed in her adoration of her husband: 'I shall ever be happy to kiss dearest beloved Papa's hand for you; I should like often and often to fall at his feet – for I feel how unworthy I must be of one so great and perfect as he is!'[75]

Victoria kissed Albert's hands, she lay herself at his feet, receiving a foretaste of paradise itself. When he died, it was as if the ground had been pulled out from under her:

> Indeed 'Why may the earth not swallow us up?' Why not? ... Oh! I who prayed daily that we might die together and I never survive him! I who felt, when in those blessed arms clasped and held tight in the sacred hours at night, when the world seemed only to be ourselves, that nothing could part us ... I never dreamt of the physical possibility of such a calamity – such an awful catastrophe for me for all.[76]

For a long time after 1861 deep despair, mourning and abject depression filled Victoria's letters to her daughter. As their addressee, Vicky became a central figure in Victoria's expansive process of mourning, allowing her mother, during the seclusion of the subsequent years, to find in letterwriting an outlet for her laments and a means of shaping her identity as a widow. Vicky was fellow mourner, comforter and witness to her worship at the altar that Victoria erected to Albert.

Motherhood

Victoria later became an imperial super-mother and she would take great care to see that her daughters married royalty. In her epistolary opinions on childbirth, however, she remained quite close to her own natural body, as if the letter to her daughter was the place where she needed to impart its secrets. The contradictory statements Victoria made about childbirth in her letters show particularly clearly that the imperial succession and the trials of pregnancy and birth, which she hated from experience, were addressed by her in the proper place – in public congratulations and the private letter, respectively. Here we find no idealisation of birth akin to that of marriage, but rather an insistence on the profane, on an attitude that would never have been permitted to a queen in the Theresian mould, and that was ultimately a slap in the face of the bourgeois ideology of the family as well. In their brutal candour, the letters she wrote to Vicky during her first pregnancy were probably not exactly encouraging to her daughter:

> What you say of the pride of giving life to an immortal soul is very fine, dear, but I own I cannot enter into that; I think much more of our being like a cow or a dog at such moments; when our poor nature becomes so very animal and unecstatic ... I positively think those ladies who are always enceinte quite disgusting; it is more like a rabbit or a guinea-pig than anything else and really it is not nice ... but for you, dear, if you are sensible and reasonable not in ecstasy nor spending our day with nurses and wetnurses, which is the ruin of many refined and intellectual young lady, without adding to her real maternal duties, a child will be a great resource.[77]

After all, dynastic considerations also had to be taken into account:

> As it is – it is a great happiness it should be a boy for the country and for you all, but I own I much wished for a girl, as boys cause so much suffering, and sometimes one buys the experience with one's first child and therefore a girl is sometimes better ...[78]

In Victoria's eyes it was this excessive number of births, this animalistic and ruinous experience – 'one becomes so worn out and one's nerves so miserable'[79] – that constituted woman's unequal lot, and that occasioned her own secret discontent with her otherwise ideal husband. As she remarked to her daughter on the subject of childbirth, it is 'dreadful what we have to go through and men ought to have adoration for one, and indeed do everything to make up for what after all they alone are the cause of!'[80] Her royal cynicism gave Victoria a clear-eyed view of the fate of the unwanted princess in the dynastic succession, whom she refers to in one letter as 'this unwelcome little thing'. Albert had been the member of the English royal family most concerned with childcare: 'Dear Papa always directed our nursery and I believe that none was ever better.'[81] Victoria's relationship to babies appears to have been marked by the same disdain she felt for her own pregnant body. Quite unlike her daughter, who relished her role as a mother, she could feel no tenderness for these small creatures

> till they have become a little human; an ugly baby is a very nasty object – and the prettiest is frightful when undressed – till about four months; in short as long as they have their big body and little limbs and that terrible froglike action. But from four months they become prettier and prettier.[82]

Nevertheless, her letters represent a paradox, for they are full of childish figures, and of eagerness to hear as much as possible about them, as well as constant mentions of new babies being born in her circle. These passages in the correspondence bring up elements of Victoria's own biography, of a childhood she always characterised as a lonely world surrounded by adults, populated by a legion (132) of dolls.

Queen

As a reigning queen, Victoria regarded herself as being in an 'anomalous and trying position', although she never permitted any doubts to arise that she was queen of England.

> One great drawback you all (our daughters I mean) will have, which I have not viz: the being exiled from your native land. This is a great necessity. One great advantage however you all have over me, and that is that you are not in the anomalous position in which I am, – as Queen Regnant. Though dear Papa, God knows, does everything – it is a reversal of the right order

of things which distresses me much and which no one, but such a perfection, such an angel as he is – could bear and carry through.[83]

Victoria tells her daughter quite plainly that her conduct as queen was wholly dependent upon Albert's aid and advice, and that he was part of her political royal body. When he died she became an apparent amputee, in need of help. In her letters, Victoria's laments about the nightly torments of loneliness and her physical longing, 'that dreadful, weary, chilling, unnatural life of a widow',[84] merge seamlessly with her horror at the loss of the political head beside her.

> What is to become of us all? Of the unhappy country, of Europe, of all?... But how I, who leant on him for all and everything – without whom I did nothing, moved not a finger, arranged not a print or photograph, didn't put on a gown or a bonnet if he didn't approve it shall be able to go on, to live, to move, to help myself in difficult moments? How I shall long to ask his advice! ... The day – the night ...

In order to act as a queen, Victoria tried over and over again, as her letters in the years that followed show, to call up the internalised ghost of Albert. Convinced 'that his pure and perfect spirit is guiding and leading and inspiring me!' she promised 'I will do [what] I can to follow out all his wishes'.[85]

She tried to imagine what would he have thought or felt in politics or family matters, which were often dynastic ones, to discover what his guiding ideas had been, what he had written on this or that subject, and wondered whether she was capable of interpreting it properly. Victoria was a widow not just as a private individual but also as a royal personage in the political sense. Over the years she had constituted her monarchical existence as male and female, as a couple. Weintraub even speaks of an 'informal dual monarchy'.[86] She indicated as early as 1862 that she did not feel equal to the task on her own, complaining that

> the life of utter depression, of objectless pleasurelessness is dreadful and wears me away ... Every Day makes me feel that my position is ruined ... A woman in my position and of my nature cannot stand alone, and you will see that a new state of things will in a little while not be looked upon as misfortune.[87]

Apart from her diary, the letters to Vicky were the screen upon which, after Albert's death, Victoria projected the male figures who over the years may have appeared as substitutes for her idealised husband. Her nights and days appear to have been split between her descriptions of two men.

Beginning in 1865, her letters to Vicky also sketch the figure of her ideal Highland servant, John Brown, the man who, according to D. Thompson, was intended to fill the gap 'of the loving and supportive companion'[88] that Albert's death had left in the household – and perhaps also in her nights. In order to do so, however, he, too, had to be idealised. Victoria transplanted him to that landscape which she celebrated in the *Leaves of our Life in the Highlands*.[89] Composed at this period as 'an exact account of our happy life, as a picture of it',[90] an ideal inside view of her earlier happy married and family life and her closeness to the common people,[91] the work was insufficiently appreciated by Vicky.[92] Of Brown she wrote that

> he is indeed one in a thousand for he has feelings and qualities which the highest Prince might be proud of – viz: unflinching straightforwardness and honesty; great moral courage; unselfishness and great and rare discretion and devotion. This quite independently of his excellence as a good, handy. thoughtful servant ... this good, tender, devoted, and truly noble-hearted creature ... and there is something peculiarly touching in seeing this in a strong, hardy man, a child of the mountains.[93]

The role of political adviser was also gradually filled, here, too, with an idealised figure, Disraeli, later Lord Beaconsfield, whom she also felt close to because of her own literary aspirations and his poetic ambitions. The romance was now played out on the political stage.

> Mr. Disraeli will, I think, make a good Minister and certainly a loyal one to me, for he has always behaved extremely well to me, and has all the right feelings for a Minister towards the Sovereign. I enclose you a copy of his first letter to me which might interest you. He is full of poetry, romance and chivalry. When he knelt down to kiss my hand which he took in both of his he said 'in loving loyalty and faith'.[94]

At the same time, in 1868, a letter to Vicky indicates that Victoria was preparing the official biography of the prince consort, and indeed that she intended to write it herself.[95] It would become a hagiography and nothing would be allowed to disturb the legend of this saint. Towards the end of 1868 the crown princess, who was clearly somewhat unnerved by John Brown and Disraeli, as well as by her mother's thirst for publication,[96] wrote (after seeing Victoria in Windsor), in her own affectionate style: '... Goodbye, darling Mama. May God ever bless, support and protect you. This heart will never cease to pray for you and love you with all the love it has – and all the gratitude it can give. Far or near you are ever in my thoughts, dearest beloved Mama.'[97]

During the forty years that Victoria reigned after Albert's death Vicky, too, would become a central partner in discussions of all political matters; a flood of commentaries, everyday impressions, reflections and gossip concerning all the main events and personalities pours out in the correspondence. The more self-confident Vicky became, and the less merely Victoria's English ambassador-in-exile, the more heated their exchanges of liberal, conservative and radical positions became. The two women negotiated their own place in the familial, dynastic and political arena openly and vigorously. Through this consistently spontaneous, at times both nerve-racking and pleasurable, and above all affectionate, communication the correspondence, especially in its secret elements, affords a unique glimpse of the inner workings of the female monarchic experience of politics and representation in the second half of the nineteenth century.

Déjà Vu

On 23 July 1885, nearly thirty years after Vicky's wedding, Victoria's youngest daughter Beatrice married Prince Henry of Battenberg. Before the wedding, Victoria, who hated to let go of her last daughter, wrote to Vicky from Aix-les-Bains:

> I count the months, weeks and days that she is still my own sweet, unspoilt, innocent lily and child. That thought – that agonising thought which I always felt, and which I often wonder any mother can bear of giving up your own child, from whom all has been so carefully kept and guarded – to a stranger to do unto her as he likes is to me the most torturing thought in the world. While I feel no girl could go to the altar (and would probably refuse) if she knew all, there is something very dreadful in the thought of the sort of trap she is being led into.[98]

Victoria's diary contains the following entry for the day of the wedding:

A happier looking couple could seldom be seen kneeling at the altar together. It was very touching. I stood very close to my dear child, who looked very sweet, pure and calm. Though I stood for the ninth time near a child for a fifth time near a daughter, at the altar, I think I never felt more deeply than I did on this occasion, though full of confidence. When the blessing had been given, I tenderly embraced my darling 'Baby'.[99]

Two days later, after the couple's departure, she wrote to Vicky, 'I bore up bravely till the departure and then fairly gave way. I remained quietly upstairs and when I heard the cheering and "God Save The Queen" I stopped my ears and cried bitterly.'[100]

Royal Portrait and Victorian Novel

Maria Theresa trained the world in her own image, while Victoria described the world and herself as a queen in it. I would like to compare the relationships shaped in the secret correspondences of mothers with their daughters once again on four levels: the image, the textual genre, the secret and, finally, the female royal body.

Maria Theresa was not looking for her daughter's 'natural' beauty. In her wish for a portrait of her daughter, she felt no longing for a likeness, but only impatience. Maria Theresa's letters themselves constituted work on her daughter's portrait, on her body politic, which would be represented in the portrait. What mattered was representation. Maria Theresa clothed the body in a system of rules and regulations, systematically polishing its appearance. She traced a choreography that defined its place in the political space of the courtly world, and in the royal *tableau*. She wanted to see the figure 'in your finery' (*in ihrem Staat*), 'in court dress', equipped with the splendid symbols of absolutist power – for Marie-Antoinette was to be queen at the very court where the portrait of a ruler that remained the prototype far into the nineteenth century, the portrait of Louis XIV by Hyacinthe Rigaud, had also created the pictorial model for the queen.[101] And 'this great portrait' was to hang in the Habsburg palace at Schönbrunn, it was 'destined for a hall housing the entire family hung in life-size [portraits]'.[102] In this way the French queen could make her entry into Vienna; the portrait of the Habsburg mother of the French dauphin hung in the ancestral portrait gallery of the monarchic dynasty. The alliance between the Habsburgs and the Bourbons was sealed and publicly represented on the pictorial plane as well. Marie-Antoinette's individual face and subjective aura were beside the point; what mattered was that she adapted to the model.

In the nineteenth century, in the Victorian era, we can trace the growing cracks in the genre of royal portraiture. Private life invaded monarchical imagery; queens wearing their hair loose, royal genre scenes, family tableaux in a bourgeois style, intimate portraits, pictures for the selection and recognition of potential marriage partners and photographs of countless children fill the picture galleries that open up in the letters of Victoria and Vicky.

The rigid portrait that Maria Theresa expected of Marie-Antoinette corresponded to the tone of her letters. Building on instructions whose uniformity we can also trace in her letters to other married princesses and princes, they established an epistolary relationship that may be regarded as a female equivalent to the education of princes. In its aristocratic and monarchic way, this relationship conveyed transnational standards of kingship in developing nation-states. Since the foreign courts at Naples, Parma or Versailles were precarious and surrounded by traps, and marriages were contracted between strangers, a set of rules of conduct and advice was required to guarantee that the parties kept in mind the proper form and objective of matrimonial transactions. Another form was also preserved: Maria Theresa's didactic, reproachful and imploring letters to Marie-Antoinette and the latter's replies always – even on the verge of desperation – maintained the safe set phrases of affectionate and respectful address. We know from accompanying letters that these were often mere set phrases – that individual life and subjectivity mattered only marginally, that they could erupt unexpectedly, even catastrophically at times, but ultimately were not envisaged. Maria Theresa's love for her daughter appears to have allowed her no life of her own beyond her political destiny.

The secrecy of the correspondence, the *Correspondence secrète*, thus had nothing to do with an intimate mother-daughter relationship. Like the instructions, it served a political function. It marked the place in the fabric of exchange and the management of knowledge and news between the courts. Maria Theresa wrote her letters to Marie-Antoinette, but she discussed these 'secret' letters with her ambassador and spy Mercy-Argenteau, sharing with him her impressions of her daughter, and sending him copies of letters which Marie-Antoinette believed to be 'secret' and intended for her mother's eyes only, and thus safe. Instead, Maria Theresa discussed with Mercy the measures necessary to prevent Marie-Antoinette from suspecting the surveillance network around her. In this way, Marie-Antoinette could not tell her mother anything that she had not already heard from Mercy. Which secret pact was relevant here – or was it the multiplicity of overlapping streams of information? Cornelia Bohn has pointed out that in sixteenth- and seventeenth-century theories of the monarchical state, the term 'arcanum' became a key concept in the doctrine of political conduct, and that secrecy was considered a necessary practical and rational precondition for successful policy. Secrecy served to maintain control over communications and one's own actions. Well into the eighteenth century, simulation and dissimulation were viewed as the exercise of prudence.[103] Nevertheless, the correspondence between Maria Theresa and Marie-Antoinette does contain moments of secret intimacy. Perhaps they were also cracks, obstinacies, a non-functioning of the system of absolutist secret policy, which may already have hinted at a changing meaning of the secret, and occasionally also at emotions of elation or desperation that sought to break through the stereotypical quality of the epistolary codes. Perhaps Maria Theresa's call for the portrait was also an attempt to hold onto a collapsing figure of rule, as if the portrait could save the queen, as if it could show her the essence of the real queen – beyond Marie-Antoinette's letters and Mercy's grim reports. For Maria Theresa suspected that when forms and representation fell apart, the court too would crumble.

The letters in Victoria's and Vicky's correspondence, which were carried by special messenger, demonstrate the fundamental transformation in the concept of secrecy and its location in the eighteenth and nineteenth centuries. The secret had withdrawn into the private sphere, 'which was accordingly constituted as a secret realm of a new quality,'[104] a sphere of secrecy and at the same time of femininity, sexuality and love. It is in this realm of 'intimacy' that a large portion of Victoria's letters to Vicky belong, and this is true above all of these letters, since she felt herself to be 'on a par' with her eldest daughter.

Victoria seems to have grasped the world less in pictures than through writing itself – 'I must write it down'. Her pleasure in and mania for writing – impulsively and associatively – were boundless. It has been estimated that Victoria's writings, had they all been published in book form, would have filled some 700 volumes. One could regard her 3,777 letters to Vicky as part of her 'Victorian epistolary novel', exchanged between virtual equals, middle-class, sentimental and subjective. For her mother, Vicky appears to have been the ideal reader, with whom she could share her own self-projections, and in whose life she saw her own reflected. Her immense curiosity is witness to her need for control, but the knowledge she acquired in this manner also fills her own poetic projects. Almost more than her diary, her letters to Vicky were the place where she analysed her feelings and spread out the tableaux of her psychic landscapes. Her daughters' marriages and romances offered potentials for identification, they reflected Victoria's own unique love story, the waves of yearning for an ideal husband and of physical desire. She could be close to her daughter because she could appropriate her story, could narrate it and integrate it into the romance of her own life. Her daughter's marriage, however, also told of her mother's abandonment, and Vicky's pregnancies released Victoria's other self-perception of her corporeality and perhaps of her childhood – the alien quality and the burden of her childbearing body and the animalistic, almost uncanny being it brought out. The ambivalences in 'Victorian' self-perception thus expressed themselves in idealised paeans to the Other – but above all to the beloved consort – on the one hand, and melodramatic, tearful scenes on the other.

It seems as if Victoria was also very much the queen of her own imagined people. Her autobiographical publications were an immense success among the reading public, far more than among her children. As she herself wrote to Vicky, the people loved her in her romantic texts, which wallowed in middle-class family idylls and a romantic enthusiasm for nature. Just as she shared the middle-class cultural tastes of 'her people' – unlike Vicky, she loved melodramatic operas (above all Verdi), sentimental novels and moral homilies[105] – she had also mastered the semantics of the world of the post-Richardsonian novel and located part of her Self within it.

Beyond all of the diverse contexts and forms, however, the letters also contain moments and fissures in which the suffering of this woman shines through in a direct and almost creaturely manner, in which her desolation and the fragility of her body become visible. But there are also sudden moments of the comic and the grotesque, and of mirth, of uninhibited, booming 'fits of laughter',[106] which shake the body of the queen.

Notes

1. *Maria Theresia und Marie Antoinette. Ihr geheimer Briefwechsel*, ed., commented and translated into German by Paul Christoph, first complete edition (Vienna, 1952), 32 (letter of 1 November 1770). The French edition of 1874–75 cited here is incomplete, giving a censored version of the correspondence, and I have drawn upon the French originals of the letters published in German only in order to get a more precise impression of Maria Theresa's writing style. Marie-Antoinette, *Correspondance secrète entre Marie Thérèse et le Cte de Mercy – Argenteau avec les lettres de Marie-Thérèse et de Marie-Antoinette*, eds. Alfred von Arneth and Matthieu Auguste Geffroy (Paris, 1874).
2. *Geheimer Briefwechsel*, 219 (letter of 29 June 1770).
3. On the relationship between portraits and representation, see Louis Marin, *Portrait of the King* (Minneapolis), 1988, 207ff.; originally published in French as *Le Portrait du Roi* (Paris, 1981); Konrad Repgen, *Das Herrscherbild im 17. Jahrhundert* (Münster, 1991); Annette Dixon (ed.), *Women who Ruled: Queens, Goddesses, Amazons in Renaissance and Baroque Art* (London, Ann Arbor, Mich., 2002); Ilsebill Barta-Fliedl, *Familienporträts der Habsburger: dynastische Repräsentation im Zeitalter der Aufklärung* (Vienna, 2001); Muriel Vigié, *Le portrait officiel en France du Ve au XXe siècle* (Paris, 2000).
4. Cf. Franz Herre, *Maria Theresia. Die große Habsburgerin* (Munich, 2004).
5. *Geheimer Briefwechsel*, 15–16 (letter of 21 April 1770). Cf. the first and second very similar 'instructions' for Maria Carolina, queen of Naples and the Two Sicilies of 1768, or that given to Maria Amalia in 1769 after her marriage to Ferdinand of Parma in '*Aus mütterlicher Wohlmeinung*', *Kaiserin Maria Theresia und ihre Kinder. Eine Korrespondenz*, ed. Severin Perrig (Weimar, 1999), 113ff., 145ff.
6. *Geheimer Briefwechsel*, 18.
7. See Maria Theresa's reflections as expressed to Mercy and her worry that Marie-Antoinette might suspect something in *Correspondance secrète*, Vol. 1, 182. Particularly illuminating is the letter that Maria Theresa wrote to Mercy after the death of Louis XV on Marie-Antoinette's coronation as queen of France: 'I am most grieved to hear this and still more worried about the fate of my daughter, which may be either quite splendid or terribly unfortunate … she herself is young, has never had a head for serious pursuits and will never have one, or only with great effort. I believe that her beautiful days are over, far earlier than was the case for me. I enclose the letter I wrote to her; … In future I shall arrange myself according to what you dictate. Spare neither couriers nor express post, any detail, even the most insignificant, is a great comfort to me and serves to guide me.' Letter of 18 May 1774 (original in French), *Correspondance secrète*, Vol. 2, 149.
8. *Geheimer Briefwechsel*, 19 (letter of 4 May 1770).

9. Ibid., 19–20.
10. Ibid., 85 (letter of 3 January 1773).
11. Ibid., 86.
12. Ibid., 112 (letter of 3 April 1774).
13. Ibid., 108 (letter of 3 October 1773).
14. Ibid., 333 (letter of 2 August 1780).
15. Cf. the correspondence with Florimond comte de Mercy-Argenteau in *Correspondance Secrète*, Vol. 1, e.g. 182.
16. *Geheimer Briefwechsel*, 20 (letter of 4 May 1770).
17. Ibid., 129 (letter of 16 July 1774).
18. Ibid., 28 (letter of 1 November 1770).
19. Ibid., 35 (letter of 11 February 1771).
20. Ibid., 50–51 (letter of 17 August 1771).
21. Ibid., 43 (letter of 5 May 1771).
22. Ibid., 84 (letter of 31 January 1773).
23. Ibid., 84–85.
24. Ibid., 43 (letter of 8 May 1871).
25. Ibid., 27 (letter of 1 November 1770).
26. 'Je voudrais avoir un portrait de ma fille en grand deuil, habillée comme elle l'est, on dit même sans poudre. Si le portrait même n'était pas si ressemblant, je voudrais voir l'habillement et le tableau au plus tôt.' Marie-Antoinette, *Correspondance secrète*, Vol. II, p. 154 (letter of 25 May 1774).
27. Ibid., 144 (letter of 5 May 1775).
28. Ibid., 198 (letter of 1 October 1776). On public perceptions of Marie-Antoinette's predilection for expensive jewellery and the extent of the scandal, see the chapter on the diamond necklace affair in Sarah Maza, *Private Lives and Public Affairs: The Causes Célèbres of Prerevolutionary France* (Berkeley, Los Angeles and London, 1993), 167–211. Cf. also Lynn Hunt, 'The Many Bodies of Marie-Antoinette: Political Pornography and the Problem of the Feminine in the French Revolution', in *Eroticism and the Body Politic*, ed. Lynn Hunt (Baltimore, 1991), 108–31; Joan Landes, *Women and the Public Sphere in the Age of the French Revolution* (Ithaca, 1988), esp. chap. 3, and most recently Evelyne Lever, *L'affaire du collier* (Paris, 2004).
29. *Geheimer Briefwechsel*, 193 (letter of 2 September 1776).
30. Ibid., 241 (letter of 1 February 1778).
31. Ibid., 205 (letter of 2 January 1777).
32. Ibid., 160–61 (letter of 30 June 1775). Here, Maria Theresa already raises a criticism of Marie-Antoinette that would recur repeatedly in the pamphlets against her and in the historiography on the French Revolution. See Maza, *Private Lives and Public Affairs*, esp. 167–211; Regina Schulte, 'Der Aufstieg der konstitutionellen Monarchie und das Gedächtnis der Königin', *Historische Anthropologie. Kultur – Gesellschaft – Alltag* 6, 1, (1998), 76–103, here 76–77.

33. Maria Theresa was familiar with this 'compulsive gambling' from personal experience. At the beginning of her reign she had bet large sums at pharoan, a card game, incurring the criticism of her chaperone Count Emanuel Tarouca, who planned her daily schedule. Edwin Dillmann, *Maria Theresia* (Munich, 2000), 98–99.
34. *Geheimer Briefwechsel*, 147 (letter of 2 June 1775).
35. Ibid., 237 (letter of 5 January 1778).
36. Ibid., 230 (letter of 5 November 1777).
37. Ibid., 237 (letter of 5 November 1778).
38. Ibid., 252 (letter of 2 November 1778).
39. Ibid., 263–64. (letter of 1 June 1778).
40. Ibid., 261 (letter of 17 May 1778).
41. Letter of 20 and 24 December 1778 from Mercy to Maria Theresa, in *Geheimer Briefwechsel*, 287–88.
42. Ibid., 290 (letter of 1 April 1779).
43. Ibid., 331 (letter of 30 June 1780).
44. Cf. ibid., 239 (letter of 5 January 1778). In 1771 she had received a portrait in pastels 'that is a very good likeness', but probably not the portrait ordered. 'It is in my study, while the first portrait … is in my bedroom, where I work in the evenings. In this way I always have you with me, before my eyes. You are forever deep in my heart'. Ibid., 50 (letter of 17 August 1771).
45. Ibid., 290 (letter of 1 April 1779).
46. In fact, Maria Theresa used to dictate the majority of her letters to her secretary Pichler, adding from time to time personal notes with her own handwriting. Cf. introduction Marie-Antoinette, *Correspondance secrète*.
47. Ibid., 119f. (letter of 30 May 1774).
48. *Queen Victoria in her Letters and Journals*, selected and edited by Christopher Hibbert (London, 1984), 99 (letter of 22 October 1855 to Augusta of Prussia).
49. Stanley Weintraub, *Victoria: Biography of a Queen* (London, 1996), Vol. 1, 287. See also Dorothy Thompson, *Queen Victoria. Gender and Power* (London, 1990), 132.
50. Letter of 12 February 1766 from Maria Theresa to her friend Countess Enzenberg, quoted in Dillmann, *Maria Theresia*, 112.
51. *Queen Victoria in her Letters and Journals*, 98.
52. 'I sent for Albert; he came to the Closet where I was alone, and after a few minutes I said to (him), that I thought he must be aware why I wished (him) to come here, and that it would make me too happy if he would consent to what I wished (to marry me); we embraced each other over and over again, and he was so kind so affectionate; Oh! To feel I was, and am, loved by such an Angel as Albert was too great delight to describe! He is perfection; perfection in every way – in beauty – in everything! I told him I was quite unworthy of him and kissed his dear hand … I told him it was a great sacrifice, which he wouldn't allow… I feel the happiest of human beings'. Ibid., 57.

53. Cf. Thompson, *Queen Victoria*, 50; Weintraub, *Victoria*, Vol. 1, 150.

54. *Dearest Child. Private Correspondence of Queen Victoria and the Crown Princess of Prussia, 1858–1861*, ed. Roger Fulford (London, 1964), 28 (letter of 2 February 1858).

55. Ibid., 30 (letter of 4 February 1858).

56. Ibid., 194 (letter of 4 June 1859).

57. Ibid., 183–84 (letter of 20 April 1858).

58. *Letters and Journals*, 99–100 (letter of 6 October 1856).

59. *Dearest Child*, 179 (letter of 16 April 1859).

60. Ibid., 181 (letter of 18 April 1859).

61. Ibid., 70 (letter of 5 March 1858).

62. Ibid., 190 (letter of 30 April 1859).

63. Ibid., 48 (letter of 17 February 1858).

64. Ibid., 32 (letter of 6 February 1858).

65. Ibid., 35 (letter of 7 February 1858).

66. Ibid.

67. Ibid., 49 (letter of 18 February 1858).

68. Ibid., 47 (letter of 17 February 1858).

69. Ibid., 27 (letter of 25 January 1858). This letter was written on the day of the wedding and is the first in the collection.

70. Ibid., 44 (letter of 15 February 1858).

71. Ibid., 69 (letter of 2 March 1858).

72. Ibid., 44 (letter of 15 February 1858).

73. Ibid., 254 (letter of 16 May 1860).

74. Ibid., 45 (letter of 15 February 1858).

75. Ibid., 48 (letter of 17 February 1858).

76. *Dearest Mama. Private Correspondence of Queen Victoria and the Crown Princess of Prussia, 1861–1864*, ed. Roger Fulford (London, 1968), 23.

77. *Dearest Child*, 115, 195 (letters of 15 June 1858 and 15 June 1859).

78. Ibid., 164–65. (letter of 5 March 1859).

79. Ibid., 195 (letter of 15 June 1859).

80. *Dearest Child*, 165 (letter of 9 March 1859).

81. Quoted in Thompson, *Queen Victoria*, 46.

82. *Dearest Child*, 191 (letter of 4 May 1859).

83. Ibid., 67–68. (letter of 1 March 1858).

84. *Dearest Mama*, p.142 (letter of 2 November 1862).

85. Ibid., 23 (letter of 18 November 1861).

86. Cf. Weintraub, *Victoria*, Vol. 1, 171.

87. *Dearest Mama*, 62ff (letters of 20 and 27 May 1862).

88. Thompson, *Queen Victoria*, 79.

89. Victoria, *Leaves from the Journal of our Life in the Highlands from 1848–1861*, ed. Arthur Helps (New York, 1868), appeared early in 1868, and on 21 December 1867 Victoria wrote to Vicky that 'it has been an interest and an occupation – for no-one can conceive the trouble of printing a book, and the mistakes, which are endless'. *Your Dear Letter. Private Correspondence of Queen Victoria and the Crown Princess of Prussia, 1865–1871*, ed. Roger Fulford (London, 1971), 166.

90. Letter of 28 March 1863, announcing the work, in Ibid., 219.
91. Victoria felt that Vicky did not respect her enough as an author. See *Your Dear Letter*, 171 (letter of 18 January 1868). 'I send you again several newspaper articles about the book, the effect produced by which is wonderful, and will I know gladden your heart from the extreme loyalty it displays. From all and every side, high and low, the feeling is the same the letters flow in, saying how much more than ever I shall be loved, now that I am known and understood, and clamouring for the cheap edition for the poor – which will be ordered at once. 18,000 were sold in a week. It is very gratifying to see how people appreciate what is simple and right and how especially my truest friends – the people – feel it. They have (as a body) the truest feeling for family life.' She had already complained on 23 December 1865 that Vicky had ignored the first, private edition of the work. 'You have also never said one word about my poor little Highland book'. Ibid., 51.
92. See also Weintraub, *Victoria*, Vol. 2, 382–83.
93. *Your Dear Letter*, 23, 48 (letters of 12 April and 5 December 1865).
94. Ibid., p.176 (letter of 4 March 1868).
95. *Your Dear Letter*, 170 (letter of 15 January 1868), n. 1. See also Weintraub, *Victoria*, Vol. 1, 336–37.
96. On Disraeli, she replied to her mother on 1 March 1868, 'It is absurd to have an aristocratic prejudice against Mr. Disraeli – on account of his being a Jew and an adventurer. A person that rises to a high place by his abilities has surely a good right as anyone to be your Prime Minister. My fears were that his other qualities were not such as to enable him to fill the place well'. *Your Dear Letter*, 175.
97. Ibid., 213 (letter of 29 November 1868).
98. *Dearest Child*, 186 (letter of 15 April 1885).
99. *Letters and Journals*, 294 (letter of 23 July 1885).
100. *Beloved Mama. Darling Child. Private Correspondence of Queen Victoria and the Crown Princess of Prussia, 1878–1885*, ed. Roger Fulford (London, 1976), 195 (letter of 25 July 1885).
101. See Rainer Schoch, *Das Herrscherbild in der Malerei des 19. Jahrhunderts* (Munich, 1975), 18–22; Gabriele Christen, *Die Bildnisse der Kaiserin Elisabeth*, in Juliane Vogel, *Elisabeth von Österreich. Momente aus dem Leben einer Kunstfigur* (Frankfurt, 1998), 177–222, here: 177f.
102. *Geheimer Briefwechsel*, (letter of 29 June 1877).
103. Cornelia Bohn, 'Ins Feuer damit: Soziologie des Briefgeheimnisses', in *Schleier und Schwelle. Geheimnis und Öffentlichkeit. Archäologie der literarischen Kommunikation* V/1, ed. Aleida Assmann and Jan Assmann in collaboration with Alois Hahn and Hans-Jürgen Lüsebrinck (Munich, 1997), 42–51, here 41–42. See also Barbara Stollberg-Rilinger, 'Das Verschwinden des Geheimnisses. Einleitende Bemerkungen', *Zeitsprünge. Forschungen zur Frühen Neuzeit, Das Geheimnis am Beginn der europäischen Moderne*, 6, nos. 1–4 (2002), 229–33, here 229–30.

104. Stollberg-Rilinger, 'Das Verschwinden', 230.
105. The correspondence with Vicky demonstrates this repeatedly. See also Weintraub, *Victoria*, Vol. 1, 180.
106. This reflects Vicky's fantasy about Victoria's typical reaction to grotesque visitors: 'He would put you into fits of laughter …', in *Your Dear Letter*, 172 (letter of 21 January 1868).

Part III

Queens of Modernity

9

Queen Margherita (1851–1926)

'The Only Man in the House of Savoy'

Catherine Brice

T he intention of this contribution is not to provide yet another biography of Queen Margherita of Savoy, but rather to explore the symbolic place she occupied alongside her husband Umberto I within the House of Savoy.[1] Towards the end of the nineteenth century, queens were assigned a political role orientated towards the new parameters of constitutional monarchy in the age of the masses. Victoria, queen of England and empress of India, served as an archetype here. Her example also left a deep impression on *fin de siècle* Italy.[2] Margherita was quite conscious of this, even if she sought to distance herself from it – not without sarcastic undertones: 'Everyone ran to see this short, fat, not at all aesthetic old woman simply because she embodies all the pride, strength and power of that tenacious and admirable nation!'[3] she wrote to Colonel Osio in 1898.

The room for manoeuvre available to these queens was nevertheless strictly limited, on the one hand by their sex and on the other by the nature of constitutional monarchy, as Margaret Homans has explained for Victoria: 'By the curious twist of British constitutional logic, the Queen is obliged to retain her prerogatives just as she is obliged to perform her duties ... Victoria's power resides in her resistance to using her power'.[4] Thus according to British law, the queen could not act: she had no power over parliament, but had to be present in order to ratify the decisions made there, since they could not take effect otherwise. This paradox did not apply to Margherita, however, who had no governmental duties whatsoever – a fact expressly emphasised by her 'hagiographic' biographer Onorato Roux: 'At the Italian court –

fortunately for the Italians – women have the unique advantage of not intervening even indirectly in affairs of state. Queen Margherita was the outstanding example of the most conscientious abstinence from any type of intervention'.[5] Roux stressed that she had never possessed her own party at court. This assertion requires some qualification, since even if she had no party in the strict sense of the word, she was nevertheless surrounded by a group of intimates, who were hostile to the group around Litta, the king's official mistress.[6] The opposing factions exerted little political influence, however.

The Political Convictions of Margherita of Savoy

Margherita of Savoy nevertheless held political opinions which, if not always marked by great intellectual acuity, reflected the liberal thought widespread in the Italy of the Risorgimento. She considered the people to be fundamentally good and educable, but believed that, since they had not yet reached sufficient maturity, they were easily misled by dangerous doctrines. 'For I believe that the masses, who have been deceived for many years, now understand that they were betrayed by their superiors and that neither the golden age nor the age of equality will ever come; they have abandoned theories,' she wrote in 1898 on the occasion of the Milan uprisings.[7] She acknowledged social inequality and called for a more equitable social order, without, however, taking into consideration any means of attaining it beyond moderation and charity. Like the anti-parliamentary discourses one finds in contemporary political literature and newspapers, she had only contempt for parliament and parliamentarians: 'Take the parliamentary regime, for example! It is impossible for countries to continue to permit themselves to be ruled by a herd of ill-mannered blackguards, who, scarcely inside parliament, appear to be gripped by a raging madness. What do the people think of this?'[8] As she elaborated in 1892, 'What a mess in the chamber! How many useless and disrespectful speeches, one shouldn't allow them to say certain things at all![9] In 1894, she wrote '... there is nothing alive there apart from the parliament with its bursts of outrage and its sad gossip, which have so little importance for the country, but nonetheless exert a pernicious influence over the course of public life because of the power of the organisations; it is a terribly sad thought'.[10] These brief statements suggest two basic convictions: on the one hand, that in her opinion the people and the parliament essentially had little in common, with the former being betrayed by the latter (an all-too-familiar topos in late nineteenth-century Italy, which persists into the present), and a deep mistrust of what she calls the 'organisations', that is, the political parties, which in 1894 were increasingly opposition parties, while the only genuinely impartial representative of the people – who allegedly united all Italians – was the king. Margherita kept herself informed about the affairs of the country and sought the counsel of important politicians, which strongly influenced her opinions. In the notes for his diary, Francesco Crespi mentions numerous conversations with the queen in which they apparently discussed national and international affairs quite uninhibitedly and directly. Thus on 2 January 1897, for example, after the New Year's receptions and the proclamation of a political crisis, he supposedly told the queen: 'The king is bound by strict regulations. He is governed by others, and does not himself govern. And that is not right'.[11] Another interlocutor was Marco Minghetti, whose 'pupil' Margherita had been in the early 1880s, and with whom she maintained an intensive correspondence.[12] She also plainly expressed her antipathy towards those who did not show the proper respect for the monarchy. Thus Ruggero Bonghi found himself banished from the Quirinal by the queen after he published quite a critical article entitled 'The Office of the Prince in a Free State' in the *Nuova Antologia* in 1893.[13]

Another notable characteristic of Margherita's political views was her love of Italy, which at the end of the period studied here became an intense nationalism. As a great devotee of the army, she wrote to Colonel Osio in 1895 that 'I feel the greatest admiration for our military and regret that I am not a man, for if I were, this admiration would not remain Platonic!'[14] and added that the Italian virtues found their place in the army, and not in the political arena. During the First World War the queen mother, ever mindful of the well-being of the troops, turned her Roman palace (the Palazzo Piombino, which had been renamed Palazzo Margherita) into a Red Cross hospital.

On the other hand, one could say of her, as of Victoria, that 'she accomplished the creation of the nineteenth-century monarchy largely through representations. She could manipulate her public image to the extent that her culture permitted; yet many of her representations were made by others', and we must also keep in mind that Victoria 'participated in the creation of the royal public image, while at the same time remaining subject to the Victorian image of woman'. These statements also apply to Margherita of

Savoy, I believe. She was adept at manipulating her public image, an image of the monarchy and the queen, while slipping into the pre-existing forms expected of women, and only occasionally revealing a sort of 'modernity' of function and personality – a shift that was always duly noted.

How was this 'modernity' expressed? We must read this very vague term in the nineteenth-century context in order to grasp the extent to which the 'queen' was capable of behaving in a 'modern' manner.[15] Naturally, one could locate Margherita of Savoy's modernity in her personality or her leisure pursuits, such as her love of aviation and automobiles or her skills as a mountain climber. She possessed qualities and inclinations that were perfectly in tune with the spirit of the turn of the century, but which I see as corresponding to the general development of the European aristocracy around 1900, whereas she presented herself as a 'monarch of the modern age'. What made the first queen of Italy modern was chiefly the way in which she actively sought to promote the process of 'nationalising' the Italians at the side of Umberto I. Seen from this point of view, when Margherita advocated rather traditional opinions suitable for a queen, she managed to highlight them in a very particular way and to make them known to broad segments of the population, revealing a firm grasp of what we might now call political communication. On the occasion of her death in 1926, one of her biographers wrote, doubtless somewhat indulgently: 'Margherita of Savoy's particular duty, first as the wife of the heir to the throne and then as queen, consisted in seeing to cohesion and assimilation in a country such as Italy, which for historical and ethnic reasons tended more to division and fragmentation than to unity under the strong but gentle pressure of national sentiment. ...' He went on to praise 'the charisma of this Queen Margherita of Savoy, who captured the hearts of poets and members of all parties and even opponents of the monarchy. She was particularly adept at fulfilling a great national task and thus accomplished for Italy – through the great sympathies accorded to her by the people and her humblest subjects – a genuinely moral and voluntary unity, which wars and plebiscites had created on the political level only.'[16]

These reflections bring me to the following hypothesis: the modernity of Margherita of Savoy was only partially rooted in the themes or values she championed and supported. Her modernity is evident far more in her grasp of how a constitutional monarchy worked, and in her adeptness at addressing the masses within the limitations of the privileges available to her, whereby she took into account the innovations in the political system, particularly the possibility of influencing public opinion, of which she was highly aware. I would add that her popularity as well as the success of this undertaking must, paradoxically enough, be attributed to rather conservative values: piety, benevolence and poor relief, the cult of the family and admiration for the army, to name just a few. To cite the title of Alberto Maria Banti's fine book, *La nazione del Risorgimento. Parentela, santità e onore alle origini dell'Italia unita* (The Nation of the Risorgimento. Kinship, Sanctity and Honour in the Origins of United Italy), let us note that by championing these 'ideals of the Risorgimento' (family, religion and honour) Margherita lent them new force and efficacy.

Beauty as a Political Weapon

Margherita of Savoy's physical qualities are naturally significant in the context of problematising the meaning of the queen's 'body'. Before turning to this, however, I should like to address the ambivalence of relationships towards the body. At the end of the nineteenth century, two different views of the body of public personalities intersected. According to the traditional view expressed for centuries, virtues were visible in a person's outer appearance. Perceptions of the queen were accordingly influenced by the discourse about her: to mention her beauty was to attribute virtues to her, and to speak of her virtues was to point to her beauty. The register here was an abstract one, with texts and commentaries predominating. A the same time, though, the queen's physical appearance was set in scene for the largest possible public, facilitated by the explosive development of mass media of communication (photography, newspapers, etc.), which culminated for the individual observer in the sense of being able to 'actually meet' the queen. This was the birth of the star cult with all of its psychic and emotional implications, evoked by identification with the queen or the longing for her, and in the years that followed these developed further (and continue to the present day). The queen's body, her beauty, her posture and her wardrobe thus formed a relationship axis to the 'people' or the court that appeared anything but coincidental. On the contrary, this was one of the motivating forces behind her popularity and thus also an arena for her political manoeuvres.

Margherita of Savoy has been called 'the only man in the House of Savoy'. Her biographer used this surprising description to indicate the important role the queen played, and to emphasise that she was not satisfied to serve as a mere companion or decorative supernumerary in court ceremonial. 'Margherita of Savoy operated according to a precise plan, which pursued two objectives with absolute coherence: dynastic interests and the prestige of the crown'. In order to achieve her aims, 'I dare to assert that Queen Margherita – long before fascism – understood the necessity of gaining mass support. In her day the governments were liberal, suffrage was restricted, politics was elitist but the Crown had to belong to the masses, eternally supported by the people, and the fact that she had to drag along a lazy and not always available consort only served to make the plan more exhausting', writes a recent biographer of the queen.[17] In view of the queen's active role in the defence and representation of the dynasty, Prince Bernhard von Bülow informed Emperor Wilhelm II that 'the queen is concerned exclusively with the fame and honour of her country and her dynasty. She embodies, as it were, Italian raison d'état – and she does so with wit and grace'.[18] We can trace this effort to embody raison d'état intelligently and gracefully almost to the beginning of the young woman's 'political' career. At the time of her marriage to Umberto I in 1868, one of her closest friends, Countess Irene della Rocca, with whom she maintained an especially frank correspondence throughout her life, wrote that,

all of your desires and deeds, my dear little daughter, must be directed towards two great and noble objectives: love for your husband and the good of the nation … You must become a Garibaldi of peace, that is, a – sometimes real, sometimes fantastic – creature whom the Italians will invoke to free themselves of all ills and to lift themselves out of the mire. In the mind of the masses, Garibaldi could banish Italy's external enemies with a single musket shot. The same masses must believe and say that Margherita is able with a smile to deliver them from their internal enemies: discord, division, misery, and the vexations of government.

The countess continued (now writing in French)

Therefore do not fear too greatly the sight of suffering, of misery. Tolerate the importunate when they are unhappy. I dare not advise you to intervene in politics; the terrain is perilous and full of treacherous surprises, where the best intentions are turned against their authors, but keep abreast of all serious and important questions, so that those who approach you realise that you live the life of the country.[19]

She describes here quite precisely the relationship to politics that Margherita would maintain throughout her life: she was interested in political questions and attracted what we may refer to as genuine popularity. She knew how to activate the hidden powers so essential for nation building thanks to her sure feeling for gestures and words calculated to be picked up and commented upon repeatedly in the press, and contributed in this way to the emergence of a widespread royal legend. Margherita summarised her stance very aptly in a letter of 1918 to Natalia Morozzo della Rocca: 'I believe that subtle forms of propaganda, which continuously disseminate patriotic and lofty ideas, are very useful'.[20]

Very much a child of her time, Margherita adopted a highly ambivalent attitude towards the Italian people. Her correspondence testifies to a distinction between the educable and thus likeable people on the one hand and the essentially dangerous masses on the other. Of the 'educable' people she wrote in 1898: 'What great power education exerts, and what guilt is incurred by governments who do not educate their peoples!'[21] She expressed quite different sentiments on 22 April 1897 after a large public demonstration in support of the king, following Acciarito's assassination attempt:

> The demonstration on the same evening there belongs to the most impressive experiences of my life. When the king appeared on the loggia a single, prolonged shout arose from the crowd, it was a shout of joy, a howl of revenge and protest, a very strange thing. The mere thought sends a cold shiver down my back! It seemed as if human passion was speaking from the united soul of this crowd of people![22]

This fear of the 'savage' masses was doubtless shared by even her most enlightened contemporaries.

But what possibilities for action did the queen have? She was, after all, a queen, who had no practical opportunity to communicate using language. At this point I would like to draw attention to an aspect that seems particularly important to me. Rereading the biographies written during the queen's lifetime or shortly after her death, I was particularly struck by the fact that the authors, without exception, depict her as a personality without a voice. In her

repeatedly rewritten legend, the queen is constantly being
constructed as a model on the basis of her gestures and actions,
which were intended to symbolise her mental attitudes. When her
own words are cited, it is always intimate speech, even in public
contexts. She always addresses individuals (women, children,
occasionally politicians or heads of state), but gives no speeches. At
the end of the nineteenth century there was no place for the queen
to speak 'officially' (with the exception of Queen Victoria, who
assumed the business of state in her own right, and who was
authorised by law to give a royal address – which, however, she
refused to do for many years). It was generally uncommon for
women to speak in public, as Michela di Giorgio has emphasised:
'For women it is no easy matter to speak from a public lectern', and
the first who dared to do so were women, often of aristocratic
origin, who, when not reading aloud texts written by others,
lectured on selected themes such as flowers or horticulture, which
were hardly calculated to inspire polemical reactions.[23] For her
part, the queen liked to attend public lectures. Thus, for example,
the lectures held by the *Società per la promozione delle donne*
(Society for the Promotion of Women) were sophisticated cultural
events, in which ladies could participate even without male escort.
The queen was certainly not lacking in humour and critical acuity,
as reflected by a letter she wrote to Irene Rocca di Castiglione on 12
January 1893 after hearing a lecture by Arturo Graf,

> I like what he writes very much, but speaking, especially before so many
> women, is another matter altogether! Such a large number of married
> women is evidently more intimidating than a lecture hall full of learned
> men. The result is often deplorable, since the fear of appearing pedantic
> and the desire to put himself on our level causes the speaker to offer
> nothing but banalities. It is humiliating to admit it, but we make them
> more superficial![24]

This background explains the importance of mediating accounts
(eyewitness reports, the press, biographies) that sought to
summarise anew the queen's exemplary conduct or to disseminate
her words publicly.

   The queen thus rarely had a chance to deploy her verbal skills,
but she played very consciously with her image by using her beauty
as a gender-coded weapon. Without wishing to devote undue
attention to this aspect, it is still impressive how frequently texts

about her mention her beauty, grace and smile, how much attention she herself paid to her appearance and what effects this 'star behaviour' had. For segments of the aristocracy and the Italian middle classes, Margherita became an exemplary figure, and she was admired by a large portion of the Italian population. In the ideal image devised by her biographers, beauty, virtue and intelligence were mutually interdependent, to be sure, but spectacular political conversions and unexpected seductive power, made possible only by Margherita's 'neutrality', were attributed above all to her grace and smile: 'Not one but many political conversions were generated by Margherita's grace, cultivation and amiability', writes one biographer.[25] This woman succeeded in changing the mind of a relentless opponent of the monarchy, Nicotera, along with the Socialist Alessandro Fortis from the Romagna and Matteo Renato Imbriano Poerio, a Republican member of parliament, as well as the pro-clerical aristocracy of Rome: 'In Rome, Margherita succeeded, with her grace, in breaking the ice that distanced the majority of the Italian high aristocracy, which remained loyal to the Vatican, from the court'.[26] Even if the success of this campaign to charm the aristocracy was more modest than Onorato Roux suggested, it is certain that in the years after the taking of Rome (1869), Victor Emmanuel II (who was no longer officially married), relied far more on Margherita than on the crown prince in his attempts to win over Rome for the monarchy, while himself sojourning in the capital only very rarely.

The great passion that Margherita inspired in the writer Carducci, a political enemy reportedly overwhelmed by the queen's beauty, may be regarded as an impressive triumph. The story is almost too good to be true: the dyed-in-the-wool republican Carducci had initially refused to go to the railway station in Bologna to welcome Margherita (then still a princess), but in 1878, on the occasion of the attempted assassination of Umberto I by Passanante, he wrote an 'Ode to Queen Margherita', thus performing a political about-turn so apparently contradictory and irrational that people were tempted to attribute it to love. He had indeed been enchanted by the young queen when she stopped in Bologna during a journey shortly after the coronation of Umberto in the autumn of 1878. Bologna had the reputation of being a 'difficult' city in which anti-monarchist feeling ran high. The journey was correspondingly carefully planned and members of any potential opposition had been temporarily banished from the city. The success of Margherita's stay, however, exceeded all expectations of a visit cautiously controlled and stage-managed from above. The queen in particular received a warm welcome. Alessandro Guiccioli, who accompanied the royal couple, noted in his diary: 'the success of the queen here in Bologna, as a woman and as a sovereign, is indescribable'.[27] As one of countless spectators, Carducci saw the queen ride by and then later watched her greet the crowd alongside Umberto from the balcony on the Piazza San Petronio. According to his own account, the effect was palpable:

> These two young people greeting the cheering throng with great courtesy from a place where the papal legates otherwise show themselves to announce blessings and condemnations and to impose sentences of execution, rewards, the damages and disgrace of slavery and other vileness upon life and upon Italy, must, I feel, necessarily touch those who believed in a common future for the monarchy and the country.[28]

The next day Carducci was received, together with the professors of the university. And here, planned or not, the poet was struck as if by lightening by the queen's charm. She was not merely beautiful, and 'rose with an unusual purity of pose and lovely attitude,[29] but was also familiar with the *Odes Barbares* and informed Carducci that she found them splendid. The poet thereupon wrote the following ode: 'I regarded the queen, emerging in mild white, blonde and bejewelled, from the darkness broken but not conquered by that strange dazzle and wavering sound. And a fantasy gripped me. ...'[30] A few weeks later he published the *Ode to the Queen*, which appeared at the time of the assassination attempt in Naples. In this euphoric homage to the queen Carducci asserted that he had expressed in verse the thoughts circulated in the streets and squares, in other words, that he had simply made himself the herald of public opinion. This unleashed a storm of dismay in all political camps, royalist as well as republican. To be sure, in 1859 Carducci had already penned a song addressed to the 'beautiful and silvered cross of Savoy, which shines in our eyes and smiles at our hearts',[31] in which he had praised the Piedmontese monarchy over the Tuscan grand duchy. This fact notwithstanding, until 1878 he had continued to announce his distaste for the institution of the monarchy publicly, going so far as to refuse the order of the *Merito civile di Savoia* because he would have had to swear on the Bible his loyalty to the king and his successors. In 1888, at the time of the University of Bologna's jubilee celebrations, Carducci became an unerring defender and admirer of the queen. He wrote numerous additional eulogies, poems and odes, earning the scorn of his republican friends, who regarded his actions as a sort of betrayal. At that time Carducci saw the queen frequently. He visited her in Gressoney Saint-Jean, where Margherita spent her summers far from the 'golden cage of the Quirinal', enjoying the fresh air, taking mountain walks or hunting chamois. These meetings, which we naturally know of only from Carducci's accounts, were apparently wholly devoted to learned conversation and the poet reading from his works, to the intellectual exchange of an at once sophisticated and educated salon culture. The queen copied one of Carducci's sonnets, *Rêverie*, in order to put it to music, solely so that he might claim the honour of asking her for the manuscript written in her own hand. Was this love, emulation of courtly lifestyles, or perhaps fetishism? Carducci was clearly fascinated by the queen's beauty, but also by her cultivation. Margherita, in contrast, was possessed by the desire to prove herself intellectually, and doubtless felt flattered by the poet's interest in her. It is unlikely, however, that the two had an affair, as some authors have suggested.

Margherita was highly skilled at cultivating what we would nowadays call her 'image'. She did so on the one hand by disseminating reproductions of her portrait throughout the country, and on the other thanks to the use of symbolic identifying marks, such as the daisies (*margherita* in Italian) that women and children carried at her royal entries. Many little girls were named after her. 'The popularity of the house of Savoy can be measured in the frequent use of the names Umberto (also in the variant Umberto Primo) and Margherita with the variants *Regina Margherita* or *Margherita Regina*,[32] writes Stefano Pivato, who has studied the distribution of first names in nineteenth- and twentieth-century Italy. And we should not forget that Carducci himself advised his daughter Beatrice to name her baby daughter Margherita.

A further sign of the queen's popularity was the appearance of periodicals with her name in the title. The first of these, *Margherita*, was launched by the Treves brothers in Milan in 1878. It was a lavishly produced weekly for Italian ladies, with the queen's portrait gracing the front cover. A number of more or less successful rival magazines calling themselves *Margherita* or *La Margherita* followed. As a veritable *vade-mecum* of elegance and distinction, *Margherita* described the queen's costumes down to the most minute detail, so that readers of more modest means could emulate them in somewhat less extravagant versions. These only apparently unimportant details, I believe, point to the heart of a process in which the queen in a constitutional monarchy became fundamentally differentiated from her absolutist version. The process of 'privatising' royal persons had already reached a high point on the scaffold, as Fanny Cosandey has noted in the instance of Marie-Antoinette.[33] This privatisation, that is, the abolition of royal holiness, made it possible for the first time for subjects to identify with the queen. Under an absolutist monarchy, such identification was neither desirable nor truly conceivable. Submission, respect and emulation in the field of fashion doubtless represented possible attitudes towards a female absolutist monarch, whether she reigned in her own right or was the king's consort. The possibility of identifying with her, though, of seeing in her a kindred model partly rooted in 'normality', was a giant step taken only after the desacralisation of monarchical office – at the same time as the accompanying so-called *embourgeoisement* of the ruling dynasties. Here, where social needs and 'propaganda' intersected, the sense of identification assumed a new dimension.

Portraits of monarchs had existed for quite some time. The portrait of the absolutist monarch, however, remained coded, hierarchical and to a certain extent unrealistic. It reflected an ensemble of rules orientated towards depicting, and thus establishing in the first place, the majesty of the model. 'The portrait is the mirror, the "very pure glass" of the qualities in which person joins Idea, beyond attributes and ornaments. In the picture, this conjunction is symbolised by beauty', Edouard Pommier commented on a portrait of Louis XIV by Le Brun.[34] The portrait of the king is an 'inimitable original'. The dissemination of the king's portrait in engravings or copies also remained quite limited. The broad dissemination of pictures (including in the press) is clearly a phenomenon of the late nineteenth century. In the early nineteenth century, when the inhabitants of an Italian city wanted to burn a portrait of Napoleon in a symbolic act, they had to find a noble house and force the owners to turn over the only available portrait of the 'tyrant' in town. Fifty years later, matters had changed dramatically. The dissemination of illustrated periodicals, methods of mass reproduction and the care taken by monarchs to have their portraits published everywhere permitted a large majority of Italians to 'recognise' the king or queen, or at least to be familiar with their idealised portraits, since the production and distribution of pictures of the royal couple were subject to censorship. In addition, Margherita of Savoy modelled for a number of sculpture busts and, albeit less frequently, for monumental statues; one also finds her likeness on vases, plates, porcelain, etc. The depictions of Margherita – like those of Victoria – thus reflected an established female ideal on the one hand, while initiating certain changes on the other.

It is impossible even to guess at the exact number of depictions of Margherita or the royal couple circulating in Italy. The fact that the magazine *Margherita* offered its readers a photograph of the king and queen with the first number is an indicator of the extent of this dissemination. The documents referring to the queen in the archives of the *Casa Real* also contain references to countless photographs of Margherita bearing personal dedications sent out to people who had explicitly requested them, or who had sent her gifts.[35] Margherita's face is readily recognisable in the gallery of surviving photographs, paintings and engravings: her coiffure, which remained practically unchanged from the first paintings to the last photographs, her rather prominent nose, her generally melancholic and peremptory gaze. Within the unchanging schema one can distinguish three phases of representation: first, the young girl reading or watching a bird, then the queen of Italy portrayed in numerous variants, and finally the widow of the period 1900–1926, shown in widely varying 'poses'.

In portraits of Margherita as a young girl, the melancholy and wistfulness which seemed to fill the future queen of Italy are especially striking. From her time as queen, we must distinguish between the 'official' portraits that depict her alone or alongside her husband and the (although equally official) pictures that show her on the borderline between the public and the private, or altogether in private. The official portraits primarily demonstrate what made her the 'queen of pearls', that is, the ropes of pearls that became more numerous from year to year, which she wore either wrapped closely around her throat or as long necklaces, and which became Margherita's true trademark. Umberto reportedly gave both his wife and his mistress, Countess Litta, a rope of pearls every year. These official photos also show what people found so fascinating, or so ridiculous, about the queen: her excessive but not always very sure taste for complicated costume.

Margherita's relationship to 'fashion' deserves particular attention. In the women's magazines, but also in newspaper or other accounts of her journeys, one is particularly struck by the media obsession with her wardrobe. The 1881 account of the royal couple's journey to Sicily notes in great detail the gowns worn by the queen, as well as the other ladies present, whether they belonged to the royal retinue or to the Sicilian nobility who turned out to welcome the king and queen.[36] Fabrics, colours and jewellery are all described layer by layer, without commentary beyond admiration for their splendour, while the apparel of the men is not mentioned at all. The same applies to sober occasions such as the opening of a session of parliament, a solemn affair in Italian political life at which the king gave a royal address: the press commented upon and emphasised the queen's presence solely with reference to her wardrobe:

> The queen's gown was of brocade with large, finely worked coral-coloured velvet flowers on a grey background and an immense train; over it she wore a short cape made of a curious stuff, half Turkish, half Persian, embroidered in gold and trimmed in red velvet, a gift only recently made to her by the king. Diamond pins were stuck into her red-gold hat, she wore a wide diamond bracelet on her left arm, a diamond butterfly on her little muff – and altogether her rosy white complexion stood out against such a magnificence of strong colours. The ladies of honour formed a dark backdrop in sombre violet, dark green, plum with huge diamond earrings, with the royal monogram on their shoulders.[37]

This extensive description underlines the queen's 'shimmer' in an assembly of parliamentarians in frock coats and women in sombre colours,[38] for even the ladies of the court were dressed in shades of plum and violet; the mention of the king's gift stressed the continued existence of the royal 'couple' – in spite of the well-known fact that the king kept mistresses. Above all, this description shows us the limits of Margherita's scope of action: she is reduced to her appearance. The fact that the king was dressed in uniform or civilian clothing is mentioned only in passing – but he was the one giving a royal address to the parliament.

There is no question that Margherita must have been 'coquettish': her expenditures for clothing were frequently the subject of rather meticulous negotiations with the king or the treasury as part of budget deliberations. We scarcely have any accounts or commentaries from the queen herself; in a brief letter to

Natalia Morozzo della Rocca, however, she expressed her views rather wittily:

> It seems that Rembrandt hats are back with a vengeance, which pleases me very much, since they are most flattering to those of us approaching forty (how unfortunate to reach and surpass this age!). Particularly in one's manner of dress one does not wish to make oneself too youthful, nor to make oneself a grandmother yet, quite an awkward situation! The Rembrandts, the compassionate shade of whose broad wings hide a multitude of things![39]

Some observers criticised the queen's taste, finding her unforgivably badly dressed by the fashion standards set mainly in Paris. The response to these critics was that, as a good Italian woman, Margherita dressed 'nationally', defending local fashion designers and refusing to submit to French dictates. Paris, by the way, already felt insulted by the queen's preference for the Germans ('it is always better to be on the German side than the other one'[40] she declared on 12 March 1899 to senate president Domenico Farini, who was close to the court). Her references to Italian alterity were well received and appreciated, and yet this did not really achieve the desired effect, since Italian fashion continued (in contrast to much of the twentieth century) to be overshadowed by Paris. As a consequence, some admired Margherita with her pearls, feathers and elaborate gowns while others deemed her hopelessly provincial. As long, however, as one does not argue from the perspective of foreign fashion, one can probably agree with Bracalini that 'Margherita's provincial and garish elegance increased the fascination of the royal dynasty in Italy'.[41] In fact the queen's gowns appear to have met with approval in the newly unified state, appearing to a certain extent to have corresponded to public expectations. The queen embodied the possibility of being at once the same and different. Her taste resembled that of the provincial bourgeoisie, although she wore gowns whose splendour, price and originality of cut, which could be copied, were unique. Here we come to the heart of the dialectic of popularity hinted at above: the phenomenon of the queen created by these expectations cast back a reflection, a distortion, that was supposed to serve as an example.

Although the attention paid to the queen's clothing, hairstyle and jewellery was not a purely Italian phenomenon, in the period in question it was nonetheless intensified in the context of the newly created Italian court. To be sure, Italy had had its courts before 1861: those of the grand duchy of Tuscany, of Naples, Parma or Turin, but no 'national' court. And at the centre of power, in Rome, the Vatican court was exclusively male, and chasubles and vestments, though certainly magnificent, were tied to and regulated by religious ritual. The presence of the Italian court on the Quirinal Hill, which was enlivened by Margherita and her ladies-in-waiting, made it possible for the first time to establish a connection between everyday life and the court, between ordinary mortals and the monarchy. Splendour and luxury, which were so important for the very essence of the monarchy (including constitutional monarchy), offered a means of expression, even if they were harshly criticised by republican or socialist public opinion. This extravagance, which was only counterbalanced by the good works of the royal couple, was accordingly still an integral part of the functioning of political representation. And Margherita was the protagonist of this strategy, which would disappear at the end of the century. The next queen, Elena, along with her daughters, mixed with the masses: their clothes, pastimes and haircuts became 'normal'. Margherita of Savoy, in contrast, occupied a transitional space; she was, on the one hand, one 'of the most important feminine representations of power' and, on the other, a woman who was unusual, to be sure, but who could be emulated and formed anew by her female contemporaries.

The physical appearance of Queen Margherita, her (doubtless genuine) beauty, repeatedly cited in newspapers and books, her elegance and grace certainly played an important role in the establishment of the monarchy in Italy. We will never know for sure whether the queen herself was fully aware of the aims she served and the politics of the image that she projected (despite the lack of any scope for political action). But Margherita's consciousness of the status of the monarchy and her love for Italy, which appeared to be without any ulterior motives, make it likely that she represents an early form of the star cult, which was calculated to evoke interest, affection and even identification. The queen is a woman like any other, but at the same time her otherness makes her unattainable and thus particularly desirable.

Queen Margherita's body was, accordingly, not unimportant for the popularity enjoyed by the Italian monarchy at the end of the nineteenth century, which is largely underestimated today.[42] This was merely one of the fields of activity of a queen who also sought to develop a new relationship with the Catholic Church[43] and practised a well-organised poor relief policy, which contributed greatly to increasing the acceptance of the monarchy in Italy until at least the mid-1890s.[44]

Translated by Pamela Selwyn

Notes

1. On the biography of Queen Margherita, see Romano Bracalini, *La Regina Margherita, la prima donna sul trono d'Italia*, with a preface by Ugoberto Alfassio Grimaldi (Milan, 1983); Antonio Monti, *Donne e passioni del Risorgimento* (Milan, 1935); C. Casalegno, *La Regina Margherita*, Turin, 1956; Onorato Roux, *La prima regina d'Italia* (Milan, 1901); Arturo Santini, *La leggenda di Margherita di Savoia nei secoli futuri: conferenza letta a Bologna, Torino, Moncalieri, Courmayeur, Gressonez, S. Jean etc.* (Milan, 1901).
2. See Margaret Homans, *Royal Representations. Queen Victoria and British Culture (1837–1876)* (Chicago, 1998).
3. 'Tutti correvano per vedere questa piccola vecchia signora, grassa, niente estetica, solamente perché personifica tutto l'orgoglio, tutta la forza e il potere di quella tenace, ammirevole nazione!'
4. Homans, *Royal Representations*, xx–xxi.
5. 'Nella corte d'Italia, fortunatamente per gli Italiani, le donne hanno il singolare pregio di non immischiarsi neppure indirettamente, nelle faccende di Stato.' Roux, *La prima regina*, 447–48.
6. Thus in 1897, after a provocative article by the Italian politician Sidney Sonnino, entitled 'Torniamo allo Statuto' appeared in the *Nuova Antologia*, Margherita supported Sonnino, while Santa Fiora (the king's mistress) defended Di Rudini and Litta sided with Pelloux. The king certainly could not ignore the divergent positions adopted by his 'women', but it remains to be proven that they influenced his own position in any way.
7. 'Perché credo che le masse, illuse per molti anni, ora hanno capito che sono state ingannate dai capi loro, che l'età dell'oro e dell'uguaglianza non verrà mai; ed hanno abbandonato le teorie.' Letter to Osio, 9 August 1898, in *Oggi* IX, 29 (28 July 1953), 29.
8. 'Il regime parlamentare per esempio! E impossibile che i paesi seguitino a lasciarsi governare da quella mandra di maleducati malvagi, i quali appena entrano in Parlamento, sembrano per di più essere colti di pazzia furiosa. Che cosa ne pensa il popolo?' Letter to Osio, 2 August 1899, in *Oggi* IX, 29 (28 July 1953), 25–26.
9. 'Quanti pasticci alla Camera! Quanti discorsi inutili e poco rispettosi, veramente certe cose non le dovrebbero lasciar dire!' Letter to Osio, 15 June 1892, in *Oggi* IX, 29 (28 July 1953), 28.

10. '... non vi è di vivo che il Parlamento con le sue ire ed i suoi tristi pettegolezzi, che importano poco al paese, ma che poi per la forza delle organizzazioni hanno una grande e perniciosa influenza sull'andamento della vita pubblica; è un tristissimo pensiero'. Letter to Osio, 8 June 1894, in *Oggi* IX, 29 (28 July 1953), 28.

11. 'Il re è legato alle formule. E retto dagli altri, non regge. E governato, non governa. E questo non va'. Istituto per la storia del Risorgimento, Carte Crispi, 668 (1), 1897.

12. *Lettere fra la Regina Margherita e Marco Minghetti (1882–1886)*, ed. Lilla Lipparini (Milan, 1957).

13. R. Bonghi, 'L'Ufficio del principe in uno stato libero', *Nuova Antologia* 3rd series, XLIII, Fasc. 2 (1893), 340–55.

14. Letter to Osio, 1 August 1895, in *Oggi* IX, 30 (23 July 1953), 28.

15. The position of the queen in the modern period and in Victorian England has been the subject of various studies. See, for example, Fanny Cosandey, *La reine de France. Symbole et pouvoir* (Paris, 2000). A thorough investigation of the position of the female constitutional monarch in Europe remains to be written, however.

16. 'Ma doveva essere compito specialmente di Margherita di Savoia, dapprima come sposa del principe ereditario e poi come Regina, il fare operazione di coesione e di assimilazione in un paese che, come l'Italia, è portato per ragioni storiche e etniche a dividersi e a frazionarsi piuttosto che a tenersi uno sotto la forte, ma delicata pressione del sentimento nazionale ... questo fascino personale di questa Regina Margherita di Savoia che seppe, sì, conquistare l'animo dei poeti e degli uomini d'ogni partito anche avversi alla monarchia, ma seppe in modo speciale adempiere ad un grande compito nazionale all'Italia, con le simpatie cosi largamente tributate dal popolo e dagli umili, quell'unità veramente morale e volontaria, che le guerre e i plebisciti avevano creato solo politicamente'. Monti, *Donne e passioni*, 146.

17. 'L'unico uomo in casa Savoia', 'Margherita di Savoia si muove in un preciso programma che persegue con assoluta coerenza due obiettivi: l'interesse dinastico e il prestigio della Corona ... Oso dire che la Regina Margherita ha capito – assai prima del fascismo – la necessità di poggiare sulle masse. Ai suoi tempi, i governi sono liberali, il suffragio è costretto, la politica è elitaria ma la Corona deve essere di massa, perennemente plebiscitata, e il fatto di doversi rimorchiare un consorte pigro e non sempre disponibile non fa che rendere più faticoso il programma'. Bracalini, *La Regina*, 11.

18. 'La Regina non ha altra cura che la gloria e l'onore del Suo paese e della Sua casa. Ella incarna, per cosi dire, la ragion di Stato italiana, e ciò con spirito e con grazia'. Bernhard von Bülow, *Memorie* (Milan, 1931), 662.

19. 'Tutti i vostri desideri, tutte le vostre azioni, mia cara figliola devono tendere verso due grandi e nobili scopi: l'amore del vostro marito e il bene della Nazione ... Bisogna che voi diventiate il Garibaldi della pace, cioè un essere di volta in volta reale e fantastico che gli Italiani invocheranno per liberarsi e risollevarsi dai loro mali. Nello spirito delle

masse, Garibaldi può con un colpo di moschetta cacciare i nemici esteri dell'Italia. Le stesse masse dovranno credere e dire che con un sorriso Margherita può e sa liberarli dai loro nemici interni: la discordia, la divisione, la miseria, le vessazioni governative ... Ne craignez donc pas trop la vue de la souffrance, de la misère. Tolérez les importuns quand ils sont malheureux, je n'ose pas vous dire mêlez vous de politique; le terrain est dangereux, plein de traîtres surprises qui font retourner contre leurs auteurs les meilleures intentions, mais tenez vous au courant de toutes les questions sérieuses, intéressantes pour ceux qui vous approchent sentent que vous vivez la vie du pays'. Archivio di Stato Torino, Carte Malgrà, fasc. 180–81, letter from Countess Irene della Rocca to Margherita, published in Margherita di Savoia, *Lettere 1862–1924*, ed. Aldo di Ricaldone (Rome, 1989), 52.

20. 'Je crois que les formes de propagande menues qui sèment avec continuité des idées patriotiques et élevées est (sic) très utile'. Margherita di Savoia, *Lettere*, 418 (letter of 30–31 August 1918).

21. 'Che grande forza ha l'educazione e quanto sono colpevoli i governi che non educano i popoli!' Letter to Colonel Osio (1898), in *Oggi*, 23 July 1953.

22. 'La dimostrazione la sera stessa qua fu una delle cose più impressionanti che abbia mai sentito quando il Re apparve alla loggia si alzò da quella moltitudine un solo lungo grido prolungato, era grido di gioia ed urlo di vendetta e di protesta, una stranissima cosa e che mi fa scendere il freddo per la schiene solo a pensarvi! Sembrava la passione umana che parlasse in un anima sola formata da tutta quella folla!' Letter of 27 June 1897, in ibid.

23. 'Per le donne, non è conquista facile prender parole, pubblicamente, su un podio'. Michela di Giorgio, *Le italiane dall'Unità ad oggi* (Rome and Bari, 1992), 398.

24. The queen wrote the letter in French (with at times rather unorthodox syntax). 'J'aime beaucoup ce qu'il écrit mais de parler et surtout devant beaucoup de femmes est bien autre chose! Une masse de femmes mariées (car évidemment le grand nombre doit être ainsi intimide ces messieurs plus qu'un auditoire des savants. Le résultat est souvent déplorable car la peur d'être pédant et le désir de se mettre à notre niveau fait qu'ils nous servent beaucoup de banalités. C'est humiliant à avouer, mais nous les aplatissons!' Margherita di Savoia, *Lettere*, 184.

25. 'Non una, ma molte conversioni politiche generarono dalla grazia, dalla cultura e dall'amabilità di Margherita'. Giovanna Vittori, *Margherita di Savoia* (Assisi, 1935–38), 73.

26. 'In Roma, Margherita, con la sua grazia, riuscì a rompere la barriera di ghiaccio che ancora divideva dalla corte la maggioranza dell'alta aristocrazia italiana devotissima al Vaticano'. Roux, *La prima regina*, 450.

27. 'Il successo che ha la Regina qui a Bologna, come donna e come sovrana, è indescrivibile'.

28. 'Quei due giovani, risalutanti con effusione di gentilezza il popolo salutante, da quel luogo dove i legati pontifici s'affacciavano a spargere le benedizioni per la morte e le maledizioni e le impiccagioni e le taglie e tutti i danni e disonori della servitù e della viltà su la vita e sull'Italia, doverono, io lo sento, toccare il cuore ai credenti di fede nelle sorti della monarchia unite alle sorti della patria'. Quoted in Ugoberto Alfassio Grimaldi, *Il Re 'buono'* (Milan, 1970), 133.

29. 'Ella sorgeva con una rara purezza di linee di pose nell'atteggiamento'.

30. 'Io guardai la regina, spiccante mite sul bianco, bionda e gemmata, tra quel buio rotte ma non vinto da quegli strani baglliori e da quel rumore fluttuante. Ed una fantasia mi assali ...'

31. 'Bella e argentea Croce di Savoia che splende agli occhi e arride ai cuori ...'

32. Stefano Pivato, *Il nome della storia. Onomastica e religione politiche nell'Italia contemporanea* (Bologna, 1999), 82.

33. Cosandey, *La reine*.

34. 'Le portrait est le miroir, la "glace très pure" des qualités dans lesquelles la personne se rencontre avec l'Idee, au delà des attributs et des ornements. Cette rencontre est signalée, dans le tableau, par la beauté'. Edouard Pommier, *Théories du portrait de la Renaissance aux Lumières* (Paris, 1998), 225–26.

35. A.C.S., Real Casa, *Casa della Regina Margherita e Regina Madre.*

36. I. Castrogiovanni Tipaldi, *I sovrani in Sicilia nel 1881, Cronica* (Palermo, 1881).

37. 'L'abito della regina era di broccato a fondo grigio con grandi fiori cesellato coralli, con un strascico immenso; sopra una visite in stoffa strana, un po' turca, un po' persiana, tutti ricami d'oro, tutta riporti di velluto rosso, un regalo fattole da poco dal re. Sul cappello roso e oro vi erano dei fermagli di brillanti, un largo braccialetto di brillanti al braccio sinistro, una farfalla in brillanti sul piccolo manicotto – e insieme un candore roseo di carnagione che resisteva a tanta magnificenza di colori forti. Le dame d'onore formavano un fondo bruno, di violetto cupo, di verdone, di prugna, con orecchini enormi di brillanti, con la cifra reale sulla spalla. *Cronaca Bizantina,* 1 December 1882.

38. 'Di colore ve ne erano poche' is how the *Cronaca* put it.

39. 'Il paraît que l'on reporte avec fureur les chapeaux Rembrand ce qui me fait beaucoup de plaisir, car ils vont bien même à nous qui frisons les 40 si malheureux à toucher et à passer! Surtout, en fait de manière de s'habiller, on ne veut plus faire les jeunesses, on ne voudrait pas encore faire les grand mères et c'est très embarrassant! Les Rembrand, sous l'ombre pietosa de leurs grandes ailes cachent finalement bien des choses!'. Margherita di Savoia, *Lettere*, letter of 12 September 1889, 320.

40. 'È sempre meglio stare coi Tedeschi, che con gli altri'. Domenico Farini, *Diario di fine secolo*, ed. Emilia Morelli (Rome, 1961–62), II, 1455.

41. 'L'eleganza provinciale e chiassosa di Margherita accrebbe il fascino della regalità in Italia'. Bracalini, *La Regina*, 113.

42. See Catherine Brice, 'La Monarchie, un acteur oublié de la "Nationalisation" des Italiens?', *Revue d'Histoire Moderne et Contemporaine* 45, no. 1 (January–March 1998), 147–69 and now Catherine Brice, La monarchie et la construction de l'identité nationale italienne (1861–1911). Thèse de doctorat d'Etat (Paris, 2004).
43. Catherine Brice, 'I viaggi della Regina Margherita', in *Altrove. Viaggi di donne dall'Antichità al Novecento* (Rome, 1999), 201–23.
44. Cf. Silvano Montaldo, *Patria e affari. Tommaso Villa e la costruzione del consenso tra unità e grande guerra* (Turin, 1999), esp. 179–249.

10

The Double Skin

Imperial Fashion in the Nineteenth Century

Juliane Vogel

Robes of state no longer suited the kings and queens of the nineteenth century. They had lost their power to persuade. Their glamour, cut and fit could not conceal the fact that they no longer fulfilled their purpose. Even the most splendid covering could not transform the body of the ruler into an authoritarian sign of power,[1] nor could the power of the garment be transferred to it. The link between the body political and the body natural had been broken; the one was no longer contained within the other, their twin nature abolished. In a famous satirical drawing, the English novelist William M. Thackeray pointed to the discrepancy between the royal body and royal apparel (Figure 10.1). He chose his victim not from among his contemporaries, but rather from among the absolutist rulers of a past which, looking back from the perspective of the year 1840, he denied all dignity and majesty. His depiction of Louis XIV is more of a dressing down than a dressing up. The splendour of the Sun King, we surmise from the caricature, lay exclusively in his clothes, which disguised his pathetic and not at all sun-like physique, a disguise that could no longer function in the age of bourgeois revolutions. Thackeray's satire was directed first of all against the *portrait d'apparat*, a rhetorical pictorial schema that presented absolutist rulers in magnificent robes and amidst their insignia.[2] It refers particularly to the 1701 portrait of Louis XIV by Hyacinthe Rigaud, which depicts the king wearing a wide, sweeping ermine robe and a full-bottomed wig and striking a dancerly pose, a picture in which body and costume combined to form a perfect whole. Compared to the body politic, which was represented by the signs of rule, the ageing body natural was insignificant. By 1840, however, no amount of clothing could hide the weakness of the royal flesh. Clothing and body contrast satirically and reveal their incompatibility. It is no accident that Ernst Kantorowicz chose Thackeray's drawing to illustrate the construction of the king's dual dignity.[3]

In his caricature, Thackeray sought to weaken the great royal singular. He presents not one but three figures. The portrait of the monarch, whose uniqueness evoked comparison with the sun, must accept both multiplication and fragmentation. Multiplication moves the sublime portrait into the comic sphere, while fragmentation destroys the king's dual nature. Next to Rigaud's figure of the sovereign we see the body natural of Louis XIV, which in its frailty retains only the pose and the *negligé*, and the dummy in an ermine robe on the other side. The Sun King's robe of state is placed on a mannequin, which reveals the absence of a body capable of filling the garment. In the state of separation, the robe, like the ruler's physique, is divested of pictorial power.

Thus Thackeray's mannequin is not an effigy, one of those dummies that served as deputies of the dead or absent king and

Figure 10.1 Caricature of the Portrait of Louis XIV (Hyacinthe Rigaud) by William M. Thackeray.

received the homage due to him. Devoid of all royal authority, it retreats into the royal wardrobe, but not to disappear there forever, as one might assume from the caricature, but rather in order to begin a second, secular career. The mannequin steps out of the *ancien regime* and into the fashion age. Thackeray's royal dummy is not simply a spectre of lost royal glamour, it is also a parvenu of a post-revolutionary order of monarchical representation, devoted no longer to the timelessly valid signs of power but to fashion. Tailors' dummies appeared at the courts: 'that is, dress-stands in human form made of wicker, wood or tow, which could be adapted to the measurements of certain ladies of the court',[4] also known as 'mannequins', the protagonists of nineteenth-century fashion. A few years after Thackeray held kings up to ridicule Empress Eugénie of France, wife of Napoleon III, used such deputies to keep her gowns tidy.[5] At her own request, the empress's body natural was replaced by wooden or straw-filled dummies, which were transported to her dressing-room, wearing the gown she had chosen, in a special lift. Dummies populated the dressing-room of a lady whose ambition was to be not just empress of France, but also queen of fashion.

Eugénie sought to solidify her fragile position as empress above all with the instruments of fashion. Since as the daughter of a wine merchant and a Spanish noblewoman she could point to no royal antecedents, and since she was married to Napoleon III, a political parvenu who had attained his position as head of state by a coup, she veiled the deficiencies of her origins with variegated and continually renewed play with clothing, masks and roles. Her constant changes of dress constituted the structure and the central efficacy of imperial appearances in public and at court under the Second Empire. She gave brilliant costume balls and kept the court world in a continual state of masquerade.[6] The court's guests had to submit to an elaborate dress code of her own devising. The court staff were decked out like an operatic chorus. The daily imperial schedule was a careful composition of fashion tableaux, which necessitated minute attention to the details of clothing care. The increased importance and the courtly elaboration of wardrobe played a central role in the strategies of an imperial court regarded as parvenu, which sought to ennoble itself with the aid of an artificial etiquette not provided by tradition. Among the court's strategies for confronting the loss of tradition caused by two revolutions were strict, if imaginative, imperial dress codes, which were at the same time subject to fashion, i.e. to a principle of accelerated change. Only the

Second Empire made the notion and the dictatorship of fashion possible. After an era of slow and virtually imperceptible evolution, after decades of stagnation, which had brought little alteration in the basic cut of clothing,[7] an unprecedented acceleration in changing dress began and established rapidly obsolete innovation as the motive force in the fashion world. Only now did the garment industry become a fashion industry and *haute couture* a national business. Thus the culture of costume at the court of Napoleon III and Eugénie initially served a heightened and insatiable hunger for distinction – the desire to emphasise differences through dress, above all when another desire for genealogical difference and distinction could not be satisfied. At the same time, however, the imperial court's textile displays also served to promote the French fashion industry of the Belle Epoque. The empress's luxurious apparel was not simply intended to obscure the gaps in her family tree, it also promoted textile production and established France as the leading arbiter in matters of dress.

After all, when Empress Eugénie spoke of her oft-cited *robes politiques*,[8] what she really had in mind were her *robes économiques*. Her political gowns represented not the 'dynasty' but rather, in this case, a 'manufactory'. The richness of their fabrics advertised the products of the French textile industry, particularly fostering the prosperity of the Lyon silk manufacturers, whose products could be presented on the expansive exhibition surfaces of the imperial crinolines.[9] They not merely demanded more than ten widths of cloth,[10] but promoted and indeed required the interplay of several types and layers of fabric and trimmings, so that a remarkable density of commodities piled up on the steel hoops.

Yet fashion was a dangerous herald of imperial glory. Since a fashionable frock did not outlast the season, it could only ever represent a fleeting order. While crowns and insignias announced the ruler's timeless glory, fashion was a protagonist of time and change. The fashion mania of the Napoleonic court was thus interpreted as a symptom of political instability. Where fashion attained such significance, people also lived in the expectation of political change.[11] It represented in perfect form a political condition whose temporary glamour rested not on strong political traditions but on the mass production of novelties – *nouveautés*. For that reason alone the empress's gowns lacked the force of a strong dynastic sign,[12] and could not constitute a body politic because they were constantly being replaced and renewed. The loss of political credibility that unsettled the regime of Napoleon III from the beginning and provoked a proliferation of compensatory symbolic forms was shaped by the accelerated shifts of fashion around 1850 and the hypertrophy of fashionable forms themselves. With the crinoline, a hollow space inhabited the core of the modistic will to style, which was perceived as an emanation of excess. A 'walking hot-air balloon, a swollen, speeding yeast dumpling',[13] it was prey to the same charge of *vanitas* as contemporary financial speculation. The mass of fabric hid an expansive void, which no longer maintained formal relations to the clothed body, a gigantically extended nothing in which legs walked without contact with skirts.

The new fashions of excess could look back on noble models. On this point Eugénie, urgently in need of monarchical genealogy, followed her predecessor Marie-Antoinette, whose life and relics she celebrated in a cult that her contemporaries found embarrassing.[14] The empress of France propagated a fashion à la Louis Seize, a neo-rococo for the industrial age, with the steel bell of the Belle Epoque crinoline repeating and exceeding the farthingales of the pre-revolutionary court.[15] The frame, which transferred the constructions of contemporary steel architecture to the arena of dress,[16] without recourse to the soft support of countless petticoats,[17] cited and monumentalised the hoop skirt of the Louis Seize period, whose basket structure had still been composed of whalebones held together by fabric and wire. The *ancien régime* had also translated the excessive magnification of outlines and volumes to the field of coiffure and, in the run-up to the Revolution, had expanded skirts and hairstyles alike in hyperbolic progression. These exaggerations could not, however, guarantee the dignity of the body politic in either era. On the contrary, this immoderate magnification indicated the reduction of the monarchical principle, and caricature became its constant companion.

Couturier to Queens – Charles Frederick Worth

The mobilisation of fashion, the establishment in the Second Empire of *haute couture* as the central arbiter of European fashion, could not, however, simply be accomplished by the traditional ladies' tailors. Fashion interests and economic interests had to be harmonised on a large scale, and the production of exclusive original pieces profitably combined with modern mass production. What was needed was an impresario of outfitting, an imperialist of fashion, who could found an international fashion empire that reached beyond France's borders, which would dress not just the rich and the distinguished of the era, but also see to the dissemination of inexpensive copies and off-the-rack models. The man who set the guidelines of international fashion for decades was the Englishman Charles Frederick Worth (1825–95), who lived and worked in Paris. The trend-setting female shape of the second half of the nineteenth century was designed, marketed and further developed in his salon in Rue de la Paix. From there he regulated the relationship between the original and mass production. At the same time, within only a few years he attained the position of unchallenged fashion designer to the European high nobility and made dresses for Empress Eugénie, Queen Victoria, English princesses and Russian grand duchesses, for Queen Margherita of Italy and Elisabeth, empress of Austria, among others.[18] He was the constructor of queenly contours and figures, and chiefly responsible for deciding how the bodies of queens should be represented according to the stage directions of an industrialised society.

Primal Scene of a Couturier – The Rainbow Portrait

At the beginning of his career as a fashion designer, however, stood the encounter with an overwhelming body politic and its costume. The primal scene of his career, at least according to the memoirs of his son Jean Worth, already revolved around an imposing royal gown.[19] Even as a child, Charles Worth had been fascinated by a portrait of Elizabeth I, the famous 'Rainbow' portrait, which he saw in the National Gallery in London (Figure 1.1).

Every moment that was not occupied by Allenby's he spent in the museums and art galleries, studying the great paintings. Those whose subjects flaunted elaborate costumes fascinated him before all others. One in particular, that of Queen Elizabeth in her velvet gown embroidered with ears and eyes, signifying that she saw everything and heard everything, was destined to become the love of his life. Young as he was, he understood the meaning of the strange design and was so struck by its quaint symbolism, so impressed by the luxuriousness of the painted velvet, that he exclaimed never dreaming that it would come to pass, 'If I ever am rich enough, I shall have that copied. I'll have stuff made like that with eyes and ears.'[20]

More than the figure of the queen herself, we see, it was the ingenious and precious gown she wore in the painting that captured his imagination. A perfect textile shrine, it transfigured the sovereign's body natural into a splendid body of state. It transformed the mortal shell into a symbol of power – not just because of the preciousness of the worked brocade, but mainly because of the eyes and ears, which served the queen as additional sensory organs. In the painting Elizabeth I wears a gown that can see and hear in all directions, which dramatically expands her spectrum of perception and makes her an absolute and inescapable figure of control and arbiter of knowledge. Enchanted by this picture, Worth devoted himself once and for all to the fashion arts, and to the figure of *the* queen.

Yet Charles Worth was never to encounter and dress an imperial or royal equivalent of the virginal Elizabeth among his contemporaries. The nineteenth century produced no convincing monarchical bodies. The 'new clothes' circulated under the conditions of a secularised modern age, which had exposed the royal flesh, revealing its nakedness and frailties. The power of the robe, which the 'investiture' of the body politic had established, had to be reinterpreted after the latter's decay. This power was transferred to fashion, which transformed the 'heavy' signs of the past into 'light' ones and treated empresses, too, like mannequins.[21] Under the conditions of the mass production of clothing, the body of the customer, even if she was a queen, became abstract. The couturier's frame of reference was less the individual physique as a set of measurements and numbers, lengths and widths.[22] Worth did not need the future wearer at all costs. He easily designed patterns without actually measuring the customer's body, and made even spectacular originals as if for an imaginary mass production. A unique gown for a queen or empress could be copied, multiplied and worn by other women. Even *haute couture* ad/dressed not just the individual visitor to a couturier's salon, but always also the absent and unknown customer. It was no accident that the telegraphic apparatus accepted a large portion of orders at Rue de la Paix, since the woman wishing to be dressed often lived hundreds of miles away.[23] Worth emancipated the gown and treated it as an autonomous commodity independent of its actual wearer, with rights, a will and a destiny of its own.

Worth was also the first to employ live fashion models. The true wearer of his gowns was not the customer, with all of her deficiencies, but the *mannequin vivant*.[24] While Eugénie housed straw dummies in her apartments, Worth commanded a whole corps of living statues. If the tailor's dummy was 'a chimera, in which the body and fashions are amalgamated,[25] how much truer this was of the fashion model, who lent the gown nothing but her measurements and volume. In his salon, the latest fashions were presented by women without qualities but with perfect measurements, whose figures in no way reflected those of potential customers, but who were all the more successful as figures in the mirror and as dream imagos for customers. The invention of the fashion model, the clothing of a model by a model, of the perfect body by the perfect dress, once more presupposed the separation of person and clothing. What is more, the fashion body, a mere function of the gown, was a constructionist derivative, which guaranteed the optimal and unwrinkled presentation of the gown. They showed the clothes in their ideal form and promoted their autonomisation. From now on, clothes would pursue a career independent of the wearer and her body.

Thus Worth also worked for empresses and queens without ever seeing or touching their bodies. Elisabeth, Empress of Austria, who never entered the salon in Rue de la Paix, still wore gowns from the House of Worth.[26] 'Elisabeth, Empress of Austria, never came to Paris, but nevertheless ordered three or four dresses every year from us.'[27] The most spectacular gowns she ever wore in public were designed here. They included the white gown decorated with stars that she wears on the famous state portrait of 1864 by Franz Xaver Winterhalter, as well as the dress she wore for her coronation as queen of Hungary in 1867,[28] which contributed to the success of a moment of intense historical significance for the Habsburg monarchy. This gown, which gracefully cited elements of Hungarian aristocratic costume, corresponded to the nationalist interests of the people whom the 'Compromise' of 1867 had given preference over the other peoples of the Habsburg Monarchy. The Austrian empress dressed up as a Hungarian here, not unlike the Hungarians themselves, who only began to recall their traditions of national costume during these decades.[29] Nevertheless, this creation came from a famous Parisian fashion house, and was designed by a virtuoso of masks and costumes, who made liberal use of historical and national clothing traditions. Even for her coronation as queen of Hungary, the icon of Hungarian nationalism, Elisabeth, queen of Austria, who had spoken up for Hungarian interests for many years, was outfitted by a representative of international couture. And despite its nationalist character, the coronation gown from the House of Worth appealed above all to the operetta tastes of international high society, which thrilled to the romantic and rebellious aura of Hungarian drawing-room heroism. In an atmosphere of growing nationalism, the queens of nations ordered their gowns from Paris. In Rue de la Paix Charles Worth centralised royal fashion; from here he developed a luminous art of female appearance, which – like the capital that financed it so lavishly – was no respecter of borders. The royal customers, who were beholden to national interests, invented ruses in order to have their gowns made by Worth without ruffling feathers at home. As Jean Worth reports, they became clandestine recipients of his designs, acquiring the gowns they desired via local middlemen.[30]

Heraldry in Crisis

It is thus not surprising that the tailor to queens had neither knowledge of nor an interest in the field of dynastic heraldry. The science of the symbols of imperial and royal authority was incompatible with the couturier's ambitions. As a young entrepreneur, Worth had designed a costly train, shown at the Paris Exhibition of 1855, which he hoped would attract the attention of the imperial court and gain illustrious customers for his designs. This time, at least, his plans failed, since the ornaments appliquéd on the train so resembled the Bourbon fleur-de-lis that the courtiers of Napoleon III suspected him of harbouring sympathies for the dethroned Louis Philippe.[31] The ambiguous signs on the train temporarily prevented the development of business ties between the court and Charles Frederick Worth.[32] This incident, which not coincidentally occurred at the Paris Exhibition and not at court, nevertheless throws some light on a serious crisis of royal representation in the nineteenth century. For the couturier, at least, the Bourbon lily no longer possessed any dynastic or political significance. He added it to the inventory of fashion as one ornament among others, and used it in a playful way that no longer had any dynastic loyalties. When a symbol previously tied to a strong sphere of power was turned over to fashion, its dignity, but above all its exclusivity, was at an end. The 'heavy' sign became a 'light' one. What had become the object of playful variation and further dissemination could no longer refer to and empower the body politic. As an ornament, a mere gambling chip, a weakened sign with no basis in a functioning system of monarchical representation, it became lost in endless free reproductions and in the hereafter of its traditional meaning. The eyes and ears of the 'Rainbow' portrait, which Worth had admired on Queen Elizabeth I, also ended as a grotesque and incomplete Elizabethan citation on a fashionable Parisian fabric:

> [T]he first of the materials especially made for Worth was the famous brocade with eyes and ears worn by Queen Elizabeth in the portrait that had so fascinated my father as a boy in London. Through some oversight the first he ordered was made only with eyes, when it should have had both eyes and ears. Therefore, some ten or fifteen years later, my father had the pattern made again, this time accurately in a new material, velours au sabare, of the sort that was woven under Louis XVI, but not so fine in quality.[33]

The remake of the Elizabethan brocade could no longer transfer power to its wearer. The loss of the sense of hearing points to its 'organic' deficiency, but also to the priorities of an epoch that overestimated the sense of sight to the detriment of sound. Even the second attempt to copy the 'Rainbow' fabric, however, was marked by difference rather than exact replication. In the eclectic manner of historicism, Worth was not satisfied by a single – Elizabethan – citation, he also combined it with a second from the more recent history of the French kings. But if eyes and ears appeared here not on brocade but on velvet, which was used under Louis XVI, then it was a multiply devalued background. Jean Worth himself conceded the imitation's inferiority to the original. Above all, however, as in the Empress Eugénie's playing at Marie-Antoinette, the regime mentioned by name here is one that ended with the beheading of its monarch and the destruction of the body politic. The mere mention of Louis XVI extracts the political power from the old fabric. In the age of its reproducibility, the gown that was capable of forming a splendid body politic squanders its entire symbolic capital. And yet Eugénie would scarcely have been the appropriate wearer of a gown adorned with eyes and ears. The empress of France put far more energy into the *donner voir*, the desire to display, to be seen, than in her own desire to see and hear. Through the medium of fashion she caught the public eye. Instead of equipping herself with a hundred eyes, she presented herself as a pretty picture.[34]

Tulle Illusion or the Gown in Glory

In the years that followed Charles Worth pursued modern and industrial methods in order to compensate for the loss of traditional monarchical glory with contemporary glamour. He enveloped his customers in a new fabric. He surrounded countless gowns he designed with a textile halo, doubling them with *tulle illusion* – a transparent and ethereal material that was only developed in France in 1827 and began to dominate evening dress beginning around 1840. *Tulle illusion*, a machine-made silk product,[35] lent women the appearance of fairies, higher beings from a never-never land, transported to inaccessible realms of illusion. The qualities of *tulle illusion* were exclusively prismatic in nature. In itself a transparent nothing, it guided and refracted light in a flattering manner and surrounded the wearer with a filmy white and shiny cloud of gauze.[36] It transformed women into apparitions with luminous edges. The figure dressed in tulle was enveloped in a secular halo, it moved in a vague, restless field of light, which made its contours disappear and obscured its true position in space. Its use in countless creations of the House of Worth demonstrated the high importance the couturier accorded to light. Thus he experimented in his salons with the interplay of gaslight and fabric. When women came for a fitting, they also went into a specially equipped room to test the effect under artificial light. One salon of the workshop in Rue de la paix, in which a twelve-armed gas lamp[37] simulated the lighting in a ballroom, was devoted exclusively to experiments with light.

> Next to the fourth salon was the salon de lumière. The walls of this room were completely covered with mirrors, and the curtains were always drawn. Hissing gas flames behind movable shades bathed the room in a bright light. The lady trying on her new ball gown here saw herself in the mirror exactly as others would see her the next evening in the Tuileries.[38]

The dresses were subjected to different illuminations and their effects tested. In order to be shown to their best advantage, the models needed professional light direction, but as the products of light they were at the same time designed for specific and unrepeatable moments, and calculated to make a momentary and transient impression. *Tulle illusion* was an indispensable component of an ephemeral fashion, and it was correspondingly perishable. A single day sufficed to produce a gown,[39] and a single night to destroy its magic.[40] The transience of light and the fabric counteracted the heaviness and girth of the steel hoop, which always made the wearer appear as a colossal figure. The fairy-like quality of the tulle and the monumentality of the steel construction, the phantasmagoria and the megalomaniac substructure, appeared in an endless interplay.

The fascination that Worth's fashions gained from light also explains his predilection for white gowns.[41] As ideal reflectors they offered a blank surface onto which the light could fall, which at the same time suggested the hypothetical and blank white of the female body. Eugénie in particular was transformed by white gowns into a white screen, whose blinding highlights far outshone the gleam of jewels of state and other dynastic symbols. Her abstinence from jewellery, with the exception of white pearls, was grounded not just in the perfection of her white bosom, but also in the knowledge that the glamour of her appearance owed more to modern lighting than to the delegitimated state jewels of a government brought to power by a coup d'état.[42] As an industrial producer of glamour, Charles Worth outdid centuries of Christian and dynastic imagery.

Queens of the Night – Star-spangled Gowns at Court

It is also against this background that one should view the famous portrait that Franz Xaver Winterhalter painted of the empress of Austria (Figure 10.2). Her white tulle gown was a typical Worth creation.[43] As Gabriela Christen has noted, it was far more appropriate to the queen of the ball than the empress of a vast empire. Although Winterhalter takes up elements of traditional royal portraiture in his depiction of Elisabeth, and although he still operates within the iconographic framework of the *portrait d'apparat* – a portrait schema that surrounded the king's official body with an aureole and placed it outside of time – the painting captures a fleeting appearance: 'The empress, dressed as for a ball, appears for only a brief moment as a romantic vision bathed in bright light.'[44] Thus even the empress of Austria appears in the picture frame as an ephemeral being, her splendour unfolding in a moment of evanescent presence, amidst uncertain lights, not in the eternity of dynastic authority and dynastic pretensions of eternity. Insignias and heraldic symbols have disappeared from the picture plane. The empress wears no crown; also absent is the *tabouret*, the low table with which royalty was usually portrayed and on which their symbols of power were displayed. The tiara, in contrast, is doubly occupied, on the one hand by the natural insignia of the empress's hair, which was always regarded as Elisabeth's true crown, and whose fame was far greater than that of the Habsburg insignias

Figure 10.2 Empress Elisabeth by Franz Xaver Winterhalter (1864).

kept in the treasure-house of the Hofburg,[45] and on the other by a ring of single diamond stars cut by the Viennese jeweller Köchert, which were attached to the empress's plaited coiffure. The royal tiara has been replaced by individual stars, and thus by the ascendants of those that adorned the *tulle étoilé* of hoop skirts. As cosmic images of the greatest possible universality, they avoid any precise dynastic or heraldic reference, as literal 'heavenly bodies'[46] they embody no specific dynastic tradition, and emanate a less exclusive glamour. To be sure, the imperial ring of stars cites the Virgin Mary's crown of stars in the secular setting of a ballroom,[47] just as the tulle draping the gown wreathes the empress in a secular halo. The headdress in particular was a legacy of Christian iconography, so that Elisabeth too appears as a higher being in a pseudo-sacred sphere. The stars are primarily accessories, however, and belong to the world of fashion, which was open not just to the empress but also to office girls and courtesans, a world of devalued and endlessly reproducible signs. In addition to the nine stars visible in the painting, Elisabeth owned at least twenty-seven pieces by Köchert, among other jewellers.[48] The splendour of heraldic as well as religious symbols was transformed into the modern glamour of orchestrated light and illumination, insignias in costume jewellery with heightened luminosity. Thus the empress of Austria, who preferred to entrust her self-presentation to a professional light director rather than to court etiquette,[49] may also be considered a forerunner of the modern stars who also like to underline their status with star jewellery. Charles Frederick Worth, as this example shows once again, was far more interested in outfitting the queen of the ball than the body politic of the Habsburg Empire.

And yet a shadow of irony fell onto this famous starry gown from an unexpected quarter. The design of the empress's gown also reveals much about the iconographic intrigues of a fashion house that had to serve not one queen alone, but queens of all sorts and nations. The world of the French imperial court had already seen the star-spangled ball gown, but more particularly the stars in the empress's crowning glory. As Franz Xaver Winterhalter's model, the Austrian empress, whose rank placed her above all comparison, wore an inverted costume citation. A few years before Charles Frederick Worth designed the tulle gown for Elisabeth, he had dressed Virginia Countess Castiglione, Napoleon III's mistress, as the Queen of the Night. A photograph of 1858 shows her in a magnificent black gala gown, whose crinoline is covered by four wide sashes adorned with stars (Figure 10.3). Her coiffure and hair ornaments in particular – stars in an artfully plaited crown of hair – strikingly anticipate Winterhalter's famous portrait of the empress of Austria. The black mistress and the white empress wore stars as signs of a secular, dynastically unspecified glamour, both appeared in the light of publicity as 'stars' in the modern sense of the word.

In view of this prehistory, a small if quiet scandal remains. For even if the empress was enchanted by the more spectacular gown, looming white out of the Winterhalterian twilight, her frock was nevertheless an answer, an inverted reply, ironic counterpart to a model initially presented by a lady of inferior rank and doubtful intentions. Elisabeth of Austria moved into second place, playing second fiddle in a dialogue of star-spangled dresses, a little fashion drama, which was staged even without the knowledge of the two protagonists and over a period of ten years. The case is also rendered

Figure 10.3 Contessa Castiglione (1858).

more interesting by the fact that Countess Castiglione was no mere bed-mate of the French emperor. As a kinswoman of the Italian politician Cavour, she had been sent to the court of Napoleon III to gain his support for Italian unification. 'Accomplish your mission, dear cousin, by any means that appear appropriate to you, but accomplish it.'[50] And as the mistress of the French emperor she was supposed to devote herself to the objectives of Italian nationalism, which collided dramatically with Austrian interests in Italy. The customer of the House of Worth, Virginia Contessa Castiglione, intrigued against the Habsburg monarchy, which sought to assert its territorial and hegemonic rights against the movement for Italian unification. On the stage of couture, Worth orchestrated a theatrical duet for Odette and Odile, for black and white, the Queen of the Night and her illuminated double, for negative and positive in a world of balls and nights at the theatre.[51] He operated with the blasphemous irony of a politician of *haute couture*, who was willing to emancipate gowns even at the expense of his royal clientele. If, however, it is true that the empress of Austria drew the inspiration for her own starry adornments from a theatrical costume for Mozart's *Magic Flute*,[52] we need to inquire again into the close ties between stage costumes and royal fashions, or into why the figure of the Queen of the Night inspired the outfitting of mistress and empress alike.[53] The intimate dialogue between the two star gowns also speaks of the triumph of theatrical fashion over the weakened symbolic systems of nineteenth-century neo-absolutist governments, the textile versions of which referred to and were inspired by the theatre. Monarchical representation unmasked itself by borrowing theatrical masks and using them to replace their own forms. Elisabeth's hairdresser, Frau Feifalik, had once worked at Vienna's Burgtheater.

Skin and Gown – The Return of the Dual Body

The empress of Austria did not depend solely on the splendid effects of Worth's ball gowns. Over the course of her life as empress she undertook radical changes of dress policy. Although she repeatedly emphasised the importance of the monarch's wardrobe, and lamented that her royal contemporaries dressed like philistines, the unusual quality of her appearance did not relate solely to the fashions she wore. In the House of Worth, the empress of Austria was considered a regular but unenthusiastic customer: 'Clothes meant little to her. She affected the greatest simplicity, and wore mostly white, pearl grey, or very, very pale violet.'[54]

Since royal robes had become suspect as carnival costumes, which could not longer secure the dignity of their wearers, Elisabeth of Austria concentrated on the body rather than the gown. She drew her own consequences. Since the insignia of monarchy had lost their credibility, the royal flesh itself had to be transmuted into a timeless symbol. Since fashions lasted only a season and were soon outmoded, the body natural of the ruler had to prove its own immortality. The empress of Austria deployed her own body as an incorruptible (in both senses of the word) sign. Under the bell of Worth's crinoline, but particularly after its disappearance, she prepared another, far more reliable and less perishable work of art. She became famous not for her clothes, but for the strict rituals she devoted to the preservation of her beauty. Over the years she devised an artificial and self-determined figure, whose naturalness was to be completely transfigured. Not only did she lace her waist, an effort that could take up to an hour, but she did all she could to perfect and preserve her famous silhouette and make her body immortal, despite the vagaries of fashion. She rode, walked and performed gymnastics to keep age and fat at bay. By refusing solid food and increasingly replacing it with liquid nourishment, milk, meat juices and violet ice, she risked malnutrition to protect her figure from the ravages of time.[55] Sport, cosmetics and diet, not the grace of God, raised her above decay.

Her gowns, too, had to fit her body so perfectly that skin and fabric were practically indistinguishable. Since Elisabeth would accept neither hooks nor buttons – items that reminded one that a dress could be put on or taken off, rendering tangible the difference between body and costume, skin and fabric, she was sewn into her gowns.[56] Thus she covered herself with a skin-like membrane, a second skin, which encompassed her body with an organic fit. Later, when the crinoline had disappeared from the fashion world, she abandoned voluminous petticoats and replaced them with close-fitting suede underwear, which surrounded her like another second skin.[57]

Yet her skin was not merely doubled, but also preserved. She was subjected to radical cosmetic treatments which marked the empress as a modern martyr. By submitting to the tortures of extravagant skin care, she propagated a modern version of eternal life. In contrast to the Christian saints, who had suffered for the salvation of their souls, Elisabeth of Austria suffered for the beauty of her membranes, risking 'the terrible death of many a Christian martyr.'[58] She sought to combat age with the aid of 'muscle waters' and icy 'gladiator baths', while at the same time her skin was supposed to cheat the passage of time with steam baths and baths in nearly boiling oil. Face masks of raw meat and strawberry purée also contributed to keeping her skin supple.[59] Cosmetic treatments, not clothing, ensured the dignity of the ruler, and only with their help could the gap between the king's two bodies be closed. The empress's hair, skin and figure constituted an imperial icon of the Habsburg monarchy, which recaptured through the transfiguration of the body natural the respect lost because of the appearance of her royal contemporaries.[60] The empress's preserved and muscular body succeeded in covering up the crisis of royal clothing rhetoric and deciding it in her favour. Only when transmuted into a shiny cosmetic product was the body natural safe from Thackeray's satire.

This icon, however, could no longer be encountered in that public space where kings and emperors went about the business of representation; it withdrew from the public perception generally devoted to royal display. Its magic is a version of uncertainty, withdrawal and refusal. The empress's black silhouette, which grew ever thinner, was a symbol far more of absence than of presence and her perfection of form can be described only in negative terms. The unity of the body natural and the body politic can be realised only in an act of disappearance. The sight of the dual body, in which skin and gown had merged to the point of indistinguishability, finally disappeared into endless journeys, behind parasols and fans. By leaving the public sphere behind her, and refusing the duties of representation, Elisabeth of Austria developed her image beyond the field of vision of the watching world. By instituting a strict prohibition on pictures of herself, she preserved an image that could no longer be tested. What remained was the negative of a royal portrait, the negative of imperial presence, but also the negative of a photograph, on which Charles Frederick Worth's white ball gown was transformed into a black one that fitted as snugly as a second skin. For his part, Charles Frederick Worth had whole pieces of silks and brocades from the gowns of his royal clients sewn into the upholstery of the sofas at Suresnes, his splendid estate.[61]

Translated by Pamela Selwyn

Notes

1. Cf. Albrecht Koschorke, 'Macht und Fiktion', in *Des Kaisers neue Kleider. Über das Imaginäre politischer Herrschaft. Texte. Bilder. Lektüren*, ed. Thomas Frank et al. (Frankfurt a.M., 2002), 73–85, 79. 'In the political code ... clothing marks the link between the empiricism of the body and that element of social organisation that is not immediately accessible to the senses, and consequently of a transcendental nature'. Clothing, the side of official power visible to the gaze of subjects, must, according to Koschorke, be ratified by respect – a recognition often refused in the nineteenth century.
2. Rainer Schoch, *Das Herrscherbild in der Malerei des 19. Jahrhunderts* (Munich, 1975), 18–22.
3. Ernst H. Kantorowicz, *The King's Two Bodies: A Study in Mediaeval Political Theology* (Princeton, New Jersey, 1957), 423 and figure 26.
4. Katharina Sykora, *Unheimliche Paarungen. Androidenfaszination und Geschlecht in der Fotografie* (Cologne, 1999), 44.
5. Annie Latour, *Magier der Mode. Macht und Geheimnis der Haute Couture* (Stuttgart, 1956), 89. Dummies had been set up in the Tuileries palace and dressed in the empress's gowns to prevent them from acquiring the slightest wrinkle.
6. Maurice, Comte de Fleury, *Memoiren der Kaiserin Eugénie*, Vol. 1 (Leipzig, 1921), 317ff.
7. Jean Philippe Worth, *A Century of Fashion*, trans. Ruth Scott Miller (Boston, 1928), 4. 'Prior to this, the change in styles from year to year was hardly perceptible.'
8. 'The number of silk looms operating in Lyon doubled between 1860 and 1870.' Latour, *Magier der Mode*, 75.
9. Worth, *A Century of Fashion*, 42.
10. Latour, *Magier der Mode*, 77. A crinoline could swallow as many as thirty metres of cloth. Fleury speaks of steel cages that 'devour an entire shop full of fabric'. (Fleury, *Memoiren*, 355).
11. The privileging of temporary effects disconcerted those who placed their hopes in long-term political securities or in the continued existence of the monarchies. When the brother of the Austrian emperor Francis Joseph II arrived in Paris, he wrote: 'The image of the momentary is everywhere visible here; everything is quite brilliant, but unmistakeably calculated only for the moment – the idea of the permanent arises nowhere'. Quoted in E.A. Reinhardt, *Napoleon III. und Eugenie. Tragikomödie eines Kaisertums* (Berlin, 1930), 140.
12. Jean Baudrillard, *Symbolic Exchange and Death*, trans. Iain Hamilton Grant (London, 1993), 87. The dynastic symbols of the old world belonged to a limited because referential order of signs, which disappeared in the age of fashion. 'There is no longer any determinacy internal to the signs of fashion, hence they become free to commute and permutate without limit.'

13. Friedrich Theodor Vischer, 'Vernünftige Gedanken über die jetzige Mode', in *Kritische Gänge*, ed. Robert Vischer, Vol. 5 (Munich, 1921), 339–65, 343.
14. Juliane Vogel, *Elisabeth von Österreich. Momente aus dem Leben einer Kunstfigur* (Frankfurt a.M., 1998), 115; Iréneé Mauget, *L'Impératrice Eugénie* (Paris, 1909), 15, 53 , 81, 281.
15. 'On her table lay a register of the *toilettes* of Marie-Antoinette, which had been found in the archives and which the empress had preserved as a particular treasure'. Latour, *Magier der Mode*, 89.
16. James Laver, quoted in Latour, *Magier der Mode*, 77.
17. Latour, 78. The multiplicity of supporting underskirts was reduced to one or two muslin skirts.
18. Latour, *Magier der Mode* and Worth, *A Century of Fashion*, 39ff. and 133ff.; Aileen Ribeiro, 'La mode dans l'oeuvre de Winterhalter', in *Franz Xaver Winterhalter et les Cours de l'Europe de 1830 à 1870*, exhibition at the National Portrait Gallery, 12 February to 7 May 1988 (London, 1988), 66–72, 69. Ribeiro calls Worth the 'dictateur de la haute couture, non seulement en France, mais partout ailleurs dans un monde qui s'élargissait de plus en plus grâce à l'amélioration des communications et au développement des voyages.'
19. Worth, *A Century of Fashion*, 7.
20. Ibid., 7–8.
21. Baudrillard, *Symbolic Exchange*, 87.
22. Latour, *Magier der Mode*, 65ff.
23. See, for example, Worth, *A Century of Fashion*, 122.
24. Cornelia Vismann, 'Gewandstudien', in *Vom Griechenland*, eds. Friedrich Kittler and Cornelia Vismann (Berlin, 2001), 91–111, 102. The first model to present Worth's creations was Madame Worth. Worth had married the ideal mannequin.
25. Sykora, *Unheimliche Paarungen*, 43.
26. Worth, *A Century of Fashion*, 204. See also Johannes Thiele, *Elisabeth. Das Buch ihres Lebens* (Munich and Leipzig, 1996), 427.
27. Worth, *A Century of Fashion*, 204.
28. Ibid., 353.
29. Katalin F. Dóza, *Letûnt idok, eltûnt divatok* (Past Times and Forgotten Fashions) http://www.idg.hu/expo/divatcsarnok/divat/.
30. Worth, *A Century of Fashion*, 116, 195.
31. Latour, *Magier der Mode*.
32. Latour, *Magier der Mode*, 72.
33. Worth, *A Century of Fashion*, 80.
34. Fleury recalls the empress's early days, 'when the eyes of France and all of Europe were trained upon Eugenie; for we must always keep in mind the extent to which the Second Empire, then at the pinnacle of its power, was the focus of all attention'. Fleury, *Memoiren*, Vol. I, 353.
35. On the primacy of tulle, see Ribeiro, *La mode*, 67, 70. Cf. Worth, *A Century of Fashion*, 27.

36. Edith Saunders, *The Age of Worth. Couturier to the Empress Eugenie* (London, 1954).
37. Latour, *Magier der Mode*, 82.
38. Latour, 146–7. See also Worth, *A Century of Fashion*, 186: 'the evening dress must be shown by artificial light, as it is impossible for daylight to do justice to the robes de soirées.'
39. Worth, *A Century of Fashion*, 26, 191. The short life of Worth gowns was matched by the rapidity with which they were produced.
40. On the fragility of tulle see Ribeiro, *La mode*, 70.
41. Ibid. See also Saunders, *König der eleganten Welt*, 64ff.
42. Gabriela Christen, 'Die Bildnisse der Kaiserin,' in Juliane Vogel, *Elisabeth von Österreich. Momente aus dem Leben einer Kunstfigur* (Frankfurt a.M., 1998), 164–91, 172.
43. Worth used *tulle étoilé* here, a speciality of the house of Worth. Ribeiro, *La mode*, 70.
44. Christen, *Die Bildnisse*, 169.
45. Cf. Thomas Frank, 'Höfische Mode', in Thomas Frank et al. eds., *Des Kaisers neue Kleider. Über das Imaginäre politischer Herrschaft. Texte. Bilder. Lektüren* (Frankfurt a.M., 2002), 197–205, 202ff. Cf. Vogel, *Elisabeth*, 82.
46. Richard Dyer, *Heavenly Bodies. Film Stars and Society* (London, 1986).
47. Revelation (12:1) 'And a great portent appeared in heaven, a woman clothed with the sun, with the moon under her feet, and on her head a crown of twelve stars ....' This sentence was the basis of the iconographic tradition of representing the Virgin Mary with a crown of stars.
48. Irmgard Köchert-Hauser, *Köchert* (Florence, 1990), 73, for further star designs, see 148.
49. Vogel, *Elisabeth*, 94ff.
50. Original quotation attributed to Cavour and cited in Maurice Paléologue, *Cavour. Ein großer Realist* (Berlin, 1928), 136.
51. According to information from the house of Köchert, the empress of Austria also received the inspiration for her star headdress from a performance of Mozart's *Magic Flute*.
52. Information from the house of Köchert. See also Christen, 'Die Bildnisse', 177, with stronger reference to Winterhalter's portrait of Elisabeth as Diana with a crescent moon.
53. Vogel, *Elisabeth*, 82.
54. Worth, *A Century of Fashion*, 204.
55. Brigitte Hamann, *Elisabeth. Kaiserin wider Willen* (Vienna and Munich, 1982).
56. Hamann, *Elisabeth*.
57. Hamann, *Elisabeth*, 209. On the psychoanalysis of the dual skin, see Claudia Benthien, *Haut. Literaturgeschichte – Körperbilder – Grenzdiskurse* (Frankfurt a.M., 1999), 154. In the case of men's fashion, skin-tight clothing was realised in the uniform. The well-fitted garment

in which office and person merged was the military uniform. On the militarisation of male fashions at court, see Frank, *Höfische Mode*, 202.

58. Marie Freiin von Larisch Wallersee, *Meine Vergangenheit. Wahrheit über Franz Joseph/Schratt/Kaiserin Elisabeth/Andrassy/Kronprinz Rudolf/Vetschera* (Berlin, 1913), 54.

59. Hamann, *Elisabeth*, 592ff.; cf. Vogel, *Elisabeth*, 140ff.

60. On the relationship between royal reputation and royal appearance, see Koschorke, Macht und Fiktion, 79.

61. Latour, *Magier der Mode*, 83.

11

Theatrical Monarchy

The Making of Victoria, the Modern Family Queen

Bernd Weisbrod

When Diana died – England's rose and queen of hearts – there was a short moment when it almost seemed as if the monarchy itself was at stake.[1] Some commentators may be forgiven for having thought at the time that all the outer signs of a revolutionary situation were at hand: the people were out on the streets, forcing the monarch to return to the capital and to bow to public sentiment and the flag. As we know, nothing came of it. On the contrary, Diana's death probably laid to rest what doubts there may have been about the future usefulness of monarchy in Britain. It was her royal innocence, her seriousness in charitable work, her fate as a 'wronged woman' which in her tragic end obscured the extent to which her tabloid life of jet-set glamour and her bitter fight with Charles had undermined the credentials of monarchy in the public eye. In many ways she fell victim to her own theatrical self, her battle for emancipation skilfully played out against the expectations of a mass audience which was heavily engaged in royal imaginings. The monarchy has always been what it was believed to be, but the monarchy as a media event is of rather recent origin: like many of those 'invented traditions' which came with the test of national nerve in the nineteenth century, theatrical monarchy was the legacy of Victoria, the First Family Queen on the British throne.[2]

To mobilise the nation in grief – in a global media event – this smacked of almost democratic feelings, but this illusion is precisely what theatrical monarchy is all about. Everybody could share the 'royal touch' on this occasion, especially women who felt with the orphaned children, and that 'constituency of the rejected' who were craving salvation. And she did touch not just the mourners but AIDS victims as well; as she made abundantly clear, she meant to touch both metaphorically and physically. She performed a last remnant of that old privilege which Queen Anne had exercised on young Samuel Johnson in 1715, who was brought to her with the 'mal du roi' or 'King's evil': but alas, even then, as Johnson later dryly reported, her touch did not help very much.[3] With Diana the crowd witnessed a sentimental sacralisation of a royal persona which fed primarily on her youthfulness and femininity, her charm and looks, the 'body of the Queen' indeed, but also, let us not forget, on her political powerlessness which brought her so close to the hearts of every man and – more so – every women.

In historical terms, the political framing of the monarchy and its symbolic reinvention was the outcome of Victoria's long reign, from 1837 to 1901, which in itself gave the impression of triumphant resilience and moral stamina in the face of turbulent change. Victoria, mother of nine, grandmother of thirty-six and great-grandmother of thirty-seven children, presided over the strange transformation of Britain from aristocratic self-government to political mass market, from Reform crisis and Chartist turmoil to the glory of Empire, without the flare of revolution which in most continental countries was due in no small part to the fierce reprisals which the established powers took against the rising spirit of bourgeois emancipation.[4] 'She succeeded to the throne', as Dorothy Thompson, the accomplished scholar of the Chartist movement, argues in her admirable biography, 'under threat from popular republicanism and ultra-right absolutism and left it sure enough to survive a half century of war, depression and scandal until the advent of another female sovereign continued and reinforced the trends her reign had set in motion.'[5]

This was quite a feat, but it was certainly not all of her doing. It can be argued that the defeat of revolutionary expectations was due to the sensible response of people like Sir Charles Napier, the Commander of the Northern Division, who credited the Chartists with a real cause and thereby saved the crown. But it can also be said that it was the political framing of monarchy which saved Britain from a revolution, and here certainly, to quote Thompson again, 'the special conditions which told against revolutionary action ... included the gender of the monarch'.[6] The queen was eighteen and blissfully innocent in political terms when she succeeded to the throne. She had been born in a dynastic race to Victoria of Leiningen, a widowed mother of two with nothing to her name but the principality of Amorbach, and Edward August, the Duke of Kent, whose draconic severity was as notorious as his debts; and she was brought up after his early death by her mother and her uncle, Leopold of Saxe-Coburg, later King of Belgium, in royal poverty and ambition. From early on she was a pawn of the reform party simply for not being like her 'wicked uncles' and she served as the perfect stopgap in 1837 against Ernst August, the ruthless Duke of Cumberland, who showed his high Tory credentials in his own Kingdom of Hanover when he drove such famous Göttingen-professors from the seat of learning in the same year. As Lytton Strachey remarked in his famous biography of 1921, it was the political victory of the Reform Party in 1832 which transformed Victoria from being the 'protégé of an opposition clique' to a valuable 'asset' of the 'official majority of the nation': 'The Princess Victoria was henceforward the living symbol of the victory of the middle classes.'[7]

But Victoria also stood in the line of female royalty who had already fuelled the fires of popular monarchism. Queen Caroline of Brunswick, the 'wronged woman' of George IV, had come back to London on the accession of her estranged husband in 1820 to claim her rights to the roaring applause of radical London. Since John Wilkes's day, speaking out against the corruption and the perversion of court life had never been easy; it was inscribed on the body of the wronged Queen in numerous pamphlets and songs although her life abroad was no proof of sanctity either, if the counter-propaganda of the court was to be believed. But she profited as a mother from the romantic wave of sympathy with her daughter, the wife of the above Leopold of Saxe-Coburg, Princess Charlotte who died giving birth to a stillborn boy in 1817. There was a sense of 'national tragedy', and not just in Byron's poems. Just as in the case of Diana the tragic death filled with doom those who had hoped for a 'renewal and cleansing of the monarchy'.[8] One year after the Peterloo massacre of protesting workers in Manchester, the public showdown of the Queen Caroline affair was a dangerous precedent of what the case of a 'wronged woman' and 'injured queen' could do to the monarchy. When Caroline symbolically took hold of the city in procession she mobilised the 'reversionary interests' of all those who sought redress for political wrongs, and when her name was to be struck from the official liturgy, she was included in the prayers, as the House of Commons were told, of all those, 'who are desolate and oppressed'.

The young Peel, reforming hopeful of the Tories, sensed the political dimension of this affair which died down as quickly as it had started:

> 'I do think the Queen's affair very formidable. It is a famous ingredient in the cauldron which has been bubbling a long time, and upon which, as it seems to me, the Government could never discern the least simmering. They added a blow-pipe, however, when they omitted the queen's name in the Liturgy: when they established a precedent of dethronement for imputed personal conduct. Surely this was not the time for robbing Royalty of exterior marks of respect and, for preaching up the anti-divine right doctrines ... What is to be the end of it?'[9]

The end of it was the rapid decline in the open display of the monarch's political ambition and the rise in her public influence as a symbol of national unity and imperial glory, epitomised in the Golden and Diamond Jubilees of 1887 and 1897. The 'Bedchamber' crisis of 1839 is somewhat peevishly said to have been the last royal veto on 'political appointments', but the Queen had no choice but to work with Peel after the Tory victory of 1841 and felt more and more comfortable with this under the guidance of the Prince Consort, her beloved Albert, who strove to build his own reputation on a new alliance with middle-class values in public rather than in Parliament.[10] In times of crisis Victoria as a woman appeared less threatening politically, and as a matriarchal figure more acceptable, even to republicans who never really dared to take her head-on, in spite of their constant protesting against the civil list for the 'royal tax-eaters'. As the century went on, the 'trivialisation' of the figure of the monarch was in effect a source of her strength.[11] This was the new theatrical power of modern monarchy: whereas the courtly splendour of old had been a display of real power, the semblance of power was the spectacle of modern monarchy.

Strangely enough, this applies to all stages of Queen Victoria's long career: as the 'innocent queen', the married women, the homely mother figure, and even more so after Albert's death in 1861, when she disappeared at the age of forty-one from public sight – 'a retired widow with an unemployed child', i.e. the Prince of Wales, as Walter Bagehot jibed in his famous essay, *The English Constitution*, which spoke of the unabashed self-consciousness of the new political class.[12] Even the open rumours about the concubinary behaviour of 'Empress Brown' in Balmoral could not deflect from the sentimental attachment which grew apace in the heyday of Empire. Dorothy Thompson argues that in 'times of separate spheres the life of Victoria was an example of role reversal'.[13] But only through role assertion, it seems. Victoria certainly managed to embody the 'feminisation' of a once powerful male symbol. But, at the same time, of course, the price of feminisation, as in many other respects, was the downgrading of a gendered power structure.

This is not to argue that the Queen was without power or influence. The royal prerogative prevailed, and not just in diplomatic relations, in which, in the course of the nineteenth century, a new culture of transnational governance was established in the pomp and circumstance of royal visits and courtly and marriage rituals.[14] In addition, Victoria almost managed to plant her daughter Vicky, as 'Empress Frederick', close to the heart of the German Empire, very much to the dismay of Chancellor Bismarck who feared nothing more than some kind of German liberal Gladstonian Cabinet.[15] Royal performances like the jubilees even acquired cult status in the rising mass media and provided the nation with an icon of national identity in the ups and downs of a political mass market which was highly competitive and volatile and which still excluded women until after the Great War.[16] Across Europe this revival of the theatre of monarchy was part and parcel of the 'invention of tradition' which – as Eric Hobsbawm has shown – was a concomitant of the new nationalism of the late nineteenth century. Even the oldest monarchy reinvented itself, recovering much of the old 'theatre of power' of the Stuart monarchy, after the dismal show of the Hanoverian court, which had given rise to the powerful self-assertion of the landed elite in the eighteenth century and which had led the way in uniting the nation against the Catholic foe, Napoleonic France.[17] In the case of Victoria, two aspects stand out in this process of 'theatricalisation': one is the integration of the Celtic fringe in the romantic picture of the royal family as Highland clan and the 'tartan Queen';[18] the other the Indian Empire, the 'jewel in the crown', with which Benjamin Disraeli flattered her and lured her back into a public display of royalty in 1876, when she opened Parliament for the first time since Albert's death.[19] The Commons only reluctantly enthused about the aggrandisement of royal power in the Royal Titles Act and left much of the pomp at the time to Her subjects in Delhi, whereas Victoria

Regina et Imperatrix took it to heart and enjoyed it more and more, as was to be seen in her use of the regalia of Empire in later life.

By the time of the jubilees she was undoubtedly the 'mother of the nation', 'Victoria the Good', the completely removed but thoroughly natural paragon of a civilised nation. Empire was commodified in her image – 30,000 schoolchildren who celebrated in Hyde Park in 1887 took home a mug with her image.[20] Already in 1851 when the royal family opened the Great Exhibition – clad in kilts and sporrans, with seven children to show like a perfect middle-class family – popular monarchism was extolled as civic virtue and bestowed some of the royal patronage on the causes of industrial progress and civilised supremacy, while at the same time holding on to the ultra-conservative symbolism of royalty. A Whig success story, so it seems, but in no way a forgone conclusion, and highly dependent on the men behind the queen, especially Prince Albert.

From the start it was Lord Melbourne who took the coronation of the young queen to be a show of defiance against the Tory ultras. With hindsight it may have looked a rather 'shabby coronation' and the funeral rites for the Duke of Wellington in 1851 certainly attracted more people, in memory of Waterloo, but the coronation procession of Victoria to Westminster Abbey, which had not been seen since the coronation of George II, was a popular success. 'Millions of my loyal subjects', she wrote in her Journal, 'were assembled in every spot to witness the procession. I really cannot say how proud I feel to be the Queen of such a Nation'.[21] But as Charles Greville – who was well pleased with the 'remarkable union of *naivité,* kindness, nature, good nature, with propriety and dignity' in the young queen – dryly remarked in his memoirs, the real object of the show was not the queen, it was 'the people': 'The great merit of the Coronation is, that so much has been done for the people: to amuse and interest *them* seems to have been the principle object.'[22]

Outside London, especially in the industrial North, this royal show did not go down well, the 'national holiday' in some places even turned into a show of defiance that was hushed up in the national press.[23] The Manchester and Salford Trade Unions professed their loyalty, but objected to 'idle pomp and useless parade':

We [...] find the wealth in and out of parliament conspiring against the labouring poor to deprive them of the rights of industry, and withholding from them the political rights and liberties of freeborn British subjects; at the same time they call upon us to testify our allegiance to that very system of government which offers us no protection – which manifests no sympathy for the destitute poor of our country, but upon all occasions takes advantage of the power they possess to treat us as slaves, stigmatize us as combinators, and persecute us as criminals.[24]

In Leeds the official procession degenerated into a mock funeral march; in Huddersfield the tricolour flag was shown, inscribed with 'Liberty and Love'; and radical Oldham held its own holiday with its own rites and slogans. Royal parades in honour of the Queen's birthday which were meant to frighten off the Chartists had to be abandoned altogether after 1840. In the industrial North the Queen was clearly seen as a symbol of the hated Whig reform which prevented the full extension of the franchise and she was even – in spite of her sex and youthfulness – the object of the vitriolic attack of the anti-poor law movement.

This is a stark reminder that one of the main symbolic functions of the Victorian monarchy was the integration of the nonconformist and radical parts of the nation into the London political theatre, where the aristocratic court and radical Westminster had been at loggerheads with each other over reform.[25] It provided a national platform for what Walter Bagehot called the 'secret republic', in giving symbolic expression to compromise, the liberal instincts of the 'middle way', a symbolic politics above politics in a 'peaceable kingdom'. This new political key was due to another man at Victoria's side, Prince Albert, the Prince Consort, whose constitutional position was less clear to Victoria than his good looks. He was refused full royal status and his civil list income was slashed by a confident House of Commons which mistrusted that 'German prince', who, with an income far above Saxon-Coburg's total budget, was considered a burden on the taxpayer, like every single one of his nine children.[26] Albert was much too shrewd to be permanently annoyed by this unfriendly treatment. It endeared him even more to his loving wife, who came to trust him fully in political matters. He had produced a programme of reform which was well advised and more and more respected. This made him the unofficial leader of the broad-based movement for the promotion of arts and sciences in a civil society, which was bent on combining public esteem with royal privilege in the cause of social improvement.[27]

There is no question that Victoria dearly loved him, she was ravished by his romantic bravado, enjoyed his companionship and came to adore him for his diligence and seriousness. Even in old age, on the day he would have celebrated his eighty-first birthday, she remembered him with true affection and idolatry and confided to her Journal that he was 'a blessing to so many, leaving an imperishable name behind him'.[28] In the 'lottery of life' – in which 'the poor woman is bodily and morally the husband's slave'[29] as she confessed to her 'Dearest Child' Vicky – she had won the first prize: 'There is a great happiness and great blessedness in devoting oneself to another who is worthy of one's affection', she wrote to Vicky to start her in married life, 'still men are very selfish and the women's devotion is always one of submission which makes our poor sex so unenviable. This You will feel hereafter – I know; though it cannot be otherwise as God has willed so.'[30] And she continues in the same letter, as if to come clean on this issue: 'You know, my dearest, that I never admit any other wife can be as happy as I am – so I can admit no companion for I maintain Papa is unlike anyone who lives or ever lived and will live'.[31] And two days later she completed her symbolic submission: 'I shall ever be happy to kiss Pap's hand for You; I should like often to fall to his feet – for I feel how unworthy I must be of one so great and perfect as he is.'[32] It was a price she had to share with his favourite daughter, whose political thoughts and correspondence, as the Queen knew, were reserved for her Dearest Papa.

Albert also proved to be highly effective in managing the royal household. He increased the revenue of the Duchies of Cornwall and Lancaster to win independence from parliamentary grants, thereby putting together the 'money-spinning machine' which, after the waiver of hereditary and income tax at the turn of the century, made the monarchy the most profitable family business in the country.[33] This was in stark contrast to Victoria's humble beginnings. He also built the two family homes, on the Isle of Wight (Osborne) and in the Highlands (Balmoral), where court life acquired a highly publicised outdoor and family atmosphere for which she knew – even in her English correspondence – only one word: *Gemütlichkeit!* His own image as the queen's romantic lover faded into the more masculine status of the royal huntsman, standing near to and yet high above bloody nature, as in Landseer's many oil paintings, which adorned the walls of the most prominent country houses – here with the queen on horseback watching with delight and (an omen of things to come) with her Scottish servant John Brown holding the bridle, who was later charged with holding the key to her empty throne.[34]

The Queen's body was highly charged with these images of her husband's body, especially in the new medium of photography which she readily embraced, first as his devoted wife and the mother of his children and later as his loyal and inconsolable widow (Figure 11.1).[35] These photographs, set-pieces of homeliness and respectable sobriety, presented a traditional role model of female submission even on the throne to the calculated modernity of the popular imagination. It is, therefore, no mistake to conclude from this body imagery that her mind was equally charged by his mind. His untiring professionalism and seriousness about 'good causes' endeared the least aristocratic court in Europe to the industrious middle classes and cast Victoria herself in the light of 'progress' and 'reform'. Crystal Palace was the glittering icon of this new civil monarchy. Albert not only befriended the arts and sciences, practical crafts and singing, he personally looked into the building of 'model dwelling houses' for the London poor and chaired many a charity dinner as a royal figurehead for bourgeois philanthropy.[36] He established 'slumming' as a secular version of the 'royal touch' – as in the professional 'sainthood' of the great philanthropist Lord Shaftsbury – and he laid the cornerstone for

Figure 11.1 The Queen and the Prince Consort (1861). Photograph by John Mayall.

the modern 'welfare monarchy' (Frank Prochaska) with its promise of symbolic inclusion well before the modern welfare state crowded out the deterrent Poor Laws.[37] The 'middle-classness' of the British monarchy may have been a matter of the Queen's body – of seeing her in due submission to her female role in giving birth again and again and not meddling with politics – but it was certainly also the outcome of the reformed mind of a German prince who was playing out royalty to a new middle-class audience.

Ironically, maybe Albert's greatest contribution to this new civil monarchy was, his early death in 1861, which left Victoria, at forty-one, with most of her children yet unmarried, to pine after him for another forty years. It was a shock not just to her, but to the nation: *The Times* achieved its maximum circulation of 89,000 copies at Albert's death.[38] Victoria's long retreat into grief and seclusion in Balmoral made her almost invisible; it transported monarchy onto the 'moral high ground' above politics and it opened up an imaginative space for the general public, which revelled in royal fetishism and clamoured for signs of royal grace. The great prime ministers of the day knew perfectly well that republicanism was no

Figure 11.2 The Queen (1867).

real danger, but the presence of the Queen was requested on frequent occasions as a prop for political action. But she was not to be moved; the picture of the mourning queen even acquired cult status (Figure 11.2).[39] Absenteeism – usually associated with irresponsible landlords – added to trivialisation in a perfect symbolic spectacle. Her faithful citizens paid up for the memory of the object of her grief in 'Albertopolis', the great memorial for arts and sciences in Kensington, and she herself was replaced at the opening of Parliament by her state robes draped on an empty throne. She might have stood down for her son Bertie, later to become Edward VII, but, as at her accession, even for republicans she seemed to have been the lesser evil.[40]

When Disraeli, her favourite prime minister, took the 'leap in the dark' in 1867 and enfranchised the urban male householder, the Queen had become a political pawn of substantial weight, metaphorically and physically. The Scottish matron with her servant lover John Brown engaged the public imagination and –for all we know – made her even more popular with the common people, simply for being ridiculed by the well-heeled and the snob aristocrats. But for the 'secret workings' of the constitution she was a godsend, as Walter Bagehot, the founder of the *Economist*, pointed out in his famously self-assured middle-class reading of the 'English(!) Constitution' in 1867. The powers of the crown were still substantial, i.e. 'the right to be consulted, the right to encourage, and the right to warn', but in his view, this was little more than a smokescreen for real political power:

> No one can approach to an understanding of the English institutions [...] unless he divide them into two classes ... : first, those which excite and preserve the reverence of the population – the *dignified* parts, if I may so call them; and next, the *efficient* parts – those by which it, in fact, works and rules.[41]

This secret rule was not achieved by means of the 'Queen in Parliament' or even by a clear separation of legislative and executive powers, but simply by cabinet rule, whereas the 'theatrical parts', the Crown and the House of Lords, provided a sense of national unity and grandeur, especially for the newly enfranchised masses.

> 'The elements which excite the most easy reverence will be the *theatrical* elements – those which appeal to the senses, which claim to be embodiments of the greatest human ideas, which boast in some cases of far

more than human origin. That which is mystic in his claims; that which is occult in its mode of action; that which is brilliant to the eye; that which is seen vividly for a moment and then is seen no more; that which is hidden and unhidden ... ; this howsoever its form may change, or however we may define it or describe it, is the sort of things – the only sort – which yet comes home to the mass of men.'[42]

This 'double government' provided the perfect match, because real democracy, as Bagehot believed, was something for Americans, not for the 'deferential classes' of England: 'I do not count as an anomaly the existence of our double government, with all its infinite accidents, though half the superficial peculiarities that are often complained of arise out of it. The co-existence of a Queen's seeming prerogative and a Downing Street's real government is just suited to such a country as this in such an age as ours.'[43]

The public enthusiasm shown on the occasion of the royal marriage of the Prince of Wales with the beautiful Alexandra of Denmark in 1863 confirmed Bagehot in his judgement that it was of great advantage to have 'a family on the throne': 'It brings down the pride of the sovereign to the level of petty life ... The women – one half of the human race at least – care fifty times more for a marriage than a ministry.'[44] This is something which was understood almost instinctively by the Queen. Her demonstrative family life and her affection for her Munshi was more than just a fad of the old lady, it was a political demonstration not just for the people but also for her ministers and bureaucrats. In that, she was Bagehot's match, who seemed to believe that the 'dignified parts' of the constitution were but a 'theatrical show', and 'the climax of the play was the Queen.'[45]

The Queen's body lives on, and still is the powerhouse of representation for 'timeless values' which refurbish the identity-kit of a radically modernising nation. As it was said by Queen Elizabeth II on the occasion of her jubilee in 2002: 'Change has become a constant; managing it has become an expanding discipline.'[46] The self-mystification of Victoria, who came to be her own legend during her lifetime, is a good case in point. She provided the powerful idiom of the modern family queen as *regina intacta*, which reappeared in the public imagination about Diana's tragic death. But she also orchestrated, as David Cannadine reminds us in his review of Stanley Weintrouitis biography, the tough political message hidden under the motherly charm of theatrical monarchy: she was, after all, a highly reactionary, unenlightened and tyrannical person, in

Cannadine's words a clear case of 'upper-class paranoia of an advanced kind'.[47] Even her most private secretary was sometimes at a loss to understand how the dated spectacle of the queen's Tory 'ultra partisanship' could be kept on stage wielding real power in the face of royal absurdities.[48]

This double message is borne out nicely in the famous postcard image of Margaret Thatcher's head superimposed on the queen's body (Figure 11.3). Victoria was the embodiment of the stern morality and the double-edged promise of self-help and sobriety, but at the same time she provided a fiercely competitive society with a national icon of political neutrality while shoring up the defences of the established class system. 'Victorian Values' were as ambivalent as the 'popular monarchism' which grew up in the imagination of the queen's invisible but familiar body.[49] Victoria, the modern family queen, can be credited with the transfer of theatrical

Figure 11.3 Maggie Regina, postcard by Peter Kennard.

monarchy as a highly political institution into our time: 'In a country frequently described as rational, capitalist and democratic, the monachy remained–along with many others–a secretive, unaccountable, self-perpetuating and arguably corrupt institution'.[50] But it also fills the gap in national identity politics which other nations have filled with revolution or aggressive nationalism. Maybe this too was, like Victoria herself, a lesser evil – or at least a remarkable historical exercise in benign self-deception.

Notes

1. For a German version of this argument see Sabine Berghahn and Sigrid Hoch-Baumgarten, eds., *Mythos Diana – Von der Princess of Wales zur Queen of Hearts* (Gießen, 1999).
2. David Cannadine, 'The Context: Performance and Meaning of Ritual. The British Monarchy and the Invention of Tradition', in *The Invention of Tradition*, ed. Eric Hobsbawm and Terence Ranger (Cambridge, 1984), 104–164.
3. James Boswell, *The Life of Samuel Johnson* (Cambridge 1992; first edn. 1791), 21.
4. For the first critical and highly influential account see Lytton Strachey, *Queen Victoria* (Harmondsworth, 1971; first edn. 1921); for modern scholarship see Stanley Weintraub, *Victoria* (London, 1996) and Christopher Hibbert, *Queen Victoria. A Personal History* (London, 2000).
5. Dorothy Thompson, *Queen Victoria: The Woman, the Monarch and the People* (New York, 1990), xiv (same as: *Queen Victoria: Gender and Power* (London, 1990). See also her: *The Chartists. Popular Politics in the Industrial Revolution* (London, 1984).
6. Thompson, *Queen Victoria*, xvi.
7. Strachey, *Queen Victoria*, 29.
8. Thompson, *Queen Victoria*, 7.
9. Peel to Croker, quoted in John Stevenson, ed., 'The Queen Caroline Affair', in *London in the Age of Reform*, (Oxford, 1977), 117–148, here 126.
10. Robert Rhodes James, *Albert. Prince Consort: a Biography* (London, 1983), 120ff.
11. Thompson, *Queen Victoria*, 139.
12. Walter Bagehot, *The English Constitution* (London, 1974; first edn. 1867).
13. Thompson, *Queen Victoria*, 144.
14. Johannes Paulmann, *Pomp und Politik: Monarchenbegegnungen in Europa zwischen Ancien Regime und Erstem Weltkrieg* (Paderborn, 2000).

15. See Wolfgang J. Mommsen, *Das Ringen um den nationalen Staat. Die Gründung und der innere Aufbau des Deutschen Reiches unter Otto von Bismarck, 1850 bis 1890* (Berlin, 1993), 679ff.
16. John M. MacKenzie, ed., *Imperialism and Popular Culture* (Manchester, 1986), see also Susan Kingsley Kent, *Sex and Suffrage in Britain 1860–1914* (Princeton, 1987).
17. Linda Colley, 'The Apotheosis of George III. Loyalty, Royalty and the Britisch Nation 1760–1820', *Past and Present* 102, (1984), 94–129; idem, *Britons. Forging the Nation 1707–1837* (New Haven, 1992).
18. Hugh Trevor-Roper, 'The Invention of Tradition: the Highland-Tradition of Scotland', in *Invention*, Hobsbawm and Ranger, ed. 15–42; see also Robert Colls and Philip Dodd eds., *Englishness. Politics and Culture 1880–1920* (London, 1986).
19. Robert Blake, *Disraeli* (London, 1969), 562ff.
20. Thompson, *Queen Victoria*, 122.
21. Entry of 28 June 1838, in Christopher Hibbert ed., *Queen Victoria in her Letters and Journals* (London, 1984), 34.
22. Entry of 29 July 1839, in *The Greville Memoirs 1814–1860*, Vol. 4, ed. Lytton Strachey and Roger Fulford (London, 1938), 72f. See also Strachey, *Queen Victoria*, 62.
23. John Knott, *Popular Opposition to the 1834 Poor Law* (London, 1986) (Prologue: Pomp and Protest).
24. Knott, *Popular Opposition*, 2.
25. Eugenio F. Biagini and Alastair J. Reid (eds.), *Currents of Radicalism. Popular Radicalism, Organised Labour and Party Politics in Britain 1850–1914* (Cambridge, 1991).
26. Asa Briggs, 'Prince Albert and the Constitution', in *Deutscher und britischer Parlamentarismus*, Adolf Birke and Kurt Kluxen ed. (Munich, 1985), 45–56.
27. Stanley Weintraub, *Albert. Uncrowned King* (London, 1997), 213ff.; Asa Briggs, 'Prince Albert and the Arts and Sciences', in *Prince Albert and the Victorian Age*, John S. Philips ed. (Cambridge, 1981), 51–78.
28. Journal, 26 August 1900, in Hibbert, ed., *Queen Victoria*, 346.
29. 16 May 1860, in Hibbert, *Queen Victoria*, 104f.
30. 15 February 1858, in Roger Fulford ed., *Dearest Child. Private Correspondence of Queen Victoria and the Princess Royal , 1858–1861* (London, 1964), 44.
31. Fulford, *Dearest Child*, 45.
32. 17 February 1858, in Fulford, *Dearest Child*, 48.
33. Phillip Hall, *Royal Fortune: Tax, Money and the Monarchy* (London, 1992).
34. *The Highland Idyll. Prince Albert as seen by Landser, 1860*, in Hibbert, *Queen Victoria*, fig. 17.
35. *The Queen and the Prince Consort, 1861*, in James, *Albert*, fig. 23b. On the familiarisation of the monachy through the mass circulation of

these royal celebrity photographs, see John Plunkett, *Queen Victoria. First Media Monach* (Oxford, 2003), ch. 4: Photography and the Royal Family.

36. Frank Prochaska, *Royal Bounty. The Making of the Welfare Monarchy* (New Haven, 1995), especially chapter 3: Queen Victoria and Prince Albert: Civic Pride and Repectability.

37. Lynn Hollen Lees, *The Solidarity of Strangers. The English Poor Laws and the People, 1700–1948* (Cambridge, 1998).

38. Briggs, 'Prince Albert and the Constitution', 55.

39. 'Whatever the poor Queen can do she will; but she will not be dictated to, or teased by public clamour into doing what she physically cannot.' In Hibbert, *Queen Victoria*, fig. 24.

40. Thompson, *Queen Victoria*, 114ff.

41. Bagehot, *Constitution*, 3f.

42. Ibid., 7

43. Ibid., 258; see also David Cresap Moore, *The Politics of Deference. A Study of the Mid-Nineteenth Century English Political System* (London, 1976).

44. Bagehot, *Constitution*, 34.

45. Ibid., 236.

46. 'The Queen's Jubilee Speech', in Westminter Hall, BBC 30 April 2002.

47. David Cannadine, *The Pleasures of the Past* (New York 1989), ch. 3: Queen Victoria (from the *New York Review of Books* XXXIV, 23 April 1987), 29.

48. William M. Kuhn, *Henry and Mary Ponsonby. Life at the Court of Queen Victoria* (London, 2002), 206ff.; see also Mary Ponsonby's debunking exercise after Queen Victoria's death, 246ff.

49. James Walvin, *Victorian Values. A Companion to the Granada Televison Series* (London, 1987); T.C. Smout, *Victorian Values. A Joint Symposium of the Royal Society of Edinburgh and the British Academy, December 1990* (Oxford, Press 1992), proceedings of the British Academy 78.

50. Cannadine, *Pleasures*, 30.

12

The Unmanly Emperor

Wilhelm II and the Fragility of the Royal Individual

Martin Kohlrausch

After a number of contributions on queens, this essay will examine a king. It will treat a phenomenon we shall refer to as the individualisation of the monarch.[1] This phenomenon, the hypothesis runs, is the precondition for problematising the monarch's masculinity, or perhaps even his sexual orientation. The asserted correlation will be examined using the example of the reign of Kaiser Wilhelm II, and more particularly the so-called Eulenburg scandal. For that reason, I shall base my argumentation mainly on newspaper articles, that is, on the interaction between the monarch and public opinion.[2] I shall illuminate three central questions against this background: first, the relationship between the attempt to decipher the character of the monarch and the breaking of taboos; second, the degree to which the masculinity of the monarch was challenged; and third, the role that the king's body played in all this.

The Construction of the Royal Individual

The attribution of individual character traits was certainly not unique to monarchs of the late nineteenth century. Studying the case of the eighteenth-century French kings, Ivo Engels has shown that there was a strong tendency even then to 'humanise' the king, for example in the figure of the king as 'neighbour'. In this way, 'his person and his actions appear to have gained a more decipherable meaning for most of his subjects ...'.[3] This applies only partially to the post-revolutionary period. According to Monika Wienfort, in England the sovereign was expected quite early on to participate in the destiny of his people, a phenomenon that took hold later in Germany. The monarch was integrated into society,[4] a development that would accelerate in the nineteenth century. The notion that the suppressed individuality of the king needed to be liberated from the bonds of protocol and ceremonial became extraordinarily popular.[5] As Juliane Vogel has shown for Elisabeth of Austria (known as Sissi), however, this development had inherent limits: to be sure, there were efforts to equip the empress generously with sentiments appropriate less to a representative of a dynasty than to a bourgeois woman. Since, however, 'only the clichés of emotion-driven inwardness' were available to depict her psyche, this attempt to individualise the empress failed.[6] The language used to describe the queen was by no means individual, but instead quite schematic.

Despite this very clear evidence of earlier and parallel developments, I will argue here that the publicly discussed individuality of Wilhelm II was marked by a new quality. One must take into account that discussions of Wilhelm II both intentionally and unintentionally abandoned traditional restrictions. The language used shifted from one of distancing to one of closeness. There were various reasons for this. Contemporaries widely viewed the industrial age as particularly individualistic. To that extent the times demanded particularly individual persons, especially as political leaders. People were convinced as a virtual dogma that modern monarchy had to have an individual character.[7] This notion meshed perfectly with the fact that Wilhelm II himself was regarded almost universally as having a particularly individual nature. After he ascended the throne, a wave of laudatory newspaper articles and pamphlets appeared. All of them made much of the emperor's youth. Also prominent was the emphasis on Wilhelm's 'character' and individualism.[8]

The individuality of the monarch and the cult of the young emperor were closely related. As Stefan Breuer has noted, there was a strong tendency within Wilhelminism 'to stage the struggle for symbolic power as an intergenerational drama'.[9] This was particularly true of the highly sensitised *Jüngstdeutsche* (youngest or most recent German, a reference to the Young German movement of the 1830s) writers, for whom the purported individuality of the young emperor appeared significant to the extent that they viewed it as the most outstanding trait of their own generation. One of these authors, Konrad Alberti (the pseudonym of

K. Sittenfeld, 1862–1918), confronted the emperor with the expectations of the young generation immediately following his coronation, addressing Wilhelm II as a member of that generation.[10] Hermann Conradi (1862–90) did likewise in his *Wilhelm II. und die junge Generation. Eine zeitpsychologische Betrachtung* (Wilhelm II and the Young Generation. A Contemporary Psychological Perspective).[11] This went beyond merely equating the young generation with the youthful emperor; individualism functioned as a key concept here. In the 'historically powerful' year of 1888 Germany had 'experienced its true Storm and Stress'; 'a young emperor had ascended the throne, having scarcely had a chance to warm up as a crown prince, who had matured in the sultry hothouse air of compact, confused troubles and fears, and to whom anybody would have to reorganise the angle of his personal relationship, which had so recently been directed and orientated towards Kaiser Friedrich', Conradi wrote.[12]

Georg Hinzpeter, the emperor's former private tutor, had finally elucidated this individual maturity in detail in a separate and widely read book, thus introducing it authoritatively into the public discussion. Hinzpeter's study, Conradi and nearly all commentators agreed, contained the 'most interesting and valuable material' on the young emperor.[13] Hinzpeter pointed quite rightly to the strongly individual character of Wilhelm II. This predestined the young monarch to be the representative of his generation. This 'Young Generation' of those born between 1855 and 1865 'bore quite a different type of burden than that which the older generation had carried and still carried.' The older generation had become ossified into a 'machine-like civil service', while the young generation was characterised by individualism.[14]

In his study, *Kaiser Wilhelm II. Eine Skizze nach der Natur gezeichnet* (A Sketch from Nature), Hinzpeter had confidently announced that he would and could satisfy curiosity about the true character of Wilhelm II. He addressed with astonishing openness the problems he had encountered in educating the heir to the throne. In this context the strict Calvinist mentioned the prince's 'peculiarly strongly marked individuality' and his inner being, which developed solely 'in accordance with his own nature', 'touched, modified and directed, but never essentially changed or shifted, by external influences.'[15] According to Hinzpeter, no one had succeeded in disrupting the 'flight path' of the 'young eagle', and no one, not even his parents, had the right to do so.[16]

Hinzpeter's foray into the public sphere was certainly unusual in light of the traditional reticence observed in regard to the mental disposition of the monarch. This is even truer of a pamphlet that appeared (tellingly enough) anonymously in Zurich in 1892 and whose title asked, *Wilhelm II. Romantiker oder Sozialist?*[17] The author did evoke the topos of the young emperor once again, to be sure, but only in order to criticise him. While previous authors had only claimed great individuality for Wilhelm II in the abstract, this text inquired into Wilhelm's actual mental prerequisites. The author asserted that he 'had not had to go through any transitional period'. Strictly speaking, he had no personal past. This was the origin of the 'fearful, intimidated ignorance of the German people in regard to the psyche of the young emperor when he firmly grasped the reins of empire …. Prince Wilhelm's young figure blurred into the dusky darkness'.[18]

The author recognised, quite astutely, that it was only against this background that Hinzpeter's pamphlet had succeeded in gaining such influence, by claiming to have unlocked the psyche and individuality of Wilhelm II.[19] Other problems in the public perception of the new emperor were addressed plainly here for the first time as well, though. These included the standards set by Wilhelm's Hohenzollern ancestors in conjunction with the hopes awakened by the change in government. To be sure, the latter occurred with any new monarch,[20] but in the case of Wilhelm II there was much evidence that the old paths, especially those of Hohenzollern tradition, were about to be abandoned. Wilhelm II, it appeared, would indeed be a modern ruler – which was also what the author desired. After all, the emperor himself referred to his era as a 'transitional stage', and was at the same time 'the most perfect, interesting type of this age of transition: at once a Romantic and a Socialist, and yet neither of them fully!'[21]

But apart from its emphasis on the highly individual and sometimes even modern character of the monarch, this pamphlet contains a further instructive vein of information. The author admonishes Wilhelm II quite explicitly to respect freedom of expression. This (in itself not particularly original) demand becomes interesting because it is imbedded in notions of masculinity. Thus the author rhetorically asks the emperor whether he really wants a 'churchyard full of unmanned men'. Referring to a speech by the emperor that received much attention at the time, in which he called upon grumblers to leave the country, the pamphlet declares:

'No, true manliness does not flee, it stands fast and fights!' and defended the opposition and '"grumbling" – not, to be sure, in the petty philistine sense'. The author mused suggestively: 'And as I imagine the figure of Wilhelm II, is he himself not a friend of self-confident, honourable manliness?'[22]

Here one finds an illuminating equation of opposition, frank talk and masculinity. Ultimately, the author asserted, he and his readers were living in an effeminate age: 'Every honest German must notice a terrible regression in the expression of German public opinion.'[23] The emperor, and this too was a key motif, was misinformed about public opinion. There could be no other explanation for his speeches. In the modern state, the sovereign depended upon competent advisers, since he could no longer maintain a complete overview on his own. In the absence of such advisers, the German people must rise up 'against the mediocrity and unmanliness that had taken hold at court', for an 'undignified, obtrusive, servile generation' appeared to be 'pressing itself upon the young monarch and beguiling his manly heart with flattery.'[24] The themes of masculinity, of advisers and public opinion came together here with the discourses concerning generations, decadence and decline. But the individuality of the monarch and masculinity were also linked here.

The extent to which the author of this pamphlet sought to reconcile the public figure of the monarch with the public longing for a visible individual is remarkable. This occurred in a surprisingly reflective discourse, of which I would like to cite only a few examples.[25] In 1908 the *Leipziger Tageblatt* newspaper reported the results of a conversation between the French scientist Mabilleau and the emperor. After analysing the emperor's statements as manifestations of his individuality, the article ended with the thesis that it was precisely the emperor's constantly changing opinions that constituted his individual character. Like Heine – this was not intended ironically – the emperor could assert: 'I do not always agree with myself.'[26] In its article 'Das psychologische Moment', the *Hannoversche Courier* praised Wilhelm II for not being one of the many monarchs who cut off access to his 'ego'.[27]

This tendency is probably clearest in the popular analogy drawn between artists and monarchs in the area of 'representation'. 'In this creative idealism they – the emperor and the artist – who appear eternally separate to the casual glance, in the chaos of surfaces, are one', noted Georg Fuchs in 1904. This theme, developed in a far more sophisticated manner, would form the foundation of Thomas Mann's

novel *Königlicher Hoheit*.[28] Even the specifically Wilhelmine notion
of divine right was regarded as an expression and description of
Wilhelm II's individuality.[29]

Many aspects of Wilhelm II's government were criticised early on,
but not his individuality. This served instead as an excuse that could
be deployed in a myriad of ways. The monarch, a certain Caliban
explained, merely claimed 'the right to hold and express his own
opinion'. It was still difficult for people, Caliban argued, to
understand a king 'who is a human being of flesh and blood like
ourselves, with the same feelings.'[30] The positive interpretation
placed on the monarch's individuality is also revealed quite vividly
in the constant contrasting of Wilhelm with the 'philistine', a
negative obsession of the period.[31] According to Radkau, 'since the
eighteenth century philistine was a term of contempt used by
students to mock the average citizen hemmed in by obligations. The
term first became politicised in the period preceding the Revolution
of 1848: it referred to the humdrum citizen deaf to the idea of
liberty, but also to the (regional) particularist horrified by the idea of
the nation-state.'[32] Wilhelm II, in contrast, was considered the very
prototype of the anti-philistine. Rudolf Borchardt lauded the
emperor, who 'so detested going along with the trend of the
moment'. Thus it is hardly surprising that Bülow's *bon mot* about
the emperor, 'a philistine he is not' was cited so frequently.[33] The
emperor, even his critics admitted, was an original.[34]

Wilhelm II's speeches in particular – despite or precisely because
of the criticisms of them – were viewed as expressions of his
individuality. Royal speeches had been introduced into Prussia by
Friedrich Wilhelm IV. The degree to which Wilhelm II used the
medium to express his opinions, however, was doubtless wholly
novel.[35] Contemporaries recognised this, too. Alfred Kerr presented
Wilhelm as somebody who knew 'how to enjoy life', for he expressed
his world-view uninhibitedly in extemporaneous speaking and saw
'these statements immediately disseminated to all corners of the
earth'.[36] In his speeches, Kerr believed, one could find 'Wilhelm the
Second's strong sense of individuality, which had so often been
confirmed'.[37] For his contemporaries, the monarch was not just a man
with every opportunity to realise himself, but above all someone who
made use of these opportunities. As a newspaper wrote on the
occasion of his fiftieth birthday, the Kaiser was a man who could 'live
his life' as 'his high spirits dictated'.[38] 'Self-enjoyment' and 'self-
gratification' (*Selbstvergnügen* and *Selbstgenuß*) were regarded as two

of Wilhelm's II character traits.[39] To the extent that individuality was deemed a sign of modern times, a 'complicated character' was certainly no disgrace.[40] To cite Borchardt again: the emperor 'put something of the egocentric excess of his epoch into his concern for himself, into his self-scrutiny and self-penetration'.[41]

If the monarch was justified by his complicated personality, it was up to his subjects to understand him and, in the long term, to accustom themselves to this personality. Nearly every newspaper stressed the necessity of discovering new aspects of this imperial individuality. In 1900, Reichstag president Ballestrem emphasised that the emperor's unique position could be attributed above all to his great individuality. In a time of 'publicity and responsible citizenship', Ballestrem believed, it was up to the people to recognise the emperor's intentions, particularly by interpreting his speeches.[42] Only a year later, a pamphleteer argued that one could not help but fault the German people 'for not acquainting themselves with the psyche of their emperor, for failing to understand him not simply as a ruler, but as a human being who is just as subject to the vagaries of emotional life as any other man.'[43]

Wilhelm II offered them an opportunity to do just this in 1907 when he explicitly touched on the theme of individuality. In an address to the Westphalian provincial diet in Münster, the monarch complained that 'During my long reign – it is now the twentieth year since I assumed office – I have dealt with many people and have had to put up with a good deal from them, often unconsciously and, alas, also consciously, they have wounded me bitterly.'[44] Even beyond the usual hagiography writers admitted that Wilhelm's remark represented something new and very positive. Commentators believed that they had witnessed a deep transformation in the emperor's character: 'Never before has he spoken to his people in this manner', one newspaper noted.[45]

The whole extraordinarily agitated and extensive discussion of the Münster speech can also be read as a sort of official revelation of a problematic relationship between monarch and people. In 1907 and 1908, when the Wilhelmine monarchy was for various reasons gripped by its most severe crisis, a virtual debate arose over how to deal with Wilhelm II's individuality. Not all commentators were prepared to condemn subjects for their failure to understand the monarch. Some of them saw very clearly the problems of the language that had been used up until that point. As early as 1907, the newspaper *Der Tag* had reminded the emperor of his responsibility to respect the personality of his subjects, too, who after all also lived in an age of individuality.[46] One year later Ludwig Thoma questioned the idea of the imperial individual when he insisted that 'There is nothing unusual about the Kaiser. Nowhere in his speeches does one find a surprising thought or an original word.'[47]

Nevertheless, all of these quotations – whether positive or negative in tenor – demonstrate an obsession with the individuality of Wilhelm II. They also, however, underline that this was no random development, but rather that the remarkable curiosity about the person of the monarch was necessarily linked with the emergence of a mass public. The media revolution of the late nineteenth century meant an enormous boom for the individual brand-name product that was Wilhelm II. To that extent, the individualisation of the monarch Wilhelm II was a genuinely Wilhelmine phenomenon. Finally, this was also quite evidently a highly equivocal development for the ruler, and nowhere more so than in the arena of political scandal.

The Eulenburg Scandal

Prince Philipp Eulenburg may with good reason be called Wilhelm II's best friend.[48] The monarch and his most important adviser met outside the court in the context of the so-called Liebenberg Circle, named after Eulenburg's country estate.[49] Here, Wilhelm II noted years later, he had encountered people who 'understood my individuality' and 'found my friends, my interests, everything that I had previously missed.' Liebenberg was, not least, a place where Wilhelm II could adopt a feminine role.[50]

This was exactly what Maximilian Harden, probably the most important political journalist of Wilhelmine Germany, criticised. He commented sarcastically on the Liebenberg Circle: 'What lovely people. Musical. Poetic, spiritualistic; so pious that they expect more healing power from prayer than from the wisest physician; and in their intercourse, both verbal and epistolary, so touchingly friendly.' This, Harden generously admitted, 'would be their private affair, if they did not belong to the emperor's closest company at table ...'[51] Harden aimed at certain – from his perspective – unsatisfactory political developments in the past. He suspected that the atmosphere prevailing at Liebenberg had dissuaded the emperor from taking the tough foreign policy line that Harden considered necessary.[52]

These were sufficient grounds for the journalist to launch a campaign against 'Wilhelm the Peaceful' via Eulenburg and his circle. Harden, who had criticised Eulenburg and the monarch for many years, finally began his direct assault in 1906.[53] Over and over again he provoked a few selected members of the Liebenberg Circle with constant references to their presumed abnormal sexual proclivities. In conjunction with other statements in Harden's magazine *Die Zukunft*, these hints could be read as accusations of homosexuality against Eulenburg. This accusation formed the core of Harden's campaign. To be sure, the journalist claimed that he could always distinguish between Eulenburg's political influence more generally, which he rejected, and his alleged homosexuality,[54] but in fact for him the two things were inextricably linked.[55]

Finally, Moltke, another friend of the emperor's, brought a libel suit against Harden. This trial and the ones that followed, in which Eulenburg also became increasingly entangled, not least because of his own misjudgement of the situation, comprised what later came to be known as the Eulenburg scandal. Although Harden never succeeded in proving Eulenburg's homosexuality in a court of law, he was still in a position, month in, month out, to present material about the emperor's inner circle which was, to put it mildly, bound to have a highly bewildering effect upon the German public.

Eulenburg presented an almost perfect target for Harden's attack. His enormous political influence as an adviser, quite out of keeping with his political position, was deemed extremely problematic. Eulenburg's purportedly active role in the dismissal of imperial chancellors Bismarck and Caprivi seemed to confirm this influence.[56] In addition, Eulenburg was known to be a devotee of spiritualism, and there was speculation that this had helped him to win the emperor's friendship.

Karsten Hecht is doubtless correct in his conclusion that 'this multiply vulnerable, always sickly "weakling" at the imperial court, whose only "power base" was his personal friendship with the emperor, provided a phenomenal target. He could count on neither the military nor the bureaucracy'.[57] More important still, however, Harden could evoke the firmly entrenched idea of a fateful combination of homosexual orientation and negative political activity.[58] Homosexuality also served as an efficient catchword for describing undesirable political developments.[59] Eulenburg was regarded as particularly dangerous for two reasons: first, it was generally assumed that homosexual tendencies were more widespread at court than elsewhere – even beyond the equally common notion of a certain aristocratic predisposition.[60] Second – and this was more problematic still – homosexual influence at court was considered politically disastrous.[61] In agreement with contemporary scientific opinion, Harden described homosexual men as 'less productive in their essential character than normal men', which made such advisers even more dangerous for the emperor and the country than 'flatterers of normal disposition'.[62] In addition, it was considered certain that homosexuals, with their alleged tendency to forge 'a tight ring around the emperor', were predestined to separate the monarch from his people.[63] To this extent it was not mere convenience that led Harden to use weapons from the sexual arena for his campaign.

To a far greater extent than the case of Oscar Wilde, the Eulenburg scandal brought together perceptions of the general political situation with perceptions of men's own bodies. To be 'hard' enough for a supposedly difficult political situation became a virtual paradigm. The extent to which the sexualised body and politics were intertwined in the scandal described here is quite obvious.[64] Since his personal relationship with Wilhelm II formed the basis of Eulenburg's power, Harden sought, logically enough, to render this very relationship socially impossible by claiming that Eulenburg and some of his friends were homosexual. The political consequences were far-reaching, since everyone realised that Eulenburg had merely served as a lightening rod to catch criticism actually aimed at the emperor.[65] Without the obvious connections to Wilhelm II, Harden would have had no reason to take action.

Why was Harden able to exploit this theme so successfully? It appears that two important strands of discussion came together here: the construction of a royal individual and the obsession with hardness and manliness.[66] We must not forget that Wilhelm II loved presenting himself in extreme masculine poses. What his subjects saw was a monarch equipped with the so-called *Es-ist-erreicht* (approximately: 'We have done it') moustache,[67] and characterised by vigorous speeches and an ostentatiously military bearing.[68] The monarch was quite obviously reacting here to tendencies that were gaining ground in any case, but which were intensified by his hyper-masculine symbolic promises. By accepting and exaggerating these tendencies, Wilhelm II made himself vulnerable. Contemporaries already saw in Wilhelm's all-too hearty displays of manliness attempts to hide the feminine, if not homosexual, side of his character.[69] In a discourse on political rule that increasingly relied on the ideal of the tough leader, this was bound to gain enormous significance.[70]

The matter was a good deal more complex, though. Many contemporaries believed in a decisive connection between power and homosexuality. As George Mosse has shown, while the homosexual aesthete was an accepted *fin de siècle* figure, a homosexual statesman was utterly unimaginable. It was quite in keeping with this finding when the court-marshal Robert von Zedlitz-Trützschler declared that the problematic nature of the homosexual question lay less in whether homosexuals followed their inclinations or not, and more in the fact that they could be politically dangerous because of their 'effeminate attitudes, their weak and fantastic natures ... particularly in the entourage of Wilhelm II'.[71] Zedlitz believed that it was the allegedly disastrous influence of homosexuals on the emperor rather than the mere existence of homosexuals at court that had prompted Harden's actions. After all, as indicated above, a strong semantic connection existed between masculinity and the clear light of publicity on the one side and homosexuality and obscure political practices on the other. In an open letter, Harden called upon the emperor to leave the stuffy air of the eunuch press and heed the warnings of sensible monarchists.[72] One of the commentators on the Münster speech, obviously cast in the same mental mould, believed that with this speech the emperor 'was undertaking a kind of escape from the sultry atmosphere of courtly flatterers, in order to approach again the hearts of the nation, and that he had recognised the value of loyal resistance and the justification of independent public opinion, and was seeking its approval'.[73]

Not surprisingly, authors contrasted moral decay and the suppression and manipulation of channels of information with specifically bourgeois values. At the height of the sexual scandal surrounding Eulenburg in 1907, Paul Michaelis commented in the *Berliner Tageblatt* newspaper that it was telling that degeneration appeared in particular 'where people are demonstratively devoted to the attitudes of earlier times, wallowing in vague sentiments and seeking to breathe new life into nebulous romantic notions. The swamp blossom of sexual perversity has grown in the soil of reaction and finds its nourishment there.' One must combat the 'poisonous plant of the camarilla' with 'open air and publicity'.[74] In this view,

moral decay and political obscurity necessarily belonged together and
the camarilla was an obsessively deployed image of this relationship.

The Destruction of the Monarch's Aura

There is some evidence that suspicions about the true role played by
the monarch were chiefly responsible for the unusual intensity of
public interest in the Eulenburg scandal. During the first two trials
alone, the opposing parties directly mentioned the emperor more
than eighty times in court.[75] This circumstance assumes significance
when one considers the enormous press coverage of the trials. For
two years, even the smallest regional newspapers reported almost
daily on the trial accounts, disseminating details of internal matters
concerning the imperial court. The trials were described practically
blow by blow, with verbatim accounts and extensive commentaries.
In both breadth and depth, this style of reporting was something
completely new for the German media, and contemporaries
recognised it. The public treatment of sexual matters in particular
was considered unprecedented.[76]

Against this backdrop, we can distinguish three main lines of
interpretation of Wilhelm II's role in the Eulenburg scandal.

1. The official and dominant line of interpretation was that the
   emperor had unwittingly surrounded himself with dubious
   individuals. This gave the public the opportunity to place a
   positive interpretation on the whole affair. According to this
   view, the monarch had finally become aware of the true
   character of his entourage and could now begin anew after a
   process of cleansing. The emperor was now 'free', crowed
   Harden, after the removal of Eulenburg from the court.[77]
2. A second question is how the sensationalistic drama played out
   in the courtrooms of Moabit was received by those who did not
   simply accept the official interpretation. The commentators
   even publicly mused over how Wilhelm II – with his knowledge
   of human nature, which was considered a cardinal virtue of
   kings – could have misjudged the true nature of his entourage so
   thoroughly. Some members of this entourage, the trial revealed,
   regularly referred to the emperor in their letters as 'the darling'
   (*das Liebchen*).[78]

   How problematic the image of the unknowing monarch was is
   underlined by the tenor of many commentaries. The senior

police official Hans v. Tresckow, who was also involved with the Eulenburg case, complained: 'Had the emperor only consulted the register at the time, he would have been informed about his entourage , and the subsequent sensationalist trials, which did so much to damage the reputation of the Crown, would have been avoided.'[79] The monarchical ideal contrasted sharply with the image of a ruler who had apparently managed to go for twenty years without the slightest suspicion of matters whose true nature was completely obvious to the public after only a few days.[80] Count Günther von Schulenburg summarised this dilemma quite aptly: 'His Majesty is still surrounded by fairies (*warme Brüder*). Even if he does not approve of the tendency as such, he is all the more under the spell of such people, for he is already so spoilt that he won't listen to the truth anymore.'[81] Eulenburg, 'our emperor's friend', according to Busching, had never been taken seriously by politicians: 'Only the emperor stood by him.' It was 'too bad for the emperor', that a figure like Eulenburg headed the entourage with which he had surrounded himself.[82] At best, the emperor lacked the abilities required for his office, and at worst he was a dubious character himself.

3. Thirdly, after all that had been made public in the courtroom, one could ask whether Wilhelm II's character, and indeed his sexual orientation, were not problematic. Not surprisingly, the newspapers almost never posed this question openly.[83] The taboo surrounding the imperial body was preserved, at least superficially. That Wilhelm II had been in closer contact with members of his entourage than he admitted, however, appeared quite probable given all that had come out during the trials. If the monarch had been in such close contact with proven homosexuals for so many years, was it not likely that he had at least homoerotic tendencies?

The debates on the court camarilla implied that the emperor's friendships were being investigated. This is true, for instance, of an article that appeared in the *Kölnischen Zeitung*, which declared that the emperor must experience it as a 'breach of trust and a disgraceful betrayal' when men he had honoured with his friendship secretly harboured inclinations that he detested and the law punished.' Herein lay, 'psychologically speaking, the heart of this repugnant story'.[84] The conceivability of the monarch's homoerotic tendencies is also discernible when commentators felt the need to stress the emperor's ideal family life over and over again.[85]

For the monarch, the most delicate matter was surely the existence, which soon became known, of letters to Eulenburg of supposedly compromising content. Wild speculations about their contents ensued (Figure 12.1).[86]

Figure 12.1 In a pertinent cartoon, Augustus, plainly identifiable by his striking beard as Wilhelm II, laments the loss not of his legions but of compromising letters. In the background, a humiliated Eulenburg makes the direct connection between the monarch and the scandal abundantly clear. Th. Th. Heine, Simplicissimus 22 June 1908.

One commentator speculated on the 'friendship between man and man', which was 'a peculiar thing'. Here one could find the 'most affectionate modes of expression', which were committed to paper at moments of when people 'pour out their hearts confidentially'. This should not become public, which was understandable, all the more when, as turned out to be the case here, one of the friends was an 'unworthy man', who had 'led a disgraceful life' and was 'beneath the honour of possessing the love and trust of a real man'. Here the 'guilt and disgrace of the one cast a dark shadow over even the tenderest and most noble sentiments of the other, which had found expression in such intimate exchanges of thoughts and feelings'.[87]

People wondered how the emperor could have given his friendship to a man like Eulenburg, 'that he could have favoured him with so much love and accorded him such a prominent place in his heart'.[88] In addition, the Eulenburg scandal evoked memories of the Krupp affair. Alfred Krupp, also known as a friend of the emperor's, had committed suicide in 1902 after his homosexuality had become public knowledge. Wilhelm II, who spoke at the funeral, had defended Krupp vigorously at the time.[89] Similar inclinations among the emperor's living relatives, as well as Frederick the Great, were also openly discussed.[90]

The comments made in letters were more explicit still. Harden wrote to his friend Walther Rathenau in 1908: 'If the tarring of the most imperilled person is to be avoided, justice must treat this like any other case … His Majesty's complete indifference must be established. The matter is dangerous in the extreme. I prefer not to discuss details.'[91] When Harden spoke of 'tarring', he was quite capable of envisioning the emperor's forced abdication. He informed chancellor Bülow that he would not hesitate to publish material demonstrating Wilhelm's II relevant contacts in Bavaria.[92]

To be sure, commentators repeatedly invoked the consensus that the person of the emperor should be kept out of the debate. This in itself, however, shows how fragile the monarch's position was.[93] The mere fact that Wilhelm was mentioned in the same breath as the scandals sufficed to discredit him.[94] Quite early on, in 1910, the physiognomist Rudolf Kassner recognised that imperial greatness was inconceivable after the Eulenburg scandal.[95] Even Wilhelm II, who rarely had a sense of the perils facing the monarchy, realised that the Eulenburg affair had placed him 'in an unprecedented situation for a monarch'.[96]

Certainly, sexual scandal was nothing new in the political arena,[97] and explicit attacks on the king's sexuality had been made before. This early twentieth-century German example, however, differed sharply from others, for example those Lynn Hunt has described for late eighteenth-century France.[98] In France, addressing the king's sexuality had served a particular purpose. One might even say, with only slight exaggeration, that it did not matter whether the accusations were true or not.

In the case of Wilhelm II, the attack was generally on the weak, unmanly man who indulged in bizarre romantic friendships. Thus his possible homoerotic tendencies only came to light rather covertly. They were less the means to an end than stages and elements in a process of getting to grips with the monarch, of exploring the royal individual. This investigation and scrutiny were concerned above all with the psyche of Wilhelm II. In Wilhelmine Germany the – politically very powerful – [99] king was transformed into an individual, someone his subjects wanted to understand as thoroughly as possible. To this extent, every aspect of the monarch's character assumed significance. Highly self-confident mass media equipped with a strong liberal, middle-class impetus also believed they had the right to know all of this. In this sense, I would like to argue, the individualisation of the emperor was the precondition for confronting him with his sexual orientation, or at least with his masculinity.

Against this background one can observe a reciprocal process of taboo breaking. This applies to references both to the individuality of the monarch and to his sexual orientation. The ambivalent results of the individualisation of the emperor become clearly evident here. However much this process also helped the emperor to gain substantial sympathy and to deflect and divert criticisms of his person, the same phenomenon could also boomerang. In that case, the construction of the royal individual became an invitation to place everything under the microscope – including the king's own body.

Put another way, once the monarch had been unmasked as the unmanly emperor, both his body natural and his body politic became problematic. This is true to the extent that Wilhelm II's reputation suffered on two levels. The monarch now appeared to be not merely unmanly, but also potentially homosexual. The two aspects were closely intertwined. Even if the emperor's body itself was not problematic, there were enough reasons to abandon the dogma of the manly emperor. A monarch who not only urgently needed political counsel, but also sought this advice from highly dubious, effeminate men, and thus showed that he could not bear manly, open talk, who was not man enough to recognise the true character of those around him, and ultimately needed assistance to rid himself of his unworthy advisers, was little more than a figure of fun when compared to the model of a strong and manly ruler that had still been largely intact until the time of the scandal, and continued to exist as an ideal. In 1919, a critic noted that one could not blame the now ex-emperor for everything. 'But that he tolerated all this for decades, and did not feel in his heart the impulse to breathe the free and invigorating air of true manliness, and that he could not see to it personally that his throne was surrounded by men and that all of the grovelling rabble reaped the scorn they deserved' – that had been his fault alone.[100]

Translated by Pamela Selwyn

Notes

1. Individualisation refers to two things here: first, to the individual character traits, opinions, etc. actually displayed by the monarch; and second, to the obsession with these same traits of royal individuality, which was independent of them. The term thus encompasses qualities generally described as personalisation and subjectivation.

2. The role of the media in Imperial Germany as well as the significance of the *fin de siècle* for media history has been thoroughly reconceptualised in recent years. Cf. Jörg Requate, 'Öffentlichkeit und Medien als Gegenstände historischer Analyse', *Geschichte und Gesellschaft* 25, (1999), 5–32; Axel Schildt, 'Das Jahrhundert der Massenmedien: Ansichten zu einer künftigen Geschichte der Öffentlichkeit', *Geschichte und Gesellschaft* 27, (2001), 177–206; Andreas Schulz, 'Der Aufstieg der "vierten Gewalt". Medien, Politik und Öffentlichkeit im Zeitalter der Massenkommunikation', *Historische Zeitschrift* 270, (2000), 65–97; and Bernd Weisbrod, 'Medien als symbolische Form der Massengesellschaft: Die medialen Bedingungen von Öffentlichkeit im 20. Jahrhundert', *Historische Anthropologie* 9, (2001), 270–83.

3. Jens Ivo Engels, *Königsbilder. Sprechen, Singen und Schreiben über den König in der ersten Hälfte des 18. Jahrhunderts* (Bonn, 2000), 232.

4. Monika Wienfort, *Monarchie in der bürgerlichen Gesellschaft. Deutschland und England von 1640 bis 1848* (Göttingen, 1993), 137.

5. Juliane Vogel, *Elisabeth von Österreich. Momente aus dem Leben einer Kunstfigur* (Frankfurt a. M., 1998), 63. On this issue, see also Thomas Rahn, 'Masse, Maske und Macht. Psychologien des Zeremoniells im 20. Jahrhundert', in *Zeremoniell in der Krise. Störung und Nostalgie*, ed. Bernhard Jahn, Thomas Rahn and Claudia Schnitzer (Marburg, 1998), 129–48. See also the introduction to this volume.

6. Vogel, *Elisabeth*, 64. See also Regina Schulte, 'Der Aufstieg der konstitutionellen Monarchie und das Gedächtnis der Königin', *Historische Anthropologie*, 6 (1998), 76–103.

7. Hermann Oncken asserted that the constitutional type achieved too little, was 'boring and dispensable' to modern society, and stood in contradiction to the age's 'culture of personality'. Wilhelm II, however, represented the individualistic character of the epoch. Hermann Oncken, *Der Kaiser und die Nation. Rede bei dem Festakt der Universität Heidelberg zur Erinnerung an die Befreiungskriege und zur Feier des 25jährigen Regierungsjubiläums Kaiser Wilhelms II.* (Heidelberg, 1913), 19. See also the examples cited in Thomas Kohut, *Wilhelm II and the Germans. A Study in Leadership* (New York, 1991), 169, and Elisabeth Fehrenbach, *Wandlungen des deutschen Kaisergedankens, 1871–1918* (Munich, 1969), 90.

8. John C.G. Röhl, *Wilhelm II. Der Aufbau der Persönlichen Monarchie. 1888–1900* (Munich, 2001), 42.

9. Alongside the novels by Alberti and Conrad, which will be discussed below, Breuer mentions 'the rebellion of "the young" within Social Democracy (1890), the secessionist movements in art and the polarisations within important associations, such as the Verein für Sozialpolitik (Association for Social Policy) or the Evangelisch-Sozialen-Kongreß (Protestant Social Congress) ...' Stefan Breuer, 'Arthur Moeller van den Bruck: Politischer Publizist und Organisator des Neuen Nationalismus in Kaiserreich und Republik', in *Kritik und Mandat, Intellektuelle in der deutschen Politik*, ed. Gangolf Hübinger and Thomas Hertefelder (Munich, 2000), 143. On generational problems in Imperial Germany, see also Thorsten Bügner and Gerhard Wagner, 'Die Alten und die Jungen im Deutschen Reich. Literatursoziologische Anmerkungen zum Verhältnis der Generationen 1871–1918', *Zeitschrift für Soziologie* 20, (1991), 177–90.

10. Konrad Alberti [Sittenfeld], *Was erwartet die deutsche Kunst von Kaiser Wilhelm II.?, Zeitgemäße Anregungen* (Leipzig, 1888). See also the same author's *Die Alten und die Jungen, Sozialer Roman*, 2 vols. (Leipzig, 1889). One should mention Michael Georg Conrad in this connection. In 1885, the Naturalist author (1846–1927) founded the journal *Die Gesellschaft*, the 'central organ' of the 'Youngest German' movement. His novels repeatedly treated the theme of the monarchy. In 1894, the disillusioned Conrad allowed Ludwig Quidde to use his journal as a platform for the scandalous criticism of Wilhelm II in his *Caligula*. Cf. Gerd Fesser, 'Kaiser Wilhelm II. und der Wilhelminismus', in Karl Holl and Gerd Fesser, *Caligula – Wilhelm II. und der Caesarenwahnsinn. Antikenrezeption und wilhelminische Politik am Beispiel des'Caligula' von Ludwig Quidde* (Bremen, 2001), 117–152.

11. Hermann Conradi, *Wilhelm II. und die junge Generation, Eine zeitpsychologische Betrachtung*, in *Gesammelte Schriften*, Vol. III, ed. Gustav Werner Peters (Munich, 1889).

12. Conradi, *Wilhelm II*, 311.

13. Ibid., 314.

14. Ibid., 316–17.

15. Georg E. Hinzpeter, *Kaiser Wilhelm II. Eine Skizze nach der Natur. Gezeichnet von G. Hinzpeter*, 9th edn. (Bielefeld, 1888), 7.

16. This fact was welcomed by many commentators. See Anonymous, *Die 'eigene Flugbahn'. Wer will sie stören? Auch ein Beitrag zur Zeitgeschichte* (Berlin, 1889), 4.

17. Anonymous, *Wilhelm II. Romantiker oder Sozialist?* (Zurich, 1892).

18. Ibid., 3.

19. Ibid., 5.

20. As the author put it, 'It is an old phenomenon that upon assuming office each new ruler awakens hopes impossible under his predecessors. … The first year of the reign of every ruler provides fertile soil for rosy and weedy desires.' Ibid., 5.

21. Ibid., 7ff.

22. Ibid., 17, 19, 22.

23. The author continues, 'The German conscience is becoming increasingly emasculated and de-germanified. To be German is to be open, loyal and honest – traits one cannot claim for current public opinion. On the contrary, it is furtive, dishonest and cowardly.' Ibid., 25.

24. Ibid., 31.

25. Paul Busching, 'Der Kaiser', *Süddeutsche Monatshefte*, 5 (1908), 614–20, 620.

26. Quoted in 'Das psychologische Moment', *Hannoverscher Courier*, 10 July 1908 (no. 273).

27. Ibid.

28. Georg Fuchs, *Das Kaiser-Buch. Der Kaiser, die Kultur und die Kunst. Betrachtungen über die Zukunft des Deutschen Volkes aus den Papieren eines Unverantwortlichen* (Munich and Leipzig, 1904), 176. See also Rudolf Borchardt, 'Der Kaiser', *Süddeutsche Monatshefte* 5 (1908), 237–52. Very important in this context is Thomas Mann's novel, *Königliche Hoheit* (Berlin, 1909). On the concept of representation in Mann's work, see Dieter Borchmeyer, 'Repräsentation als ästhetische Existenz. Königliche Hoheit und Wilhelm Meister. Thomas Manns Kritik der formalen Existenz', *Recherches Germaniques* 13, (1983), 105–36; Hinrich Siefken, 'Thomas Mann and the Concept of "Repräsentation": "Königliche Hoheit"', *The Modern Language Review* 73, (1978), 337–50.

29. See the examples in Aristides, *Der Kaiser und die Nation* (Leipzig, 1909), 9; Ernst v. Reventlow, *Kaiser Wilhelm II. und die Byzantiner*, 2nd edn. (Berlin, 1906), 42–43 as well as Borchardt, 'Kaiser', 250. The commentators referred in particular to speeches given by Wilhelm II at the banquet of the provincial diet at Königsberg on 15 May 1890, and at the banquet of the Rhine Province Koblenz (31 August 1897), and the virtually classic emphasis on Wilhelmine divine right. Cf. Ernst Johann (ed.), *Reden des Kaisers. Ansprachen, Predigten und Trinksprüche Wilhelms II.* (Munich, 1966), 51, 73.

30. Caliban, 'Die goldene Medaille', *Die Gegenwart* 46, (1894), 332–33.

31. Lamar Cecil, 'The Creation of Nobles in Prussia 1871–1918', *American Historical Review*, 75 (1970), 757–95, here 757.

32. Joachim Radkau, 'Nationalismus und Nervosität', in *Kulturgeschichte Heute*, ed. Wolfgang Hardtwig and Hans-Ulrich Wehler, Geschichte und Gesellschaft, Sonderheft 16 (Göttingen, 1996), 292–93.

33. Conradi, *Wilhelm II.*, 311, 319, 382, 408; Borchardt, Kaiser, 245, 249; 'Kaiser Wilhelm II.', *Hamburger Nachrichten*, 14 June 1908 (no. 412); Friedrich Naumann, 'Die Politik des Kaisers', *Die Hilfe* 14 (1908), 718–20, here 719.

34. Cf. the statement of Moritz von Egidy: 'Because our king – much to the joy of every German to whom the right of personality means anything – is a personality, a Self, a man, and through this quality is however set apart from thousands of his compatriots, those who seek to profit from the king's power and splendour are anxious to sacrifice their own selves to the majesty of this prince who is also so superior in inner strength. Moritz von Egidy, 'Servilismus', *Versöhnung*, 2 February 1896 (no. 109).

35. On Wilhelm's speeches, see Sonja Reinhardt, '"Wie ihr's euch träumt, wird Deutschland nicht erwachen." Formen der Herrschaftslegitimation in ausgewählten Reden von Kaiser Wilhelm II. und Adolf Hitler' (Ph.D. diss., University of Hannover, 1994), 10ff.

36. Alfred Kerr, *Wo liegt Berlin?. Briefe aus der Reichshauptstadt*, ed. Günther Rühle (Berlin, 1997), 497. See also the paradigmatic newspaper articles 'Und weiter sprach der Kaiser …', *Berliner Zeitung*, 9 September 1898 (no. 217); 'Wenn der Kaiser spricht …', *Pfälzische Volkszeitung*, 4 September 1907 (no. 213) and 'Kaiser Wilhelm II. als Redner', *Deutsche Zeitung*, 1 June 1907 (no. 124).

37. Kerr, *Wo liegt Berlin?*, 602.

38. 'Zum Geburtstag des Kaisers', *Augsburger Abendblatt*, 26 January 1908 (no. 26).

39. According to the article 'Alle Menschen sind wie Du', 'And he in particular, in the untrammelled development of all his talents, has recognised his ideal in the self-enjoyment and self-gratification of his own ego and repeatedly claimed the right to live it out'. Spectator, 'Alle sind Menschen wie Du', *Der Tag*, 31 September 1907 (no. 419).

40. On this nexus after 1918 see, for example, Conrad Bornhak, *Deutsche Geschichte unter Kaiser Wilhelm II.* (Leipzig and Erlangen, 1921), 47 and Josef Sonntag, *Schuld und Schicksal. Die Tragödie Wilhelms II.*, 2nd edn. (Leipzig, 1927). In Imperial Germany the chief proponent of this idea was Karl Lamprecht. Cf. his article 'Zur Lage', *Münchener Allgemeine Zeitung*, 14 November 1908, and the tenor of his book *Der Kaiser* (Berlin, 1913).

41. Borchardt, ,Kaiser', 242.

42. Friedrich Zipfel, 'Kritik der deutschen Öffentlichkeit an der Person und an der Monarchie Wilhelms II. bis zum Ausbruch des Weltkrieges' (Ph.D. diss. Berlin, 1952), 94.

43. Gustav Adolf Erdmann, *Der deutsche Kaiser und sein Volk* (Leipzig, 1901), 7–8.

44. Johann, *Reden des Kaisers*, 120ff.
45. R. Falke, 'Der religiöse Standpunkt unseres Kaisers', *Der Tag*, 6 September 1907 (no. 247). On the response in the press, see BAL, Reichslandbundarchiv 8034 II, no. 4009, Blatt 81ff.
46. Spectator, *Alle Menschen*, 2.
47. Ludwig Thoma, 'Der Kaiser', *März. Halbmonatsschrift für deutsche Kultur* 2 (1908), 249–53, here 251. See also Paul Liman, *Der Kaiser. Ein Charakterbild Wilhelms II.* (Berlin, 1904), esp. 10, 21ff.
48. See John C.G. Röhl, 'Philipp Eulenburg, the Kaiser's Best Friend', chapter 2 of *The Kaiser and his Court: Wilhelm II and the Government of Germany*, trans. Terence F. Cole (Cambridge, 1995).
49. Isabel V. Hull, *The Entourage of Kaiser Wilhelm II 1888–1918* (Cambridge, 1982), 45ff. and 'Kaiser and "Liebenberg Circle"', in *Kaiser Wilhelm II: New Interpretations*, eds. John C.G. Röhl and Nicolaus Sombart (Cambridge, 1982), 193–220.
50. Hull, *Entourage*, 20. Röhl emphasises that, particularly after harsh public criticism, it was important for the emperor to be able to seek refuge with the Liebenbergers. Röhl, *Wilhelm II. Der Aufbau*, 939.
51. Quoted in Karsten Hecht, *Die Harden-Prozesse – Strafverfahren, Öffentlichkeit und Politik im Kaiserreich*, (Ph.D. diss. Munich, 1997), 30.
52. Harden considered the fact that the notorious French embassy official Lecomte was able to enter the emperor's most intimate circle through Eulenburg's mediation to be final proof of this. Hecht, *Die Harden-Prozesse*, 401ff. Hellige suspects that 'the permanent juxtaposition of the "true" "charismatic leader", equipped with the highest degree of manliness and professional and personal authority with the decadent ruler surrounded by effeminate courtiers and afflicted with imperial mania was influenced to a significant degree by Harden's own conflict with his father and his "rebellion against hermaphroditism"'. Introduction to Hans Dieter Hellige and Ernst Schulin eds., *Walther Rathenau-Gesamtausgabe*, Vol. VI: Walther Rathenau to Maximilian Harden, *Briefwechsel 1897–1920* (Munich, 1983), 127.
53. Hecht, *Die Harden-Prozesse*, 38–39.
54. Ibid., 156.
55. At any rate, despite supporting the abolition of §175, Harden shared many of the significant common prejudices against homosexuals. Hull, *Entourage*, 134.
56. 'Kaiser und Bismarck und Fürst Eulenburg', *Münchner Neueste Nachrichten*, 16 May 1908 (no. 230). See also Liman, *Der Kaiser*, 30–31. On the facts of the case, see Hans Wilhelm Burmeister, *Prince Philipp Eulenburg-Hertefeld (1847–1921). His Influence on Kaiser Wilhelm II and his Role in the German Government. 1888–1902* (Wiesbaden, 1981), 46–47.
57. Hecht, *Die Harden-Prozesse*, 19ff., quotation on 28.

58. The attacks on homosexuals, argues Fout, 'illustrate real concern about the kind of masculinity that the male homosexual had come to represent. He was now clearly perceived as some novel but unacceptable masculine creature, who manifested behaviour that contradicted a newly emerging redefinition of hypermasculinity.' John C. Fout, 'Sexual Politics in Wilhelmine Germany: The Male Gender Crisis, Moral Purity, and Homophobia', *Journal of the History of Sexuality* 2, (1992), 388–421, here 413. 'Like women, homosexuals were thought to be marionettes of their sexual desires.' In addition, homosexuals were often assumed to have a female soul in a male body. On this view, see Franz X. Eder, 'Sexualised Subjects. Medical Discourse on Sexuality in German-Speaking Countries in the Late 18th and in the 19th Century', in *Civilization, Sexuality and Social Life in Historical Context. The Hidden Face of Urban Life*, ed. The Institute of the History of Medicine and Social Medicine (Budapest, 1996), 17–29, here 24–25.

59. On the contemporary debate on homosexuality, see George L. Mosse, 'Manliness and Homosexuality', in *Nationalism and Sexuality. Respectability and Abnormal Sexuality in Modern Europe*, ed. George L. Mosse (New York, 1985), 23–47, here 40. He also remarks upon the increasing critical scrutiny of 'male friendship', 31. At the same time as the Eulenburg scandal, the abolition of §175 was also being debated, albeit not very widely. For an article that presented medical arguments in favour of abolition, see 'Die Aufhebung des §175', *Berliner Tageblatt*, 15 November 1907 (no. 582). For a general account of the debate, see Angela Taeger and Rüdiger Lautmann, 'Sittlichkeit und Politik. §175 im Deutschen Kaiserreich (1871–1919)', in their essay collection *Männerliebe im alten Deutschland. Sozialgeschichtliche Abhandlungen*, Sozialwissenschaftliche Studien zur Homosexualität, 5 (Berlin, 1992), 239–68. Eulenburg consequently also saw himself as a victim of a new era in whose cult of tough masculinity more sensitive natures like his own and those of his friends no longer had a place. Hull, *Entourage*, 59. In 1902, Werner Sombart described the 'coming generation' (*heranwachsende Geschlecht*) as a 'harder and less emotional type of human being, who looks down upon the sentimentality of early generations as 'gushing' and has already internalised modern 'restlessness'. Joachim Radkau, *Das Zeitalter der Nervosität. Deutschland zwischen Bismarck und Hitler* (Munich and Vienna, 1998), 391.

60. Angela Leuchtmann, *Der Fall Philipp Eulenburg. Anfang und Ende einer Karriere im wilhelminischen Deutschland* (Munich, 1998), 203ff.

61. Homosexuals, it was regularly argued, must be regarded as completely out of place in the circle around the monarch. Hans v. Tresckow, *Von Fürsten und anderen Sterblichen. Erinnerungen eines Kriminalkommissars* (Berlin, 1922), 112.

62. Hecht, *Die Harden-Prozesse*, 16ff. The phrase Harden used was 'in ihrer Gesamtwesensleistung geringer einzuschätzen'.

63. Cf. the article 'Prozeß Moltke vs. Harden', *Vossische Zeitung*, 24 October 1907 (no. 499). Moltke's testimony was repeated in nearly all reports from the courtroom.
64. It is remarkable that Harden's impetus, if not always his methods, was largely accepted. Hecht, *Die Harden-Prozesse*, 148–49.
65. Hull, *Entourage*, 47.
66. Cf. Thomas Kühne, *Männergeschichte als Geschlechtergeschichte*, in *Männergeschichte - Geschlechtergeschichte. Männlichkeit im Wandel der Moderne*, ed. Thomas Kühne (Frankfurt a.M., 1996), 7–30. Robert A. Nye, *Masculinity and Male Codes of Honour in Modern France*, Studies in the History of Sexuality 3, (Oxford, 1993).
67. Gisela Brude-Firnau, *Die literarische Deutung Kaiser Wilhelms II. zwischen 1889 und 1989*, Beiträge zur Neueren Literaturgeschichte, 148 (Heidelberg, 1997), 19.
68. Hull, *Entourage*, 18.
69. Brude-Firnau, *Literarische Deutung*, 130ff.
70. See Martin Kohlrausch, 'Die Flucht des Kaisers – Doppeltes Scheitern adlig-bürgerlicher Monarchiekonzepte', in *Adel und Bürgertum in Deutschland II: Entwicklungslinien und Wendepunkte*, Heinz Reif ed. (Berlin, 2001), 65–101.
71. Robert von Zedlitz-Trützschler, *Zwölf Jahre am deutschen Kaiserhof* (Stuttgart, 1924), entry for 26 November 1907, 171.
72. Brude-Firnau, *Literarische Deutung*, 46.
73. F. St. V., 'Der Kaiser nach zwanzigjähriger Regierung', *Tägliche Rundschau*, 14 June 1908 (no. 275).
74. Paul Michaelis, 'Politische Wochenschau', *Berliner Tageblatt*, 27 October 1907 (no. 547).
75. This figure is based on the trial minutes provided by Hugo Friedländer, *Der Beleidigungsprozeß des Stadtkommandanten von Moltke gegen Maximilian Harden*. Digitale Bibliothek, 51, 3948ff.
76. Cf. the article 'Hofskandal', *Leipziger Neue Nachrichten*, 1 June 1907 (no. 150).
77. Hellige, *Briefwechsel*, 165.
78. As Röhl notes, Moltke, Varnbühler and Eulenburg actually called Wilhelm II 'Das Liebchen'. Röhl, *Aufbau*, 643.
79. Tresckow, *Fürsten*, 116.
80. In the thirteenth letter, dated 12 June 1907, Schneidt finally refers to the Eulenburg scandal. 'Millions of good Germans, Herr Kaiser, think just as I do. It is inconceivable to all of them how it was possible that persons whom any ordinary citizen would go out of his way to avoid were able to cross your path daily and hourly, that they could gain influence over your thoughts and deeds, which was indeed unavoidable with a certain degree of contact, and that nobody possessed the courage to warn you openly and honestly'. Karl Schneidt, *Briefe an den Kaiser*, Sonderabdruck aus den Jahrgängen 1906–1908 der Tribüne (Berlin 1909), 109–10.

81. Tresckow, *Fürsten*, 199.
82. Busching, *Der Kaiser*, 363.
83. Wilhelm II's role in the scandal as such, how much information he possessed and his personal sentiments remain vague. Leuchtmann, *Fall Eulenburg*, 259. Using an article from the *Tägliche Rundschau* annotated by the emperor, Rogge was at least able to show how he viewed the trial. Helmuth Rogge, *Holstein und Harden. Politisch-Publizistisches Zusammenspiel zweier Außenseiter des Wilhelminischen Reichs* (Munich, 1959), 233ff. Spitzemberg wondered why the emperor was not informed earlier of how matters stood with Eulenburg. Rudolf Vierhaus ed., *Am Hof der Hohenzollern. Aus dem Tagebuch der Baronin von Spitzemberg 1865–1914* (Munich, 1965), entry for 31 May 1907, 472.
84. 'Schmutzige Wäsche', *Kölnische Zeitung*, 15 June 1907 (no. 630). Even the *Kreuzzeitung* wrote: 'the longer this continues, the more sensible one becomes of how grateful one should be to the emperor for not becoming a misanthrope after all the bitter experiences of the past two years. One recalls his speech at Münster, which shows us how his faith in God has saved him from bitterness towards man. At that time one could scarcely imagine how soon the emperor would be subjected to such an ordeal'. 'Zum Prozeß Moltke-Harden', *Neue Preußische Zeitung*, 28 October 1907 (no. 506).
85. 'Ein "Beschwichtigungshofrat"', *Kölnische Volkszeitung*, 6 November 1907 (no. 963).
86. 'Fürst Eulenburg', *Fränkischer Kurier*, 16 May 1908 (no. 134).
87. Karl Schneidt, 'Kaiserbriefe an Eulenburg', *Die Zeit am Montag*, Berlin, 18 May 1908 (no. 20).
88. Schneidt, *Kaiserbriefe*. Apparently Schneidt knew more about the correspondence than he admitted publicly. Suspicions of the emperor's homosexuality are obvious between the lines.
89. Wilhelm's eulogy at Krupp's funeral was viewed as a sign of solidarity. Johann, *Reden des Kaisers*, 104. Wilhelm II had chosen the wrong advisers and friends. See also Conrad Bornhak, *Deutsche Geschichte unter Kaiser Wilhelm II.* (Leipzig and Erlangen, 1921), 43.
90. For examples among the emperor's relatives, see Röhl, *Aufbau*, 694ff.
91. Hellige believes that Harden possessed information that would have allowed him to force the emperor to abdicate. Harden to Rathenau 8 May 1908, Hellige, *Briefwechsel*, 553ff. On this see also Norman Rich ed., *The Holstein Papers, The Memoirs, Diaries and Correspondence of Friedrich von Holstein, 1837–1909*, 4 vols. (Cambridge, 1955) IV, no. 1151 and Röhl's Introduction to his edition, *Philipp Eulenburgs politische Korrespondenz*, 3.vols, Deutsche Geschichtsquellen des 19. und 20. Jahrhunderts 52 (Boppard am Rhein, 1976–83), 46–47.
92. The contacts referred to here were to the fisherman Jakob Ernst and Friedrich Kistler, Eulenburg's former secretary. Holstein to Fürst

Bülow, 16 November 1908. Rogge, *Holstein und Harden*, 386–87. In April 1909 Harden announced to Ballin that, by introducing new witnesses, he would 'give the matter a scope which he had been "trying for years to avoid, among sacrifices of the harshest kind"'. BAL, N 2106, no. 2. (1909). Vergleich Moltke-Harden, Blatt 6. He goes on to say 'I therefore believe that we will be forced into the ghastly matter against the will of plaintiff and accused, because the courage and energy for a serious intervention are everywhere lacking. Perhaps also because somebody desires this explosive eruption ...' Holstein to Prince Bülow, 20 November 1908. Rogge, *Holstein und Harden*, 396.

93. Hull, *Entourage*, 142–43.

94. Wilhelm II's involvement in the scandal surrounding Moltke and Eulenburg became particularly evident in the course of the pertinent trials. The emperor was also always indirectly present. Harden had at least considered subpoenaing the crown prince. Uwe B. Weller, 'Maximilian Harden und die "Zukunft"', *Deutsche Presseforschung*, 13 (Bremen 1970), 188. On the plan to serve a summons on the emperor – which was intended to turn him against Harden, see 'Fürst Eulenburg', *Fränkischer Kurier*, 16 May 1908.

95. 'An emperor is great as emperor; it is his imperial actions that matter and not those in his private life, historically and politically speaking, that is'. Rudolf Kassner, *Von den Elementen historischer Größe* (Leipzig, 1911), 50.

96. Weller, *Maximilian Harden*, 185.

97. John B. Thompson, *Political Scandal: Power and Visibility in the Media Age* (Cambridge, 2000).

98. Lynn Hunt, *The Family Romance of the French Revolution* (Berkeley and Los Angeles, 1992).

99. Röhl, *Wilhelm II. Der Aufbau*, passim.

100. Heinrich Binder, *Die Schuld des Kaisers* (Munich, 1919), 15.

Part IV

Visual Metamorphoses

13

The 'Berlin' Nefertiti Bust

Imperial Fantasies in Twentieth-Century German Archaeological Discourse

Claudia Breger

E uropean modernity defines itself in part as the time in which
kings (and queens) were dethroned and decapitated. This
implies, however, not so much that royalty lost its central
socio-symbolic position but rather that it gained other contours – in
literature, culture and science. Connoted as 'traditional' and
'premodern', monarchs serve to a certain degree as figures of alterity
in the European modern imagination. One sign of this royal distance
from the modern norm(ality) is the gender trouble ascribed to
courtly life. In the discourses of bourgeois self-empowerment,
which gained their contours from the eighteenth century on in part
with the help of the rhetoric of 'natural' masculinity, the courtly
practices of self-representation were recoded as feminine – and, by
association, sexually deviant.[1] In addition, ethnic difference is also
closely related to the attribution of historical alterity in European
modern thought. Ethnography and archaeology, the sciences which
helped to shape the contours of modern European identities in the
nineteenth century by offering counter-images and images of
origins, associate the 'other' with the 'old', the 'traditional' or the
'uncivilised'.[2] The 'other' culture thus becomes the realm of kings.
As Hollywood occasionally reminds us, today the figure of the king
as such harbours a more or less latent 'oriental despot'.[3] In the
context of modern debates about identity and power, these 'other'
kings serve as figures both of the problematic of power and
domination and that of (lost) greatness, grandeur and splendour.

One stage upon which the dichotomy between the ('anti-progressive') Orient and (Western) modernity develops – and is, at the same time, complicated – is the discoursivisation of pharaonic Egypt, which produced the stone sculptures and gold treasures that served as a continuous source of fascination for the scientific community as well as the public in the twentieth century. This Egyptian – and Egyptological – terrain has a very complex position in the topography of European modernity. While Egypt served in European memory up until the eighteenth century as a land of (one's 'own') cultural heritage, this high estimation was rewritten – though not completely replaced – by a discourse around 1800 that eroticised Egypt. On the one hand, Egypt was now perceived as part of the 'Orient', which, following Herder, could be idealised as a source of European culture that was inevitably past, and that could be dominated culturally and politically in the present. On the other hand, during a time of increasing racist codification, this land on the 'Black' continent was differentiated from the central Asian territories under consideration in the 'Aryan' genealogy of European peoples.[4] But it was not quite possible to bring the land of the pharaohs under political, scientific or imaginary control. The military failure of Napoleon's soldiers on the Nile may have contributed to the representation of the scientific 'conquest' of Egyptian monuments – initiated by Napoleon's troops – as a situation in which the *conquistadors* were themselves overpowered by the force of sublime historical ruins.[5] The lasting impact of older discourses on Egypt as well as the European iconography of Africa (as a 'wild' continent) also interfered with the fantasies of European dominance. While European colonial discourses characteristically feminise the 'other' culture, the monumentality of the pyramids, obelisks and the (ambiguously gendered) sphinx added a 'masculine' touch to these cultural relics. As a result, Egyptological texts convey highly ambivalent fantasies of 'phallic' female rulers (for example the figure of Cleopatra or simply Rider Haggard's *She*). In the course of the twentieth century this imaginary configuration has been newly displaced. As the historiographic paradigm of progress which had encouraged the devaluation of 'conservative' Egypt lost its legitimacy, a process of 'reclaiming' the Egyptian 'heritage' (as a world culture, i.e. a European heritage) set in, which culminated in the contemporary boom in Egyptological theories of 'cultural memory'.[6] This did not mean, however, that racist differentiations were completely erased.

No less complex than the position of ancient Egypt in the intellectual topographies of modern Europe is the position of archaeology in the modern *dispositif* of the arts and sciences. Like ethnography or history, archaeology is a science of the other (the 'foreign' and/or earlier) culture. However, in comparison to ethnography, a discipline that gains its legitimacy through fictions of cultural contact, or to modern European history, which operates with a stronger affinity for the concept of continuity, archaeology's precondition is the lack of just such a presence or continuity. Foucault's use of the archaeological metaphor for his intervention in historiographical contexts[7] reflects the potential affinity of the discipline – given its search for what is lost and gone, buried, fragmentary remnant – to projects that deconstruct identities. Long before the late twentieth century, the self-understanding of the discipline was influenced by the methodological paradigm of active reconstruction.[8] While archaeology as a discipline can thus be said to bear certain affinities to postcolonial paradigms, it has on the other hand also taken active part in the construction of imperialist thought and activity in the last two hundred years. The archaeological objects in European (and North American) metropolitan museums lend the countries of origin and the appropriating countries metonymic re-presentation. The choice of objects, their classification and presentation contribute to the construction of the alterity of 'foreign' cultures and 'other' times, which simultaneously functions as a medium for constructing modern Western identities.[9] Framed by scholarly and popular texts about their cultural context and artistic value, and, above all, by the archaeological process of their discovery,[10] these objects function as the focus of and a medium for imperial(ist) fantasies – as I would like to show here with the example of the famous Nefertiti bust in the Egyptian Museum in Berlin.

My use of the term 'imperialist fantasies' implies the proposition that even beyond the reach of overt colonial or imperialist activities, the culture of European modernity is influenced by structures of thought (and action) that subject non-European cultures and peoples to European authority and domination. These fantasies, as they are developed in literature and film as well as archaeology and ethnography, contribute substantially to shaping individual and collective identities which are (literally and/or metaphorically) 'imperialist'. In this process, the use of royal/imperial figures from 'other' places can play a central role, as I will show. Because the period of overt colonial activity by German and German-speaking countries encompassed a relatively short period, the history of German imperialist fantasies has long been neglected. In contrast to Edward Said's thesis that the lack of actual German colonies (at least up until 1871) made German discourses about non-European cultures 'more abstract, scholarly, and by implication, less powerful' than their French and British equivalents, Susanne Zantop has argued that German colonial fantasies gained their specific power as '*Handlungsersatz*, as substitute for the real thing, as imaginary testing ground for colonial action'[11] and thus helped to prepare its ground. I am interested here in the time *after* Germany's colonial period, of which something similar can be argued: the production of imperialist fantasies, which has continued throughout the twentieth century, functions as both a substitute for concrete imperialist activities and simultaneously as a continuation of them, for example in the field of archaeology.

In the realm of archaeology, imperialist fantasies are shaped in no small measure by popular reports on the excavations – paradigmatically embodied by Howard Carter's report on how he broke the pharaonic seal at the entrance of Tutankhamen's tomb. He describes how he inserted his torch, illuminating the 'wonderful things' inside: gold objects arranged – in both a real and an imaginary way – around the wrapped body of the dead king. These stories are, of course, stories about gender and sexuality, race and 'civilisation', power and domination. Through the process of the excavation and interpretation of old kings, the new heroes, the archaeologists, are conferred a royal dignity – not one associated with an authority that has been handed down, but rather a dignity of an 'other' type of sovereignty that has been gained through the heroic fight against established limits and recognised authorities. They are men of the frontier whose identities, as in the American Westerns, are constituted in the act of transgressing (geographic and legal) borders.[12] Thus, in his classic text *Götter, Gräber and Gelehrte*, C.W. Ceram (i.e. the German journalist Kurt Marek) writes, as stated in the subtitle of his book, the 'novel on archaeology' as a story about shady adventurers, who are notoriously in conflict with both the European and the local authorities and who compete with both ancient and modern tomb raiders.[13] In the footsteps of Napoleon, whose military excursion to the Nile initiated the scientific exploration of ancient Egyptian culture, they are unmistakably portrayed as the new 'conquistadors'.[14] Their conquest, however, is a 'conquest of the intellect'.[15] Since Napoleon's undertaking in Egypt was a military failure, scholarly domination became a substitute for rather than a complement to political control – at least according to Ceram's novel (first published in 1949), which presents the history of archaeology after the end of the Nazi period as an 'alternative', quasi-pacifist way of heroically entering into the big, wide world (largely ignoring, as it were, the British protectorate in Egypt and the French control over the *Department des Antiquités*). Thus, the archaeological colonisers, distinguished by their fight to preserve the relics of 'old' cultures, discover their 'cultural mission' as the explorers of 'universal history' (*Weltgeschichte*).[16] And the fantasy of this heroic task is doubtless a central facet of the archaeological adventure's appeal. In their specific scholarly form, the imperialist projects of German archaeology could be carried on without reservation not only after the end of the colonial period in 1918/19 but also after 1945 – in the service of re/constructing a cultural and national identity. The immense and lasting success of Ceram's *Roman der Archäologie*[17] indicates the cultural significance of archaeological imperialist fantasies in the postcolonial period – and specifically in post-fascist Germany. Among the ruins of the *Kulturnation* (in a literal and a metaphorical sense) the time of the archaeological hero arrives – whose specialty, after all, is the rubble of grandeur. He may find sheep grazing 'where kings once ruled', but the ruins in which he digs with his spade are witness to 'greatness, splendour and past magnificence'.[18]

In this context I would now like to discuss the politics – both material and phantasmatic – of the German appropriation of the colourful 'Berlin' bust of Nefertiti. Nefertiti was the famous wife of a no less famous husband, the pharaoh of the eighteenth dynasty who called himself Akhenaten and whose religious and cultural reforms made him a favourite among the Egyptologists at the turn of the twentieth century, as I will further explicate below. The Nefertiti bust, which has become the landmark of Berlin's Egyptian Museum (and of Berlin's cultural landscape), was found during an excavation by the German Orient Society led by Ludwig Borchardt in 1912/13. The history of this excavation and the transport of the bust to Berlin unfold at the margins of the law, in accordance with the topoi of heroic archaeology mentioned above in the context of Ceram's best-selling novel. After the official unveiling of the bust in the 1920s, controversy arose when a representative of the Egyptian government demanded the return of the bust, a demand that was repeated often in subsequent years. According to Philipp Vandenberg in his bestseller *Nofretete. Eine archäologische Biographie*, the 'coup' was 'adventurous and beyond comparison' with which Borchardt tricked the Egyptian administrators of ancient artefacts into underestimating the value of the bust during the division of the find prescribed by law after the excavation. Vandenberg's words are meant less as a critique than as a means of characterising colonial heroes.[19] Does the 'case of Nerfertiti' show that the excavators were in fact grave robbers?

Gert v. Paczensky and Herbert Ganslmayr's documentation of the events in their 1984 book *Nofretete will nach Hause* poses the more fundamental question of how European museums profited from the art treasures of colonised countries – as well as what the political consequences of this historical process should be. They conclude that the events leading to the division of the excavation find, as well as the question of whether or not there was a 'deliberate deception', can no longer be adequately reconstructed.[20] But at least one thing is certain based on the museum's files: the circumstances which led to the bust not being shown for over ten years after its discovery, despite the fact that a larger exhibition in 1913/14 presented to the public the results of the Amarna digs, can be traced back to an explicit policy initiated by Borchardt to keep the excavation find a secret.[21] Given this, the question of the legality of the transfer of the bust to Germany becomes more pressing – unless one wants to accept the even more adventurous alternative explanation for Borchardt's worries, which is based on the circumstance that on the day of the excavation of the bust, his royal highness Prince Johann Georg and Princess Mathilde von Sachsen were visiting the site. According to this story, Borchardt had the piece 'faked, buried and dug up again on December 6 in order to impress the visitors, who had announced their arrival in advance, with the discovery of a colourful showpiece'.[22] In any case, 'Cairo reacted with astonishment and indignation'[23] when the bust was finally presented to the public in 1924.[24] In the ensuing controversy the Egyptian claim on the basis of the available documents and the agreement from 1912 could not be legally established, and the subsequent recurring proceedings on the subject emphasised the legitimacy rather than the legality of the bust transfer.[25] On this matter the museum was no more judicious at the turn of the twenty-first century than in the 1920s, and the bust has remained in Berlin to this day.

Long located at the Egyptian Museum in Berlin-Charlottenburg, the collection will be transferred to the Museumsinsel in Berlin-Mitte after reconstruction work is finished there.[26] At the Egyptian museum, the bust is exhibited in a separate room in which the otherwise plain, dark-grey walls are bare but for a description of the bust translated into several languages, and a memorial plaque for James Simon,[27] the sponsor of the excavation campaign, explaining that he donated the bust to the museum. Separated from the rest of the Amarna collection, a warm light illuminates the colourful bust, which is kept at a distance from viewers behind glass and an additional, thin rope. It is positioned such that viewers can admire the 'queenly thing' from all sides. Otherwise the room contains only two benches that invite viewers to contemplate the work. With recourse to James Clifford's description of the 'art-culture system' of the post/colonial *dispositif* as a square with corners designated 'art' and 'culture' (in the wider anthropological sense), 'not art' and 'not culture',[28] this installation can be interpreted as singling out the Nefertiti bust as an (authentic) 'work of art' from a display of historical 'culture', which is presented by the arrangement of the rest of the Amarna collection in a (more) ethnographic perspective.[29] In comparison to the remnants of a past culture, the documentation of which allows the museum visitors a glimpse of 'exotic' rituals and ancient ways of thinking,[30] the limestone bust – 'as atypical for its time as its time is atypical for ancient Egyptian art and religion'[31] – becomes a constituent part of transhistorically valid (universal) art. In this way the bust helps to negotiate, displace and mediate Egypt's ambiguous, overdetermined position on the historical map of European intellectuals.

The room next door documents the history of the work of art – including that of its excavators and the scholars who studied it. A display case exhibits photographs, Borchardt's diary (which is opened to the page on which he reports the find), an open box of index cards, as well as a few smaller pieces from the find: metonyms of a heroic excavation event. The informational plaques on the 'modern history' of the bust make the claim that Egyptian authorities showed no interest in it during the legal proceedings which divided up the find between the excavators and the Egyptians, and that only later when the bust became world famous did the controversy ensue. The museum's narrative of legitimisation is not uninteresting from the perspective of the history of discourses. Taking this narrative at face value means restoring contingency to the alleged timeless beauty of the bust. The assignment of a status that distinguishes 'our' Nefertiti from the continuum of ancient Egyptian culture has, in fact, a history; it is the effect of a socio-symbolically overdetermined process of ascription that is closely related to the process of material appropriation. Perhaps on first view some of those involved perceived the bust as lacking a unique artistic value[32] and therefore as second-rate. After all, it was possibly unfinished (the bust has only one eye) and is apparently merely a model. Furthermore, with its bright colours, it provided flashy evidence of the multiple colours used in ancient art, the theoretical recognition of which researchers of antiquity had long struggled over in the nineteenth century.[33] Borchardt defended himself with the claim that he did not immediately recognise the full (presumably objective) value of the bust,[34] a formulation which, however, does not correspond to the pathos which he creates in his diary entry. In his *Porträts der Königin Nofretete*, in which the excavator wants to make the bust 'generally known',[35] Borchardt situates his individual pathos in the context of diverging evaluations of the portrait as a 'work of art':

> I have never heard an evaluation that was somehow disparaging, but often expressions of enthusiasm. For one person the bust is the highest expression of ancient Egyptian art, for another it extends beyond all limitations of time and space, yet another holds it to be one of the most magnificent works which is lacking, however, in that which he calls 'quality', though I cannot identify, despite my great effort to do so, what he means to express with the word quality ... Observing this work of art, anyone who has a feeling for art will have an individual perception of it ... I will therefore limit myself to an exclamation from my diary: 'Description does no good, you must look at it!'[36]

The location of the bust in the art-culture system occurs here with recourse to the 'omnipotence of the aesthetic gaze', which functions in an individualised way and which measures the success of one's social education in tastes.[37] In the 'wide field' of post/colonial space, this undertaking proves to be precarious. What constitutes quality?

In 1930 the bust was almost given back to Cairo. After the failure of earlier attempts to employ moral and practical measures to force the return of the bust to Egypt (e.g. by refusing to grant further concessions for digs), an offer for an exchange was submitted which had been agreed upon taking the German demands into account. In early April, reports in nationwide and local Berlin newspapers declared that the negotiations had almost come to a close. In these reports, the position formulated 'in museum circles' was almost unanimously adopted, i.e. that the art works offered in exchange for the Nefertiti bust, including a statue of Ranofer from the ancient empire, were in fact more valuable than the bust. The exchange was thus said to be advantageous for the Germans.[38] When controversy ensued in the following weeks concerning the exchange of the bust, James Simon, who felt himself to have a certain authority in this matter due to his sponsorship of the piece, also urged the Germans to accept the exchange. Although the bust may have a 'certain affective value', he said, its 'popularity among a large audience' should not be conflated with the 'unanimous judgment of the real experts'.[39]

The 'colourful Nefertiti' appeared to be a favourite among, above all, the people (who had, by implication, an aesthetically unsophisticated taste). This cannot be said unequivocally, however, given that the newspapers reporting on the bust in April 1930 did not all report the same story in relation to its reputed popularity: 'One would like to believe that a large audience is taking leave' of the Nefertiti every day, wrote Karl Escher in an article entitled 'Visiting a Queen' in the *Berliner Morgenpost* on 11 April 1930, '[b]ut no, she stands there all alone', unapproachable behind her glass dome. Just two days before, however, the *Deutsche Zeitung* had reported a great throng of visitors in the new museum, apparently in response to the nationwide press about the planned exchange; and the stereotypical reference to the great 'popularity' of the bust returned in the news reports. The bust was celebrated in Berlin as having 'great success in the women's world' and as having 'received the honor of roses being laid down' in front of it (*Der Tag*, 8 April 1930). Thus already in 1930 the bust was discursively created as the 'star object'[40] which it still is today in the Berlin museum.

The concept of a 'star' is to be taken quite literally in this context. It refers to a second mode of reception of the bust, which overlaps in a complex and precarious way with the assignment of a status as timeless 'art' and which is conveyed via the positioning of the object in the exhibition as described above. A museum visitor of average height is presented with the carefully lit bust at an angle from below, which lends the face 'something majestic', as Borchardt remarked.[41] The bust is thus exhibited as the royal object of a modern cult. Within these perimeters, the ancient artefact, which according to ethnographic research was possibly used for religious purposes, takes on a contemporary status as post-secular, transcendental majesty: as a ruling instance in the (media) empire of the audience, the star becomes the successor of the royal majesties, who have often been deposed in the art and culture of modernity. Like the monarchs (at least according to Kantorowicz's classic representation of early modern political theology, the topoi of which have been cited and recontextualised in various ways in modern texts), the star has two (textual) bodies which interact in complex ways. Richard Dyer has described the 'total star text' as a 'hall of mirrors' in which the body of the 'star-as-image' (created in the interplay between role images) is closely interwoven with the body of the 'star-as-real-person' through a series of mirror-relations.[42] Of course these two bodies cannot be equated with those of the king in early modern theory. But even Kantorowicz associated the legal theorem he analysed with 'one of the most startling features of royal duplication contrived in modern times: the rites connected in France with the king's effigy' which were integrated into fifteenth-century French burial ceremonies.[43] According to Kantorowicz, these effigies can be read as the visualisation of the otherwise invisible 'political body' of the king, a symbol of immortal dignity. The image, studded with insignia, is accordingly honoured as an embodiment of royal authority, as a 'holy image'.[44] The body images of stars are not invested with the artificial decoration of political insignia. Typically presented in close-up shots of their faces as a sign of 'natural' individuality, they transfer the authority of these royal images into a modern order. This order displaces the charisma of royal power from Europe's castles to Hollywood's villas and from the discursive spaces of political institutions to those of 'natural' humanity – or, according to the dominant gender coding of the star-spectacle, femininity.[45] Their doubled *natural* body creates the historical vanishing point of a problematic, which Kantorowicz refers to as the 'human background'[46] of the burial ceremonies: the theory of the immortality of dignity heightens the perception of a 'discrepancy between the transience of the flesh and the immortal splendour of a Dignity which that flesh was supposed to represent'.[47] The science and culture of the following centuries have been obsessively preoccupied with fantasies of overcoming this discrepancy – with mechanisms for extending and preserving life in order to make the 'natural' body a reliable vehicle for sovereignty. Thus the eternal 'natural' second body of the stars, created with the help of plastic surgery and photography, should not be understood as merely 'mortal'; its presentation with the camera represents a new mode of making the king's double body transcendental. The star's reception, which raises the person depicted out of the timeframe of natural deterioration and phantasmatically makes them immortal, transforms them into a higher, hyper/natural being.[48]

The newspapers from 1930 were aware of the potential inherent in such figures of royal stardom, and thus the (image of) Nefertiti became the new monarch for the people of the Weimar Republic who had just been 'robbed' of their emperor. They never tired of personifying the bust, whereby the attribute of the 'queen' competed with that of (today's) 'woman'.[49] The cult object was thus not to leave Berlin, according to the newspapers in 1930, particularly given the 'state authorities' all too intentional sell-out of the art treasures of the former royal houses'.[50] In the *Berliner Börsenzeitung* on 11 June 1930 the bust was described in one of the most telling formulations of the press campaign against the exchange as the 'most precious ... stone in the setting of the diadem' from the art treasures of 'Prussia-Germany'.[51] On 22 June, the decision not to accept the exchange was published.[52] In the name of a nation whose contours were established in possession of monarchical art treasures, and with the consumption of them in museums, the position prevailed that the Nefertiti bust belonged along the Spree River. The 'national meaning' of the painted stone was formulated in the press occasionally with consideration of the Egyptian point of view, but at the same time Germany's claim to it always won out: 'we should recognise the Egyptian art administrator's sense for quality and their national feelings, but we should not be put second to them'.[53] As a valuable piece from the 'Prussian-German' Diadem (i.e. a sign of Hellenistic, late Roman and Byzantine imperial dignity), the bust was to help re/figure German national identity as imperial after 1918.

In this way the object in the museum became a 'metonym of the state'[54]: the 'colourful queen' functioned as an insignia of national identity. This appropriation of the bust was not restricted to the Weimar Republic, but could also be applied to the Federal Republic, the successor state to Prussia. This is exemplified, for example, in a lecture by Reinhard Mußgnug for the Berlin Juridical Society in 1976. By this date, the bust had become the object of diplomatic debates between the two German states. During the Second World War it had been stored in Thuringia, but by 1945 it made its way back to Berlin via Wiesbaden, thus landing in what was to become West Germany. Citing the 'Haag Convention for the protection of cultural goods in armed conflicts', in the 1970s the German Democratic Republic demanded rights to the artwork because it had earlier been located on its territory.[55] Mußgnug dismisses the East German claims. In order to do so, he refers, with the intention 'to learn from the state's practices in similar cases', to the 'treasures and insignia of the Holy Roman Empire of the German Nation, above all the crown of Charlemagne'.[56] This crown had, as he claims, arrived in Vienna's Hofburg during the wars following the French Revolution 'in exactly the same manner' as the Nefertiti arrived in Charlottenburg,[57] and it had stayed there despite repeated attempts to reclaim it. Introduced as an example, the imperial insignia become a metaphor for the meaning of Nefertiti at the moment when Mußgnug relates historical arguments directly to the topic of his lecture: 'According to this view of things, the former location implies no rights, especially when in this location, 'new symbols' have been created with the hammer and sickle and new signs of world class status with Olympic gold medals.'[58] In this disagreement between the two Germanys, the royal metonymy of Prussian–German identity becomes an indirect sign for the Federal Republic's adherence to the Prussian cultural tradition. This kind of functionalisation of the Nefertiti bust, which is, for example, also reproduced in a 1989 series of German postage stamps, is not limited to 'conservative' or nationalistic discourses. In the 1999 election campaign, to take another example, a reproduction of the Nefertiti bust appeared on a poster for the Greens/Bündnis 90 as a promise for a cosmopolitan, potentially multicultural and egalitarian city – with the slogan: 'Strong women for Berlin!'[59]

But what produced the extraordinary attraction of the bust as a sign of national identity, which was recreated again and again throughout the twentieth century with recourse to an imperial(ist) imaginary? One aspect of the genealogy of its fame is undoubtedly the context created in the 1920s with the sensational Tutankhamen excavation. The glowing gold treasures dug up by Howard Carter and his team called forth not only an international wave of more intensive Egyptomania, but also a national(ist) wave of irritation with the great fortune of the British 'gold diggers'. In this trans/national game, which discursively produced 'ancient Egyptian mass suggestion',[60] 'Prussia-Germany' was able to score points with the Nefertiti bust, whose colourfulness had a similar effect as that of the Tutankhamen gold – which was itself of suspect taste on a scale of 'high culture' norms.[61] But to the misfortune of the Brits, Nefertiti, unlike Tutankhamen, did not land in Cairo. A few years after the German empire's colonial period of 'catching up' was forced to an end, international competition in the field of Egyptology continued. And Germany, the German press insisted, was in a position to prove its significance as a *Kulturnation*.[62]

But perhaps even more important to the development of the bust's fame – and its continued status today – was the role played by the bust in twentieth-century discourse on the Amarna, i.e. Akhenaten's period of reform. After his archaeological 'rediscovery' in the course of the nineteenth century,[63] this pharaoh, whose name is missing in the written historical records, became an important node of identificatory visions for Egyptologists and enthusiasts in an otherwise 'foreign' ancient Egyptian cultural history. His seemingly radical revision of traditional ideas made him an anomaly in the Egyptian cultural continuum as it was perceived by Orientalists, and it made it possible to associate him with progress and modernity.[64] The earlier monographs on Akhenaten, which significantly shaped the reception of him in the first half of the twentieth century, praise him for being the 'first individual in human history'[65] and stylise his teachings as the 'prototype' of Christianity.[66] The appropriation of this figure implied an exclusion of Judaism from the genealogy of monotheism.[67] Having been 'Aryanised'[68] by the presupposition of an 'Asian' lineage,[69] Akhenaten found a place not only in the early twentieth-century literary avant-garde,[70] but also in German and European fascism.[71] In comparison to the 'Black Egyptian darkness', he shone '[l]ike a flash of blinding light'.[72]

But from the beginning this discursive construction was offset by the 'shadows' cast on the figure of 'the ruling sun', which constantly confused the archaeologists and made them perform endless hermeneutic tasks. The art of the Amarna period appeared to show the pharaoh in a 'womanish and bizarre shape'. With his 'elegantly curved, swan-like neck', his 'wide hips', 'swollen breasts', and 'full thighs', the men on the dig could hardly distinguish him from his wife Nefertiti.[73] However, within the perimeters of the discursive appropriation of the Amarna period as 'Egyptian modernity', this art was deemed 'realistic' and (according to the rules of bourgeois intimacy) 'natural' – in contrast to the otherwise austere aesthetic of representing rulers in Egyptian art. Given the contemporary norm of masculinity, which corresponds better to the heroism of traditional Egyptian art than to the representation of Akhenaten, his body became a problem for the archaeologists to the extent that the realism thesis held (and still holds today). As the quote above shows, the subject of gender dominated the discourse of pathology which evaluated his 'oddness'. The subject of 'race', which was used as a means of distinguishing Akhenaten, was left out here. That race played, however, an unconscious role can be read in a comparison of the iconography of Jewish and Black masculinities – as well as in reference to the reception of this figure in Black movements from the Harlem Renaissance to contemporary ghetto art.[74]

The tensions inherent in the appropriation of Akhenaten for modern European fantasies of domination lend this 'most remarkable of all the Pharaohs'[75] an apparently irresolvable ambivalence which condenses in his reputed 'ugliness'. The 'Berlin' Nefertiti bust, the 'beautiful one who has come',[76] on the other hand, offered possibilities for displacement and an imaginary resolution to this problematic. My thesis is that the central position of the Nefertiti bust in the Egyptological discourse of the twentieth century cannot be separated from the complications related to the figure of Akhenaten as outlined above. In the representative configuration outlined here, he serves as Nefertiti's shadow in the background (see Figure 13.1, in which this configuration is visualised) or as her precarious sidepiece. Indeed, in the current exhibition of the Charlottenburg museum discussed above, a largely disintegrated Akhenaten bust, which is still extremely fragile in its 'restored' condition,[77] is positioned at the side entrance to the room that is dedicated entirely to the Nefertiti bust.

Figure 13.1 Cover plate of the exhibition catalogue *Nofretete Echnaton*, Ägyptisches Museum Berlin 1976.

The 'Berlin' bust serves to constitute the extraordinary beauty of the queen – somewhat androgynous, but in comparison to her husband identifiably gendered – as a perfect combination of exotic and yet familiar, i.e. 'European' characteristics. The press coverage of the proposed exchange in 1930 manifests this, for example, in the story on a 'cheeky teenage girl' who reacted to the bust by commenting that underneath the crown of the 'brown Egyptian queen', her hair was probably styled in a fashionable bob.[78] As an 'image of woman that seems to belong to neither a specific time nor place',[79] the bust fills in the abyss which was a constant threat in the attempted appropriation of the Egyptian pharaoh by the imperialist imagination. It is no surprise in this context that speculations about Nefertiti's 'Asian' lineage were even more persistent than those about Akhenaten.[80] Thanks to her appeasing looks, the limestone queen was perfectly suited to function within the *dispositif* of realism into which Amarna art had fallen during its modern reception. As suggested above, the relationship between the two bodies of the royal figures in this *dispositif* had taken on a new quality. While Kantorowicz's early modern texts give an abstract account of the inseparability of the two bodies[81] (the body politic being ultimately invisible), by 'in-built means of authentication'[82] the two 'natural' bodies of the stars are enclosed in a hall of mirrors, where their reflections mutually constitute their identity. In other words: 'Stars are a particular instance of the supposed relation between a photograph and its referent', the incorporation of an 'existential bond'[83] secured by 'an infinite regress by means of which one more authentic image displaces another'.[84] Unlike the representations of her husband, Nefertiti's limestone image did not produce fantasies of pathologised 'gender trouble'. It thus made possible the appropriation of the Amarna period in the form of an (eternally young) object of German (male heterosexual) desire, and as such ultimately advanced the bust of Nefertiti as the 'legitimate' royal representative of the German *Kulturnation*.

Even Hitler is said to have particularly admired the Nefertiti bust.[85] Its functionalisation for fascist discourse, which built upon the Amarna reception of the early twentieth century, can be pursued in a series of narrative texts from the 1930s[86] which negotiate the tensions inscribed into the figure of Akhenaten by framing the narrative of his greatness and failure with a story about the colourful bust of Nefertiti. The fantasies developed in these texts, however, also point to the complexities which haunt the production of the royal star object as an object whose bodies are bound together in a relation of identity in the imperialist realm – a realm structured by the categories of race and gender. For example, Max Kronberg's novel *Nofretete* (first published in 1934) portrays Akhenaten as a great artist and intellectual and spiritual leader whose 'unmanly' pacifism, however, threatens to destroy the Egyptian empire (it is not surprising that this topos is the focus of fascist Akhenaten reception).[87] The empire is saved only because Haremheb, the 'loyal soldier', takes over rule and is able to halt the further disintegration of the provinces as well as the intrigues of the murderous Amun priests. This historical plot is framed by the story of the bust. At the beginning of the novel, Akhenaten commissions the artist Thutmes to create a 'true to life' portrait of his wife. But the representational function of the bust is in vain: By the time the portrait is finished, the queen's beauty has been compromised by her grief over the disastrous politics of her husband. The bust thus remains in the artist's studio – until the soldiers in the service of the Amun priests throw it into the pit from which archaeologists will later recover it. But even these soldiers, who are described as 'vandals', have some respect and a sense of taste such that the bust is only minimally damaged – unlike the bust of Akhenaten, which the German excavators of the twentieth century will find in pieces next to the Nefertiti.

In resolving the Amarna problematic, Kronberg's historical narrative does not simply contrast the 'beautiful' woman with the 'ugly' king, but also Nefertiti's eternal (naturalistic) body in art with her original 'natural' body, which is surrendered to its death in a double sense. After the loss of her beauty, Nefertiti, whom Haremheb loves, sacrifices herself by the end so that he may remain pure and fulfil his duties. Thus 'the beautiful one who has come' survives only as an art object in a Berlin museum, signifying the dominance of male archaeologists over the historical real. She does not survive, however, as an (imaginary) living representative of a history or a culture which is not exhausted by an archaeological perspective, or as a (feminine coded) alternative to the military sacrifice of the soldier's body. In relation to the above-mentioned French burial rites, Kantorowicz notes that the use of the image adds a 'triumphal element' to the ceremony.[88] In Kronberg's novel the two 'heterogeneous ideas' which are brought together here, the 'triumph of death' and the 'triumph over death',[89] are clearly allocated to the figures of the Egyptian woman and the European archaeologist. This phantasmatic configuration of death and survival is not limited to fascist discourses; it is also found in modern European imperialist fiction. This literature shows that in nineteenth- and twentieth-century discourses, survival is closely tied to certain gendered and racial positions identified with exceptional humanity. This complicates the formula for the star script described by Dyer: not only do critical deconstructive performances produce differences between the bodies of the stars, but so does the ideological-normative interplay of bodies. Perhaps the paradigmatic figure of this difference in Egyptological discourse is the mummy.

Since the nineteenth century, the Egyptian techniques for mummification, i.e. the preservation of the 'natural' body, have been one of the main sources of public fascination with the pharaohs. This practice of simulating life was a very ambivalent affair – for example in Karl Freund's classic film *The Mummy* from 1933, in which Boris Karloff plays the role of a crumpled up and crumbling 'ancient' Egyptian who is brought back from the dead, or in the 1999 Hollywood film of the same title, in which the mummy is reconfigured with recourse to the iconography of the *Alien* films as a more 'juicy' figure. In their half-rotten state, the undead mummies with uncanny abilities embody both the limits of creating life, which at the level of plot is related to 'ancient' Egyptian magic – i.e. the realm of the 'other' – and also the archaeological enterprise of deciphering this magic. Furthermore, the project of creating (the semblance of) life is metaphorically related also to the medium of film, which has itself been theorised in terms of a 'mummy complex'.[90] At the turn of the twenty-first century, however, this set of motifs has been displaced. In the 1999 mummy productions, and above all in the 2001 sequel (*The Mummy Returns*), the point of emphasis in the fiction of the undead monster is displaced onto the perfect body of an Egyptian man, who according to the plot is regenerated (not unlike a vampire) by the juices and organs of the mummy's victims (in part one this happens gradually throughout the film, in part two the process is accelerated). In this fiction, the 'ancient Egyptian' – a figure in which the markings of 'European' history, 'Oriental' origins and the 'African'-barbarian other are conflated in an uncanny way – is able to break through distinct historical epochs into the fictive world of the twentieth century with the power of a 'natural' male body. In the age of cloning, the transitory nature of life and the differences in the interplay of historical bodies seem to be fictively annulled. If it were not for the intertextual aesthetics of the movie – i.e. its open display of its own reproductive practices – we could conclude that the appropriation of the 'Egyptian' other has reached an imaginary state of perfection in the transhistorical identity of royal masculinity.

In the case of Nefertiti, the process of appropriation is not yet complete. In a summer 2001 article in the academic journal of Egyptology, *KMT*, Susan James presents the 'natural' equivalent to the 'Berlin' bust of Nefertiti. According to her argument, a mummy from the Cairo Museum, usually called the 'Elder Lady' and which has been associated with various historical figures since its excavation, can be identified as Nefertiti. James establishes her interpretation in particular with recourse to new technologies of photographic reconstruction, which allow the 'elegant bone structure, hyperelongated neck, (and) finely formed features'[91] of the mummy to be compared with the facial characteristics of 'various surviving [sic] portrait heads', above all – of course – the 'Berlin' bust of Nefertiti (Figure 13.2).[92] According to James, this method proves not only the probable identity of the 'Elder Lady', but also the naturalism, the 'veracity' of the portrait itself.[93] Although the realism thesis has been increasingly replaced by interpretive considerations of the theological character of Akhaton art in more recent Egyptology publications on the Amarna period,[94] 'harder' scientific methods can still be used to carry on the fiction of archaeological access to the truth of ancient Egypt – and also to perpetuate the imperialist fantasy of the beautiful Nefertiti in the hall of mirrors of her star personae. It is said that a DNA analysis will soon confirm the identity of the mummy. But this would require not only a (conceivable) further perfection of this technology, but also the availability of the 'natural' body of Nefertiti and at least one immediate relative. And considering that the mummy of the 'Elder Lady' is missing at the moment, and Nefertiti's origins are still as controversial among archaeologists as the identity of the other embalmed finds from the Amarna period, presumably this hunt for the identity of the royal body of the 'ancient' Egyptian woman will continue for some time to come.

Translated by Christina White

Figure 13.2 'Bunte Büste' and 'Elder Lady'.

Notes

1. See Thomas A. King, 'Performing "Akimbo": Queer Pride and Epistemological Prejudice', in *The Politics and Poetics of Camp*, ed. Moe Meyer (New York, 1994), 23–50.
2. See Johannes Fabian, *Time and the Other: How Anthropology Makes Its Object* (New York, 1983).
3. See Andy Tennant's *Anna and the King* from 1999.
4. On Orientalism, see Edward Said, *Orientalism* (New York, 1978); on the racist exclusion of Egypt from European history see Martin Bernal, *Black Athena. The Afroasiatic Roots of Classical Civilization*. Vol. 1: *The Fabrication of Ancient Greece 1785–1985* (New Brunswick, 1987).
5. Napoleon is said to have exclaimed to his troops, who were 'overwhelmed' with images of ancient Egyptian relics: 'Soldaten! Vierzig Jahrhunderte blicken auf euch herab!' ('Soldiers! Forty centuries are gazing down upon you!') W. Ceram (a.k.a. Kurt Marek), *Götter, Gräber und Gelehrte. Roman der Archäologie* (Reinbek, 1999), 81, 114.
6. Jan Assmann, *Das kulturelle Gedächtnis. Schrift, Erinnerung und politische Identität in frühen Hochkulturen* (Munich, 1999).
7. See Michel Foucault, *The Archaeology of Knowledge*, trans. A.M. Sheridan Smith (New York, 1972), 7.
8. See Christiane Zintzen, *Von Pompeji nach Troja. Archäologie, Literatur und Öffentlichkeit im 19. Jahrhundert* (Vienna, 1998).
9. See for example Tim Barringer, ed., *Colonialism and the Object. Empire, Material Culture, and the Museum* (New York, 1998).
10. For a paradigmatic example see Howard Carter and A.C. Mace, *The Discovery of the Tomb of Tutankhamen* (Mineola/New York/Dover, 1977 and earlier editions).
11. Susanne Zantop, *Colonial Fantasies. Conquest, Family, and Nation in Precolonial Germany, 1770–1870* (Durham, 1997), 7, 6.
12. See for example Richard Dyer, *White* (New York, 1997), 32ff. on the constitutive ambivalence inscribed in this form of white, imperialist masculinity.
13. Ceram often emphasises the moment of transgressing norms, laws and borders which is related to the archaeological adventure into the 'dark' empires of long-buried epochs (see for example Ceram, *Götter, Gräber und Gelehrte*, 61). Winckelmann's homosexuality (ibid., 29), Belzoni's 'gold-digging methods' (ibid., 120) and Schliemann's 'dubious personality' (ibid., 61) construct the archaeologists as 'outsiders' (ibid., 62). The negative double of the archaeologist is the thief – repeatedly evoked by Ceram as by Carter before him through this analogy. While both figures appropriate royal treasures, Ceram insists that they are distinguished by their different intentions (see ibid., 149 and 173f.).
14. Ibid. 84, 38, see also 63.
15. See Zantop, *Colonial Fantasies*, 31ff.
16. See Ceram, *Götter, Gräber und Gelehrte*, 82f.
17. According to the cover of the German 'anniversary edition' of 1999,

Ceram sold over three million copies of the German edition, and the book was translated into twenty-six languages, making Ceram 'the most successful German non-fiction author'.

18. Ceram, *Götter, Gräber und Gelehrte*, 53.
19. Philipp Vandenberg, *Nofretete. Eine archäologische Biographie* (Bern, 1975), 55.
20. Gert v. Paczensky and Herbert Ganslmayr, *Nofretete will nach Hause. Europa – Schatzhaus der 'dritten Welt'* (Munich, 1984), 266ff., see also Rolf Krauss, '1913–1988: 75 Jahre Büste der NofretEte/Nefretiti in Berlin', *Jahrbuch des Preußischen Kulturbesitzes* XXIV, (1987), 87–124, here 105ff.
21. See Paczensky and Ganslmayr, *Nofretete*, 262, 269.
22. According to Krauss, '1913–1988', 92. Of course, the strange coincidence of the find and the royal visit can also be explained in a more harmless way – for example, that the bust had been found earlier and buried again in order to be dug up to please the royal guests. After a brief hesitation, Krauss dismisses the above rumour – which was not as present in the public debate about Nefertiti as the robbery issue was – with the argument that contemporary analyses (from 1987–88) of the bust would have discovered the lime-gypsum-anhydrous mixture typical of the Amarna period which was unknown at the time of Borchardt's excavation, and, he notes in addition, the plastic form of the bust is largely congruent with another object found during the dig; ibid., 93.
23. Paczensky and Ganslmayr, *Nofretete*, 266.
24. The bust was presented to the public in Borchardt's text on the Nefertiti portrait, dated 1923 but published in 1924, as well as through the exhibition of the bust beginning in March; see Krauss, '1913–1988', 100.
25. See Paczensky and Ganslmayr, *Nofretete*, 289. The subject was brought up again by Egypt not only after the Second World War and the founding of the Federal Republic (see ibid., 299), but again in 1995 when the Egyptian cultural minister suggested the symbolic return of certain art works from Western museums during the planning of a new museum – and in June 2003 when representatives of Egypt protested the bust's use in an artistic installation, which combined the royal head with a naked body; for details see Claudia Breger, *Szenarien kopfloser Herrschaft – Performanzen gespenstischer Macht. Königsfiguren in der deutschsprachigen Literatur und Kultur des 20. Jahrhunderts* (Freiburg/Br., 2004).
26. During the debates about the future of Berlin's museums it was decided in 1990 that the resources of both Egyptian collections should be united in the (war-ravaged) Neues Museum. With the integration of works from the Bodemuseum into the museum in Charlottenburg a temporary solution was found. It is the politics of this exhibition that I discuss with first-hand knowledge.
27. Simon (1851–1932) was a merchant in Berlin and co-founder of the German Orient Society.

28. James Clifford, *The Predicament of Culture: Twentieth Century Ethnography, Literature, and Art* (Cambridge, MA, 1988), 224.

29. This is surely not intended as a pure division. Nonetheless, Clifford's categories for measuring the (post)colonial field are not irrelevant here, as can be seen for example in the fact that the interim solution after Germany's unification at first (from 1994 to 1998) arranged that the Amarna 'art' was exhibited in Charlottenburg and the 'cultural' artefacts in the Bodemuseum. See Dietrich Wildung, 'Späte Offenbarung. Die Neuaufstellung der Berliner Amarna-Sammlung', *Jahrbuch Preußischer Kulturbesitz* XXXI, (1994), 84.

30. The exhibition objects are categorised thematically ('images of royalty', 'the sun god'), and the accompanying texts contribute ethnographic knowledge about the historical figures as well as more general contexts such as 'ancient gods', 'economic life', or 'women and music' [*sic*].

31. Dietrich Wildung, *Ägyptische Kunst in Berlin. Meisterwerke im Bodemuseum und in Charlottenburg. Ägyptisches Museum und Papyrussammlung Staatliche Museen zu Berlin – Preußischer Kulturbesitz* (Mainz, 1999), 30.

32. The function of the bust is still a source of controversy (see Krauss, '1913–1988', 102; Dietrich Wildung, 'Einblicke. Zerstörungsfreie Untersuchungen an altägyptischen Objekten', *Jahrbuch Preußischer Kulturbesitz* XXIX, 133–56, particularly 148 with a reference to another oppositional position represented by Werner Kaiser).

33. See Zintzen, *Von Pompeji nach Troja*, 111ff.

34. See Paczensky and Ganslmayr, *Nofretete*, 291.

35. Ludwig Borchardt, *Porträts der Königin Nofretete. Aus den Grabungen 1912/13 in Tell El-Amarna.* (1923) (Osnabrück, 1968), 1.

36. Ibid., 38.

37. Pierre Bourdieu, *Distinction: A Social Critique of the Judgement of Taste*, trans. Richard Nice (Cambridge, MA, 1984), 61.

38. See the collection of newspaper clippings (which unfortunately end in mid-April 1930) at the Central Archive of Berlin's Staatliche Museen, Preußischer Kulturbesitz (files of the Egyptian Museum, folder of newspaper clippings 1927–49), from which the following citations stem. They are referenced by place of publication and date. Newspaper articles which do not appear in this collection are listed individually in the bibliography. This quote: *Berliner Tageblatt*, evening edition 4 April 1930.

39. Quoted in Paczensky and Ganslmayr, *Nofretete*, 304f.

40. Joyce Tyldesly, *Ägyptens Sonnenkönigin: Biographie der Nofretete*, trans. Christa Broermann and Karin Schuler (Munich 1999), 289.

41. Borchardt, *Porträts der Königin*, 35.

42. Richard Dyer, 'Charisma, *A Star Is Born* and the Construction of Authenticity', in *Stardom: Industry of Desire*, ed. Christine Gledhill (New York, 1991), 57–59, 132–39, specifically 136.

43. Ernst Kantorowicz, *The King's Two Bodies: A Study in Mediaeval Political Theology* (Princeton, 1957), 419–20.

44. Ibid., 427.
45. I describe this displacement and its gender politics in more detail in my reading of the film *Queen Christina*; see Claudia Breger, 'Queens und Kings, oder: Performing Power', *Amerikastudien/American Studies* (special issue on *Queer America*, ed. Katrin Gersdorf and Ralph Poole), 46, 1, (2001), 105–21.
46. Kantorowicz, *The King's Two Bodies*, 436.
47. Ibid., 436.
48. See Dyer, 'Charisma', 57.
49. See for example the *Vossische Zeitung*, 8 April 1930 (morning edition) on the 'emigration of the graceful princess' (to Germany), who has become so 'volkstümlich' because she is 'a woman', or the *Weser-Zeitung* from 9 April, according to which the 'beautiful queen' with the 'very modern face of the greatest nobility' is leaving Germany (*Deutsche Zeitung Berlin*, 9 April).
50. Hermann Schmitz, 'Nefretete, bleibe bei uns!', *Berliner Börsen-Zeitung*, 8 May 1930, 4.
51. See Paczensky and Ganslmayr, *Nofretete*, 302.
52. Apparently, it was made by the Prussian cultural minister together with the general director of the state museums and against the vote of the director of the Egyptian department (see Krauss, '1913–1988', 109f.).
53. Schmitz, *Nefretete*.
54. See Barringer, *Colonialism*, 17, referring to the museum as a whole.
55. Together with a great number of less impressive pieces from the former Preußischer Kulturbesitz (for a brief summary of the debates see Krauss, '1913–1988', 136).
56. Reinhard Mußgnug, *Wem gehört Nofretete? Anmerkungen zu dem deutsch-deutschen Streit um den ehemals preußischen Kulturbesitz* (Lecture held before the Berlin Juridical Society on 1 December 1976) (Berlin and New York, 1977), 29.
57. Ibid.
58. Ibid., 37.
59. In the *tageszeitung*'s coverage of the election campaign, the poster is mentioned as a backdrop to a statement by the Turkish–German candidate for the Lower House, Özcan Mutlu. See Dorothee Winden, 'Nofretete zwinkert für die starken Frauen', *die tageszeitung* 10 September 1999, 20.
60. The German-language newspapers accused the British of creating this mass suggestion. See Judith Wettengel, 'Tutanchamun – das "Riesenshowgeschäft" um den "Superstar aus dem alten Ägypten"', in *Mythos Tutanchamun*, ed. Wolfgang Wettengel (Reimlingen, 2000), 18–45, here 38f.
61. For contemporary evidence of this see Dominic Montserrat, *Akhenaten. History, Fantasy and Ancient Egypt* (London and New York, 2000), 75; and in general Wettengel, *Tutanchamun*.
62. In relation to this, the press coverage of the reopening of the German Institute in Cairo in March of 1924 is interesting, in which the

Vossische Zeitung reports that this event corresponds to 'the role ... played by the German *Kulturnation*' in Egypt. See 'Deutsches Institut in Kairo wiedereröffnet', *Vossische Zeitung*, 16 March 1924.

63. For an overview of the archaeological history of this pharao see Montserrat, *Akhenaten*, 55ff.

64. See ibid., 6.

65. J.H. Breasted, *A History of the Ancient Egyptians* (New York, 1908), 265.

66. Arthur E.P. Weigall, *The Life and Times of Akhnaton, Pharaoh of Egypt* (Edinburgh and London, 1910), 117; see Montserrat, *Akhenaten*, 98ff.

67. See Weigall, *Life and Times of Akhnaton*.

68. See Bernal, *Black Athena*, 383f.

69. See Weigall, *Life and Times of Akhnaton*; Breasted speaks of a white Egyptian-Asian 'race' in general; quoted in Montserrat, *Akhenaten*, 102, 109.

70. Rilke adored the bust of this king and Werfel adapted the *Sonnengesang* attributed to him; see Alfred Grimm, *Rilke und Ägypten* (Munich, 1997).

71. See Montserrat, *Akhenaten*, 108ff.

72. Weigall, *Life and Times of Akhnaton*, 117.

73. According to Cyril Aldred, *Akhenaten. Pharaon of Egypt: A New Study* (London, 1972), 145f.

74. See Sander L. Gilman, *The Jew's Body* (New York, 1991) and *Rasse, Sexualität und Seuche. Stereotype aus der Innenwelt der westlichen Kultur*, trans. Helmut Rohlfing (Reinbek, 1992) on the pathologising of Black and Jewish bodies in nineteenth- and twentieth-century discourses; on the reception of Echnaton in Afro-American and Black British communities see Montserrat, *Akhenaten*, 116ff.

75. Breasted, *A History of the Ancient Egyptians*, 265.

76. 'Nefer' in Nefertiti's name is usually translated as 'beautiful', but the word also evokes associations with wholeness and vitality (Montserrat, *Akhenaten*, 16).

77. It is the bust which is said to have been found next to that of Nefertiti (see Borchardt, *Porträts der Königin*, 6, 31).

78. *Deutsche Zeitung Berlin*, 9 April 1930. The words 'face of an unknown flower' also exoticise the bust (*Berliner Morgenpost* 11 April), but at the same time the 'light brown ... face of a woman' (*Berliner Morgenpost*, 11 April) is apparently also 'just like yesterday and today'; with its 'suggestive, slightly ironic' look – and given a modern hat rather than a royal crown – an explicit analogy has been made to a film diva (*Berliner Zeitung*, 11 April, evening edition).

79. Johannes Guthmann, 'Zum Endkampf um Nofretete. Man soll nicht tauschen!', *Deutsche Allgemeine Zeitung*, 16 May 1930 (evening edition), 2.

80. See for example Vandenberg, *Nofretete*.

81. Kantorowicz, *The King's Two Bodies*, 9.

82. Dyer, *Charisma*, 135.

83. Ibid.
84. Ibid., 136.
85. On the creation of this legend see for example Jeanette Greenfield, *The Return of Cultural Treasures*. 2nd edn. (Cambridge, 1996), 287: 'Story has it ... that Hitler himself upon seeing the bust determined that its obvious Aryan qualities meant that it must stay in Germany'; for an attempted reconstruction of the negotiations to return the bust after 1933, which were apparently hindered by Hitler, see Rolf Krauss, '1913–1988: 75 Jahre Büste der NofretEte/Nefret-iti in Berlin', *Jahrbuch des Preußischen Kulturbesitzes* XXVIII, (1991), 123–57, specifically 123ff.
86. For more detail see Breger, *Szenarien kopfloser Herrschaft*.
87. Max Kronberg, *Nofretete. Roman einer Königin* (Berlin, 1947).
88. Kantorowicz, *The King's Two Bodies*, 423–24.
89. Ibid., 429.
90. I.e. by André Bazin. This subject as well as phantasmatic negotiations of gendered and cultural identity in mummy films from 1933 to 2001 are discussed in detail in: Claudia Breger, 'Alien Egypt, oder: Die Rückkehr der Mumie', in *Techniken der Reproduktion. Medien – Leben – Diskurse*, ed. Ulrike Bergermann, Claudia Breger and Tanja Nusser (Königstein/Ts., 2002).
91. Susan James, 'Who Is the Mummy Elder Lady?', *KMT. A Modern Journal of Ancient Egypt*, 12, 2, (2001), 42–50, specifically 43.
92. Ibid., 47.
93. Ibid., 45.
94. See for example Dorothea Arnold, *The Royal Women of Amarna. Images of Beauty from Ancient Egypt* (with contributions by James P. Allen and L. Green) (New York, 1996), 17ff.

14

Imagined Queens between Heaven and Hell

Representations of Grace Kelly and Romy Schneider

Alexis Schwarzenbach

The very successful movie careers of the actresses Grace Kelly (1928–82) and Romy Schneider (1938–82) both began in the early 1950s. Grace Kelly won an Oscar in 1954 for her part in *Country Girl* and achieved ever-lasting fame because Alfred Hitchcock cast her for *Dial M for Murder, Rear Window* and *To Catch a Thief* (1954–55). Simultaneously European cinema-goers from Spain to Greece were enchanted by Romy Schneider's appearances in the most successful Austrian films ever made, Ernst Marischka's *Sissi* trilogy (1955–57). In German cinemas alone 6.5 million saw the first, 6.4 million the second and 5.8 million the third episode of this romantic costume drama about the life of the Austrian Empress Elisabeth (1837–98).[1] Even today the *Sissi* films are regularly shown on television throughout Europe, thus reaching millions every year.[2] The careers of both Grace Kelly and Romy Schneider were based to a large extent on the successful construction of their public image, their personae. Analysing contemporary newspaper and magazine articles as well as photographs of these two actresses contained in various archives in London, Berlin and Zurich, this article will argue that one of the key features of the personae of both actresses was that they contained strong royal elements.[3] It is the construction and the development of the royal personae of Grace Kelly and Romy Schneider that this article focuses on, not only during the lifetime of the two actresses but also after their almost simultaneous, premature deaths in 1982.

In order to understand the development of the royal personae of
Grace Kelly and Romy Schneider it is necessary to examine the
historical context in which this took place. In the 1950s Grace Kelly
and Romy Schneider were of course not the only women with royal
personae. The most important royal persona of that decade certainly
belonged to the British Queen Elizabeth II. At the death of her father
the 25-year-old ascended the throne in 1952 and quickly became very
popular, both in Britain and abroad. This was not only due to her
youth. Much of the new queen's popularity was based on her
household's efficient publicity management. Especially important was
her coronation in June 1953. The elaborately planned and splendidly
staged event in Westminster Abbey was broadcast globally by means of
the relatively new medium of television. Moreover, a documentary
film was made with royal consent: *A Queen is Crowned*. It too became
an international box-office success.[4]

The enormous international popularity of the young British queen
quickly attracted the attention of the American and the European film
industry. After the coronation of Elizabeth II, a large number of films
appeared centred around the life of a princess, queen or empress. In all
of these films the female protagonist was involved in some sort of
dramatic love story. Although most of these films were based on
historical persons or events, none of them claimed to be historically
accurate, least of all when it came to telling royal love stories. Thus
not only entirely fictional films with royal themes but also those based
on historical facts were films about imagined queens. In the 1950s,
apart from Grace Kelly and Romy Schneider, other actresses such as
Audrey Hepburn (*Roman Holiday*, USA 1953), Jean Simons (*Désirée*,
USA 1954), Ingrid Bergman (*Anastasia*, GB 1956) and Lilli Palmer
(*Anastasia, die letzte Zarentochter*, FRG 1956) successfully played
imagined queens.

Grace Kelly – From American Lady to Princess of Monaco

Grace Kelly's cinema career was short but phenomenally successful.
From 1950 until 1956 she made eleven films, won the most desired
cinema award in the world and by the time she left the film industry
in 1956 she was one of Hollywood's greatest stars.[5] One of the most
important reasons for this splendid career was the successful
construction of her persona by the publicity emanating from her
studio, MGM. During the 1950s the capacity of the Hollywood

studios to generate the persona, or, as it was usually called at the time, the 'image' of a star, was at its peak. Even before actors ever appeared in a movie the studios began to distribute photographs, press releases and gossip about them. The press then communicated these tailor-made personae to potential movie goers, usually without questioning or changing the information with which the studios had provided them.[6]

In 1957 the film historian Thomas Harris analysed all publicity and press material related to the construction of Grace Kelly's persona. This useful study revealed that there were two major themes used by Grace Kelly's studio MGM in the process. Firstly, her respectable family background. Almost no article about Grace Kelly failed to mention the fact that she came from a wealthy, Catholic Philadelphia family and that her father had been successful both in the sports and in the business world. Secondly, most articles about Grace Kelly emphasised her ladylike character. In most cases this was explained as being direct consequence of her privileged background. Interestingly it was Grace Kelly's co-stars who kept on praising her, while the actress herself almost never made a statement about herself. The aim of this publicity strategy was, of course, to show that Grace Kelly was a real lady and as such far too well educated and reserved to make public statements about private matters.[7]

Grace Kelly's off-screen lady persona was reinforced by her film roles. In her most successful films, the ones directed by Alfred Hitchcock – *Dial M for Murder* (1954) *Rear Window* (1954) and *To Catch a Thief* (1955) – she always played an attractive upper-class single woman wearing pearls and carrying a handbag. What Thomas Harris wrote in 1957 is therefore not surprising: 'Terms like "cool", "lady", "genteel", "elegant", "reserved", "patrician" are as frequent in the features and reviews of her film roles as they are in her personal publicity.'[8] Grace Kelly's persona was therefore that of a lady; in other words, she was represented in an aristocratic if not yet in a royal way.

Apart from magazine and newspaper articles, photographs were among the most important means to bolster Grace Kelly's aristocratic persona and to communicate it to the general public. One frequently reproduced image shows the perfect Kelly family 'looking over the wall at their Ocean City House', as one contemporary caption stated (Figure 14.1).[9] This, of course, reinforced the theme of her family's affluence, as only rich people were able to afford a house in a fashionable beach resort. The fact that the entire family and not only

Figure 14.1 The Kelly family, Grace in the middle, c. 1950.

one daughter were very attractive was, naturally, further proof of the impeccable pedigree of Hollywood's new star. Another interesting image shows Grace Kelly arriving at Cannes railway station for the film festival in 1955. Her lady persona in this off-screen appearance is underlined by her white gloves, her simple yet elegant dress and her handbag. This exceptional photograph by the Irish society photographer Edward Quinn is rounded off by the inclusion of a newspaperman trying to sell a cinema magazine to the arriving guest. On the cover one can easily make out a portrait of Grace Kelly wearing expensive jewellery.[10] Figure 14.2, on the other hand, was made by Cecil Beaton in 1954. In addition to being an internationally successful society photographer, Beaton was also one of the most important official photographers of

Figure 14.2 Grace Kelly photographed by Cecil Beaton, 1954.

the British royal family. By the time Beaton photographed Grace Kelly, he had already taken the picture of Queen Elizabeth II several times, most importantly during her coronation in 1953. Thus the fact alone that Cecil Beaton, the Winterhalter of the twentieth century, made a portrait of the actress Grace Kelly associated her directly with the photographer's aristocratic and royal patrons.

In 1955, Grace Kelly met Prince Rainier of Monaco; they got engaged and she married him in April 1956. Like the coronation of Queen Elizabeth II, Grace Kelly's wedding was televised all over the world and a documentary film, *The Wedding in Monaco*, was produced by her studio MGM. Her marriage not only transformed the commoner Grace Kelly into Her Serene Highness Princess Grace of Monaco, it also transformed her already aristocratic persona into a royal one. On the narrative level, the metaphor most frequently used to describe this transformation was the Cinderella fairy tale. The opening sentences of one of the most successful biographies of Grace Kelly published immediately after her wedding provides an especially striking example. Gant Gaither began his 1957 account of Grace Kelly's life with the remarks: 'Every small girl at some time or another imagines herself a princess – a princess so beautiful that a handsome, dashing prince falls in love with her, asks her to marry him and to live with him happily ever after in a great palace. ... On April 19, 1956, [a] girl, whose name was Grace Patricia Kelly, ... stood before the altar besides a handsome, dashing prince who had fallen in love with her, asked her to marry him, to live with him happily ever after in a great palace; and with a gently spoken "oui" became ... Son Altesse Sérénissime la Princesse Grace-Patricia de Monaco!'[11]

Figure 14.3 Official wedding photograph of Grace Kelly and Prince Rainier, 1956.

One of her last film roles also contributed to Grace Kelly's royal transformation. In *The Swan* she played for the first time the role of a princess, Alexandra. Against her will she has to marry the crown prince of an unspecified Central European monarchy. To be sure, Grace Kelly's only imagined-queen movie was not very successful. The script was rather weak and the film was released while Grace Kelly's fans were already eagerly waiting for the live broadcast of her real wedding in Monaco. And while in reality a dream seemed to come true, *The Swan* had to fight for the audience's favour without the support of a happy end.

Grace Kelly never got the title of a royal highness because Monaco is merely a principality. Yet the *mise-en-scène* of her wedding, the protocol of her official functions and, most importantly, her constitutional position as the wife of a sovereign made Grace Kelly's persona take a royal turn. A couple of photographs illustrate this point quite well. Figure 14.3 is the official wedding photograph of Grace and Rainier. She is the perfect bride while he is the dashing prince who has brought home Cinderella to his palace. Figure 14.4 is also an official photograph. It shows the Monegasque sovereigns with their first-born child, Princess Caroline. These and other images of Grace during official engagements or while performing representational duties do not in any way differ from images made of other European sovereigns at the same time. At least in the eyes of the general public Princess Grace had thus become firmly integrated into the community of royal women, including, of course, Queen Elizabeth II.

Figure 14.4 Official Portrait of the princely couple with their firstborn child, Princess Caroline, 1957.

Romy Schneider – Crown Princess of German Cinema

Romy Schneider was ten years younger than Grace Kelly and made her film debut in 1953. By the end of the decade she had appeared in eighteen films, was the most popular German film star and had gained fame throughout continental Europe. This phenomenal career was also built to a large extent on a very efficient publicity machine. However, in contrast to Grace Kelly, who had a long-term contract with a Hollywood studio, Romy Schneider's career was managed by her stepfather, the entrepreneur and hotel owner Hans Herbert Blatzheim.[12] During the 1950s, Blatzheim and his wife Magda Schneider, Romy's mother, controlled most of her publicity and thus significantly influenced the construction of her persona.

From the beginning of her career a major element of Romy Schneider's persona was her family background. Like Grace Kelly she came from a privileged family, yet the important aspect of it was not wealth but the fact that Romy Schneider's family was presented to the public as a dynasty of actors. Both of her parents, Magda Schneider and Wolf Albach-Retty, had starred in numerous German films before and during the Second World War, and her grandmother was the still very famous Viennese Burgtheater actress Rosa Albach-Retty. Her stage name 'Romy Schneider' linked her to her mother and was obviously aimed at transferring acting prestige from one generation to the next. Furthermore, in eight out of the eighteen films in which Romy Schneider starred in the 1950s, she appeared alongside her mother. Magda Schneider often played the role of Romy's mother, most importantly in the *Sissi* trilogy, in which she got the part of the empress's mother, Princess Ludovika. The emphasis in Romy Schneider's private publicity on the off-screen mother-daughter relationship was therefore clearly intended to attract the public to the films in which both women appeared. Furthermore, the focus on Magda Schneider was publicity for the mother herself. After the end of the war in 1945 Magda Schneider had great difficulty finding a job and was desperate for a comeback. When it began in 1953, it was with the film in which her daughter Romy appeared for the first time, Hans Deppe's *Wenn der weisse Flieder wieder blüht*.[13]

Apart from her dynastic position within a family of actors Romy Schneider's persona began to include strong royal elements through her early film roles. In her third film, *Mädchenjahre einer Königin*

(1954), Romy Schneider got her first lead and played the young Queen Victoria of England. Magda Schneider got the part of Victoria's lady-in-waiting. This film clearly belongs to the category of imagined-queen films. It was probably directly inspired by the aforementioned documentary about the coronation of Queen Elizabeth II, which had been a great success in Austria as well.[14] The plot of *Mädchenjahre einer Königin* is that Victoria wants to choose a husband of her own liking. In this comedy of mistaken identity, much more inspired by Viennese operetta tradition than English history, Victoria travels incognito to Kent where she meets Prince Albert and decides to marry him and no one else. As this match had been planned from the very beginning, at the end of the film everybody is extremely happy. After the success of this film, its director, the Viennese filmmaker Ernst Marischka, came up with another imagined-queen film, a costume drama about the life of Empress Elisabeth of Austria. This eventually became the famous *Sissi* trilogy made in 1955, 1956 and 1957. In all the films Romy Schneider got the lead as Sissi, while Magda Schneider played the role of the empress's mother. In the *Sissi* trilogy the director Ernst Marischka reduced Elisabeth's life to a romantic fairy tale and only dealt with her youth – her engagement and marriage to Emperor Francis Joseph (*Sissi I*), the first years of her marriage and her involvement in Hungarian affairs (*Sissi II*), and finally her motherhood, illness and reunion with her husband (*Sissi III*). Other aspects of the empress's life – such as the violent deaths of both her son and herself – Marischka consciously left out because they were 'too problematic'.[15]

Marischka's idea of a romantic version of Elisabeth's life worked very well – the *Sissi* movies remain the most successful Austrian films made to date. Visually the films employed the same strategies as most other imagined-queen movies – they were lavish costume dramas. Interestingly, however, they also closely resembled the official self-representation of the Monegasque princely couple. A comparison between Figure 14.4 and Figure 14.5, both taken in 1957, makes this quite clear. The most important effect of the *Sissi* films on Romy Schneider's persona was that it fused with her film role. Quickly the press began to refer to Romy Schneider either by combining her name with 'Sissi' or by using that name as a synonym for her. During a promotional tour of the United States for her film about Queen Victoria – not the *Sissi* films – one German paper proudly wrote: 'Big Welcome for our "Sissi"'.[16] But not only did Romy Schneider acquire the name of Sissi, her persona also began to incorporate some of the characteristics of Marischka's romantic portrait of the empress. One journalist noted in 1957 that the adjectives which came most quickly to mind when one thought about Romy Schneider were 'clean and naive, virginal and girlish'.[17] The same can, of course, also be said about Marischka's *Sissi*.

Romy Schneider's relationship with her mother, much publicised even before the *Sissi* films, was further reinforced through Magda Schneider's appearance in the films about the empress. In this respect as well, Romy Schneider's persona fused with her film role. In the films, Princess Ludovika is the loving, caring and protecting mother of a young, pure and innocent girl who unexpectedly marries the emperor. That was exactly the way in which the Blatzheim publicity represented the mother–daughter relationship to the press. Both Magda and Romy Schneider constantly gave interviews and praised each other in the highest terms. Magda Schneider was presented as Romy's 'best friend', who frequently made statements emphasising her daughter's righteousness, girlhood and virginity. For example: 'This child ... has not yet been in touch with the filth of the world.'[18]

Figure 14.5 Filmstill from *Sissi III*, 1957: Magda Schneider (left) as Princess Ludovika, Karlheinz Böhm as Emperor Francis Joseph and Romy Schneider as Sissi.

Yet unlike Grace Kelly's overall successful publicity, the press did not unconditionally buy what it heard about Romy Schneider. Instead, the image of the happy family was often questioned and at times heavily criticised. Her stepfather's management and ruthless exploitation of his stepdaughter – Blatzheim did, for example, regularly use his stepdaughter to promote his hotels and restaurants – and Magda Schneider's constant attempts to further her second career via the success of her daughter often provoked negative or even sarcastic comments, especially during the carnival season. One paper published a photomontage of Romy Schneider riding a pig during the carnival of 1957 (Figure 14.6). The caption read: 'Also in her latest movie, "Three Pigs on the Prairie" (Sissi's ride into happiness), Romy Schneider betted on the right horse. The original title "Ride for Blatzheim" was tailored out at the very last moment.'[19] The three pigs alluded to were of course Romy and Magda Schneider and Hans Herbert Blatzheim.

To much of the general public it was thus obvious that Romy Schneider's family situation was not as perfect as her businessman stepfather wanted them to believe. Her parents were divorced and her stepfather was widely unpopular because of his pompous, *nouveau riche* behaviour. However, this was not a problem for the development of Romy Schneider's royal persona. On the contrary, even the negative aspects of her family situation were integrated into her royal persona, which further fused with her film roles. Marischka's Sissi is a young, innocent girl constantly at odds with the courtly world around her, especially with her mother-in-law, Princess Sophie. This generational conflict was of course deliberately highlighted in order to raise the audience's sympathy for the protagonist. Many journalists and fans of the young star, especially those critical of Romy's exploitation by her parents, reacted in exactly the same

Figure 14.6 Fotomontage, Carneval 1957.

way to her family situation. An article in the most important German youth magazine *Bravo* is especially revealing. At the height of the Romy mania in June 1957 it published a piece entitled 'Leave Romy alone!' It denounced the influence of her stepfather and stated that 'Mutti Magda' was just like all other mothers, namely impossible: 'She likes to treat her daughter like a child, although Romy, at 19, is not really a child anymore.' The magazine then went on to predict a fabulous career for Romy even without the publicity organised by her parents. *Bravo* came to this conclusion because Romy Schneider was 'charming' and possessed 'natural grace' – apparently all it took to build up a successful cinema career.[20] This shows that even negative reactions to Romy Schneider's publicity often had the effect of buttressing her innocent princess persona, the basis of which had been laid through the *Sissi* films.

The complicated family situation of the Schneider-Blatzheims was also expressed in press photographs. One such image shows 'Daddy' Blatzheim presenting his wife and stepdaughter to their fans in an open car. Mother and daughter are seated in the back. Romy Schneider, whose name appears above that of her mother on a publicity board on the side of the car, wears a modest headscarf and looks shyly onto her fans. Her mother, on the other hand, wears her hair open and holds her head triumphantly high. She wears an expensive fur coat. Daddy Blatzheim, the macho manager of this pair, sits in the front of the car. Interestingly, the vehicle is driven by a woman whose face cannot be seen and whose identity the caption does not reveal. Both those who believed in the Blatzheim publicity as well as those who were critical of it of course found their views confirmed in this image.[21]

Towards the end of the 1950s Romy Schneider's persona was therefore clearly dominated by royal elements. Even those critical of her publicity or her acting talents constantly used royal terminology to describe her. Romy Schneider had become the 'Crown Princess of German Cinema', as one film magazine put it.[22] As Romy Schneider had also become an important symbol of Austrian and German national identity, she could be described as the imagined crown princess of the Austrian and German nation.[23]

Beauty

What is the difference between an actress who, like Grace Kelly or Romy Schneider, becomes an imagined queen, and a princess who ascends to a throne by marriage or succession? One important difference is that the professional success of an actress directly depends upon her public. If nobody is interested in her performances, she cannot work, while princesses and queens only lose their job in the relatively unlikely event of a revolution. A major element attracting audiences to the theatre or the cinema is their physical beauty. Admittedly there were also real princesses, such as the young Elisabeth in Bavaria, whose looks their contemporaries excessively praised.[24] But even if Elisabeth had been less beautiful, by marrying Emperor Francis Joseph she would nevertheless have become empress, as so many, often much less beautiful princesses before her. Romy Schneider and Grace Kelly, however, were constantly referred to as being extremely beautiful, much more so than most real princesses or queens who lived at the same time. One need only think of the then queen of the Netherlands, Juliana, or her Greek counterpart, Frederike.

Beauty thus is an important factor enabling an actress to become queen. Yet, of course, beauty is an ambiguous term. In exactly this ambiguity lies a more specific difference between actresses and princesses who become queens. When an actress displays her beauty on stage this is to a large extent intended to arouse sexual interest in the male audience. Yet in official royal self-representation – in contrast to anti-royal pamphlets or lurid press reports – I have never found any descriptions of real queens which comment on their sexual appeal to the general male audience. Of course, the beauty of real queens was often publicly displayed. Yet the aim of this was to enhance the queen's royal status. Her sex appeal remained exclusively reserved for her husband and was not commented on in any of the cases I have analysed so far.

For the construction of the personae of Grace Kelly and Romy Schneider, their sex appeal was constantly and consciously used both in their films and in their personal publicity. Interestingly, both women were often compared to another star whose career began in the 1950s, Marilyn Monroe. Thomas Harris noted in 1957 that Grace Kelly's publicity presented her to her male public as the 'ideal mate' to get married to, while Marilyn Monroe was presented to the same audience as the 'ideal playmate' to have an affair with.[25] Simultaneously a German magazine wrote about Romy Schneider: 'If Marilyn is the woman with whom every man would love to get stuck in an elevator, Romy Schneider is the girl with whom men would most want to exchange wedding rings.'[26]

Marilyn Monroe thus incarnated the opposite of Grace Kelly's and Romy Schneider's aristocratic and ultimately domestic sexuality. Both women were thus very similar to real princesses in terms of the display of their sex appeal – a similarity which was enhanced by the fact that neither of them had an official boyfriend or fiancé during the first years of their stardom. To their male public it was clear that the sexual beauty that the two actresses displayed on the screen was ultimately reserved for the men whom one day they were going to marry. Of course, it was possible for a fan to speculate that either star would choose to get married to him. Yet in practice the chances of this were about as great as for him to get married to a real princess.

From Saint to Whore?

The royal personae of Grace Kelly and Romy Schneider continued to evolve after their initial construction in the 1950s. In the case of Grace Kelly this only set in after her death in 1982. Initially most of her obituaries repeated the well-established stereotype of her life as a fairy tale. *Newsweek*, for example, ran a cover story entitled 'The Last Fairy Tale.'[27] Grace Kelly was presented as the ideal wife, mother and conscientious princess-consort engaged in charity work, especially by the tabloids. The Monaco-based German bestselling author Johannes Mario Simmel wrote in the German weekly *Stern*: 'Princess Grace was one of the very good, very fine, very brave. She was also one of the very beautiful. She was a wonderful woman.' The last words of the princess 'knowing that she was going to die' had apparently been, wrote Simmel: 'People should not send flowers, they should make donations, please, donations, donations ... [sic]'[28]

Most of these fairy-tale reports were accompanied by photographs taken shortly before the death of the princess. They show a woman in her early fifties and make no allusion whatsoever to her sex appeal. A good example is the cover of a special commemorative issue of the German weekly, *Bunte*. In front of a black background emphasising the tragic death of the princess, a mature Grace Kelly smiles softly wearing a tame, high-necked dress. Her blonde hair is lit from above and contrasts with the darkness of the background – the effect is nothing else than a halo (Figure 14.7).

Serious newspapers and film magazines published less idealised obituaries. All the ones I have found were written by men and they all compare Grace Kelly's achievements as an actress negatively with her role as princess. Most of these articles argue more or less implicitly that her life as a princess was newsworthy only for the tabloids. On the other hand, they all emphasise her acting talent and especially her sex appeal. They all quote a remark by Alfred Hitchcock. A decade after the end of Grace Kelly's cinema career in 1966, the director of her most successful films had coined the expression of her 'sexual elegance' in an interview with François Truffaut. Hitchcock explained: 'Poor Marilyn Monroe had sex written all over her face, Brigitte Bardot wasn't very subtle either. But Grace Kelly was something different. I was after the drawing-room type, the real lady, who becomes a whore once she's in the bedroom. She was perfect for that. Just perfect.'[29] These obituaries were usually accompanied by a star photograph of the actress taken in the 1950s, such as that shown in Figure 14.8. Such images were meant to illustrate Grace Kelly's 'sexual elegance'.

A couple of years after her death, biographies of Grace Kelly started to appear. Interestingly, those sold best which claimed that they were finally revealing 'the truth' about Grace Kelly.[30]

Figure 14.7 *Bunte-Spezial* on the death of Princess Grace, 1982.

Figure 14.8 The 'sexual elegance' of Grace Kelly. Photograph by Philippe Halsman, c. 1954.

All of them did this by emphasising her pre- and post-nuptial affairs. These accounts therefore went beyond the sexual elegance stereotype and focused on the private sexual life of the actress. Robert Lacey's 1994 biography is a good example. The author writes about a great number of sexual affairs in an attempt to reinforce his central argument that Grace Kelly had been anything but a saint when it came to sex. He illustrates his point with photographs. One snapshot shows the lightly dressed Grace Kelly backstage during a break in a television production. Opposite this full-page illustration Lacey put a page entitled 'Early Lovers'. It contains six male portraits, among them the Shah of Persia.[31]

Romy Schneider's persona of the virginal crown princess underwent a transformation very similar to that of Grace Kelly, although in this case the process began much earlier. In 1958 Romy fell in love with the her French colleague, Alain Delon, whom she had met during the filming of a love story, *Christine*. This film and her much publicised move to France in order to live with Delon without being married radically changed her persona. Until then she had been the virginal German Fräulein star, now she was the sexually experienced woman *à la française*. A rather innocuous film still with Alain Delon thus became the symbol of this change (Figure 14.9).

The transformation of Romy Schneider's persona was reinforced by her subsequent films, in which she increasingly played sexually intriguing and daring women. In 1961, for example, she appeared for the first time naked in Luchino Visconti's *The Job*, which was part of Carlo Ponti's *Boccaccio 70*. Equally important were sexually charged photographs for which Romy Schneider posed and which were published all over Europe, once even on the cover of French *Playboy*.[32] An interesting example of

Figure 14.9 Romy Schneider and Alain Delon. Filmstill from *Christine*, 1958.

this kind of photograph is a portrait Helmut Newton made of Romy Schneider in 1974 (Figure 14.10). Like Grace Kelly, who had been put in line with European royalty by being photographed by Cecil Beaton, Romy Schneider's appearance in front of Helmut Newton's lens made her a member of this photographer's notorious collection of erotic women's portraits.

In 1974 the German magazine *Quick* summed up the transformation of Romy Schneider's persona in the headline: 'How a fairy-tale princess became a sex star.'[33] Many other major changes took place in her persona,

Figure 14.10 Romy Schneider seen by Helmut Newton, 1974.

for example, her love affairs and her wish to take the management of her publicity away from her mother and stepfather led to serious conflicts with her parents. Throughout the rest of her life Romy Schneider's tumultuous private life continued to fascinate the press – a fascination that the actress herself helped to keep up by regularly giving very personal interviews and participating in numerous photo sessions. By the time she died in 1982 she was twice divorced, her first husband had committed suicide and her eldest son had died in a tragic accident, all of which and more had been widely reported.

The Royal Whore

The premature and thus tragic deaths of the two women in 1982 did not kill their personae. On the contrary, the death of Grace Kelly at fifty-four following a car accident and the death of the forty-four-year-old Romy Schneider due to a heart failure were immediately integrated into their now immortal personae. Since then, the general public is always aware of the tragic ends of the two women – especially when watching one of their films on television – and is thus able to interpret their deaths like those of heroines in romantic novels. There are, for example, rumours that Grace Kelly was killed by the Mafia or that Romy Schneider committed suicide or, more romantically still, died 'of a broken heart.'[34]

Revisionist texts about the sex life of the defunct stars strongly attacked their royal personae. These texts all claimed to reveal the 'true Grace' or the 'true Romy'. Many authors even explicitly stated that they wanted to deconstruct the royal personae of the two women, that it was their intention to replace the perfect image of Princess Grace and Sissi-Romy with the biographical truth. About Romy Schneider there were reports about alleged lesbian affairs as well as sexual advances by her stepfather. The British *Observer* wrote in 1997 about a forthcoming film based on Robert Lacey's biography of Grace Kelly: 'Bitter end to Monaco's fairytale as Hollywood shoots its own princess.'[35]

This deconstruction of the royal personae of the two women by means of so-called revelations, however, largely failed to achieve its goal. Even now, the personae of the two women are heavily dominated by royal elements and the inversion of their previously positive sexual characteristics into their opposites has reinforced rather than weakened their position as imagined queens. In fact, such a narrative development, disguised as the revelation of the truth, is characteristic of actresses who become queens and is by no means an exclusively twentieth-century phenomenon. A very similar narrative development can be found already in the representations of the Byzantine Empress Theodora (c. 497–548).

Theodora was an actress in the Constantinople circus before Justinian, nephew and heir apparent of Emperor Justin, decided to make her his wife. Once Justinian had ascended to the throne, official imperial propaganda idealised Theodora as the beautiful and brave consort of the emperor, both visually and textually. The historian Procopius made a description of a statue of Theodora in Constantinople which could also have been prompted by the only surviving image of this empress, the famous Ravenna mosaic. Procopius wrote: 'The statue [of Theodora] is indeed beautiful, but still inferior to the beauty of the Empress; for to express her loveliness in words or to portray it in a statue would be, for a mere human being, altogether impossible.'[36] Like most biographers of Grace Kelly and Romy Schneider, Procopius claimed to reveal 'the truth' about the empress only after her death. While in his previous books he had praised Theodora in the highest terms, in his last work, *The Secret History*, he described her in the most evil and negative way as nothing less than a prostitute and a witch responsible for all problems that had befallen the empire. Procopius took special pleasure in describing her early days as an actress in Constantinople:

'[O]ften ... in the theatre, before the eyes of the whole people, she stripped off her clothing and moved about naked through their midst, having only a girdle about her private parts and her groins ... Clothed in that matter, she sprawled out and lay on her back on the ground. And some slaves, whose duty it was, sprinkled grains of barley over her private parts, and geese, which happened to have been provided for this very purpose, picked them off with their beaks, one by one, and ate them. And when she got up, she not only did not blush, but even acted as if she took pride in this strange performance.'[37]

This scene is highly reminiscent of articles about the excessive love life of both Romy Schneider and Grace Kelly, most of which were published after their deaths. In 1997, for example, the British *Sunday Times* published an article about a documentary on Grace Kelly. It claimed that shortly before her death the princess had become a member of a sect engaged in dubious sexual practices. 'Princess Grace "in cult sex ritual"' was the sensationalist title of this article. In the said ritual the princess allegedly 'undressed and underwent a process of "relaxation" which involved putting needles in her erogenous zones to promote sexual arousal. Afterwards, dressed in the white robes of the order, she was taken down to the priory's cellar where [two male members of the order] carried out the part-Catholic, part-occult initiation ceremony. This "led to Grace being accepted as the high priestess of the Order of the Solar temple", said [a witness].'[38]

The parallels between the representations of the Byzantine empress and former actress Theodora and the representations of Grace Kelly and Romy Schneider, the two royal actresses of the twentieth century, are extremely striking. This suggests that because of the conscious use of their sex appeal on stage, actresses who become queens or who receive a royal persona are much more likely than real queens to be first represented as virtuous spouses and then as vicious whores. In other words, royal actresses are much more likely to see the virtuous sexual aspects of their persona reversed into their opposites. This reversal is always presented as the revelation of the truth, yet in fact it is nothing more than the narrative development of the royal personae of the actresses. The persona of a real queen only changes in this way during a successful revolution – the defamations of Marie-Antoinette during the French Revolution are probably the most well-known example of this.[39] Because of the constant presence of their films and photographs on television and in the press, the personae of twentieth-century royal actresses were possibly more likely to undergo this kind of negative narrative development than was the case with their predecessors. But essentially, there is very little difference between the way in which the stories of Grace Kelly and Romy Schneider were told to a twentieth-century audience and the way in which Theodora's story was told to a Byzantine audience more than fourteen centuries earlier.

Notes

1. See Michael Jürgs, *Der Fall Romy Schneider. Eine Biographie* (Munich and Leipzig, 1991), 36.
2. See Georg Seeßlen, 'Alle Jahre wieder: 'Sissi'. Ein heimliches Nationalepos der Deutschen', *Blimp* 17, (1991).
3. I have consulted collections of newspaper and magazine clippings about Grace Kelly and Romy Schneider located in the following archives: British Film Institute, London (BFI); Archiv Renate Seydel, Berlin (ARSB); Textdokumentation Schweizer Fernsehen DRS, Zürich (SFDRS); Zoom Archiv, Zürich (ZAZ). I am especially grateful to Renate Seydel for giving me access to her vast private archive about Romy Schneider.
4. See Philip Ziegler, *Crown and People* (New York, 1978), 97–126.
5. For detailed biographies of Grace Kelly see, among others, Robert Lacey, *Grace* (London, 1995); Ronald Bowers, 'Grace Kelly', in *Films* 29, 9, (1978), 523–25; James Spada, *Grace. The Secret Lives of a Princess. An intimate Biography* (New York, 1987).
6. See Hortense Powdermaker, *Hollywood, the Dream Factory* (New York, 1979) and Richard Dyer, *Stars* (London, 1998).
7. See Thomas Harris, 'The Building of Popular Images. Grace Kelly and Marilyn Monroe', reprinted in: *Stardom. Industry of Desire*, ed. Christine Gledhill (London and New York, 1991), 40–44.
8. Harris, 'The Building', 42.
9. Gant Gaither, *Princess of Monaco. The Story of Grace Kelly* (New York, 1957), plate 14.
10. See Edward Quinn, *Fotograf, Nizza* (Zurich, Berlin and New York, 1994), 92.

11. Gaither, *Princess of Monaco*, 7–8.
12. See Renate Seydel, ed., *Romy Schneider. Ein Leben in Bildern* (Berlin, 1996), 43.
13. In this film Romy Schneider appeared as 'Romy Schneider-Albach'. However, this attempt to link her also to her actor father and grandmother was dropped in all subsequent movies. Her civil name was Rosemarie Albach.
14. See Walter Fritz, *Kino in Österreich, 1945–1983* (Vienna, 1984), 70.
15. Marischka quoted in Seeßlen, 'Alle Jahre wieder', 17: 'zu problembeladen'.
16. *Eßlinger Zeitung*, 31 January 1958, ARSB. 'Großer Bahnhof für unsere "Sissi"'.
17. *Gießener Anzeiger*, 27 January 1957, ARSB. 'sauber und naiv, jungfräulich und mädchenhaft'.
18. *Die Filmwoche*, 13 October 1956, ARSB. 'beste Freundin'; 'Dieses Kind … ist mit dem Schmutz der Welt noch nicht in Berührung gekommen!'
19. *Witzbadener Knurrier*, carnival 1957, ARSB. 'Auch in ihrem neuesten Film "Drei Schweinchen auf der Heide" (Sissys Ritt ins Glück) hat Romy Schneider auf das richtige Pferd gesetzt. Der ursprüngliche Titel "Reitet für Blatzheim" ist in letzter Minute abgeschneidert worden.'
20. *Bravo*, 2 June 1957, ARSB. 'Lasst Romy in Ruh'!'; 'Sie behandelt ihre Tochter mit Vorliebe wie ein Kind, obwohl Romy mit 19 Jahren so ein Kind doch eigentlich nicht mehr ist'; 'reizend'; 'natürliche Anmut'.
21. The image is reproduced in Seydel, *Romy Schneider*, 74.
22. *Die Filmwoche*, 13 October. 1956, ARSB. 'Kronprinzessin des deutschen Films'.
23. About Romy Schneider's role for the construction of the Austrian and German national identity see Seeßlen, 'Alle Jahre wieder' and my unpublished conference paper 'Reflections of an Imagined Empress. The Diaries of Romy Schneider During the Making of the Sissi Films', European University Insitute, Florence, 11 November 2000.
24. On Elisabeth see Brigitte Hamann, *Elisabeth. Kaiserin wider Willen* (Munich, 1998).
25. Harris, 'The Building', 42.
26. *Die Filmwoche*, 13. October 1956, ARSB. '[W]enn Marilyn die Frau ist, mit der jeder Mann am liebsten im Aufzug steckenbleiben würde, dann ist Romy Schneider das Mädchen, mit dem man am liebsten den Ehering tauscht.'
27. *Newsweek*, 27 September 1982, 32–41, Dossier *Grace Kelly*, Textdokumentation SF DRS, Zürich.
28. *Stern*, no. 39, 23. September 1982, Dossier Grace Kelly, SFDRS. 'Fürstin Gracia Patricia war eine von jenen sehr Guten, sehr Feinen und sehr Mutigen. Sie war auch eine der sehr Schönen. Sie war eine wundervolle Frau'; 'wissend, daß sie sterben müßte'; 'Die Leute sollen keine Blumen schicken, sondern Spenden, bitte, Spenden, Spenden ...'

29. Quote in: *The Guardian*, 16 September 1982, microfilm collection on Grace Kelly, BFI. See also Robert Fischer, ed., *Truffaut/Hitchcock. Vollständige Ausgabe* (Munich and Zurich, 1999), 188.
30. See, for example, Spada, *Grace. The Secret Lives*; Lacey, *Grace* and Judith Balaban Quine, *The Bridesmaids. Grace Kelly, Princess of Monaco, and Six Intimate Friends* (New York, 1989).
31. See plate section in Lacey, *Grace.*
32. *Playboy* (France), November 1980, Dossier Romy Schneider, ZAZ.
33. *Quick*, 19. March 1974, Dossier Romy Schneider, ZAZ. 'Wie aus einer Märchenprinzessin ein Sex-Star wurde'.
34. *Weltwoche*, 9. June 1982, Dossier Romy Schneider, ZAZ. 'an gebrochenem Herzen'.
35. *Observer*, 27 April 1997, microfilm collection on Grace Kelly, BFI.
36. Procopius, *Buildings* (Harvard and London, 1971), I, IX, 8–9.
37. Procopius, *Secret History* (Harvard and London, 1971), IX, 20–22.
38. *Sunday Times*, 21 December 1997, microfilm collection on Grace Kelly, BFI.
39. For Marie-Antoinette see Chantal Thomas, *The Wicked Queen. The Origins of the Myth of Marie-Antoinette* (New York, 1999).

15

Queer Queen

Elizabeth I in Sally Potter's Film *Orlando*

Katharina Sykora

> *He had been kissed by a queen without knowing it.*
> Virginia Woolf, *Orlando*, 1928

My arguments will focus on the first episode in Sally Potter's film *Orlando*.[1] Prefiguring the film as a whole, this sequence effects a complex inversion of gender and time. The close interweaving of gender, medium and historical chronology creates an optical density which develops into an emphatic self-referential gesture. Gender and history become demonstrative modalities of representation which transgress their own perimeters. The film's potential to interweave polar and linear structures, patterns of masculinity and femininity, and static as well as moving images can be traced to the central figure of this initial sequence. The imago of Queen Elizabeth I of England appears as the perfect personification of a hybrid gender and an opaque historicity.

The first episode of the film – and the Virginia Woolf novel it is based on – is set in the Elizabethan period. The Queen represents both master and mistress for Orlando, a figure created as a tribute to the author's close friend, Vita Sackville-West. In the film, the role of the elderly Queen is played by Quentin Crisp, who has the reputation of being the first 'stately homosexual of England'.[2] This characterisation refers to his role as the forerunner of an assertive homosexual lifestyle which became more accepted only with the gay movement in the 1970s. Since the 1930s Crisp's everyday public appearance presented the 'effeminate' as a complex social figure. He understood this demonstrative performance of femininity as an assertive 'missionary act' directed at a majority society which stigmatised him as a homosexual. Besides casting the role of Elizabeth I with this iridescently gendered figure, Sally Potter chose just as diverse an actress for her younger counterpart. Orlando is played by Tilda Swinton, a leading actress in Derek Jarman's 'queer cinema' of the 1980s. Queer cinema not only blurred gender categories but also created new images of the intersections between history and the present, fiction and documentary, icons and their metamorphosis.

Thus the subversion of gender categories as well as linear history – an implicit theme in Virginia Woolf's novel – is incorporated into the film with the casting itself. In addition, the medium of film itself accentuates this tendency towards inversion. On the one hand, film involves a successive scan of individual photographic images, but simultaneously it relies on the persistent illusion of uninterrupted motion. Film therefore tends towards a hermetic, teleological progression in the sense of cinematic continuity. 'Alternative cinema' often attempts to break with this secondary convention of film and exploits the potential of its static photographic images in order to represent time as discontinuous and anti-teleological. In the first episode of *Orlando*, Sally Potter therefore employs the imago of Queen Elizabeth I not only as a means of bending traditional categories of gender and time, but also as an allegory of film as a highly ambivalent medium. In her static attitude and her minimalist and thus powerful actions, Elizabeth I alias Quentin Crisp marks at once both a beginning and an end, stillness and motion, death and rebirth, thus casting the entire film as a metamorphosis that has no predetermined direction. The ambiguity in the character of Elizabeth I in Sally Potter's *Orlando* thus embodies the debates and actions in the early 1990s aimed at a bending of gender categories in the sense of 'queer performativity'. But *Orlando* also reflects a phase of filmmaking in the same period which was characterised by the blurring of the boundaries between experimental and mainstream cinema.

In order to more closely interpret the first episode of the film, it is necessary to consider the meanings originating outside the film that figure in Sally Potter's representation of the Elizabethan body. The first to consider is the image of Elizabeth I in Virginia Woolf's 1928 novel. Next, it is necessary to analyse more closely the impact of Quentin Crisp's 'male effemininity' as described in his autobiographical texts from 1968 and 1981.[3] And finally, we will consider the transformation of this imago in the 1975 film *The Naked Civil Servant*,[4] which is based on Crisp's autobiography of the same title.

The following sets of issues will inform my analysis of the visual and literary bodily images that figure in the representation of Elizabeth I in *Orlando*. First, the genre of biography and autobiography plays an important role as an act which personalises historiography and which is aimed at performativity. This genre articulates the difference between the 'script' of 'History' and the way in which it is individually enacted. Also important are clothing and transvestism as signs of authority as well as stigmatisation. Both can be understood as strategies of exclusion: on the one hand as an elite form of self-empowerment, and on the other hand as a cause for being socially excluded by others. The way in which these two forms of clothing exclude will lead back to the question of the way in which history is personalised in the case of Virginia Woolf's biographical figure of Elizabeth I, her 'male impersonator' Quentin Crisp, as well as Sally Potter's film figure. The surface of the body, as suggested by clothing, produces a gender-coded border which is often represented metaphorically as the border of a territory or a social body. A change of clothing represents not only a transgression of the usual markings of gender, topography and social norms, but also of the border between the past and a changed present. Thus the act of changing one's attire can become a central part of biographical and autobiographical projects in historiography.[5] Further, an investigation of the clothed surface of the body opens up the question of the relationship between form and content, which is always also about making distinctions between that which is shown, that which is represented, and that which remains concealed. Clothing codes and changing clothing are thus not only part of an (auto)biographical historiography, but also an explicitly visual historiography.[6]

The Queenly Effigy: Elizabeth I in Virginia Woolf's *Orlando*

The first episode of Virginia Woolf's novel is set at the end of the sixteenth century in Elizabethan England and the central figure Orlando is introduced at the prime of his youth, which is accentuated in contrast to the aging queen. Their encounters are characterised primarily through the exchange of their gazes, which never meet. One effect of this is that the readers of Woolf's novel have access to more than just the descriptions of Orlando or the Queen from the perspective of the narrator. The perspectives of the protagonists themselves take over the disembodied narrative authority, and we see the boy and the queen as subjective images that mutually create one another. These images, however, are anything but equal, given that the power of the gaze is unequally distributed between them. In the first of three encounters between Orlando and the Queen, the power differential in their gazes seems to be almost equal. Each catches a brief glimpse of the other. The first appearance of the body of the Queen in the novel is as an imago deduced by Orlando from a quick glance at her jewelled hands when he offers her a bowl of rosewater.

> Such was his shyness that he saw no more of her than her ringed hands in water; but it was enough. It was a memorable hand; a thin hand with long fingers always curling as if round orb or scepter; a nervous, crabbed, sickly hand; a commanding hand too; a hand that had only to raise itself for a head to fall; a hand, he guessed, attached to an old body that smelt like a cupboard in which furs are kept in camphor; which body was yet caparisoned in all sorts of brocades and gems; and held itself very upright though perhaps in pain from sciatica; and never flinched though strung together by a thousand fears; and the Queen's eyes were light yellow. All this he felt as the great rings flashed in the water and then something pressed his hair – which, perhaps, accounts for his seeing nothing more likely to be of use to a historian.[7]

Orlando's appearance, on the other hand, is deduced from the Queen's fleeting glance at his head during the ritual laying on of her hands:

> By the same showing, the Queen herself can have seen only a head. But if it is possible from a hand to deduce a body, informed with all the attributes of a great Queen, her crabbedness, courage, frailty, and terror, surely a head can be as fertile, looked down upon from a chair of state by a lady whose eyes were always, if the waxworks at the Abbey are to be trusted, wide open. The long, curled hair, the dark head bent so reverently, so innocently before her, implied a pair of the finest legs that a young nobleman has ever stood upright upon.[8]

From the perspective of Orlando, the body of the Queen is nothing but a hand which transcends the signs of aging and mental frailty through its powerful actions. The body, which is always more than a hand, is characterised not only as an annex, but as a negative form or an emptiness that is concealed under ostentation, attitudes, and the distinct aura of her smell. Orlando's body, although it, too, is fragmented when first perceived by the Queen, has distinct bodily markings that are aesthetic, or even erotic: his soft, curly hair, his well-formed legs, and the violet colour of his eyes. With the last attribute, the original equality of their gazes takes on an oppositional note. While his blind eyes are like violet jewels, a mere object of her visual pleasure (the scene begins with the sentences: 'The Queen had come. Orlando looked no more.'), her eyes are described as wide open and vigilant.

With this representation of the Queen's highly observant eyes, Virginia Woolf introduces another subtle meaning of the Elizabethan body: it is associated with death. The reference to the wax figure of the Queen in Westminster Abbey places her in a direct mimetic relation to her death mask (Figure 15.1).[9] Wax figures were known to be placed there after the death of a monarch to metonymically stand in for the living body of the ruler. They had the function of holding up the continuity of power in the vacuum of the interregnum until a new sovereign was proclaimed.[10] Virginia Woolf was apparently impressed by the eyes of the effigy of Elizabeth I after a visit to Westminster, which she described in a text published in the *New Republic* in 1928, the year in which *Orlando* went to press: 'Her eyes are wide open and vigilant; her nose thin as the beak of a

Figure 15.1 Funeral effigy of Elizabeth I (1760 renewed), wax figure, The Chapter of Westminster, Photograph c. 1910.

hawk; her lips shut tight; her eyebrows arched; only the jowl gives the fine-drawn face its massiveness.'[11] Here Virginia Woolf gives us a differentiated description of the surface of the Queen's body, in this case her face, but in the novel she did not. But these are only the features of a *moulage*, an imprint, a death mask. The citation of this naturalistic effigy in *Orlando* thus produces a reference to what is merely a semblance of the royal body, placing it in the same category as the guise of her attire and her jewellery. With this reference to the Westminster wax figure of Elizabeth I, Virginia Woolf reveals to us the underlying structure of the body images in her novel. Namely, the wax casts represent the 'shell of a mortal shell', an endless accumulation of surfaces. This piling up of images can be understood as a reference to the act of creating an image, in which new facets are brought forward layer by layer. Beyond this permanent process of alternately animating and petrifying images, another aspect of arresting and reanimating body images is found in Virginia Woolf's novel. It is the imago of Orlando, a fixed image which is at once the product of the Queen's gaze and that which guarantees her vivacity. It is through Orlando's image, originally created in her eyes, that Queen Elizabeth indirectly lives on throughout the novel.

The Queen's eyes transfer her presence onto the body of Orlando by producing his image, which will continue to exist throughout the story's unfolding up to the year 1928. The status of these image-producing eyes imparts a power, which is addressed in the two encounters between the boy and the Queen which follow. With each encounter, the power of the Queen's gaze intensifies as she fixes his body with her eyes. In their encounters, not only do their eyes never meet, but their bodies also never touch directly – at least not in the modern sense of skin contact. The closest physical contact is the ceremonial 'royal touch' in the first encounter. At their second meeting, Elizabeth I repeats this ritual when fastening the order of the Garter 'at the slenderest part' of Orlando's leg. They finally come closer at the third meeting in her chambers, where Elizabeth presses Orlando's face to her bodice and allows him to touch the delicate border between the natural and the representative body of the Queen: 'she pulled him down among the cushions where her women laid her (she was so worn and old) and made him bury his face in that astonishing composition – she had not changed her dress for a month – which smelt for all the world, he thought, recalling his boyish memory, like some old cabinet at home where his mother's furs were stored.'[12] The meaning of these increasingly intense encounters is very different for the two protagonists: for Orlando, the Queen represents mother and memory; for Elizabeth, he represents lover and the future.

Read from the Queen's perspective, this encounter with Orlando has a double meaning: it is a metaphor for sexual intercourse[13] as well as for her political triumph, which shows the Queen in full possession of her powers. Parallel to the erotic climax of this encounter, Virginia Woolf brings in a thunder of cannons announcing the Queen's victory over the Armada: '"This", she breathed, "is my victory!" – even as a rocket roared up and dyed her cheeks scarlet.'[14] Her victory entails the submission of Orlando's beautiful masculine body as well as the submission of a masculine military opponent in her victory over the Spanish invaders. Queen Elizabeth's pleasure derives from her double sense of control, over the physical borders of her royal body as well as the metonymically related topographical borders of England. She defines her vestments as the border of her body. Letting Orlando touch this layer/border is an expression of her absolute sovereignty, which brings her physical pleasure. And she defines the coast of England as her territorial border. Exercising the power of control over these borders as well as deciding who has the right to transgress them, and who does not, constitutes a political triumph for her.

The unity of masculine and feminine types of royal sovereignty begins to dissolve immediately after this climax. In the third and last sentence of the Elizabethan episode, the Queen is once again split into two entities, 'the old woman' and the monarch. The biological body is separated from the political body. This occurs in a scene in which Elizabeth, looking through a mirror which she always carries with her, catches sight of Orlando kissing a young girl. The Queen's reaction is vehement iconoclasm: 'Snatching at her golden-hilted sword she struck violently at the mirror. The glass crashed.'[15] With the destruction of Orlando's mirror-image, the downfall of the Queen's own physical existence is inaugurated. She soon dies, but the image she created lives on, albeit in other forms of bodily existence. What the figure of Orlando inherits from her creator is the physical structure of an effigy. As such Orlando accumulates many layers of semblances during the course of the narrative and throughout his journey through the centuries and the world, with the result that his features and his body have been thoroughly transformed: from the eighteenth century on, Orlando is a woman; beginning in the nineteenth century, she is once again geographically located in England; and in the twentieth century she has arrived on the scene of modernity. In the first episode of Virginia Woolf's text, this ability to collect layers of the body and time, expressed in the figure of the effigy as an emblem, has been transferred from the Queen to Orlando's body. From now on, he advances from an Elizabethan boy of the sixteenth century to ambassador in Constantinople in the seventeenth century, only to be transformed into an eighteenth-century Rococo lady and then a romantic Victorian figure in the nineteenth century, finally ending up in the twentieth century as a successful writer of the 1920s. The plates in the 1928 edition of *Orlando*, which all stem from Vita Sackville-West's family, also follow this narrative structure. They begin as paintings of her relatives and then finish with photographs of Woolf's friend in various poses and masquerades. These images play with clothing and sexual multiplicities, as well as with the ambiguous status of the text as both authentic document and fiction.

The Naked Civil Servant or *How to become a Virgin:* Quentin Crisp's Autobiographical Imago and William Hurt's Impersonation of It

The potential of Sally Potter's film to disrupt is intensified by the presence of Quentin Crisp and his embodiment of 'effeminate masculinity' as he describes it in his autobiography and as William Hurt embodies it in the film based on the autobiography.

'Posing was the first job I had in which I understood what I was doing.'[16] These words begin Quentin Crisp's first autobiographical text from 1968 and refer most directly to his work as a nude model for the 'life classes' at the London Art Academy. Later, when he was paid by the English government to pose as a model, Crisp called himself a 'naked civil servant', thereby coining the title of his autobiography and the 1975 film of the same title. Quentin Crisp's relationship to posing must be understood, however, as extending beyond his professional experience as a model; it is also a fundamental category of his entire 'life performance'. There is a small but significant difference between serving as a model for academic purposes versus living out a pose. For the art schools he posed as an ideal Michelangelesque masculine figure ('I tried to be as Sistine as hell'[17]), but in daily life he 'wished to propagate ... that effeminacy existed in people who were in all other respects just like home.'[18] By colouring his hair, polishing his fingernails and painting his lips bright red, Quentin Crisp enacted a visual gender bending that made him a target of intense public aggression from the 1930s into the 1960s. Because he wanted to stir up not only a verbal but also a visual disruption of gender norms, he needed a large public. And so the streets of London became his stage, and the bystanders became his audience: 'I became not merely a self-confessed homosexual but a self-evident one. That is to say I put my case not only before the people who knew me but also before strangers.'[19] By making his life a permanent act, Quentin Crisp transformed his original idea of sexual and/or physical deviance as a negative stigmatisation into an overt statement declaring deviance a positive lifestyle like any other. Clothing is the main medium through which he defines his body as situated between genders and with which he accentuates its boundaries – boundaries that are open to transgression every time he makes an appearance. His autobiography is full of encounters in which the attacks against his embodiment of an effeminate man are expressed through the violation of this significant guise, for example, his persecutors tear up his clothes, pull his hair or slap him in the face. The violent and the visual destruction of his embodied image join forces, no longer differentiating between the physical body and its guise, masculinity and femininity.

In the second part of his autobiography, entitled *How to Become a Virgin*, Quentin Crisp describes the making of the film *The Naked Civil Servant*. The film mostly follows the chronology of Crisp's autobiography, lending it, however, a different framing. At the beginning we see a short interview in which the 'real' Quentin Crisp comments on the film and his double in it, the actor William Hurt: 'They asked me how I feel about an actor playing my role on screen and I answered "I tried unsuccessfully for more than sixty years to play the difficult role of Quentin Crisp. I am sure an actor like William Hurt will do much better than I ever could."' At the end of the film Quentin Crisp alias William Hunt is shown in his 'blue period', that is, the period during which his flaming red hair was dyed bright blue. The film's biographical chronology thus comes full circle: the present time of the actor and the character which he represents are congruent by the end. This makes it possible to superimpose the images of Crisp and Hurt alias Crisp such that one serves as a double for the other and vice versa. Just as the effigy of Elizabeth I in Westminster is one of several layers that have been shed, thus bringing forth new forms of existence for the Queen, the image of Quentin Crisp created by William Hurt seems to be just another embodiment of Crisp's life performance. In Sally Potter's film, it is Quentin Crisp who plays the role of Queen Elizabeth I, thereby producing a complex, self-referential relationship between the actor and his role. As a male effeminate who embodied a fusion of gender polarities which served him as a life-long source of personal desire as well as social resistance, in *Orlando* he plays a masculine woman, Elizabeth I, who also represented the visual embodiment of gender bending in another historical period. What the two figures have in common is that both were able to transform the vulnerability resulting from their multi-layered bodies/guises into powerful body and image strategies.

My Fair(y) Lady or Queering the Queen: Elizabeth I in Sally Potter's Film *Orlando*

When Sally Potter filmed Virginia Woolf's novel, Quentin Crisp was in his mid-eighties as he played the Virgin Queen at an age of over sixty. His first appearance on the screen is announced by a counter-tenor representing the historical figure of a castrato. The castrato figure sings verses and melodies honouring the Virgin Queen, which were common in the Elizabethan court.[20] He praises the Fairy Queen who is in full command of her grace and power. This introduces us to the late period of Queen Elizabeth's reign when this kind of iconography was at its height, as manifest in Edmund Spenser's third book of the *Fairie Queen*, first published in 1590. As Susan Frye and others have shown, these songs of praise implicitly address the subject of the Queen's aging, which threatened to separate the unity of her two bodies. This was effected by the reintroduction of traditional gender roles into the concept of her physical body; the Queen's body came to represent her unconsummated and now impossible biological reproduction and, through her approaching death, represented a threat to the ruling political body. In the film this disruption is initially represented by the ambivalently gendered court singer and his encounter with Elizabeth in the context of a courtly fête. The high-pitched feminine voice from offscreen praising the authority of the Fairy Queen is imagined by the spectator as a woman's voice. The appearance of the castrato therefore disrupts our gender categories, just as the Queen's appearance must have done for her contemporaries. In the introductory sequence, these two ambiguous figures are seen sitting in ornate boats which are moving towards each other in a night scene on a river. The boat of the castrato travels from left to right, and that of the Queen from right to left, which is significant for the film's chronology. While the young singer follows a conventional linear direction of motion from beginning to end, the motion of the Queen is against the current and thus she travels in effect backwards. When the silhouettes of the two boats finally appear in the same frame, the oars of the Queen's boat stand still and are pointed by unseen rowers into the sky like totems.[21] The black river symbolises Elizabeth's Lethe or Styx, where the course of her life comes to an end. The courtly celebration of her blooming youth and her power thus takes on the character of an echo or a fading memory of what was once her present. The first close-up of the Queen shows her in profile with her chin stiffly tilted upward and her head crowned with a lacy black headdress. The image thus quotes the form of ancient coins which have depicted successive contemporary rulers' profiles since antiquity. This image lends Elizabeth I power and dignity, and it places her within the historical genealogy of 'history's great men', beginning with the first shot of her in the film. At the same time, her profile also shows us the sharp contours of an aging physiognomy and we are led back to the image of a hawk suggested by Virginia Woolf's description of the nose on the wax figure of Elizabeth in Westminster. The soft, high voice and the youthful appearance of the singer had initially evoked an image of the Fairy Queen, which does not prepare us for this dignified icon of mortality. The clash of word, voice and image in the prologue of the film in relation to the Queen's body can be understood as a paradigmatic introduction to the other incongruences, inversions and contingencies in the image of the Queen as well as in the film as a whole. In this sense it is only appropriate that the titles which follow to mark the beginning of the film's narrative defy any sense of linear development. A title announcing the date '1600' is followed by one announcing 'death'. The linear film narrative thus begins with an end: that of the Queen's existence in both body and in image. This chronological inversion, which is manifest in the filmic body of the Queen, relates also to the structure of the film as a whole. On the one hand, the film follows fairly closely the discontinuous jumps in time in Virginia Woolf's novel, which spans the period from 1600 to 1928. On the other hand, the film introduces a time reversal by giving each chapter a title that narrates a biography in reverse. After 'Death' follows 'Love', 'Art', 'Politics', 'Sex' and finally 'Birth'. All images meet with their counter-image, and teleological narratives dissolve in their own reversal.

Taking a closer look at the inner structure of the Elizabethan episode in the film, we see that it can be divided into four sequences. In the first we witness the initial encounter between Orlando and the Queen, as Virginia Woolf described it: the young noble kneels down and offers the Monarch a bowl of rosewater. No words are exchanged in this scene, directing the spectators' attention instead to the exchange of gazes between the two protagonists. Here a slight modification of Woolf's text becomes apparent. Orlando raises his eyes from the Queen's jewelled hands to look up at her face. The camera follows the upward tilting of his head and thus shows us Orlando's subjective point of view of the Queen; we see her face in full view for the first time. In an abrupt countershot we then see a close-up of Orlando's youthful face admiring the Queen. Paradoxically, it is this cut that creates an intimate connection between the two figures. The abrupt juxtaposition of these two close-ups brings an erotic relationship into play which will continue to drive the narrative forward. It is also a reflexive commentary on the medium itself, demonstrating the capacity of film to create a future sequence of time out of a moment in the present. Unlike Virginia Woolf's narrative, in which this potential is located in the persona of Elizabeth I as an effigy, here it is subtly expressed through the self-reflexive medium of film.

At their second encounter during an opulent banquet at Whitehall, the lack of words between the Queen and Orlando in the first scene has become just the opposite: the two engage in an intense dialogue in verse and prose. The film script improvises on its literary source by having Orlando recite an ode to Queen Elizabeth, praising her and at the same time dismantling her image: 'Ah! See the virgin rose / how sweetly she doeth first peep forth / with bashful modesty / that fairer seems the less Ye see her May / Ye see her after how / more bold and free / her bared bosom she doeth broad display / Ye see soon after how / she fades and falls away ...'

Sally Potter is referring here to the implicit attacks upon the aging Queen found in the courtly lyrics sung for her during her reign. But she rescues both Orlando and the figure of Elizabeth I by opening the dialogue here to a third subject of enunciation. We are introduced to the court poet who was responsible for writing the verse recited by Orlando. The filmmaker thus characterises the boy as a figure who does not speak in his own voice, thus effectively silencing him and aligning him with a purely visual status. In the narrative as well, the majestic and motherly gestures of the Queen clearly indicate where Orlando's rhetorical limits lie.

Elizabeth says to Orlando: 'Is this a worthy topic from one so clearly in the bloom of youth to one who'd desire it still?'

It is not the mute Orlando who answers, but the ambitious poet: 'Fair Virgo and gracious Majesty / Your bloom is legendary / These were of course not the sentiments of a son / but of a poet / Now, what ever would be / All of which is mine is here for your pleasure.'

And Elizabeth answers back: 'All that you call yours is mine already.'

With a slight hand gesture and these words, the Queen has regained her full sovereignty (Figure 15.2). Her gesture signals her reappropriation of all things, and the words proclaim a brazen law, namely that all things have always belonged to her and always will.

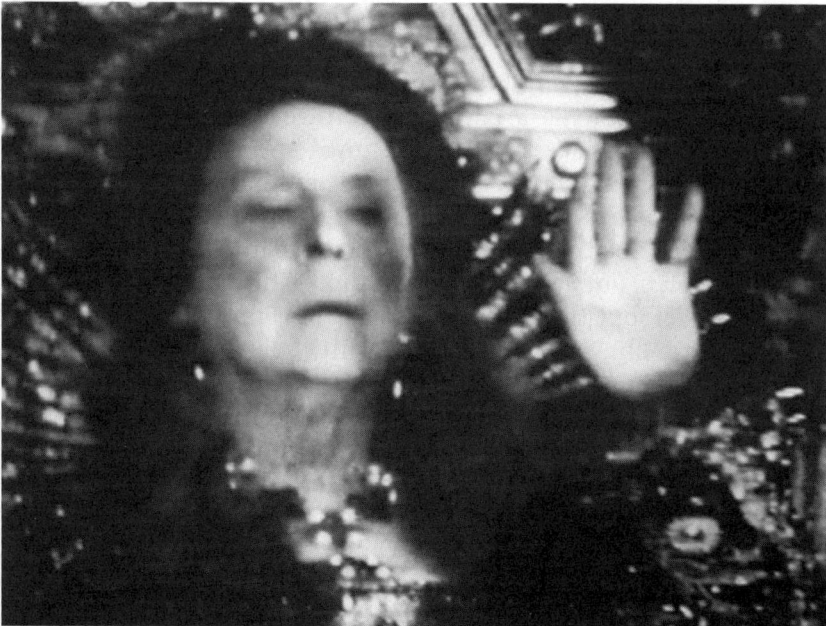

Figure 15.2 Quentin Crisp alias Elizabeth I in the banquet scene at Whitehall in Sally Potters Film Orlando in 1992, Filmstill.

Orlando and his youthful body will soon be explicitly subsumed under her power of possession. This is particularly apparent in the gentle but possessive gaze the Queen casts at him as she says the scornful words to the poet at her side. Her appropriation of Orlando's body does not happen without reciprocation, however. In the following scene set in a geometrically patterned Renaissance garden, she confers upon him the order of the Garter. During this ceremony we see the full bodies of the two protagonists in one shot for the first time, frozen in a kind of *tableau vivant* and surrounded by the courtly entourage. The Queen calls Orlando 'Sun of my old age / limb of my infirmity / my favourite / my mascot!' By declaring Orlando a physical extension of herself and an ornament for her body, she is able to incorporate his radiance, youth and virility into her own imago. This is very subtly expressed in the last term she applies to Orlando, 'mascot'. Phonetically the word unites three meanings: mask, masculinity and mascot. All three together secure the Queen magical protection, political and social power, and the possession of an erotic object.

The final scene involving Orlando and the Queen takes place in the Queen's bedchamber in Richmond. In the official ranking of royal chambers – present chamber, privy chamber and retreating rooms – the scene is set in the space most remote from the public. While Orlando is opening the final door to this most intimate of royal spaces, there is a parallel montage of her Majesty being undressed by her ladies-in-waiting until she is wearing only her corset and her petticoat. When the two are finally alone, she orders Orlando to her bed and pulls him to her corseted body, just as in Woolf's novel. She tucks the deed to an estate into his garter as a gift. The Queen lets out a sigh with the words 'This is my victory,' as in Woolf's novel, but the triumphal sound of cannon fire is not heard nor an erotic climax suggested. Her gift, however, will extend far beyond this momentary scene; the castle serves as a retreat for Orlando throughout his journeys through time all the way into the twentieth century.[22] A part of her thus accompanies him throughout his travels and his many metamorphoses. The gesture of her gift allows the Queen to transcend her own body and indirectly promises her an afterlife in him; but she also demands of him certain conditions. When Orlando attempts to graciously thank her with the words 'Your Majesty, I am forever y… ,' she cuts him off with her demand: 'But on one condition! Do not fade! Do not wither! Do not grow old!'

Queen Elizabeth's last words can be interpreted in various ways. On the one hand, they contribute to a powerful image of this eccentric Queen, whose will it is to live on forever, but whose demand calls for time to stand still and yet to continue. Virginia Woolf and Sally Potter grant this wish to her, and to us, by allowing time to move both forward and backward in the novel and in the film, and by permitting Orlando to become alternately male or female, yet never older. Taking into account the gender debates of the 1990s, one can understand the Queen's final demand as a tribute to Quentin Crisp which aims at transforming his individual practice of gender bending into a permanent and potent public affair. Through his embodiment of Queen Elizabeth, his 'queering the Queen', he has gained a wide public which extends far beyond his usual stage on the street or among the readers of his biography. He is able to recreate the figure of Elizabeth I for a worldwide cinema audience with each showing of the film by representing this figure as the effect of visual excess in terms of clothing, gender codes and age. Through his role as the powerful historical Queen, Quentin Crisp quite possibly gains the dignity and authority he needs in order to verbally and visually transform his individual pose into a powerful incantation. The medium of film is the most recent surface which allows him, in the role of Elizabeth I, to articulate their joint subversion of categories such as age, power and gender long after their physical existence has expired. He can do so because the biological body of Quentin Crisp in the guise of Elizabeth I's vestments has been fixed once and for all in analogous film images and thus lives on as a cinematic effigy. As such he has neither 'faded', 'withered', or 'grown old', remaining instead politically powerful.

Translated by Christina White

Notes

1. *Orlando*, directed by Sally Potter (UK, 1992).
2. Quentin Crisp, *How to Become a Virgin* (1981; London, 1996), 1.
3. Quentin Crisp, *The Naked Civil Servant* (1968; London, 1985); Crisp, *How to Become a Virgin*.
4. *The Naked Civil Servant*, Thames Television (UK, 1975).
5. Susan Frye has studied the intersection of bodily and topographical discourses concerning borders in the context of historical representations of Elizabeth I. Cf. Susan Frye, *Elizabeth I. The Competition of Representation* (New York and Oxford, 1993).

6. Claudia Benthien has analysed the complex relationship between surface and persona by comparing metonymic body models since the late Middle Ages, on the one hand, and anatomical body models of modernity, on the other. In the latter, skin, i.e. the body's surface, is distinguished from that which lies hidden beneath it. The models include: the anatomical machine, the romantic soul or the modern individual. Cf. Claudia Benthien, *Im Leibe wohnen. Literarische Imagologie und historische Anthropologie der Haut. Körper – Zeichen – Kultur / Body – Sign – Culture*, Vol. 4, ed. Hartwig Kalverkämper et al. (Berlin, 1998).
7. Virginia Woolf, *Orlando: A Biography* (Oxford, 1992), 21–22.
8. Ibid., 22.
9. Cf. Julius von Schlosser, *Tote Blicke. Geschichte der Porträtmalerei in Wachs. Ein Versuch*, ed. Thomas Medicus (Berlin, 1993), 43–44.
10. The English and French languages have retained the metonymic function of 'living wax pictures'. In French they are called 'représentations' and in English 'pictures', the latter of which now also refers to moving images in the cinema.
11. Quoted in Brenda Lyons, *Nachwort zu: Virginia Woolf: Orlando* (London, 1993), Note I/12, 235–36.
12. Woolf, *Orlando*, 16.
13. This sexual metaphor in Virginia Woolf's text stems from a modernist conception of the body; in the Elizabethan concept of virtue and chastity, such a metaphor would be unthinkable. Cf. Frye, *The Competition of Representation*.
14. Woolf, *Orlando*, 25.
15. Ibid., 26.
16. Crisp, *The Naked Civil Servant*, 135.
17. Ibid., 133.
18. Ibid., 33.
19. Ibid., 5.
20. Cf. Frye, *The Competition of Representation*; Louis Adrian Montrose, *The Purpose of Playing. Shakespeare and the Cultural Politics of Elizabethan Theatre* (Chicago, 1996).
21. The slow backwards movement of the Queen's boat is cinematographically reinforced by the fact that the skiff's flags are blown by a strong invisible wind.
22. It is generally known that Knole castle, in which Vita Sackville-West grew up, served as the model for the Elizabethan gift given to Orlando in Virginia Woolf's novel.

Selected Bibliography

Aldred, Cyril. *Akhenaten. Pharao of Egypt: A New Study*. London, 1972.

Alfassio Grimaldi, Ugoberto. *Il re 'buono'*. Milan, 1970.

Althoff, Gerd. *Otto III*. Darmstadt, 1996.

———— *Spielregeln der Politik im Mittelalter. Kommunikation in Frieden und Fehde*. Darmstadt, 1997.

Arnold, Dorothea. *The Royal Women of Amarna. Images of Beauty from Ancient Egypt*. With contributions by James P. Allen and L. Green. New York, 1996.

Arnold, Janet. 'The "Pictur" of Elizabeth I when Princess', *Burlington Magazine* 123, (1981), 303–4.

Assmann, Jan. *Das kulturelle Gedächtnis. Schrift, Erinnerung und politische Identität in frühen Hochkulturen*. Munich, 1999.

Auerbach, Erna. *Tudor Artists*. London, 1954.

Auerbach, Erna and Adams, C.K. *Paintings and Sculpture at Hatfield House*. London, 1971.

Axton, Marie. *The Queen's Two Bodies. Drama and the Elizabethan Succession*. London, 1977.

Balaban Quine, Judith. *The Bridesmaids. Grace Kelly, Princess of Monaco and Six Intimate Friends*. New York, 1989.

Barringer, Tim, ed. *Colonialism and the Object. Empire, Material Culture, and the Museum*. New York, 1998.

Bastl, Beatrix. *Tugend, Liebe, Ehre. Die adelige Frau in der Frühen Neuzeit*. Vienna, Cologne, Weimar, 2000.

Baudrillard, Jean. *L'échange symbolique et la mort*. Paris, 1993.

Beaton, Cecil. *Royal Portraits*. London, 1963.

Beik, William. *Absolutism and Society in Seventeenth-Century France*. Cambridge, 1985.

Benthien, Claudia. *Im Leibe wohnen. Literarische Imagologie und historische Anthropologie der Haut. Körper – Zeichen – Kultur , Body – Sign – Culture*, Vol. 4, ed. Hartwig Kalverkämper et al. Berlin, 1998.

———— *Haut. Literiturgeschichte – Körperbilder – Grenzdiskurse*. Frankfurt a.M., 1999.

Bepler, Jill. 'Women in German Funeral Sermons: Models of Virtue or Slice of Life?', *German Life and Letters* 44, (1991), 392–403.

———— 'Das Trauerzeremoniell an den Höfen Hessens und Thüringens in der ersten Hälfte des 17. Jahrhunderts', in Jörg Jochen Berns, Detlef Ignasiak, eds. *Frühneuzeitliche Hofkultur in Hessen und Thüringen*. Jena, 1993, 249–65.

———— 'Ansichten eines Staatsbegräbnisses. Funeralwerke und Diarien als Quelle zeremonieller Praxis', in Jörg Jochen Berns, Thomas Rahn, eds. *Zeremoniell als höfische Ästhetik in Spätmittelalter und Früher Neuzeit.* Tübingen, 1995, 183–97.

———— 'German Funeral Books and the Festival Description. A Parallel Development', in John Flood and William Kelly, eds. *The German Book 1450–1750.* London, 1995, 145–60.

———— 'Die Fürstin als Betsäule – Anleitung und Praxis der Erbauung am Hof', *Morgen-Glantz* 12, (2002).

Bepler, Jill, Kümmel, Birgit and Meise, Helga. 'Weibliche Selbstdarstellung im 17. Jahrhundert. Das Funeralwerk der Landgräfin Sophia Eleonora von Hessen-Darmstadt', in Heide Wunder and Gisela Engel, eds. *Geschlechterperspektiven. Forschungen zur Frühen Neuzeit.* Königstein, Taunus, 1998, 441–68.

Berghahn, Sabine and Hoch-Baumgarten, Sigrid, eds. *Mythos Diana – Von der Princess of Wales zur Queen of Hearts.* Gießen, 1999.

Berglar, Peter. *Maria Theresia.* Reinbek bei Hamburg, 1980.

Bernal, Martin. *Black Athena. The Afroasiatic Roots of Classical Civilization.* Vol. 1: *The Fabrication of Ancient Greece 1785–1985.* New Brunswick, New Jersey, 1987.

Berriot-Salvadore, Evelyne. 'Le discours de la médecine et de la science', in Georges Duby and Michelle Perrot, eds. *Histoire des femmes*, Vol. 3, XVIᵉ–XVIIIᵉ siècles. Paris, 1991, 359–95.

Berry, Philippa. *Chastity and Power: Elizabethan Literature and the Unmarried Queen.* London, New York, 1989.

Bertelli, Sergio. *Il corpo del re. Sacralità del potere nell'Europa medievale e moderna.* Firenze, 1990.

Biagini, Eugenio F. and Reid, Alastair J., eds. *Currents of Radicalism. Popular Radicalism, Organized Labour and Party Politics in Britain 1850–1914.* Cambridge, 1991.

Bijvoet-Williamson, Maya. *The Austrian Chambermaid Helene Kotanner*, in Katharina M. Wilson, ed. *Women Writers of the Renaissance and Reformation.* Athens, 1987, 326–49.

———— *The Memories of Helene Kottanner (1439–1440).* Cambridge, 1998.

Blake, Robert. *Disraeli.* London, 1966.

Bohn, Cornelia. 'Ins Feuer damit: Soziologie des Briefgeheimnisses', in Aleida Assmann and Jan Assmann, eds. *Schleier und Schwelle. Geheimnis und Öffentlichkeit. Archäologie der literarischen Kommunikation* V, 1. Munich, 1997, 42–51.

Borchardt, Ludwig. *Porträts der Königin Nofretete. Aus den Grabungen 1912/13 in Tell El-Amarna (1923).* Osnabrück, 1968.

Borchmeyer, Dieter. 'Repräsentation als ästhetische Existenz. Königliche Hoheit und Wilhelm Meister. Thomas Manns Kritik der formalen Existenz', *Recherches Germaniques* 13, (1983), 105–36.

Bourdieu, Pierre. *La Distinction: critique sociale du jugement.* Paris, 1979.

Bracalini, Romano. *La Regina Margherita, la prima donna sul trono d'Italia*, introduced by Ugoberto Alfassio Grimaldi. Milan, 1983.

Braun, Rudolf and Gugerli, David. *Macht des Tanzes – Tanz der Mächtigen. Hoffeste und Herrschaftszeremoniell 1550–1914*. Munich, 1993.

Breger, Claudia. '*Queens* und *Kings, oder: Performing Power*', *Amerikastudien/American Studies*. Special issue *Queer America*, eds. Katrin Gersdorf and Ralph Poole, 46, 1, (2001), 105–21.

—— '*Alien Egypt*, oder: Die Rückkehr der Mumie', in Ulrike Bergermann, Claudia Breger and Tanja Nusser, eds. *Techniken der Reproduktion. Medien – Leben – Diskurse*. Königstein/Ts, 2002.

Breuer, Stefan. 'Arthur Moeller van den Bruck: Politischer Publizist und Organisator des Neuen Nationalismus in Kaiserreich und Republik', in Gangolf Hübinger and Thomas Hertefelder, eds. *Kritik und Mandat, Intellektuelle in der deutschen Politik*. Munich, 2000.

Brice, Catherine. 'La Monarchie, un acteur oublié de la "Nationalisation" des Italiens? ', *Revue d'Histoire Moderne et Contemporaine* 45, 1, (1998), 147–69.

—— 'I viaggi della Regina Margherita', in *Altrove. Viaggi di donne dall'Antichità al Novecento*. Rome, 1999, 201–23.

Briggs, Asa. 'Prince Albert and the Arts and Sciences', in John S. Phillips, ed., *Prince Albert and the Victorian Age*. Cambridge, 1981, 51–78.

—— 'Prince Albert and the Constitution', in Adolf Birke and Kurt Kluxen, eds. *Deutscher und britischer Parlamentarismus*. Munich, 1985, 45–56.

Brude-Firnau, Gisela. *Die literarische Deutung Kaiser Wilhelms II. zwischen 1889 und 1989*. Heidelberg, 1997.

Bryant, Lawrence. *The King and the City in the Parisian Royal Entry Ceremony*. Geneva, 1986.

Bucholz, Robert. *The Augustan Court: Queen Anne and the Decline of Court Culture*. Stanford, 1993.

Bügner, Thorsten and Wagner, Gerhard. 'Die Alten und die Jungen im Deutschen Reich. Literatursoziologische Anmerkungen zum Verhältnis der Generationen 1871–1918', *Zeitschrift für Soziologie* 20, (1991), 177–90.

Bülow, Bernhard von. *Memorie*. Milan, 1931.

Burgess, J. Peter. 'In the Service of Narrative. Master and Servant in the Philosophy of Hegel', in Regina Schulte and Pothiti Hantzaroula, eds. *Narratives of the Servant*. Florence, 2001, 31–45.

Burke, Peter. *Ludwig XIV. Die Inszenierung des Sonnenkönigs*. Berlin, 1993.

Burkert, Walter. *Antike Mysterien. Funktionen und Gehalt*. Munich, 1990.

Burmeister, Hans Wilhelm. *Prince Philipp Eulenburg-Hertefeld (1847–1921). His Influence on Kaiser Wilhelm II and his Role in the German Government, 1888–1902*. Wiesbaden, 1981.

Cannadine, David. 'The Context: Performance and Meaning of Ritual. The British Monarchy and the Invention of Tradition', in Eric Hobsbawm and Terence Ranger, eds. *The Invention of Tradition*. Cambridge, 1984, 104–64.

Carter, Howard and Mace, A.C., *The Discovery of the Tomb of Tutankhamen;* with a new introduction by Jon Manchip White. New York, 1977.

Casalegno, Carlo. *La regina Margherita.* Turin, 1956.

Casteras, Susan P. 'The Wise Child and Her "Offspring": Some Changing Faces of Queen Victoria', in Margaret Homans and Adrienne Munich, eds., *Remaking Queen Victoria.* Cambridge, 1997, 182–92.

Cecil, Lamar. 'The Creation of Nobles in Prussia 1871–1918', *American Historical Review* 75, (1970), 757–95.

Ceram, C.W. (Kurt Marek). *Götter, Gräber und Gelehrte. Roman der Archäologie.* Reinbek, 1999.

Charlety, Sebastien. *Histoire de Lyon. Depuis les origines jusqu'à nos jours.* Lyon, 1972.

Cheal, David. *The Gift Economy.* London, 1988.

Christen, Gabriela. 'Die Bildnisse der Kaiserin', in Juliane Vogel, *Elisabeth von Österreich. Momente aus dem Leben einer Kunstfigur.* Frankfurt a.M., 1998, 164–91.

Christoph, Paul, ed. *Maria Theresia und Marie Antoinette. Ihr geheimer Briefwechsel.* Vienna, 1952.

Clapham, John. *Elizabeth of England: Certain Observations Concerning the Life and Reign of Queen Elizabeth,* eds. Evelyn Plummer Read and Conyers Read. Philadelphia, 1951.

Clifford, James. *The Predicament of Culture: Twentieth Century Ethnography, Literature, and Art.* Cambridge, MA, 1988.

Colley, Linda. 'The Apotheosis of George III: Loyalty, Royalty and the British Nation 1760–1820', *Past and Present* 102, (1984), 94–129.

——— *Britons. Forging the Nation 1707–1837.* London, 1992.

Colls, Robert and Dodd, Philip, eds. *Englishness. Politics and Culture 1880–1920.* Beckenham, 1986.

Cosandey, Fanny. *La reine de France. Symbole et pouvoir.* Paris, 2000.

Cresap Moore, David. *The Politics of Deference. A Study of the Nineteenth Century English Political System.* London, 1976.

Crisp, Quentin. *The Naked Civil Servant.* London, 1985.

——— *How to Become a Virgin.* London, 1996.

Daniel, Ute. *Hoftheater: zur Geschichte des Theaters und der Höfe im 18. und 19. Jahrhundert.* Stuttgart, 1995.

——— 'Überlegungen zum höfischen Fest der Barockzeit', *Niedersächsisches Jahrbuch für Landesgeschichte* 72, (2000) 45–66.

Dekker, Thomas. *Selected Prose Writings,* ed. E.D. Pendry. Cambridge, 1968.

Di Giorgio, Michela. *Le italiane dall'Unità ad oggi.* Rome, Bari, 1992.

Dienst, Heide. 'Frauenalltag in erzählenden Quellen', in *Frau und spätmittelalterlicher Alltag : Internationaler Kongress Krems an der Donau 2. bis 5. Oktober 1984.* Vienna, 1986, 213–41.

Dillmann, Edwin. *Maria Theresia.* Munich, 2000.

Doran, Susan. 'Juno versus Diana: the Treatment of Elizabeth I's Marriage in Plays and Entertainments, 1561–1581', *Historical Journal* 38, (1995), 257–74.

——— *Monarch and Matrimony: The Courtships of Elizabeth I*. London, 1996.

Duffy, Eamon. *The Stripping of the Altars: Traditional Religion in England 1400–1580*. New Haven, 1992.

Dyer, Richard. *Heavenly Bodies. Film Stars and Society*. London, 1986.

——— '*Charisma, A Star Is Born* and the Construction of Authenticity', in Christine Gledhill, ed. *Stardom: Industry of Desire*. New York, 1991, 57–59, 132–39.

——— *White*. New York, 1997.

——— *Stars*. London, 1998.

Ebrecht, Angelika. 'Das gläserne und das steinerne Herz. Zur politischen Psychologie der Monarchie am Beispiel von Prinzessin Diana', in Sabine Berghahn and Sigrid Hoch-Baumgarten, eds. *Mythos Diana – von der Princess of Wales zur Queen of Hearts*. Gießen, 1999, 117–32.

Eder, Franz X. 'Sexualized Subjects. Medical Discourse on Sexuality in German-Speaking Countries in the Late 18th and in the 19th Century', in *Civilization, Sexuality and Social Life in Historical Context. The Hidden Face of Urban Life*. Budapest, 1996, 17–29.

Engels, Jens Ivo. *Königsbilder. Sprechen, Singen und Schreiben über den König in der ersten Hälfte des 18. Jahrhunderts*. Bonn, 2000.

Erler, Mary C. 'Sir John Davies and the Rainbow Portrait of Queen Elizabeth', *Modern Philology* 84, (1987), 359–71.

Fabian, Johannes. *Time and the Other: How Anthropology Makes Its Object*. New York, 1983.

Fantoni, Marcello. *La corte del Granduca: forme e simboli del potere mediceo tra Cinquecento e Seicento*. Rome, 1994.

Farini, Domenico. *Diario di fine secolo*, ed. Emilia Morelli. Rome, 1961–62.

Fehrenbach, Elisabeth. *Wandlungen des deutschen Kaisergedankens, 1871–1918*. Munich, 1969.

Fesser, Gerd. 'Kaiser Wilhelm II. und der Wilhelminismus', in Karl Holl and Gerd Fesser, eds., *Caligula – Wilhelm II. und der Caesarenwahnsinn. Antikenrezeption und wilhelminische Politik am Beispiel des 'Caligula' von Ludwig Quidde*. Bremen, 2001, 117–52.

Finsten, Jill. *Isaac Oliver: Art at the Courts of Elizabeth I and James I*. New York, 1981.

Fischlin, Daniel. 'Political Allegory, Absolutist Ideology, and the "Rainbow Portrait" of Queen Elizabeth I', *Renaissance Quarterly* 50, (1997), 175–206.

Fleury, Graf von. *Memoiren der Kaiserin Eugénie*. Leipzig, 1921.

Forsyth Millen, Ronald and Wolf, Robert Erich. *Heroic Deeds and Mystic Figures: A New Reading of Rubens' Live of Maria de Medici*. Princeton, 1989.

Foucault, Michel. *L'archéologie du savoir*. Paris, 1969.

Fout, John C. 'Sexual Politics in Wilhelmine Germany: The Male Gender Crisis, Moral Purity, and Homophobia', *Journal of the History of Sexuality* 2, (1992), 388–421.

Fradenburg, Louise Olga, ed. *Women and Sovereignty*. Edinburgh, 1992.

Frank, Thomas. 'Höfische Mode', in Thomas Frank et al., eds. *Des Kaisers neue Kleider. Über das Imaginäre politischer Herrschaft. Texte. Bilder. Lektüren*. Frankfurt a.M., 2002, 197–205.

Frye, Susan. *Elizabeth I. The Competition of Representation*. New York, Oxford, 1993.

――― 'Sewing Connections: Elizabeth Tudor, Mary Stuart, Elizabeth Talbot, and the Seventeenth-Century Anonymous Needleworkers,' in Susan Frye and Karen Robertson, eds. *Maids and Mistresses, Cousins and Queens: Women's Alliances in Early Modern England*. New York, 1999, 165–82.

Fulford, Roger, ed. *Dearest Child. Private Correspondence of Queen Victoria and the Crown Princess of Prussia, 1858–1861*. London, 1964.

――― *Dearest Mama. Private Correspondence of Queen Victoria and the Crown Princess of Prussia, 1861–1864*. London, 1968.

――― *Your Dear Letter. Private Correspondence of Queen Victoria and the Crown Princess of Prussia, 1865–1871*. London, 1971.

――― *Beloved Mama. Darling Child. Private Correspondence of Queen Victoria and the German Crown Princess, 1878–1885*. London, 1976.

――― *Darling Child. Private Correspondence of Queen Victoria and the German Crown Princess, 1871–1878*. London, 1976.

Fürstenwald, Maria, ed. *Trauerreden des Barock*. Wiesbaden, 1973.

Fussenegger, Gertrud. *Maria Theresia*. Munich, 1994.

Gadamer, Hans-Georg. *Wahrheit und Methode. Werke 1*. Tübingen, 1986.

Gaither, Gant. *Fürstin von Monaco. Die Geschichte der Grace Kelly*. Bern, Stuttgart, Vienna, 1957.

――― *Princess of Monaco. The Story of Grace Kelly*. New York, 1957.

Gélis, Jacques. *L' Arbre et le fruit, la naissance dans l'Occident moderne, xvie–xixe siècle*. Paris, 1984.

Gilman, Sander L. *The Jew's Body*. New York, 1991.

――― *Rasse, Sexualität und Seuche. Stereotype aus der Innenwelt der westlichen Kultur*, trans. Helmut Rohlfing. Reinbek, 1992.

Graziani, René. 'The "Rainbow" Portrait of Queen Elizabeth I and Its Religious Symbolism', *Journal of the Warburg and Courtauld Institutes* 35, (1972), 247–59.

Greenfield, Jeanette. *The Return of Cultural Treasures*. Cambridge, MA, 1996.

Gregg, Edward. *Queen Anne*. London, 1984.

Grimm, Alfred. *Rilke und Ägypten*. Munich, 1997.

Guénée, Bernard. *Les entrées royales françaises de 1328 à 1515*. Paris, 1968.

Guy, John, ed. *The Reign of Elizabeth I: Court and Culture in the Last Decade*. Cambridge, 1995.

Hackett, Helen. *Virgin Mother, Maiden Queen: Elizabeth I and the Cult of the Virgin Mary*. New York, 1995.

Haigh, Christopher. *Elizabeth I*. London, 1988.
Hall, Phillip. *Royal Fortune: Tax, Money and the Monarchy*. London, 1992.
Hamann, Brigitte. *Elisabeth. Kaiserin wider Willen*. Vienna, Munich, 1982.
Hanley, Sarah. 'The Monarchic State in Early Modern France: Marital Regime Government and Male Right', in Adrianna Bakos, ed. *Politics, Ideology and the Law in Early Modern Europe*. Rochester, 1994.
Harris, Thomas. 'The Building of Popular Images. Grace Kelly and Marilyn Monroe', in Christine Gledhill, ed. *Stardom. Industry of Desire*. London, New York, 1991.
Hayward, John. *Annals of the First Four Years of the Reign of Queen Elizabeth*, ed. John Bruce. New York, 1968.
Hearn, Karen. *Dynasties: Painting in Tudor and Jacobean England 1530–1630*. New York, 1996.
Hecht, Karsten. 'Die Harden-Prozesse – Strafverfahren, Öffentlichkeit und Politik im Kaiserreich' (Ph.D. diss. Munich, 1997).
Heindl, Waltraud and Schulte, Regina, eds. *Höfische Welt. L'Homme. Zeitschrift für Feministische Geschichtswissenschaft* 8, 2, (1997).
Hellige, Hans Dieter and Schulin, Ernst, eds. *Walther Rathenau-Gesamtausgabe*, Vol. VI.: *Walther Rathenau – Maximilian Harden, Briefwechsel 1897–1920*. Munich, 1983.
Hennings, Fred. *Und sitzet zur linken Hand. Franz Stephan von Lothringen*. Vienna, Berlin, Stuttgart, 1961.
Heuvel, Christine van den. 'Sophie von der Pfalz (1630–1714) und ihre Tochter Sophie Charlotte (1668–1705)', in Heide Wunder and Kerstin Merkel, eds. *Deutsche Frauen der Frühen Neuzeit. Dichterinnen – Malerinnen – Mäzeninnen*. Darmstadt, 2000, 77–92.
Hibbert, Christopher, ed. *Queen Victoria in her Letters and Journals*. London, 1984.
Hilliard, Nicholas. *A Treatise Concerning the Arte of Limning*, ed. R.K.R. Thornton and T.G.S. Cain. Manchester, 1981.
Hollen Lees, Lynn. *The Solidarity of Strangers. The English Poor Laws and the People, 1700–1948*. Cambridge, 1998.
Homans, Margeret. *Royal Representations. Queen Victoria and British Culture (1837–1876)*. Chicago, 1998.
Hull, Isabel V. 'Kaiser and "Liebenberg Circle"', in John C.G. Röhl and Nicolaus Sombart, eds. *Kaiser Wilhelm II. New Interpretations*. Cambridge, 1982, 193–220.
——— *The Entourage of Kaiser Wilhelm II – 1888–1918*. Cambridge 1982.
Hunt, Lynn. 'The Many Bodies of Marie Antoinette', in Lynn Hunt, ed., *Eroticism and the Body Politic*. Baltimore, 1991.
——— *The Family Romance of the French Revolution*. London, 1992.
Ingrao, Charles W. and Thomas, Andrew L. 'Piety and Patronage: The Empress Consort of the High Baroque', *German History* 20, 1, (2000), 20–43.
Jacobsen, Roswitha. 'Religiosität und Herrschaftsrepräsentation in Funeralien sächsischer Fürsten', in Dieter Breuer, ed. *Religion und Religiosität im Zeitalter des Barock*. Wiesbaden, 1995, 163–73.

———— 'Fürstenfreundschaft. Landgraf Ludwig VI. von Hessen-Darmstadt und Friedrich I. von Sachsen-Gotha und Altenburg in ihren Selbstzeugnissen', in Ferdinand van Ingen and Christian Juranek, eds. *Ars et amicitia. Festschrift für Martin Bircher zum 60. Geburtstag.* Amsterdam, 1998, 475–502.

Jacobsen, Roswitha, ed. *Friedrich I. von Sachsen-Gotha und Altenburg: Die Tagebücher 1667–1686, Erster Band Tagebücher 1667–1677.* Weimar, 1998.

———— *Friedrich I. von Sachsen-Gotha und Altenburg: Die Tagebücher 1667–1686, Zweiter Band Tagebücher 1678–1686.* Weimar, 2000.

James, Susan. 'Who Is the Mummy Elder Lady?' *KMT. A Modern Journal of Ancient Egypt* 12, 2, (2001), 42–50.

Johann, Ernst, ed. *Reden des Kaisers. Ansprachen, Predigten und Trinksprüche Wilhelms II.* Munich, 1966.

Johnson, Paul. *Elizabeth I.* London, 1974.

Jordan, W.K. *Edward VI: The Young King: The Protectorship of the Duke of Somerset.* London, 1968.

Jürgs, Michael. *Der Fall Romy Schneider. Eine Biographie.* Munich, Leipzig, 1991.

Kantorowicz, Ernst H. *The King's Two Bodies, A Study in Mediaeval Political Theology.* Princeton, 1997.

Keller, Katrin. 'Kurfürstin Anna von Sachsen (1532–1585). Von Möglichkeiten und Grenzen einer "Landesmutter"', in Jan Hirschbiegel and Werner Paravicini, eds. *Das Frauenzimmer. Die Frau bei Hofe in Spätmittelalter und früher Neuzeit.* Stuttgart, 2000, 263–85.

Kerr, Alfred. *Wo liegt Berlin? Briefe aus der Reichshauptstadt,* ed. Günther Rühle. Berlin, 1997.

King, John N. 'Queen Elizabeth I: Representation of the Virgin Queen', *Renaissance Quarterly* 43, (1990), 30–74.

King, Thomas A. 'Performing "Akimbo": Queer Pride and Epistemological Prejudice', in Moe Meyer, ed. *The Politics and Poetics of Camp.* New York, 1994, 23–50.

Kingsley Kent, Susan. *Sex and Suffrage in Britain 1860–1914.* Princeton, 1987.

Klarwill, Victor von. *Queen Elizabeth and Some Foreigners.* New York, 1928.

Kleinclausz, Arthur. A *Histoire de Lyon.* Lyon, 1948.

Knott, John. *Popular Opposition to the 1834 Poor Law.* London, 1986.

Kohlrausch, Martin. 'Die Flucht des Kaisers – Doppeltes Scheitern adlig-bürgerlicher Monarchiekonzepte', in Heinz Reif, ed. *Adel und Bürgertum in Deutschland II. -Entwicklungslinien und Wendepunkte.* Berlin, 2001, 65–101.

Kohut, Thomas. *Wilhelm II. and the Germans. A Study in Leadership.* New York, 1991.

Komander, Gerhild. 'Tod und Trauer am brandenburg-preußischen Hof', in *Sophie Charlotte und ihr Schloss. Ein Musenhof in Brandenburg-Preußen.* Munich, London, New York, 1999.

Koschorke, Albrecht. 'Macht und Fiktion', in Thomas Frank et al., eds. *Des Kaisers neue Kleider. Über das Imaginäre politischer Herrschaft. Texte. Bilder. Lektüren*. Frankfurt a.M., 2002, 73–85.

Krauss, Rolf. '1913–1988: 75 Jahre Büste der Nofretetel/Nefretiti in Berlin', *Jahrbuch des Preußischen Kulturbesitzes* 24, (1987), 87–124; 28, (1991), 123–57.

Kröll, Joachim. 'Bayreuther Barock und frühe Aufklärung 1. Teil: Markgräfin Erdmuth Sophie (1644–1670) und ihre Bedeutung für Bayreuth', *Archiv für Geschichte von Oberfranken* 55, (1975), 55–174.

Kronberg, Max. *Nofretete. Roman einer Königin (1934)*. Berlin, 1947.

Kühne, Thomas. 'Männergeschichte als Geschlechtergeschichte', in Thomas Kühne, ed. *Männergeschichte – Geschlechtergeschichte. Männlichkeit im Wandel der Moderne*. Frankfurt a.M., 1996, 7–30.

Kurtz, Harold. *The Empress Eugénie. 1826–1920*. Boston, 1964.

Lacey, Robert. *Grace*. London, 1995.

Laqueur, Thomas. *Making Sex: Body and Gender from the Greeks to Freud*. Cambridge, MA, 1990.

Latour, Annie. *Magier der Mode. Macht und Geheimnis der Haute Couture*. Stuttgart, 1956.

Leighton, Joseph. 'Poems of Mortality in the German Baroque', *German Life and Letters* 36, (1982), 83, 241–57.

Lenz, Rudolf. *'De mortuis nil nisi bene?' Leichenpredigten als multidisziplinäre Quelle unter besonderer Berücksichtigung der Historischen Familienforschung, der Bildungsgeschichte und der Literaturgeschichte*. Sigmaringen, 1990.

Leuchtmann, Angela. *Der Fall Philipp Eulenburg. Anfang und Ende einer Karriere im wilhelminischen Deutschland*. Munich, 1998.

Levin, Carole. *The Heart and Stomach of a King: Elizabeth I and the Politics of Sex and Power*. Philadelphia, 1994.

Lipparini, Lilla. *Lettere fra la Regina Margherita e Marco Minghetti (1882–1886)*. Milan, 1957.

Llewellyn, Nigel. *The Art of Death. Visual Culture in the English Death Ritual c.1500–c.1800*. London, 1991.

Lloyd, Christopher and Thurley, Simon. *Henry VIII. – Images of a Tudor King*. London, 1990.

Loades, David M. *The Reign of Mary Tudor*. London, 1979.

——— 'Philip II and the Government of England', in C. Cross, D. Loades and J.J. Scarisbrick, eds. *Law and Government under the Tudors*. Cambridge, 1988, 177–94.

——— David *udor: A Life*, Oxford,

Longford, Elizabeth. *Victoria R. I*. London, 1964.

Machiavelli, Niccolò. *Nicholas Machievel's Prince*. London, 1968.

MacKenzie, John M. *Imperialism and Popular Culture*. Manchester, 1984.

Maclean, Ian. *The Renaissance Notion of Woman*. Cambridge, 1980.

Magnusson, Lynne. *Shakespeare and Social Dialogue: Dramatic Language and Elizabethan Letters*. Cambridge, 1999.

Manningham, John. *The Diary of John Manningham of the Middle Temple, 1602–1603*, ed. R.P. Sorlien. Hanover, 1976.

Marcus, Leah. *Puzzling Shakespeare*. Berkeley, CA, 1988.

Marin, Louis. *Portrait du Roi*. Paris, 1981.

Marshall, Dorothy. *The Life and Times of Victoria*. London, 1972.

Mauget, Irénée. *L'Impératrice Eugénie, Eugénie Kaiserin von Frankreich (1826–1920)*. Paris, 1909.

Mauss, Marcel. *Essai sur le don. Forme et raison de l'échange dans les sociétés archaïques*. Paris, 1925.

Maza, Sarah. 'The Diamond Necklace Affair Revisited', in Lynn Hunt, ed. *Eroticism and the Body Politic*. Baltimore, 1991.

——— *Private Lives and Public Affairs. The Causes Célèbres of Prerevolutionary France*. Berkeley, Los Angeles, London, 1993.

McLaren, Anne N. *Political Culture in the Reign of Elizabeth I: Queen and Commonwealth, 1558–1585*. Cambridge, 1999.

Meise, Helga. *Das archivierte Ich. Schreibkalender und höfische Repräsentation in Hessen-Darmstadt 1624–1790*. Darmstadt, 2002.

Midelfort, H.C. Erik. *Mad Princes of Renaissance Germany*. Charlottesville, London, 1994.

Mollay, Karl, ed. *Die Denkwürdigkeiten der Helene Kottannerin (1439–1440)*. Vienna, 1971.

Mommsen, Wolfgang J. *Das Ringen um den nationalen Staat. Die Gründung und der innere Ausbau des Deutschen Reiches unter Otto von Bismarck, 1850 bis 1890*. Berlin, 1993.

Montaldo, Silvano. *Patria e affari. Tommaso Villa e la costruzione del consenso tra unità e grande guerra*. Turin, 1999.

Monti, Antonio. *Donne e passioni del Risorgimento*. Milan, 1935.

Montrose, Louis Adrian. 'The Elizabethan Subject and the Spenserian Text', in Patricia Parker and David Quint, eds. *Literary Theory, Renaissance Texts*. Baltimore, 1986, 303–40.

——— *The Purpose of Playing. Shakespeare and the Cultural Politics of Elizabethan Theatre*. Chicago 1996.

——— 'Idols of the Queen: Policy, Gender, and the Picturing of Elizabeth I', *Representations* 68, (1999), 108–61.

Montserrat, Dominic. *Akhenaten. History, Fantasy and Ancient Egypt*. London, New York, 2000.

Morenz, Siegfried. 'Ägyptische Religion', in Christel Matthias Schröder, ed. *Die Religion der Menschheit*. Stuttgart, Vol. 8, 1960.

Mosse, George L. 'Manliness and Homosexuality', in George L. Mosse, ed. *Nationalism and Sexuality. Respectability and Abnormal Sexuality in Modern Europe*. New York, 1985, 23–47.

Munich, Adrienne. *Queen Victoria's Secrets*. New York, 1996.

Mußgnug, Reinhard. *Wem gehört Nofretete? Anmerkungen zu dem deutsch-deutschen Streit um den ehemals preußischen Kulturbesitz*. Berlin, New York, 1977.

Neale, John E. *Queen Elizabeth I: A Biography*. London, 1958.

Nordman, Daniel. *Un tour de France royal. Le voyage de Charles IX (1564–1566)*. Paris, 1984.

Nye, Robert A. *Masculinity and Male Codes of Honour in Modern France*. Oxford, 1993.

Opitz, Claudia. 'Hausmutter und Landesfürstin', in Rosario Villari, ed. *Der Mensch des Barock*. Frankfurt a.M. 1999, 344–70.

Paas, John Roger. *The German Political Broadsheet 1600–1700*, Vol. 1: 1600–1615. Wiesbaden, 1985.

Paczensky, Gert v. and Ganslmayr, Herbert. *Nofretete will nach Hause. Europa – Schatzhaus der 'dritten Welt'*. Munich, 1984.

Paléologue, Maurice. *Cavour. Ein grosser Realist*. Berlin, 1928.

Paulmann, Johannes. *Pomp und Politik: Monarchenbegegnungen in Europa zwischen Ancien Régime und Erstem Weltkrieg*. Paderborn, 2000.

Perrig, Severin, ed. *'Aus mütterlicher Wohlmeinung', Kaiserin Maria Theresia und ihre Kinder. Eine Korrespondenz*. Weimar, 1999.

Pirozynski, Jan. *Die Herzogin Sophie von Braunschweig-Wolfenbüttel aus dem Hause der Jagellonen (1522–1575) und ihre Bibliothek*. Wiesbaden, 1992.

Pivato, Stefano. *Il nome della storia. Onomastica e religione politiche nell'Italia contemporanea*. Bologna, 1999.

Pollock, Griselda. *Vision and Difference: Femininty, Feminism and the Histories of Art*. London, 1988.

Pommier, Edoard. *Théories du portrait de la Renaissance aux Lumières*. Paris, 1998.

Prochaska, Frank. *Royal Bounty. The Making of a Welfare Monarchy*. London, 1995.

Quinn, Edward. *Fotograf Nizza*. Zurich, Berlin, New York, 1994.

Radkau, Joachim. *Das Zeitalter der Nervosität. Deutschland zwischen Bismarck und Hitler*, Munich, Vienna, 1998.

Rahn, Thomas. 'Masse, Maske und Macht. Psychologien des Zeremoniells im 20. Jahrhundert', in Bernhard Jahn, Thomas Rahn and Claudia Schnitzer, eds. *Zeremoniell in der Krise. Störung und Nostalgie*. Marburg, 1998, 129–48.

Reinhardt, Emil A. *Napoleon III. und Eugenie. Tragikomödie eines Kaisertums*. Berlin, 1930.

Reinhardt, Sonja. *'Wie ihr's euch träumt, wird Deutschland nicht erwachen.' Formen der Herrschaftslegitimation in ausgewählten Reden von Kaiser Wilhelm II. und Adolf Hitler*, (Ph.D. diss.) Hannover, 1994.

Requate, Jörg. 'Öffentlichkeit und Medien als Gegenstände historischer Analyse', *Geschichte und Gesellschaft* 25, (1999), 5–32.

Rhodes James, Robert. *Albert. Prince Consort: A Biography*. London, 1983.

Ribeiro, Aileen. 'La mode dans l'œuvre de Winterhalter', in *Franz Xaver Winterhalter et les Cours de l'Europe de 1830 à 1870*. Exhibition organised by the National Portrait Gallery of London 12 February to 7 May, 1988. London, 1988, 66–72.

Rich, Norman, ed. *The Holstein Papers, The Memoirs, Diaries and Correspondance of Friedrich von Holstein, 1837–1909*, 4 vols. Cambridge, 1955.

Richards, J.M. 'Mary Tudor as "Sole Queene"? Gendering the Tudor Monarchy', *Historical Journal* 40, (1997), 895–924.

Roberts, Philip. *The Diary of Sir David Hamilton, 1703–14*. Oxford, 1975.

Rogge, Helmuth. *Holstein und Harden. Politisch-Publizistisches Zusammenspiel zweier Außenseiter des Wilhelminischen Reichs*. Munich, 1959.

Röhl, John C.G., *Wilhelm II. Der Aufbau der Persönlichen Monarchie. 1888–1900*. Munich, 2001.

Röhl, John C.G., ed. *Philipp Eulenburgs politische Korrespondenz*, 3.vols. (Deutsche Geschichtsquellen des 19. und 20. Jahrhunderts 52). Boppard a. Rh., 1976–83.

Roux, Onorato. *La prima regina d'Italia*. Milan, 1901.

Said, Edward. *Orientalism*. New York, 1978.

Santini, Arturo. *La leggenda di Margherita di Savoia nei secoli futuri: conferenza letta a Bologna, Torino, Moncalieri, Courmayeur, Gressoney, S. Iean, etc.* Milan, 1901.

Sarti, Raffaela. 'Telling Zita's Tale. Holy Servant's Stories and Servant's history', in Regina Schulte and Pothiti Hantzaroula, ed. *Narratives of the Servant*. Florence, 2001, 1–30.

Sauer, Birgit. 'Liebe, Öffentlichkeit und ein "Staatsbegräbnis". Über Gefühle als politische Herrschaftsressource', in Sabine Berghahn and Sigrid Hoch-Baumgarten, eds. *Mythos Diana – von der Princess of Wales zur Queen of Hearts*. Gießen, 1999.

Saunders, Edith. *The Age of Worth, Couturier to the Empress Eugenie*. With plates, including portraits. London, 1954.

Schama, Simon. *Landscape and Memory*. New York, 1995.

Schildt, Axel. 'Das Jahrhundert der Massenmedien: Ansichten zu einer künftigen Geschichte der Öffentlichkeit', *Geschichte und Gesellschaft* 27, (2001), 177–206.

Schlögl, Rudolf. 'Öffentliche Gottesverehrung und privater Glaube in der Frühen Neuzeit. Beobachtungen zur Bedeutung von Kirchenzucht und Frömmigkeit für die Abgrenzung privater Sozialräume', in Gert Melville and Peter von Moos, eds. *Das Öffentliche und Private in der Vormoderne*. Cologne, Weimar, Vienna, 1998.

Schlosser, Julius von. *Tote Blicke. Geschichte der Porträtmalerei in Wachs. Ein Versuch. (1910)*, ed. Thomas Medicus. Berlin, 1993.

Schmidt, Uta C. 'Der Antennenhut. Frauenkörper in gesellschaftlichen Mediatisierungsprozessen am Beispiel des frühen Rundfunks (1923–1933)', *Metis, Medien und Gender* 13, 7, (1998), 31–50.

Schmitter, Elke. 'Scheitern als Erfolg: Die Paradoxien der Lady Diana', in Sabine Berghahn and Sigrid Hoch-Baumgarten, eds. *Mythos Diana – von der Princess of Wales zur Queen of Hearts*. Gießen, 1999.

Schoch, Rainer. *Das Herrscherbild in der Malerei des 19. Jahrhunderts*. Munich, 1975.

Scholz, Susanne. *Body Narratives. Writing the Nation and Fashioning the Subject in Early Modern England*. London, New York, 2000.

Schulte, Regina. 'Der Aufstieg der konstitutionellen Monarchie und das Gedächtnis der Königin', *Historische Anthropologie* 6, (1998), 76–103.

Schulz, Andreas. 'Der Aufstieg der "vierten Gewalt". Medien, Politik und Öffentlichkeit im Zeitalter der Massenkommunikation', *Historische Zeitschrift* 270, (2000), 65–97.

Schwarzer, Alice. *Romy Schneider. Mythos und Leben*. Cologne, 1998.

Seydel, Renate. *Romy Schneider. Ein Leben in Bildern*. Berlin, 1996.

Shell, Marc. *Elizabeth's Glass*. Lincoln, 1993.

Siefken, Hinrich. 'Thomas Mann and the Concept of "Repräsentation": "Königliche Hoheit"', *The Modern Language Review* 73, (1978), 337–50.

Smith, Thomas. *De Republica Anglorum: A Discourse on the Commonwealth of England*, ed. L. Alston. Shannon, 1972.

Smout, Thomas C. *Victorian Values. A Joint Symposium of the Royal Society of Edinburgh and the British Academy, December 1990* (Proceedings of the British Academy 78). Oxford, 1992.

Sophie Charlotte und ihr Schloss. Ein Musenhof in Brandenburg-Preußen. Munich, London, New York, 1999.

Spada, James. *Grace. The Secret Lives of a Princess. An Intimate Biography*. New York. 1987.

Starkey, David. *Elizabeth: The Struggle for the Throne*. New York, 2000.

Stedman Jones, Gareth. *Languages of Class. Studies in English Working Class History 1832–1982*. Cambridge, 1983.

Steiger, Johann Anselm. *Schule des Sterbens. Die 'Kirchhofgedanken' des Andreas Gryphius (1616–1664) als poetologische Theologie im Vollzug*. Heidelberg, 2000.

Steiner, Uwe. 'Triumphale Trauer. Die Trauerfeierlichkeiten aus Anlaß des Todes der ersten preußischen Königin in Berlin im Jahre 1705', *Forschungen zur brandenburgischen und preussischen Geschichte* N.S. 11, (2001), 23–52.

Stevenson, John. 'The Queen Caroline Affair', in id., ed. *London in the Age of Reform*. Oxford, 1977, 117–48.

Stollberg-Rilinger, Barbara. 'Das Verschwinden des Geheimnisses. Einleitende Bemerkungen', *Zeitsprünge. Forschungen zur Frühen Neuzeit* 6, 1–4: *Das Geheimnis am Beginn der europäischen Moderne*, 2002, 229–33.

Strachey, Lytton. *Queen Victoria*. Harmondsworth, 1971.

Strong, Roy. *Portraits of Queen Elizabeth I*. Oxford, 1963.

——— *Holbein and Henry VIII*. London, 1967.

——— *The English Icon*. London, 1969.

——— *Tudor and Jacobean Portraits*, 2 vols. London, 1969.

——— *The Cult of Elizabeth: Elizabethan Portraiture and Pageantry*. London, 1977.

——— *Artists of the Tudor Court*. London, 1983.

——— *Gloriana: The Portraits of Queen Elizabeth I*. London, 1987.

——— *The Tudor and Stuart Monarchy: Pageantry, Painting, Iconography*, Vol. 1: *Tudor*. Woodbridge, 1995.

Sykora, Katharina. *Unheimliche Paarungen. Androidenfaszination und Geschlecht in der Fotografie*. Cologne, 1999.

Taeger, Angela and Lautmann, Rüdiger. 'Sittlichkeit und Politik. § 175 im Deutschen Kaiserreich (1871–1919)', in Angela Taeger, ed. *Männerliebe im alten Deutschland*. Sozialgeschichtliche Abhandlungen. Berlin, 1992, 239–68.

Teskey, Gordon. *Allegory and Violence*. Ithaca, NY, 1996.

Tetzeli von Rosador, Kurt and Mersmann, Arndt, eds. *Queen Victoria. Ein biographisches Lesebuch*. Munich, 2000.

Thiele, Johannes. *Elisabeth. Das Buch ihres Lebens*. Munich, Leipzig, 1996.

Thomas, Chantal. *The Wicked Queen. The Origins of the Myth of Marie-Antoinette*. New York, 1999.

Thompson, Dorothy. *The Chartists. Popular Politics in the Industrial Revolution*. London, 1984.

—— *Queen Victoria. Gender and Power*. London, 1990.

—— *Queen Victoria. The Women, the Monarchy and the People*. New York, 1990.

Thompson, John B. *Political Scandal: Power and Visibility in the Media Age*. Cambridge, 2000.

Trevor-Roper, Hugh. 'The Invention of Tradition: the Highland-Tradition of Scotland', in Eric Hobsbawm and Terence Ranger, eds. *The Invention of Tradition*. Cambridge, 1984, 15–42.

Turner, Victor. 'Betwixt and Between: The Liminal Period in *Rites de Passage*', in *The Forest of Symbols*. Ithaca, NY, 1967.

Tyldesley, Joyce A. *Nefertiti: Egypt's Sun Queen*. London, 1998.

Vandenberg, Philipp. *Nofretete. Eine archäologische Biographie*. Bern et al., 1975.

Veszprémy, László. 'König Stephan der Heilige', in Alfried Wieczorek and Hans-Martin Hinz, eds. *Europas Mitte um 1000. Beiträge zur Geschichte, Kunst und Archäologie. Handbuch zur Ausstellung*, Vol. 2. Stuttgart, 2000, 875–79.

Vierhaus, Rudolf, ed. *Am Hof der Hohenzollern. Aus dem Tagebuch der Baronin von Spitzemberg 1865–1914*. Munich, 1995.

Vischer, Friedrich Theodor. 'Vernünftige Gedanken über die jetzige Mode', in Robert Vischer, ed. *Kritische Gänge*, Vol. 5. Munich, 1921, 339–65.

Vismann, Cornelia. 'Gewandstudien', in Friedrich Kittler and Cornelia Vismann, *Vom Griechenland*. Berlin, 2001, 91–111.

Vittori, Giovanna. *Margherita di Savoia*. Assisi, 1935–38.

Vogel, Juliane. *Elisabeth von Österreich. Momente aus dem Leben einer Kunstfigur*. Frankfurt a.M., 1998.

Walter, Friedrich. 'Maria Theresia. Briefe und Aktenstücke in Auswahl', in Rudolf Buchner, ed. *Ausgewählte Quellen zur Deutschen Geschichte der Neuzeit. Freiherr vom Stein-Gedächtnisausgabe*, Vol. XII. Darmstadt, 1968.

Walter, Fritz. *Kino in Österreich, 1945–1983*. Vienna, 1984.

Weigall, Arthur E.P. *The Life and Times of Akhnaton, Pharaoh of Egypt*. Edinburgh, London, 1910.

Weil, Rachel. 'Sometimes a Sceptre Is Only a Sceptre: Pornography and
Politics in Restoration England', in Lynn Hunt, ed. *The Invention of
Pornogaphy*. New York, 1993.
——— *Political Passions. Gender, the Family and Political Argument in
England, 1680–1714*. Manchester, New York, 1999.
Weintraub, Stanley. *Victoria. Biography of a Queen*. London, 1996.
——— *Albert. Uncrowned King*. London, 1997.
Weisbrod, Bernd. 'Medien als symbolische Form der Massengesellschaft: Die
medialen Bedingungen von Öffentlichkeit im 20. Jahrhundert',
Historische Anthropologie 9, (2001), 270–83.
Weller, Uwe B. *Maximilian Harden und die 'Zukunft', Deutsche
Presseforschung* 13. Bremen, 1970.
Wenzel, Horst. 'Öffentlichkeit und Heimlichkeit in Gottfrieds "Tristan"',
Zeitschrift für deutsche Philologie 107, (1988), 335–61.
——— 'Repräsentation und schöner Schein am Hof und in der höfischen
Literatur', in Hedda Ragotzky and Horst Wenzel, eds. *Höfische
Repräsentation. Das Zeremoniell und die Zeichen*. Tübingen, 1990,
171–209.
——— 'Das höfische Geheimnis: Herrschaft, Liebe, Texte', in Aleida
Assman and Jan Assmann eds. *Schleier und Schwelle. Geheimnis und
Öffentlichkeit. Archäologie der literarischen Kommunikation* V, 1.
Munich, 1997, 53–69.
Wenzel, Horst and Lechtermann, Christina. 'Repräsentation und
Kinästhetik. Teilhabe am Text oder die Verlebendigung der Worte',
Paragrana. Internationale Zeitschrift für Historische Anthropologie 10,
(2001), 191–214.
Wettengel, Judith. 'Tutanchamun – das "Riesenshowgeschäft" um den
"Superstar aus dem alten Ägypten"', in Wolfgang Wettengel, ed. *Mythos
Tutanchamun*. Reimlingen, 2000, 18–45.
Wienfort, Monika. *Monarchie in der bürgerlichen Gesellschaft.
Deutschland und England von 1640 bis 1848*. Göttingen 1993.
Wildung, Dietrich. *Ägyptische Kunst in Berlin. Meisterwerke im
Bodemuseum und in Charlottenburg. Ägyptisches Museum und
Papyrussammlung Staatliche Museen zu Berlin – Preußischer
Kulturbesitz*. Mainz, 1999.
Wilhelm-Schaffer, Irmgard. *Gottes Beamter und Spielmann des Teufels. Der
Tod in Spätmittelalter und Früher Neuzeit*. Köln, Weimar, Vienna,
1999.
Wilson, Elkin Calhoun. *England's Eliza*. London, 1966.
Wiswe, Mechthild. 'Die Särge im jüngeren herzoglichen Grabgewölbe der
Hauptkirche Beatae Mariae Virginis', in Hans-Herbert Möller, ed. *Die
Hauptkirche Beatae Mariae Virginis in Wolfenbüttel*. Hannover, 1987.
Woodall, Joanna. 'An Exemplary Consort: Antonis Mor's Portrait of Mary
Tudor', *Art History* 14, (1991), 192–224.
Woolf, Virginia. *Orlando. Eine Biografie*. Frankfurt a.M., 1981.

Worth, Jean Philippe. *A Century of Fashion*, trans. Ruth Scott Miller. Boston, 1928.

Wunder, Heide. *'Er ist die Sonn, sie ist der Mond': Frauen in der Frühen Neuzeit*. Munich, 1992.

———— 'Herrschaft und öffentliches Handeln von Frauen in der Gesellschaft der Frühen Neuzeit', in Ute Gerhard, ed. *Frauen in der Geschichte des Rechts. Von der Frühen Neuzeit bis zur Gegenwart*. Munich, 1997, 27–54.

Wunder, Heide, Zöttlein, Helga and Hoffmann, Barbara. 'Konfession, Religiosität und politisches Handeln von Frauen vom ausgehenden 16. bis zum Beginn des 18. Jahrhunderts', *Zeitsprünge. Forschungen zur Frühen Neuzeit* 1, 1, (1997), 75–98.

Yates, Frances A. *Astraea: The Imperial Theme in the Sixteenth Century*. London, 1975.

Zanger, Abby. *Scenes from the Marriage of Louis XIV. Nuptial Fictions and the Making of Absolutist Power*. Stanford, CA, 1997.

———— 'Making Sweat: Sex and the Gender of National Reproduction in the Marriage of Louis XIII', *Yale French Studies* 86, (1994), 187–205.

Zantop, Susanne. *Colonial Fantasies. Conquest, Family, and Nation in Precolonial Germany, 1770–1870*. Durham, 1997.

Zemon Davis, Natalie. *The Gift in Sixteenth-Century France*. Madison, 2000.

Ziegler, Philip. *Crown and People*. New York, 1978.

Zintzen, Christiane. *Von Pompeji nach Troja. Archäologie, Literatur und Öffentlichkeit im 19. Jahrhundert*. Vienna, 1998.

Zipfel, Friedrich. 'Kritik der deutschen Öffentlichkeit an der Person und an der Monarchie Wilhelms II. bis zum Ausbruch des Weltkrieges' (Ph.D. diss.). Berlin, 1952.

Index